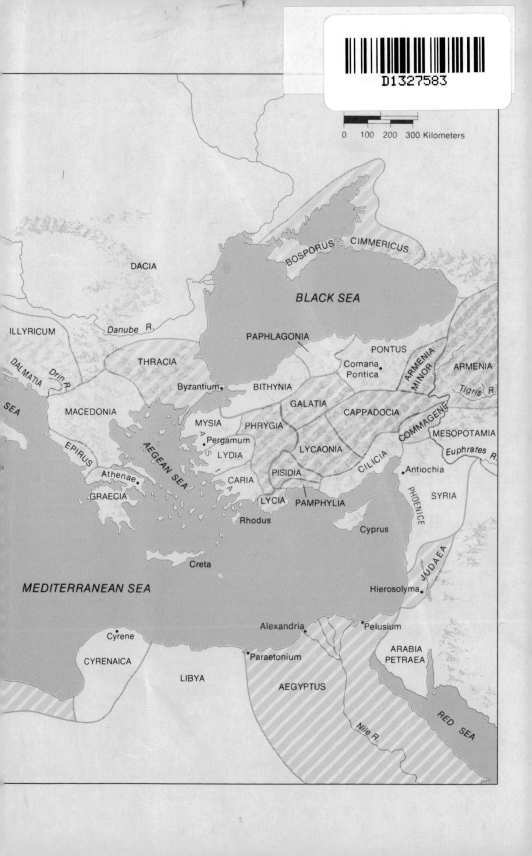

0   100   200   300 Kilometers

DACIA

BOSPORUS CIMMERICUS

BLACK SEA

ILLYRICUM

Danube R.

PAPHLAGONIA

PONTUS

Comana
Pontica

ARMENIA
MINOR

ARMENIA

THRACIA

BITHYNIA

Tigris R.

DALMATIA

Drin R.

Byzantium

GALATIA

CAPPADOCIA

COMMAGENE

SEA

MACEDONIA

MYSIA

PHRYGIA

MESOPOTAMIA

Euphrates R.

EPIRUS

Pergamum

AEGEAN SEA

LYDIA

LYCAONIA

CILICIA

Antiochia

Athenae

CARIA

PISIDIA

PHOENICE

SYRIA

GRAECIA

LYCIA

PAMPHYLIA

Rhodus

Cyprus

JUDAEA

Creta

MEDITERRANEAN SEA

Hierosolyma

Alexandria

Pelusium

Cyrene

Paraetonium

ARABIA
PETRAEA

CYRENAICA

LIBYA

AEGYPTUS

Nile R.

RED SEA

MARK ANTONY
A Biography

The John K. Fesler Memorial Fund provided assistance in the publication of this volume, for which the University of Minnesota Press is grateful.

MARK ANTONY

A Biography

Eleanor Goltz Huzar

UNIVERSITY OF MINNESOTA PRESS, MINNEAPOLIS

Copyright © 1978 by the University of Minnesota.
All rights reserved.
Printed in the United States of America.
Published by the University of Minnesota Press,
2037 University Avenue Southeast,
Minneapolis, Minnesota 55455,
and published in Canada by Burns & MacEachern
Limited, Don Mills, Ontario

Library of Congress Cataloging in Publication Data

Huzar, Eleanor Goltz.
  Mark Antony, a biography.

  Bibliography: p.
  Includes index.
  1. Antonius, Marcus, 83?-30 B.C. 2. Rome—
History—Republic, 265-30 B.C. 3. Statesmen—Rome—
Biography. 4. Generals—Rome—Biography.
DG260.A6H89   937'.05'0924 [B]   78-53133
ISBN 0-8166-0863-6

The University of Minnesota
is an equal opportunity
educator and employer.

Magistris Optimis

Harry Caplan

John L. Heller

Tom B. Jones

Sister Mona Riley

M. L. W. Laistner—In Memoriam

Gratiam maximam habeo.

Acknowledgments

This biography has been possible only with the generous counsel and help of many associates to whom I am heartily grateful. Professor Tom B. Jones was certainly Antony's *patronus*; he gave me the initial interest in the work and helped me with the publication. Professor Harry J. Brown advised me on many questions of form and endured proofreading. As assistant editor at the University of Minnesota Press, Tyna Thall Orren was wise and enthusiastically supportive; Victoria Haire, assistant editor, corrected, checked, counseled with acute skill and unflagging patience. James M. Lipsey, Amy Doll, and Peter Krafft of the Michigan State University Center of Cartographic Research expertly prepared the maps. Helen Elkiss and Susan McMahon served as unselfish and splendidly capable typists. Research grants from Michigan State University aided my studies, and a sabbatical leave enabled me to spend a happy and productive year at the American Academy in Rome, which generously welcomed me to its library and other facilities. The stimulation of many students and conversations with many colleagues broadened and brightened my efforts. Relatives and friends all deserve warm thanks for bearing with my long devotion to Mark Antony.

Contents

Mark Antony, hero too human (identification uncertain). Bust found in 1941 and dated between late first century B.C. and mid-first century A.D. Vatican Museum. Reproduced with the permission of the German Archaeological Institute, Rome. Gray marble, ht. .34m.

MARK ANTONY
A Biography

I

The Setting

Mark Antony's life (83- or 82–30 B.C.) spanned the fatal last fifty years of the Roman Republic. Born into a Rome beset with stresses of expansion and change, Antony acted as lieutenant to the leaders, then captured briefly the absolute command of the disintegrating government. His domination was challenged: by those who accused him of destroying the state and by those who judged him moving too slowly against the state. When Antony lay dead, so too did the Roman Republic.

Antony was only a final agent in the decline which had begun decades, even centuries, earlier. A state, like a man, suffers elements of decay and progresses to its death from the moment of its birth, though for a time growth and maturation dominate, and only gradually is the body politic aware' of difficulties emerging in a number of vital areas. Thus no one can assign a specific date for the onset of the republic's decline, the growth of imperial rule. But the Hannibalic wars of the third century B.C. certainly accelerated and intensified a number of Rome's problems and introduced issues which Rome had to face. In many ways Rome's wars determined its destiny. Aggressive and tenacious by tradition, in half-defensive, half-offensive campaigns, Rome expanded its borders from the tiny agrarian city-state of the sixth century B.C. until, by the early third century B.C., it controlled all Italy. But each acquisition of territory brought new neighbors, fearful, resentful, seem-ingly threatening to Rome, precipitating yet more mobilization and conquests.[1]

Expansion to Italy's coast meant that Rome's new neighbors lay overseas. Some early foreign contacts were for peaceful trade, as Rome's expanded lands became a market worth cultivating. Mighty Ptolemaic Egypt (Aegyptus) sent its first embassy in 273 B.C. Rome's first silver coinage serviceable for trade was issued in 269 B.C. under the guidance of Alexandrian moneyers. Other east-ern Hellenistic states also began tentative trade relations and cul-tural contacts. But all too readily Rome viewed its neighbors as threats. Fighting the Punic Wars, Rome forced the Carthaginian en-claves out of Sicily, then Spain, Sardinia, and Corsica, and claimed their overseas territories, not as allies or colonies of Rome—the pol-icy adopted in Italy—but as subject provinces to be ruled from and by Rome. The desperate battles in Italy itself against the Cartha-ginian armies under Hannibal devastated the land and confirmed Rome's aggressive determination never again to be invaded.[2]

Macedonia had made a brief, ineffective alliance with Hannibal. During the second century B.C., Rome turned against the east Mediterranean states. Macedonia and Greece were taken as prov-inces almost reluctantly when they proved unable to cope with the relative liberty Rome had offered after its first victories. Next the rich state of Pergamum was willed to Rome by a ruler preferring peaceful occupation to military conquest. The lesser states of Syria and Asia Minor became the pawns of Roman generals seeking power, like Pompey, and fell *seriatim*, with greater or lesser strug-gles. By the mid-first century B.C., of the great Hellenistic states only Egypt remained nominally independent; but even the Ptole-mies paid well for the privilege of ruling as Rome dictated. The ini-tial conquests had been at least half-defensive: to secure frontiers, to protect allies, to support trade. Gradually motives changed. Prov-inces were bases of power, sources of wealth, justifications for commands. The general Julius Caesar's high-handed conquest of Gaul (Gallia) in 58–49 B.C. is evidence that under the pretenses of defense and righteous causes, Roman leaders had become strongly expansionist.[3]

4

The centuries of almost constant warfare brought concomitant changes in the internal structure of Rome. The pattern of rule which Rome had established after the expulsion of the kings in 509 B.C. was a hereditary aristocracy. The patricians held the annual elective offices and received lifetime appointments to the powerful upper council, the Senate. The plebeian citizens met en masse in an assembly (Comitia Curiata) at intervals and voted in family groupings to elect hand-picked candidates and to approve or disapprove the major measures proposed by the patricians. The patricians were proudly exclusive. Their dynastically arranged marriages included only a few great families. Their allegiances, especially politically, were tied to family obligations, and though this loyalty (*amicitia*) might have to shift with developing marriage alliances or political exigencies, the ties of aristocratic *amicitia* remained strong. The patricians in many ways governed well. Despite some defects, they provided remarkably able generals for the state. Trained in family traditions of service to Rome, they held government offices responsibly. The lopsided system worked because Rome was still a small, cohesive, religion-and-tradition-bound city-state, united against the enemies which surrounded it. Plebeian protests were long muted.[4]

By immemorial custom, each aristocratic family acted as patron to a group of plebeians known as their clients. The relationship was a sacred bond whereby the patron offered military, legal, and economic protections in return for loyal services, including the clients' vote when a member of the patron's family stood for election. It seems possible that, in earliest times, every man in the small state was either a patron or a client. As Rome expanded, the small-state pattern was awkwardly imposed on diverse peoples. Free men of conquered lands were often taken as clients by either the victorious generals or the governors of the new provinces since clientage proved useful as an aspect of the administrative system. Pompey, especially, set the pattern of acting as patron to the princes of client states, even while he exploited them by demanding tribute. Such massive troops of clients inevitably were bases of political and military power for the patrons. Freed slaves were also clients of their former masters. This established patron-client system was strong and enduring. But by shifting the close personal relationships to remote, foreign obligations, Rome's expansion did contribute to the eroding of the system. By Antony's time great numbers of free men were conditioned to the status of dependents but concluded that they owed allegiance only to the leader promising them the most.[5]

This aristocratic republic, then, founded as a small cohesive, agricultural state, functioned well in many respects. Nevertheless, no human institution can remain static, and Rome expanded its problems with its territory. The aristocratic rule of the patricians continued, but with significant adjustments. The plebeians suffered the hardships of years of fighting on Rome's battlegrounds and learned that the generals could not conquer without their service. Especially as the wars moved farther from Rome, the legionnaires begrudged the prolonged campaigns which kept them from their farms and brought financial disaster to their families. The booty of victories disproportionately fell to the officers; the enemies enslaved and brought to Italy provided abundant cheap labor inimical to the free laboring class and to the small farmers who had to sell their produce in the more competitive markets. When overseas conquests were made provinces ruled by Rome, exploitation of native peoples by taxes and plunder further enriched the ruling classes. The meager wealth that filtered down to the common people came through public works and donations or through bribery by which the victorious leaders squandered their booty to win state elections and honors.[6]

Almost from the foundation of the republic, the plebeians demanded greater participation in the government and gradually won concessions. During two centuries (509-287 B.C.) of "the struggle of the orders," the plebeians gained their own elected officials, the tribunes, and the right to stand for all the offices of the state. Plebeians who held the highest offices of praetor and consul could join the previously patrician Senate in lifelong memberships as *patres conscripti*, and, though of lesser rank, their families were ennobled forever. All the male citizens met in assemblies (Comitia) and gradually reorganized them to increase their effective power. By responses to shifting needs (which became hallowed traditions), the same citizens met in three different assemblies—summoned by different officials, voting in different patterns, and deciding different problems. The ancient Comita Curiata still met under patrician officials to approve religious and family matters. Next to develop was the Comitia Centuriata, an assembly based on the fact that voting citizens were also soldiers. The consuls and the praetors had the right to serve as generals of the armies (*imperium*) and regularly summoned the soldiers to vote in military service units for issues like declaring war or peace, capital punishment, and for the annual election of their official successors. But it was the Comitia Tributa, presided over by the popularly elected tribunes, that was the increasingly influential legislative assembly.[7] It elected the lower officials (the tribunes, quaestors, and aediles) and by 287 B.C. it had won the right to initiate and pass laws valid for the state even without senatorial approval. The plebeians could now also intermarry legally with the patricians and could hold religious office in the priesthood. By the time of the Punic Wars in the third century B.C., Rome seemed to be developing toward a true political and social democracy.[8]

The overseas wars wrought such radical changes, however, that although Rome claimed to continue the old patterns, it actually lost its republic. The military men, the governors, the big businessmen (equestrians) were amassing enormous fortunes in the provinces from government contracts or exploitation of the conquered. The contrasts between these rich and the poor became ever more ugly as the ranks of the destitute swelled. The armies levied citizens from their farms or businesses for such long periods that many had to sell their land to wealthy men who could farm great estates with cheap slave labor. The dispossessed families drifted to the towns, especially to Rome, where too many of them eked out precarious lives hoping for a public dole. The discharged veterans returned to such a life as well, and Rome swelled with a discontented population whose sole asset for sale was their vote. Foreigners came to the capital as well: slaves, merchants, petitioners to the government, even artists, philosophers, and priests of strange eastern cults. An increasing number had been granted citizenship and with it the vote which was all too often for sale.[9]

In return, Romans of all ranks fought, traded, studied, or served as government officials around the Mediterranean. Especially in the eastern Hellenistic states, such Romans had to acknowledge the ancient religions, the advanced learning, the sophisticated civilizations developed centuries before Romulus had founded Rome. Italy's cultural backwardness meant that the cultivated carefully adopted, the philistine crudely aped the exotic eastern refinements. Rome's familiar ways and beliefs were mingled with, then overwhelmed by, the cosmopolitanism of a world capital. The old tales were retold, the old phrases reused; but the cohesive, consistent, committed spirit of early Rome was now a pose, not an actuality; the stern moral code based on Roman religion disintegrated with the faith. For many, self-interest, reached by any opportunism, was the only creed.[10]

The plight of growing numbers of the destitute led men to follow leaders advocating reform. Tiberius and Gaius Gracchus, the patrician brothers who became tribunes (in 133 B.C. and 123–22 B.C. respectively) to pass legislation aiding the impoverished, are only the most famous of a number of civilian reformers who denounced the conditions of the Italian poor and who proposed reforms that would help the masses by checking the excesses of the rich. Their proposals to grant plots of farmland and to establish urban colonies for the poor (and to benefit their supporters) roused their rich opponents to political manipulation, then to street violence. Murder destroyed the civilian reformers before their measures were completed. Their unintended heritage was an intensified awareness of class hostilities and bitter intransigence, an open manipulation of the laws and religious sanctions for individual ends, and an unprecedented willingness to shed citizens' blood on the streets of Rome.[11]

By Antony's time the established republican ways of meeting political and social problems were observed only in form, not in fact. The continuing, distant wars, the proliferation of provinces had made the army generals virtual rulers in their areas of conquest. Expanded commands, prolonged commands, even the *maius imperium infinitum*, which gave sole command over an extended part of the empire to a general with completion of an assigned mission its only temporal limit, began as extraordinary measures but soon became common. At the end of the second century B.C., the general and consul Gaius Marius had reorganized the army from the traditional pattern of short-term, land-owning citizen conscripts to paid, long-term, professional volunteers. The legions were strengthened by the reforms, but the state was weakened; for the soldiers took their oaths of allegiance to their general, not to the state; their lifetime loyalty was not to ideals but to the leader who would give them safety, victory, booty, and promised veterans' benefits. Such an army would follow its commander even into civil wars against Rome itself. The equestrian Marius and the patrician Sulla, in 88 B.C., were the first hostile and jealous generals to pit one Roman army against another within the gates of Rome. In their brutal ambitions they were also the first to issue the public proscription lists naming hundreds of political and economic enemies who were to be killed on sight. Leaders still claimed to be acting for the common good; in reality, not the well-being of the state but the personal honor and power of the great man determined the battles of Roman armies.[12]

Normal civilian government buckled under the open threat of the armies. Liberty (*libertas*), so cherished at least by the patricians, was almost gone. And yet the forms of constitutionality and precedent were observed. The traditional officials were elected, even though the leading candidates were allied with one or the other of the generals and served his purposes when elected. The Senate and Comitia met. During lulls the Senate could assert some of its old authority: of the purse over the sword, of control of foreign affairs, and even of granting honors like triumphs; but for the most part it was hamstrung by divisions into the factions following the competing great men. The tribunes who presided over the Comitia Tributa had come to be the tools of the generals. The chief check on a powerful man was another powerful man—the empire was so widespread that several generals could concurrently hold major commands.[13]

In traditional Roman politics a candidate was supported by a group of political adherents (a *factio*). Now, as political support, each general had his *factio*, a following of patricians, equestrians, and leading plebeians who worked for his power and presented his program. Adherents to a *factio* were drawn by personal ambitions but also by traditional family *amicitia* or understood political debts. Factions interacted, and grouped, and shifted membership for mutual conveniences. In broad terms, the men who supported leaders by appeals to traditional Roman ways, senatorial prerogatives, or patrician domination were known as the optimates. The men who supported leaders by advocating legislation on behalf of the poor, by soliciting the votes of the people, by using the tribunes to pass legislation in the Comitia Tributa were called the populares. An ambitious young aristocrat, still aspiring to the dignity of high office, had to rise through the lower offices to hold the consulship and join the Senate by attaching himself to a faction in one or the other camp, and strive to make himself visible to the "great man."[14]

Roman politics, so long the monopoly of the patricians, was still the preserve of the wealthy nobles. Men could stake fortunes on the expenses of campaigning and buying masses of votes to hold the offices which would enrich the shrewd, and unscrupulous, politician. But the unsuccessful candidate could also be hopelessly impoverished. Many an old patrician family was now bankrupt—by political losses, by extravagant living in an outrageously ostentatious age, or perhaps by inability to profit from shifting economic patterns in an expanded empire in which Italy had gradually lost economic self-sufficiency and now depended on imports from the provinces. The bankrupted aristocrats were as ready as the hopeless masses to follow the ambitious general to a political revolution.[15]

From our vantage point we know that as the republic died, the empire was being born and that a new monarchical government, strong enough to last five centuries, would carry over much that was valuable from republican times. But in Antony's age, although some leaders were beginning to look beyond the republican aristocracy to one-man rule, for most Romans only the problems were evident. Able men could not passively watch the state disintegrate. The conflicts came when politicians proposed different cures for the public ills.

Roman pride in traditions and successes ran very deep. Conservatives of all classes saw the problems as unwise deviations from the old ways and sincerely sought a healthy revival of patterns which had worked for a half-millennium. They admitted concessions when strongly pressured, like granting citizenship rights to the Italian peoples. They checked abuses in the undisciplined government of the provinces, at least enough that provincial revolts were few. They even brought officials to trial for malfeasance in such unprecedented numbers that the courts, too, became agents for political power plays. But these reforms were refurbishings of the existing system. The conservative political ideal was a republic based on the traditional *libertas*, which gave every man his place in the state, under the enlightened leadership of the Senate. It was an ideal they deemed worth fighting and even dying to maintain.[16]

The advocates of change could also be sincere. They criticized the ancient system as a selfish monopoly of power held by the nobles at the expense of common peoples and provincials, and they argued that only powerful men backed by armies could effect the needed changes to check aristocratic abuses and strengthen the tribune-led people. Marius's military attack on the patrician champion Sulla in the 80s B.C. had been in the name of popular rights. The same catchwords provided a power base for the self-styled popular leaders Pompey, Crassus, and Caesar, who in 60 B.C. disguised their animosities and pooled their political and military strengths to rule jointly as the First Triumvirate. Such populares leaders viewed ancient traditions as less functional and therefore less sacred than did their optimates opponents. Their changes and innovations were accordingly more revolutionary.

All serious statesmen knew that many institutions of their republican world were crumbling. The best men struggled to look forward, to rebuild the old government or to help the evolution into a new state. But no plan could start with a *tabula rasa*; developments seemed almost wholly determined by the past and the troubled present. Faithful republican or bold autocrat, every active leader lived in personal danger and seemed driven by the times to the reckless tenet that the end justified the means.

11

II

Heir

For Antony, born into a family of ancient lineage and high distinction, a political and military life was a foregone conclusion. The Roman aristocrat honored his distinguished ancestors in prescribed religious and public rites, and voted with the political faction engineered by generations of political favors and calculated marriage ties. Aristocracy existed for political power. Though individuals could vary in commitment and distinction, every Roman noble received his most significant inheritance in widely known family and political ties. Mark Antony's branch of the Antonii was of plebeian nobility. His plebeian ancestors had ennobled the family in perpetuity by winning high political office and sitting in the Senate. His mother, Julia, descended from the Julii Caesares, the patrician family which claimed descent from Venus and—more probably—an ancestor who came from Alba Longa to Rome at its foundation. (Indeed, Julia and Julius Caesar were third cousins, and family loyalties, although not intimate, were maintained.) Some noble families honored celebrated remote ancestors but won no present honors. Both the Antonii and the Julii achieved unprecedented reputation during the late republic, so that Antony was born to prominence and potential power, although also to the burden of high family expectations.

Of the prestigious career of his paternal grandfather, Marcus Antonius, there is substantial ancient evidence. The abilities and boldness of the man, the variety of his involvements, the range of his public responsibilities—all set traditions and commitments which would leave their mark on Antony and his career. Antonius's exceptional talent was in oratory. His speeches are not extant—he refused to publish them lest inconsistencies in his position be noted —but he wrote a book about oratory, and Cicero, who studied under Antonius, made him an eloquent central figure of his essay "The Making of an Orator." Antonius's career was filled with successes in political elections and in special pleadings. Born in 143 B.C., he was quaestor in Asia in 114 or 113 B.C. While quaestor propraetore in 113 or 112 B.C., he was one of those charged in a scandal involving the Vestal Virgins. Though technically immune from prosecution while abroad on public service, Antonius hastened to Rome and defended himself so brilliantly that (although three Vestals were condemned) he was acquitted. Clearly, the young orator was a political ally worth the winning. His political affiliations were normally with the moderately conservative faction, led by the aristocratic Metelli and opposed by the more radical followers of Gaius Marius. Antonius supported Metelli measures and he defended several members of this faction in the courts. But the shifting political scene and divisions in the Metellan faction made it sometimes expedient to side with the Marians.[1]

By 102 B.C. his political career was reaching full glory. As praetor governing the Roman port stations along the Cilician coast, Antonius was given a special commission against the pirates whose strongholds lay along this rocky southern coast of Asia Minor and who, as the policing power of such states as Syria, Egypt, and Rhodes dwindled before Rome's eastward-moving might, were dominating the eastern Mediterranean and blocking sea traffic to Italy. More concerned than the Senate for safe commerce, the business classes demanded effective suppression of piracy. Accordingly, Antonius was given Rome's first special command which included authority over other provincial governors: a power which later grew to the *imperium maius* held by generals such as his grandson over all other commanders. As praetor in 102, propraetor in 101-

100 B.C. (perhaps with proconsular *imperium*), he gathered ships and supplies from the eastern states, battled the pirates, and secured a foothold (which was to be extended by later generals into the much larger province of Cilicia) on the pirate-held coast.

Though the pirates were not eliminated, they were checked; and in December, 100 B.C., he was awarded a triumph, a statue of him was erected, and he could decorate the Rostra in Rome with the prows of enemy ships. By good luck, he and his troops were neutral during the bloody days when Marius had to take responsibility for crushing the riots instigated by his violent former allies Saturninus and Glaucia. During the disorders Antonius's troops were waiting in camp for permission to enter Rome in a triumphal procession hailing Antonius's victory. In 99 B.C. Antonius was consul; in 97 censor. By now the vacillating political alignments of the Metellan faction made it expedient for Antonius to side sometimes with the Marians, less often with the Sullans. He defended adherents of both factions in the courts and skillfully defended himself in 90 B.C. when, with a number of other senators, he was accused of treason for supporting the enemy in the Social War raging between Rome and the states formerly allied with it in Italy. The charge was invalid, but it was true that as censor Antonius followed Marius's policies in bestowing unusually generous grants of citizenship to Italians. Such grants left a legacy of gratitude among the Italians for Antonius's family. During these years of prominence, Antonius also received the religious office of augur for life.[2]

But preeminence itself was tantamount to destruction in these years of civil war. Sometime between 95 and 90 B.C. Antonius seems to have broken with Marius. He was cordially hated by the Marian supporter Gnaeus Papirius Carbo whose father's trial, disgrace, and suicide he attributed to Antonius's prosecution. When the Marians marched into Rome, Antonius advised Quintus Caecilius Metellus, who had been praetor in 89 B.C., to bring the army promptly to help the Senate against the Marian forces. With five other consulars, Antonius was proscribed by the Marians, and in 87 B.C. murder ended his distinguished career. His head was exposed to public view on the Rostra from which he had delivered his orations.[3]

Antonius was the most prominent member of his family in generations. His sons inherited his good name and record of public service, family ties with the Caesars, sympathy for provincials, loyal clients among the Italians and peoples abroad, and a willingness to support reform legislation. They were also indebted to him because his preeminence ensured their election to high offices. But his real ability in oratory, his capacity for military and political leadership, his political dexterity in adjusting to new leaders and demands of the time were to leap a generation and to reappear in his more famous grandson.

His elder son, Marcus, the triumvir's father, proved an amiable incompetent—attractive, generous with his friends, but avaricious of public moneys to fill his spendthrift purse, wholly ineffectual in the political and military leadership thrust upon him by the prestige and allies of his family. That he received power at all bespeaks the bankruptcy of senatorial leadership in this age of dictators, but perhaps also, as Cicero said, he was given power because he was too inept to use or abuse it.

Of this Antonius's earlier life during the Sullan-Marian wars which killed his father we know nothing. His political affiliations were with Marian trimmers, who had compromised to make peace with Sulla but were reasserting more popular politics after Sulla's death. By 74 B.C. Antonius was praetor when, by senatorial decree, he received a special command against the pirates who were again besetting Mediterranean shipping. The command gave him *imperium infinitum*, the first assignment of this extended power, checked by almost no time and few territorial limits. Seven years later, by the Gabinian Law, Pompey received almost as much power and used it as the foundation of his domination of the empire. But Antonius was too inept to defeat the pirates, much less build a power base. Praetor in 74 B.C., proconsul in 73-71 B.C., he demanded heavy contributions of ships and supplies from Sicily, Greece, Byzantium, and other subject states. But beyond exploitation, he had neither strategy nor tactics. He attacked Spain to clear pirates from the Mediterranean, then went to Crete as an incidental operation before launching his main attack on the Cilician pirates. The expedition was a disastrous failure, and Antonius had to negotiate with the pirates a humiliating peace, which the Senate later rejected. Mercifully, Antonius died in Crete in 71 B.C. and was awarded, posthumously and it seems derisively, the title "Creticus." The pirates, more confident and aggressive, had to be dealt with by more competent successors.[4]

Antonius's legacy to his son was, therefore, far from glorious: a fatherless home, a tarnished name, an overspent purse. But at least Antonius had lived his career in the Forum and had the political allies and loyalties so intrinsic to Roman political life. Notable as an ally was Julius Caesar, who apparently was his legate in 73 B.C.; and although Caesar had left Antonius's service before the Cretan debacle, this association may have been the basis of Caesar's later friendship with Antonius's son.

Also influencing the young Antony's career was his father's younger brother, Gaius Antonius, known as Hybrida. Like his brother Creticus, he was penalized by being born so totally a member of the senatorial nobility that he could not avoid a life of politics, but was too weak, too venal, too vacillating to prove anthing but a self-seeking toady to more powerful men of the age.[5]

He began his career as a legate of Sulla in the Mithridatic War. Here he used his rank and cavalry to plunder Greece, even holding the island of Cephallenia high-handedly as his private property. With Greek booty he returned, momentarily rich, to Rome. In Sulla's triumph he ostentatiously drove a four-in-hand chariot, which won him the further nickname Quadrigarius. But his provincial exploitation was too egregious. In 76 (or 77 B.C.), working through Julius Caesar, the Greeks charged Antonius with extortion in his province of Achaia. The praetor peregrinus, the judge with jurisdiction over foreign residents, condemned him; but Antonius avoided conviction by an appeal to the tribunes. Nevertheless, in 70 B.C., when reform censors expelled sixty-four senators as unworthy, Antonius was removed from the Senate on charges of former provincial mismanagement and current debts so heavy that a senator was judged subject to irresistible pressures and temptations. Undaunted, Antonius returned to office as promptly as possible by election as tribune of the people in 68 B.C., next as praetor in 66 B.C. In 65 B.C. he went east as a legate to Pompey's conquests, then returned to Rome from Cappadocia in 64 B.C.[6]

16

Antonius's year as consul in 63 B.C. was memorable for high drama, not because of Antonius's leadership but because of the tumultuous events which swept him along. A band of many dissatisfied and some desperate men had gathered around the reckless, dissolute patrician Catiline, determined to hold power and effect debt reforms by any means from legal elections to civil war. Other ambitious opportunists like Caesar and Crassus hovered at the edges of the gang, prepared to use or disavow the men and policies as they calculated their own gains. Antonius, a petty intriguer, debauched, and, despite periodic raids on the provincials, perennially debt-ridden, was a natural ally for the extremists around Catiline and was prominent enough politically to be welcomed to the conspiracy as a useful tool. Also involved as Antonius's ally was Mark Antony's new stepfather, Lentulus Sura.

In the fashion of Roman matrons of her class, Antony's mother, Julia, had remarried soon after Creticus's death. Unhappily, she was equally imprudent in the choice of her second husband. Publius Cornelius Lentulus Sura, gracefully dignified but morally corrupt, came from the ancient patrician house of Cornelii. He held the highest offices: quaestor under Sulla in 81 B.C., praetor in 75 B.C., propraetor in Sicily in 74 B.C., and consul in 71 B.C. But his office holding was tarnished with corruption and exploitation, for Lentulus lived extravagantly and was always deeply in debt. He was acquitted in a trial for extortion after his quaestorship, but in 70 B.C. the censors expelled him, and sixty-three others, from the Senate because of the wildness of his life. He regained his seat in the Senate by again winning the praetorship in 63 B.C., but the disgrace of expulsion plus his mounting debts probably led to his joining the Catilinarians. Lentulus, with his distinguished family name and consular rank, was the most prestigious of the gang and assumed that he would be its leader. Moreover, he was convinced of the validity of two Sibylline prophecies that three Cornelii (Sulla, Cinna, and, he hoped, Lentulus) would rule Rome and that Rome would suffer civil war twenty years after the burning of the Capitol. But his energy and competence fell far short of his ambitions, and he was merely a a tool used by Catiline.

17

Apparently, Gaius Antonius was involved in the abortive coup known as the First Catilinarian Conspiracy, which fizzled out in 65 B.C. In 63 B.C. he, Catiline, and Cicero were the leading three candidates for the consulship. Catiline and Antonius, possibly backed by Caesar and Crassus, banded together for victory and reforms.[7] But after a campaign of bribery, threats, and denunciations, conservative voters rallied to elect Cicero as the ablest man and Antonius as the least dangerous, driving the defeated Catiline to plot a violent attack upon the state. The first objective was to kill Cicero, since Antonius would then be a pliant tool of Catiline. But Cicero seized the initiative and outmaneuvered the conspirators. Antonius he neutralized by outbidding Catiline and even the suspected conspirator Crassus in promises of wealth. The consulship year was regularly followed by a one- to three-year appointment as governor of a province; the specific province was chosen before the election to lessen the still grave dangers that the governor, who was not paid, would plot to seize the wealth of the provincials. In the allotment Antonius received Cisalpine Gaul (Gallia Cisalpina), Cicero was assigned Macedonia, which Antonius deemed the more desirable province since warfare along its unstable borders could bring the glory of a triumph and the delights of plentiful booty. Cicero therefore bought Antonius's cooperation by giving him the governorship of Macedonia.[8] For this price Antonius stood aside to let Cicero begin the year as presiding consul and in that office crush the conspiracy of Antonius's former allies.

When Catiline fled north, Lentulus remained the conspiracy's leader in Rome, intending, Cicero charged, to set Rome on fire to distract the authorities, to kill Cicero and other senators, and to seize control of the government with an army of freed slaves and Gallic mercenaries. If these were his intentions, Lentulus failed completely. Instead of acting promptly and violently, he contacted ambassadors of the Allobroges in Rome to woo them to an offensive alliance which would precipitate war beyond the Alps. He even wrote letters to their chiefs in his own hand and under his own seal; and when the Allobroges gave the evidence to Cicero as consul, Lentulus was arrested on December 3 and tried by the Senate. Briefly he feigned innocence, but when he was denounced by some of his men, he was obliged to resign his praetorship on the vote of the Senate and was put into custody. On December 5 Lentulus was one of five Catilinarians executed as public enemies on the order of Cicero, and his estate was forfeited.[9]

Only when Catiline's troops stood at bay in north Italy during late January, 62 B.C., was the untrustworthy Gaius Antonius given command of the government forces against them. Even here he let Catiline mobilize troops and elude him; and when the fight began, he used the excuse of gout to transfer his command to his able subordinate M. Petreius, who finally won the desperate battle.

Gaius Antonius did govern the province of Macedonia and undertook the border wars from which he expected easy, profitable victories. The province was plundered as planned, but the Dardanian and Scythian tribes dashed his hopes by defeating him so disgracefully that when he returned to Rome during Caesar's consulship in 59 B.C., he was again brought to trial. The charge was perhaps treason for complicity with Catiline. For this the senatorial judges acquitted him; but, despite Cicero's reluctant but dutiful defense of his former colleague, Antonius was found guilty for his actions in Greece and Macedonia. Basically, his reputation was too bad to save, and, banished from Rome, he settled on the island of Cephallenia which he had seized.

Near the end of Antonius's life, his nephew Antony's power brought him once more to dignity. In 48 B.C., acting through Mark Antony, Caesar had returned many of those banished but had not included Gaius Antonius, whom he resented for many old disloyalties and antagonisms. Apparently, Mark Antony had not pleaded for his uncle then. But in 45 B.C. Caesar did recall him and restore him to the Senate, perhaps for the advantage of having another consular name added to his revolutionary roll. In 42 B.C., when Mark Antony ruled Italy, Gaius was elected censor, the state's highest office—however inappropriate the censorial office for the elderly reprobate. After 42 B.C. we hear of him no longer.[10]

Antony was probably twenty years old in 63 B.C. when his stepfather, Lentulus, who had been a carelessly congenial guardian of his three stepsons, was disgraced and executed by strangling. It seems probable, though not proved, that the young Antony covertly favored the Catilinarians, and he may have heard Cicero publicly denounce the conspirators. Certainly, this family tragedy seems the basis for some of his long bitterness toward Cicero and perhaps for some of his friendship toward Caesar, who opposed the execution.

On his patrician mother's side, Antony's ties also drew him inevitably into public prominence, although with more conservative political associations. Julia's father, Lucius Julius Caesar, like others of his family, opposed the radical Saturninus. Praetor in 95 B.C., Lucius Caesar governed Macedonia in 94 B.C. In 90 B.C. he was consul at the outbreak of the Social War in which the Italian allies fought to obtain Roman citizenship and its rights. Liberals in Rome called the demands of the allies legitimate. The conservative consul, with legates including Sulla and Crassus, fought through both victories and defeats to an exhausted and frightened stalemate. Lucius Caesar therefore presented a law, the *Lex Julia de Civitate*, that granted citizenship to the Latin and Italian allies who remained faithful to Rome. The overdue concession brought the hoped-for desertions to Rome and shattered the unity of the Italian foes. Caesar's command was prolonged into 89 B.C. when Rome was victorious. In 89 B.C. he was censor, active in enrolling the new citizens, but the paper concession was shrewdly manipulated to render the Italian vote ineffectual; and though the war was ended, allied discontent remained a grievance which later generals could exploit for their own purposes. Civil war soon followed the war against the allies, and in 87 B.C. Lucius Caesar and his brother Gaius, supporting the conservatives, were killed in the Marian proscriptions. It was the same slaughter that killed Antony's paternal grandfather, Marcus Antonius. Lucius Caesar's head, like Antonius's, was affixed to the Rostra in public spectacle.[11]

Lucius Caesar left two children: Lucius Julius Caesar and Julia, Antony's mother. The younger Lucius followed his father's aristocratic politics. Quaestor in 77 B.C., praetor in 67 B.C., and consul in 64 B.C., he was among the leading senators demanding the death penalty for the Catilinarians in 63 B.C., even though his brother-in-law, Lentulus Sura, would be among the victims. A decade later he appeared to be flirting with the popular faction and aiding his Julian cousin, for he was legate to Julius Caesar in Gaul during 52-49 B.C. and was commanding 10,000 men along the frontier when Caesar, with his lieutenant Antony, crushed the revolt of conquered Gallic tribes led by Vercingetorix. Lucius Caesar invaded Italy with Julius Caesar when the civil war began and worked with Antony to control Rome during Caesar's absence. But after Julius Caesar's death in 44 B.C. and Antony's apparent eclipse at Mutina in 43 B.C., Lucius Caesar reverted to his more traditional political allies and joined Caesar's murderers against Antony, whom he favored declaring an enemy of the state. As a result, he was second on Antony's proscription list and was rescued only by his sister Julia, who petitioned her son for her brother's life. He was spared but held office only in the religious College of Augurs until his death in 40 B.C.[12]

The role of Antony's mother was unusually prominent for a matron of her day. Pronounced dignified and virtuous even by Cicero, she showed herself also strong-minded and courageous. She struggled constantly against the financial needs of her extravagant husbands and children and tried to provide a stable home in the chaotic world of civil wars, proscriptions, and moral decay. Eventually she was active in politics herself. When Antony besieged Decimus Brutus in Mutina in 43 B.C., Julia used her full family influence in Rome to keep him from being outlawed by the Senate. After Mutina, in addition to saving her brother Lucius from Antony's proscription by personal appeal, she succeeded in saving the wealth of several Roman matrons from confiscation. In 41 B.C. she fled from Octavian to Sextus Pompey in Sicily, and was sent by Pompey to Antony with an honorable escort. She worked for peace between Octavian and Antony and with Sextus Pompey. In part the prominence of her role as Antony's mother provided the opportunities for such intervention; but in part her effectiveness was due to the strength of her personality and intellect, her experience in dominating men of affairs. In amateur psychology it is all too easy to attribute a man's character to ties with his mother; but in the case of Antony, it may be fair to ascribe his repeated rebellions against social mores and his dependence on strong-minded women like Fulvia and Cleopatra to a home governed by Julia, over her short-lived, irresponsible husbands.[13]

In sum, Antony's family bequeathed him political position that provided the opportunity, indeed the expectation, of a career all the way up the *cursus honorum* (racecourse of honors). It also established his value as an ally, and in turn gave him a multitude of influential allies in both conservative and popular camps. His two able grandfathers had been killed by the radical Marians. But the next generation, less competent and committed, had adjusted to the shifting political conditions for fortune, fame, or just safety. His father had died holding an extraordinary command given by the Senate. But in Antony's consciousness the recent flirtation of his uncle with Catiline and the execution of his stepfather as Catiline's lieutenant in the popular cause seemingly outweighed the older senatorial ties. His family made his holding political office inevitable; but it left him the option of his policies.

Into this family of traditions, prestige, alliances, strengths, and instabilities, Marcus Antonius was born in 83 or 82 B.C. Perhaps he was born during his father's exile, but certainly he was reared in Rome. His brothers Gaius and Lucius were born in such prompt sequence that the associations of the three boys must have been very close. In their tumultuous later years they remained uncompromisingly loyal, and this family loyalty was one of Antony's most attractive qualities.[14]

Despite their father's death and mother's remarriage, constant financial strains in the family, and public disorders of the day, the boys would have received the regular aristocratic education for public life. Nothing is known of Antony's education, but a boy of his class was normally tutored at home, probably by a Greek slave, in reading, writing, and arithmetic, then in grammar, oratory, and literature. Education was directed toward a career in politics, the law courts, and the army; Greek and Roman literature, traditions, mythology, and religion were stressed over science; and physical training was as important as intellectual. Plutarch says that Antony "gave brilliant promise," and certainly his later career demonstrated expertness in oratory and in the considerable skills needed to command an army or direct a state. But ancient sources never suggest that Antony developed a love of learning, awareness of beauty, or commitment to intellectual excellence. Unlike Caesar, he wrote nothing of significance even about his wars, and, typically, his last known writing before his final naval battle at Actium was flippantly entitled "On His Drunkenness."[15]

22

During these years Antony was developing into manhood. Sculptures and coin portraits confirm the accounts of the ancient writers that Antony was very handsome in a rugged way which made his proud affectation of descent from Hercules surprisingly appropriate. Curly hair and beard, broad, low forehead, large nose, jutting chin, thick neck, powerful body—all were well proportioned and made attractive by the distinguished air of a born aristocrat and the friendly manner of an open, agreeable man. To the end, despite a life of intemperance in court debaucheries and camp rigors, Antony kept his gladiatorial strength and could face any hardships aggressive and uncomplaining.[16]

His character was that of a battlefield warrior—for good and ill. Courageous, bold, loyal to friends, chivalrous to enemies, he was at his best when the challenge was the greatest and his slackest at times of ease. Kindhearted, he could be brutal in revenge; generous, he was often obtuse in knowing the hearts of others. He was superbly intelligent, but his youthful interests displayed his talents chiefly in army tactics and in solving military problems. Neither the civil strife in which he grew up nor his early military training stimulated him to develop the breadth, the vision, and the stability of long-range planning, especially in civil affairs, that made for true greatness. He seemed born to be a second in command; and Caesar, who understood him fully, trusted him completely as a lieutenant and compensated for his shortcomings. In Antony's early years he avoided great responsibilities. He let even women dominate his affairs and let his best opportunities fail by default. He acted on impulses, without long-term fixed goals. With boisterous energy he relished flouting conventions and traditions, carousing and showing off to boon companions even when crises required tact, patience, and negotiations. A simple man in character and views, he long lacked the will, the deviousness, and the ruthlessness to rule the Roman world; and it was an ironic Fate that chose him to command and forced him to realize and exert his own exceptional abilities.[17]

Antony displayed these character traits early in life. Each Roman boy dedicated his childhood toga and *bulla* to the *Lar familiaris* (family god) and assumed the toga of a man and the responsibilities of a citizen sometime between his twelfth and nineteenth year, commonly at sixteen or seventeen. No longer a school boy, the aristocrat normally attached himself to a professional man in a kind of apprenticeship for politics, the courts, or the army. For a sober young citizen, this was the gradual launching of a career. But the last century of the republic suffered the breakdown of so many familiar beliefs and traditions that the boys of the day, adrift from the secure moorings of their fathers, were tempted to impatient wildness and pleasure seeking. Antony, with profligate family, unstable paternal guidance, and an inborn inclination for a carouse, early gravitated to "the gang of young incorrigibles" led by Publius Clodius, the talented but undisciplined scion of the ancient patrician family of Claudii.[18]

One of the gang was Gaius Scribonius Curio, an ambitious and able young man, whose wealthy and conservative father had held the consulate in 76 B.C., then acted as commander in Thrace. Curio and Antony became inseparable and corrupt companions, adding to their irregular attachment affairs with women, drinking bouts, and desperately heavy debts. Debts were common for young men launching political careers: Caesar, solely on the collateral of his political and military potential, borrowed the equivalent of a million dollars. But such moneys were used for wooing allies with political favors and becoming prominent for the voters by shows and donations. Antony's debts of about one and one-half million denarii ($300,000, with four or five times the purchasing power of our money) rose owing to extravagances running from gambling to buying for about 8 talents ($10,000) two beautiful boys to serve at parties. His father had died leaving an estate so encumbered with debts that Antony had refused the inheritance—a legal but hardly filial escape—so that when, in the theater, he sat in the seats reserved for the equestrians, he was blamed for not shifting to the section assigned to the bankrupts. His stepfather had already been expelled from the Senate for debauchery and extravagance beyond his means. Curio, therefore, stood surety for Antony's mounting debts, until the elder Curio was forced to settle the account and forbade Antony access to his son. The boys would not break their association; Cicero accuses Antony of having avoided the watchmen at the gates by climbing down through Curio's roof. Still, Antony's debts continued to plague him.[19]

Perhaps a rich dowry, perhaps a flouting of aristocratic social mores, probably real affection led to Antony's first marriage, to Fadia, daughter of the wealthy freedman Quintus Fadius Gallus. It is possible that Antony was not legally married to this lower-class woman, but he did acknowledge their several children as his own. The story is little known, but Cicero's references suggest that Fadia and the children were all dead at the latest by 44 B.C.[20]

Antony next married his first cousin, Antonia, the daughter of Gaius Antonius. Their daughter, Antonia, was born between 54 and 49 B.C. In 47 B.C., Antony divorced his wife on a charge of liaison with Publius Cornelius Dolabella, tribune and ally of Antony until their friendship broke over the charge of adultery. Antony continued to provide for his daughter—it was typical of him to be solicitous for all his children—and he betrothed her in 44 B.C. to the son of Marcus Lepidus the triumvir. This politically advantageous alliance dissolved with Lepidus's power, and in 34 B.C. she married Pythodorus, a rich Asiatic-Greek of Tralles.

Antony's political career was making a limping start during these years. He may have been initiated a priest of the Lupercal brethren as an adolescent since later he appeared in this role. A priesthood in an ancient religious association was a traditional type of affiliation for an aristocratic youth. But in active politics, his sympathies were with the populares rather than the optimates faction. Publius Clodius and his "gang," optimates in family origins, like Antony were badly in debt and hostile to the government in which they found themselves debtors, in disfavor, and at the bottom rung of the ladder of political offices that would bring them to power. In the years of competition between Crassus and Pompey, Clodius and his associate Antony supported Crassus, as less in control and as promising greater bribes for support. Moreover, Pompey had condemned Antony's uncle Gaius for extortion, but Crassus had supported him and had dared to remain friendly. During the Catilinarian Conspiracy in which Antony's stepfather played such an important part, Cicero called Antony's friends "the Catiline set," but eventually their role was not prominent enough to cause their prosecution.[21]

In 60 B.C., when Clodius was brought to trial for sneaking, disguised as a woman, into the sacred female rites of the "Good Goddess," Curio worked with Crassus's money for Clodius's acquittal. When Clodius turned to the triumvirs and in 59 B.C., as tribune and their agent, succeeded in exiling Cicero on the charge of illegal execution of the Catilinarian conspirators, including Lentulus Sura, Antony probably backed Clodius and may even have participated in the razing of Cicero's house as a filial vengeance for the death of his stepfather.[22]

Such factional affiliations were setting the direction of Antony's career as an agent of the triumvirate and were building the political debts and enmities later to be paid to and by Antony. Always tenaciously loyal, Antony would continue allied with Curio through several changes of fortune until Curio's death. Commitment to Clodius was not as steadfast. At times their career ambitions and political alliances clashed. Moreover, Cicero charges that in 59 or 58 B.C., Antony had an affair with Fulvia, the politically powerful and wealthy wife whom Clodius had married in 62 B.C. It is true that Antony was to marry Fulvia in 47 B.C., immediately after his divorce from Antonia. Yet after Clodius's murder in a gang fight on the Appian Way in 52 B.C., Antony supported Clodius's nephews in prosecuting and condemning Milo as the leader who had killed Clodius.[23]

Perhaps liaison with Fulvia proved difficult, perhaps Antony had wearied of the wild life of Clodius's gang, perhaps he fled pressing creditors, perhaps, at twenty-five, he was growing up; whatever the causes, in 58 B.C. Antony retreated to Greece, ostensibly to study oratory. Such study was typical advanced training for politically ambitious young aristocrats and provided a thoroughly legitimate explanation of Antony's move. Indeed, he probably studied hard, for by now he knew the practical values of swaying men's minds. He is described as preferring the ornate "Asiatic" style of oratory, and Octavian criticized the use of archaisms in his speech; but in later years he proved a powerful orator. All through the 40s B.C. Antony continued his training under a tutor, Marcus Epidius. But concurrently he was studying military training, and this was where his heart and greatest talent lay. In 58 B.C., when Aulus Gabinius as proconsul was sailing for Syria, he easily persuaded Antony to leave his studies to become Gabinius's commander of cavalry.[24]

III

Lieutenant

Antony's career, like those of his leading contemporaries, was always to include political and military aspects. Until 58 B.C. his life at Rome had led him to political involvements based more on loyalties to family and friends than on convictions and planned policies. Now at age twenty-five, rather later than most young men of his class, he began the military career that would bring out his best qualities of courage, responsibility, and comaraderie and that would give him preeminence as the best of lieutenants.

Not that military life in Antony's class could be separated from political involvements. Aulus Gabinius, the proconsul of Syria, 57–54 B.C., who drew Antony into military life, may have granted him the command of the cavalry because of family loyalties to the Antonii: an Aulus Gabinius was quaestor against the pirates in Cilicia in 102 B.C. under Antony's grandfather. Gabinius must also have known Antony in Rome as Clodius's henchman and a supporter of the triumvirs. For Gabinius had been Pompey's serviceable ally for a decade. In 67 B.C. his tribunician Gabinian Law gave Pompey the extraordinary command of the seas against the pirates that was the real basis for Pompey's power in Rome, and Gabinius repeatedly represented Pompey's interests in Rome as he himself rose through political offices to the consulate in 58 B.C. Yet he also showed some degree of independence from Pompey by associating as well with more radical popular leaders like Catiline, Caesar, and Clodius. It was Clodius as tribune who in 58 B.C., by the Clodian Law, assigned the province of Syria to Gabinius with a special military grant to make war or peace in Syria without further senatorial authorization. Clearly, Gabinius was a leader whom the popular faction believed it could trust to hold one of the richest provinces in the east.

There was warrant for armed readiness and exceptional military powers in the troubled province. Brought under Roman control by Pompey as recently as 63 B.C., Syria stood as the buffer against the Parthian menace from the east, although it suffered from internal disorders. Particularly in Judaea in south Syria, the civil war between the brothers Aristobulus II and Hyrcanus II of the reigning Hasmonean house had invited Pompey's intervention. Pompey favored Hyrcanus and in 63 B.C. made him prince (ethnarch) of part of the former Hasmonean territory and high priest of the Jewish nation. Aristobulus and his family, who had fought the Romans bitterly, were taken as prisoners to Rome. In 57 B.C., Aristobulus's son, Alexander, escaped from the Romans, returned to Judaea, gathered a force of about 10,000 infantry and 1,500 cavalry, and held Jerusalem and a number of other forts as high priest and king. Gabinius's job was to reassert Roman rule by retaking the critical forts and cities.[1]

Antony in this, his baptism of military fire, at once proved his courage and his capacity for leadership. In the siege of Alexandrinum, a fortified town near the River Jordan northeast of Jerusalem, he was the first man on the wall and was honored for his exploit. Next he besieged the Dead Sea area forts of Hyrcania and Machaerus. Alexander sued for peace on terms. But the fighting flared again when his father, Aristobulus, escaped from the Romans and seized Alexandrinum. Antony, Gabinius's son Sisenna, and Servilius led the Roman army against Alexandrinum. Aristobulus retreated, then was defeated, and returned as prisoner to Rome.[2]

In restoring order to troubled Judaea, Gabinius treated the other members of Aristobulus's family with great leniency. Hyrcanus, although he lost his political office of ethnarch, was again made high priest. Antipater, an Idumaean, hated by the Jews as an outsider but a useful supporter of Hyrcanus and Rome, was given considerable authority—a Roman bounty and allegiance which he would soon pass on to his son Herod. Gabinius, to weaken Jewish unity, divided the country into five regions directed by councils of Jewish notables (Sanhedrins) and encouraged the leading cities to follow the Greek model of political autonomy. Although he and the other Romans like Antony profited from the booty of war—as Roman conquerors traditionally did—Gabinius sufficiently checked the unbridled rapacity of the tax collectors and moneylenders that they bitterly vilified him and his policies at Rome. In this respect Gabinius's program was essentially sound and in keeping with the most responsible Roman provincial government. The model could serve Antony well in his later administration of eastern provinces.[3]

Nevertheless, Gabinius was typically Roman also in some of the grimmer aspects of greed, ambition, and selfishness. Roman aristocrats were not paid for holding public offices at Rome, and a man who rose to high public office regularly expended huge sums from his own purse to win the elections. As the centuries wore on, the ever larger and more disparate electorate required ever greater expenditures of campaign funds, and it was accepted that these losses could be recouped by holding high office in the provinces after the praetorship or consulship in Rome. Provincials could be bullied, exploited, and in a myriad ways made to recompense the governor and his staff for their political debts. Gabinius now wanted more opportunities for the conquests that would augment his military fame and his fortune; and, without authorization from the Senate, he led expeditions beyond his province of Syria. There were minor skirmishes with the Nabataean Arabs, justified by the always threatening Arab raids through the desert frontier to the south. He also planned a major campaign against the Parthian kingdom, Rome's formidable eastern neighbor which was to destroy the army of Gabinius's successor, the triumvir Crassus, and which would force an expedition led by Antony into ignominious retreat. Gabinius, no doubt with Antony commanding the cavalry, had advanced beyond the Euphrates when an opportunity for easier and richer conquest induced him to turn south and leave the Parthian expedition to the ill-fated Crassus.[4]

The ruler of Egypt (Aegyptus), Ptolemy XI Auletes (the Flute

Player), sat precariously upon his throne. The Greco-Macedonian Ptolemaic house, ruling Egypt since the death of the Macedonian conqueror Alexander the Great in 323 B.C., had reigned strongly and wisely for several generations and had cultivated good relations with Rome as early as 273 B.C., when it had sent its first embassy to the city. But for the past century Egypt had been facing increasing internal disorder and external threat. The rulers themselves were incompetent; the economy, which had to be minutely and prudently regulated, suffered from bad management and overtaxation; the Egyptian populace were rebellious against their Greco-Macedonian overlords. The great port city of Alexandria, with its restless, heterogeneous population, was particularly explosive. And, although Egypt was still technically free, Roman legions had conquered every other land bordering the Mediterranean, and the dark threat of Roman intervention dominated all developments in Egypt. Indeed, outright annexation of Egypt as a Roman province was blocked chiefly by jealousy among the leading Romans over who should have the glory and the immense profits of the conquest.

Previous Ptolemies had had to accede to Roman demands, but Ptolemy XI became completely subservient and dependent. His claim to the throne was muddied by the suppositious will of his predecessor, Ptolemy X, who had been murdered by the people. For twenty years Auletes sought, by petitions and extravagant gifts, confirmation of his right to the throne from the Roman Senate and the Roman leaders. Only in 59 B.C., for a bribe of 6,000 talents, did Caesar pass a resolution through the Senate and Comitia recognizing Ptolemy as "Friend and Ally of the Roman People." The constant financial drain was then topped by the Roman annexation of Cyprus, Egypt's last overseas possession. The people of Alexandria revolted in 58 B.C., and Ptolemy fled to buy Roman help against his own people and his own daughter Berenice who had been elevated to his throne by the Alexandrians. The Romans were willing to support Ptolemy, for a price, but feared to grant any one general a command over the power and wealth Egypt offered. To block action, a religious prohibition was produced. In January, 56 B.C., it was announced that the ancient Sibylline books forbade the restoration of the Egyptian king by force, though they permitted friendly embassies. The discovery of this useful passage was publicly proclaimed and the credulity of the people fanned so that the Senate was able to forbid intervention of any kind on the basis of religious scruples. The tribunes vetoed this prohibition, but no troops were sent from Rome.[5]

Ptolemy, therefore, turned to Gabinius as a governor with troops in the neighboring province of Syria. Gabinius knew of the Senate's decree, but more immediate and persuasive was Ptolemy's proffered bribe of 10,000 talents. With this fortune and probably the sympathetic connivance of the triumvirate and other Roman leaders who wanted the troublesome Egyptian question laid to rest, Gabinius counted on the practical advantages of time, distance, and a *fait accompli*. Antony, alert to the wishes of the triumvirs, eager for glory and booty of war, and hardly deterred by religious scruples, urged the campaign, although most of his fellow officers were opposed.[6]

In the autumn of 56 B.C. Gabinius accused Egypt of encouraging pirates and building a fleet which would outdo that of Rome, and for these provocations he launched a swift, efficient attack. The major problems in attacking Egypt from the northeast have always been marching an army across the waterless desert area and along the fetid marshes and then forcing the narrow land bridge at Pelusium. Antony led his cavalry on the hard ride; then, aided by Jews within Pelusium who followed Antipater's advice to collaborate with the Romans against the Egyptians, he not only won the isthmus but also carried the city in a sudden attack. Gabinius, bringing Ptolemy and the main force, followed Antony. Ptolemy in his bitterness would have executed the captives in Pelusium, but Antony, showing his usual clemency to defeated enemies, protected the Egyptians he had taken.[7]

The full army now marched on Alexandria. The troops of Berenice took a stand. Bold and skillful, Antony led an unexpected dash behind the enemy's rear to surround the Egyptian forces and win the battle for Egypt. For such signal service he was rewarded and honored. A final skirmish in the outskirts carried Alexandria, though it also cost the life of Queen Berenice's consort, Archelaus of Cappadocia. No doubt Archelaus would have chosen this honorable death in battle. An ambitious troublemaker who had goaded

31

on the queen's claims and kept Egypt in turmoil, he would have been an inevitable victim of Ptolemy's brutal vengeance, which included even the killing of his daughter Berenice. Antony, whose friend and host Archelaus had once been, found and honored his corpse with a royal funeral. The generous gesture after the gallant fight won the hearts of the Alexandrians as well as the Roman soldiers, and Antony is said to have left a shining reputation in Egypt. He must also have seen Berenice's sister, Cleopatra, now named successor to Ptolemy's throne. Conceivably there is truth in the tale that the susceptible Antony loved the fourteen-year-old princess at first sight.[8]

Gabinius's tenure in Egypt was brief. A revolt by Alexander had erupted in his proper province of Judaea as soon as he had left with his army. Early in 55 B.C. he returned hurriedly to crush it in a battle against 30,000 Jews at Mount Tabor. He next campaigned against the marauding Nabataean Arabs. Antony would have left Egypt with him, although Gabinius, on his own authority, detached a contingent of Roman troops to support Ptolemy's throne against the Egyptian people and to back Rabirius Postumus, the Roman moneylender to whom Ptolemy was so deeply indebted for the money to bribe Roman officials that the king made him Egypt's chief treasurer. Gabinius counted on Rabirius's usurious tax collecting to provide the 10,000 talents promised for his Egyptian expedition, for as yet he apparently had received only expense money for his troops. Antony, too, would then have been the richer only in reputation for the illegal expedition which he had encouraged.[9]

Gabinius was to rue the adventure. He had relied on the support of the triumvirs, especially Pompey, for keeping Egypt securely within triumviral control. But the Senate and people proved too hostile to his greed and arbitrary illegality. In September, 56 B.C., when Gabinius asked the Senate for a festival of thanksgiving for his successes in the east, it was denied. In 55 B.C. tribunes hostile to the triumvirs and the populares tried to censure Gabinius's actions before the Comitia; but, with Pompey's support, the consuls maneuvered so to fill the comitial days with Senate meetings that no censure was possible. By 54 B.C., when Gabinius had to pass on his Syrian command to the new governor and return to Rome, his case was so weak that far from demanding a triumph as he had hoped, he skulked into Rome under cover of night and stayed inconspicuously at home.[10]

Charges, however, were laid against Gabinius for treason and extortion. He was tried first for the treasonable act of exceeding the authority given to him as governor of Syria in marching into Egypt. Gabinius defended himself by saying that the special *imperium infinitum* (unlimited command) which the Senate had granted him extended his authority beyond Syria. But more effective, the argument was backed by extravagant bribes to the jurors and by pressures applied by the triumvirs. Gabinius—to the disgust of Cicero and other traditional Romans—was acquitted.[11]

The tax collectors of Rome had their own grievance against Gabinius for his checking of their rapacity in Syria while he himself profited; and they next brought him to court on the charges of extortion in his province and of leaving the coast of Syria unguarded so that the pirates had kept them from collecting taxes. Pompey so pressured the reluctant Cicero that the orator defended Gabinius; but Cicero did not bring his best skill to the task. Gabinius was condemned and fined the 10,000 talents he was supposed to have received from Ptolemy. Lacking the promised reward and unable to pay without it, Gabinius went into exile. Suit under the same law was then instituted against Rabirius Postumus, who was supposed to be collecting the money for Gabinius. But Rabirius had been obliged to flee Egypt because of the people's anger at his oppressive exactions; and he too went into exile.[12]

All this public exposé of provincial corruption and the legal battles Antony avoided. Though he had been a leading participant in Gabinius's exploits and though he had established friends and commitments which would be the bases of his later eastern policies, he was so unquestionably subordinate to Gabinius and even Rabirius that he was not held accountable. Still, he escaped all responsibility for supporting Gabinius in Rome and avoided the legal squabbles by deciding in late 55 B.C. or early 54 B.C. to go directly from Syria to Gaul, where Caesar now invited him to serve as legate.

Caesar had already made Gaul a critical area of Roman conquest and party politics. In 59 B.C. he had secured an extraordinary pro-

GAUL DURING ANTONY'S CAMPAIGNS

BRITANNIA

North Sea

Thames R.

GERMANIA

Rhine R.

NERVII

EBURONES

ATREBATES

TREVERI

Moselle R.

BELLOVACI

Seine R.

Gallia
Belgica

Lutetia

VENETI

CARNUTES

Loire R.

Alesia

BITURIGES

AEDUI

Bibracte

HELVETII

PICTONES

Gallia

Comata

ARVERNI

Lugdunum.

Gallia
Cisalpina

Rhone R.

Aquitania

Gallia

Narbonensis

Argenteus R.

Narbo.

Massilia

0   50   100 Mi.

0 50 100 150 Km.

Mark Antony: A Biography by Eleanor Goltz Huzar
Copyright© 1978 by the University of Minnesota.

consular command over Cisalpine Gaul (Gallia Cisalpina) and Illyricum with three legions for five years. Later Transalpine Gaul (Gallia Transalpina), with another legion, was added to his command. Caesar had utilized this base to move into the rest of Gaul, acting arbitrarily without senatorial consultation but finding excuses in the migrations and wars of the various Gallic tribes and in the invasions of the Germans from across the Rhine. By 56 B.C. Caesar had used Roman power with lightning speed and skillful strategy to subdue all Gaul to the Atlantic and North Sea; in 55 B.C. he had crossed the Rhine to show muscle to the Germans and had made a brief sortie into Britain, which was offering aid to Rome's foes. He had molded a crack army of eight veteran legions devoted to him, and he had significantly enhanced his reputation in Rome. For Antony, to join Caesar meant both fighting under Rome's finest general and allying with the Caesarian political faction. The affiliation was to determine the direction of Antony's life.

Nothing specific is known of Antony's service as Caesar's legate from early 54 to early 53 B.C. But during this year Caesar again invaded Britain with a fleet of almost 1,400 vessels, 5 legions, and 200 cavalry. Despite the damage done to the fleet by a channel storm, Caesar crossed the Thames and captured the capital from Cassivellaunus, the British commander. The fighting throughout was arduous. No permanent occupation was attempted, and after the initial victories Caesar withdrew his entire force to Gaul. Nevertheless, the campaign had taken hostages and tribute, and the conquests reported by Caesar again thrilled Rome.[13]

Even before Caesar's absence from Gaul, disorders had erupted there. The Nervii, Treveri, Eburones, and others in Belgian Gaul (Belgica), discontented because their intertribal wars and intratribal feuds had been checked by Caesar, attacked the several winter camps Caesar had established. The fighting was severe, casualties were heavy. Upon their return from Britain, Caesar and his staff moved rapidly to relieve beleaguered camps and crush guerrilla bands. Finally Caesar was able to cross the Alps to Cisalpine Gaul for the winter reprieve from fighting and the surveillance of his political fortunes.[14]

Caesar's *Commentaries* rarely stress his junior officers, and, typically, Antony is not mentioned in Caesar's account of these campaigns. He may have been stationed anywhere in Gaul. But it seems probable that he was closely attached to Caesar. Confident of his own ability, Caesar liked able men around him whom he could drive to their best performances. Antony was relatively unknown to Caesar when he came to Gaul, but during the first year he gained Caesar's appreciation and trust, presumably by capable and gallant action in Britain and Gaul. By the spring of 53 B.C. Caesar had marked him out from among the several talented legates on his staff for a political agent and a military commander.

Accordingly, Antony was sent to Rome in 53 B.C. to stand for election to his first public office, that of quaestor. The twenty quaestors elected by the people each year were responsible for public finances. Two served at the temple of Saturn in Rome, some in Italy, and every province had a quaestor as financial secretary and aide to the higher state and military officials. Because the quaestorship was an early lap in the *cursus honorum*, superior officers were expected to guide and oversee their quaestors and provide patronage for their advancing public careers. Evidently Caesar proposed to launch Antony into public life as his man. To this end he wrote to Cicero, soliciting the distinguished orator's public endorsement; and Antony, arrived in Rome, promptly and eagerly courted him. Cicero, painfully balancing between the established power of Pompey and the growing power of Caesar, agreed to support Antony.[15] In practice, such support probably consisted only in not opposing the candidacy.

Caesar was carefully calculating his moves and placing his agents in Rome. Antony must have carried instructions well beyond winning the election. Disorders, riots, bloodshed had been wracking the disintegrating republic. The competition between Caesar and Pompey had intensified with the death in 54 B.C. of Julia, Caesar's daughter and Pompey's wife, who had been a bond between them. The triumvirate of Caesar, Pompey, and Crassus dissolved with Crassus's death in Parthia in 53 B.C. Although the two remaining colossi were still formally allied, their supporters readied for violence, and gangs of any or no political allegiance roamed the streets. The very elections for 53 B.C. were delayed for a year by riots and disorders, thus also delaying the elections for 52 B.C. which Antony sought.[16]

Especially undisciplined and dangerous were the gangs of two nobles: Titus Annius Milo, who supported Pompey and now stood for the consulship, and Publius Clodius, Antony's old friend, who was seeking the praetorship. For several years Clodius had been Caesar's man, especially useful in attacking Cicero and Cato and intimidating Pompey with his gang of bravoes. But his excesses and dangerous independence now led Caesar to set him aside. While Antony waited for Rome to grow settled enough that elections could be held, a riot in the Forum occasioned a sword attack by Antony on Clodius, who escaped only by barricading himself on the stairs of a bookshop. The rift between the former friends was notorious. Rome must have snickered when Antony virtuously claimed to be revenging Cicero for Clodius's spiteful attacks. Perhaps Cicero believed the tale; he commended the action—while disclaiming responsibility for it—and called Antony his "noble and gallant" friend. Antony had made his unlikely rapprochement with Cicero for Caesar's ends. Possibly Caesar's will also drew Antony's sword against Clodius, who now was serving Pompey more often than Caesar. But Caesar did not casually order murder in Rome, and Antony's violence may have been only a personal vendetta, perhaps even stemming from the long liaison which Cicero charged that Antony had with Clodius's wife, Fulvia.[17]

Whatever the basis of the attack, it was soon rendered unimportant by Clodius's murder by Milo, along the Appian Way on January 18, 52 B.C. The death wracked Rome. Always a popularis, Clodius by death was sanctified as the heroic defender of the common man; and the rioting mob burned down Rome's Senate house as Clodius's funeral pyre. Even constitutional supporters like Cato acknowledged that the troubled times required extraordinary measures. Pompey, already holding proconsular power, had been waiting outside Rome for the call to save the state. Now the helpless Senate voted Pompey an unprecedented and illegal sole consulship to raise troops and restore order. The medicine for the state's ills was strong, but it did effect a temporary recovery. Pompey's troops imposed order. Milo could be brought to trial for murder. But he was weakly defended by a Cicero terrified by Clodius's mob and Pompey's troops surrounding the court; and Milo had to flee into exile. Antony, accurately gauging the public passion for Clodius, had shifted position and had spoken for two hours in favor of Milo's prosecution. His popularis career might well have been ended with Clodius's life had his sword struck home in the Forum attack.[18]

For Antony, Clodius's death and the resultant disorders, bringing Pompey to power, precipitated the long overdue election. The voting gave Antony the quaestorship. The distribution of the quaestors among the provinces was regularly determined by lot. But Antony, confident that Caesar's word had precedence over law, without waiting for the drawing of the lots or for a senatorial decree, hurriedly returned to Gaul.[19]

It was more than time for Caesar's lieutenant to join his army. Caesar had been hurried from his winter stay in Cisalpine Gaul by a revolt of the previously quiet tribes in central Gaul. Vercingetorix, a young prince of the Arverni, proved a brilliant leader, and for the first time rallied the disunited and quarrelsome Gallic tribes into a powerful cooperation. Almost all Gaul eventually followed Vercingetorix as he raided southern France and checked Caesar's early attacks. But, by summer, Caesar, with his full legions supplemented by German mercenary cavalry, joined his lieutenant Labienus near Paris and trapped Vercingetorix and his infantry in the impregnable town of Alesia.[20]

Apparently, this was when Antony rejoined Caesar. The Romans fully encompassed the city and counted on the starvation of those trapped within to undermine its defense. But the Gauls were determined to rescue their allies. After a delay to settle their tribal differences and raise new levies, Gallic troops in turn surrounded the Roman besiegers with 240,000 infantry and 8,000 cavalry, five times the number of Caesar's force.[21] The pressure was critical for both sides. In Alesia famine was decimating the 80,000 soldiers and civilians.[22] Coordinated attacks from the surrounded city and the encircling Gauls threatened the double line of walls, trenches, and forts, eleven miles long on the inner side, fourteen miles on the outer line, between which the Romans were entrenched. Alesia itself, situated on a height, was surrounded by hills and two rivers, except that a plain about three miles long lay in front of the town. In Caesar's distribution of his troops and officers, Antony and Gaius Trebonius were given command of this exposed frontal plain.[23]

In the final fight to relieve Alesia, the opening battle, concentrated in the plain, raged bitterly but indecisively from noon to sunset. After taking a day to recover and to prepare equipment for breaking through the Roman defenses, at midnight the Gauls again attacked from the outer ring and from within the city. Every Roman had been assigned his post and weapons, and the fortifications held. But in the darkness casualties were heavy on both sides. Antony and Trebonius summoned troops from less hard-pressed areas and sent them where most urgently needed. The line was held; the Gauls received heavy casualties from the Roman missiles and hidden ground pits and pointed stakes; and they withdrew by daybreak.[24]

The third and final battle ensued at noon. Sixty thousand picked men attacked an upper Roman camp placed by necessity on steep, disadvantageous ground; but a simultaneous diversionary action was also begun in the plain by the Gallic cavalry and other forces. The fighting spread along the Roman fortifications on both the inner and outer ramparts. Caesar himself dispatched relief troops to the hardest-pressed defenses and ordered part of his cavalry to attack the enemy from the rear. The sight of Caesar boldly in the fray drove the Romans to their last critical effort. The Gauls beyond the fortifications fled in rout and wholesale slaughter. The Gauls still held starving within the Roman siege lines handed over Vercingetorix and all Alesia in unconditional surrender. Before winter Caesar had completed the reduction of the rebellious tribes and had settled Gallic affairs for general security. The Senate in Rome decreed twenty days of public thanksgiving for the victories.[25]

Antony's role in this campaign had been honorable. He was only one of a number of lieutenants whom Caesar mentioned, without embellishment of praise, when writing about the action; but Antony's post had been a critical one, and he had held it gallantly. Every soldier received a slave as reward, and Antony would have garnered other booty as well. Not the least reward was Caesar's approval and assignment to fresh responsibilities.

Normally, Caesar retired to Cisalpine Gaul when winter weather imposed an end to campaigning. The winter of 52-51 B.C. Caesar spent in Gaul, fearful of fresh revolts. His troops were stationed throughout the province to discourage disorders. He himself stayed at Bibracte in central Gaul, south of Alesia, and he kept Antony with him. His decision proved prudent. The Gauls plotted rebellions spread so widely that they hoped to make the Roman force ineffectual. By December 30, Caesar was marching on a forty-day campaign to reassert control over the warlike tribe of Bituriges and thus to quash other tribal insurrections. During Caesar's absence from Bibracte, Antony was left in charge of the winter quarters. Eighteen days after his return, Caesar was again marching north with fresh troops to crush the Carnutes. This accomplished, he turned still farther north against the fierce Bellovaci who were assembling a great army against neighboring Roman allies. Caesar summoned four legions, then three more; but there is no evidence that Antony was with them. The Romans finally won a major victory. The Bellovaci sought peace.[26]

Again Gaul seemed uneasily quiet. Again Caesar sought to guarantee the peace by stationing troops strategically throughout Gaul. Again he kept Antony as quaestor with him, apparently attached to the Twelfth Legion. But the peace was unstable. Reprisals against troublemakers might defuse rebellions. Caesar led his force, including a legion under Antony, northeast against the Eburones whose leader Ambiorix was a fugitive, fleeing and hating Rome. Ambiorix again escaped, but Caesar ravaged the land of the Eburones by pillage, fire, slaughter, and enslavement to leave no state to which Ambiorix could return. Caesar then left Antony with fifteen cohorts in Bellovacian territory to block any further plots of rebellion and went himself through Gaul, crushing all elements of resistance, meting out harsh punishments, then offering conciliation and security to those who had challenged Rome. By autumn Gaul seemed wholly conquered and subdued, and Caesar returned to the settled southern province of Narbonensis to regulate it before returning north to Belgica for the winter.[27]

During his trip to Narbonensis the legions had been sent to winter quarters, strategically scattered across Gaul. Four of his ten legions were stationed in Belgica under Antony, Gaius Trebonius, and Publius Vatinius. Antony's troops had settled among the Atrebates, who were almost unanimously loyal to Rome. The exception among them, however, was Commius, long faithful to Rome but now embittered by Roman treachery and recently escaped from his campaign with the Bellovaci against Rome. With a brigand band of cavalry, he patrolled the roads and raided Roman supply trains. Antony sent a cavalry squadron against him led by a commander personally hostile to Commius. The vicious hand-to-hand fighting gravely wounded the Roman commander but also destroyed many of the Gauls. Commius escaped; but now, despairing of his vendetta against the Romans, he sent hostages to Antony as a guarantee that he would be available to Antony and would accept Antony's commands. The one special concession he entreated was that he should not have to come into the presence of any Roman. Antony acknowledged that previous Roman perfidy to him made his fears justified. With a calculated clemency and boldness appropriate to Caesar, Antony took Commius's hostages and let him flee to Britain. There Commius gathered around him other escaped Atrebates but offered no serious threat to Rome.[28]

With Caesar's return to Belgica, Antony's command was over. As in Syria and Egypt, he had proved a bold fighter, a popular and effective officer, a competent quartermaster supplying needed provisions, and a thoroughly trustworthy second in command whom Caesar appreciated. He knew Caesar's friends and their abilities. His pockets were filled with Caesar's largesses and his own plunder. In another age he would have made the army a lifetime career and would have relished the reckless life of the camp. But a Roman became general through political office; elections made or broke his military record. Antony had won the quaestorship, and, as an ambitious man, was due to stand for the next offices. More important, Antony was Caesar's loyal man, and Caesar's troubled political prospects could be aided by Antony's holding political office to support him. During the winter months, Antony returned to Rome. He was never to revisit Gaul; but, like Caesar, he would profit from the thoroughness with which Gaul had been pacified. In the civil wars ahead, Gaul remained relatively uninvolved.[29]

IV

Across the Rubicon

Caesar's plans and Antony's ambitions brought Antony to Rome in 50 B.C. as a candidate for two posts: the civil rank of tribune for 49 B.C. and the lifelong religious office of augur. The augural selection came first. The regular election of tribunes was held in late July; Antony was required to announce his candidacy at least seventeen days earlier.[1]

The vacancy in the augurate which Antony hoped to fill was due to the death of the augur and orator Quintus Hortensius. Once before, probably in March, 53 B.C., Antony had tried for this post, but Cicero, supported powerfully by Pompey and Hortensius, had won.[2] Now Caesar backed Antony's candidacy; for the augur's right to declare the will of the gods from reading omens held such political and legal powers that the augur could force the abdication of officials, set aside a capital court conviction, adjourn an assembly, or cancel a law. As for the other priestly colleges of Rome, suitability for the augurate was judged not by religious faith but by political power and family prestige. Indeed, Antony claimed some hereditary right to the office which his grandfather had held. His chief competitor was the former consul Lucius Domitius Ahenobarbus. Related by marriage to Cato, Ahenobarbus was firmly anti-Caesarian. But he was already a pontifex, and it was unprecedented to seek a second major priesthood.[3]

The election for augur followed both party and personal lines. Curio campaigned for Antony with Caesar's money, and the Caesarians pulled their political strings in the Tribal Assembly where the choice was made. To swell the ranks of voters, Caesar sent soldiers to Rome on furlough and urged citizens in Gaul to make the long trip to Rome. His personal canvassing was only begun, however, when news came of Antony's elections as tribune and as augur. Domitius took his loss of the augurate bitterly, and all the Pompeians must have realized fully the legal power now concentrated in Antony's hands.[4]

Caesar had been determined to have one or more of his men among the ten tribunes; for he knew well the power of tribunician leadership in the Comitia Tributa and the effectiveness of the tribunician veto. In the elections of the previous year he had bought the loyalty of the optimate Curio, among others, by paying off his overwhelming debts. Curio had been Antony's close friend. Perhaps Antony had been an intermediary in the rapprochement, or, possibly, Curio had earlier led Antony into Caesar's following. Certainly Curio had been serviceable to Caesar and now used Caesar's money and his own great prestige with the people to rouse them even to the stage of rioting for Antony, so that some of his followers were later convicted of violence during the campaign. Stuffing ballot boxes and excluding adverse voters by ringing the voting area with armed men had become common enough devices that they too may have been used.

During the elections of 50 B.C. for various offices, the final voting essentially followed party lines, although in some instances personal debts or hatreds could overcome scruples of party loyalty. Both Antony and another Caesarian candidate, Quintus Cassius Longinus (cousin of the Cassius who later assassinated Caesar and a man whose record as quaestor in Spain was scandalous), were elected tribunes on the campaign promises of continuing the Caesarian largess to the people and the popularis policies of Curio. One of Antony's brothers, Lucius, was elected quaestor. He was to serve in Asia, and Cicero warned his superior that it was now politically dangerous to antagonize the three loyal and powerful Antonian brothers. Although Caesar's father-in-law, Lucius Calpurnius Piso, became censor, his candidates for the consulship and some other

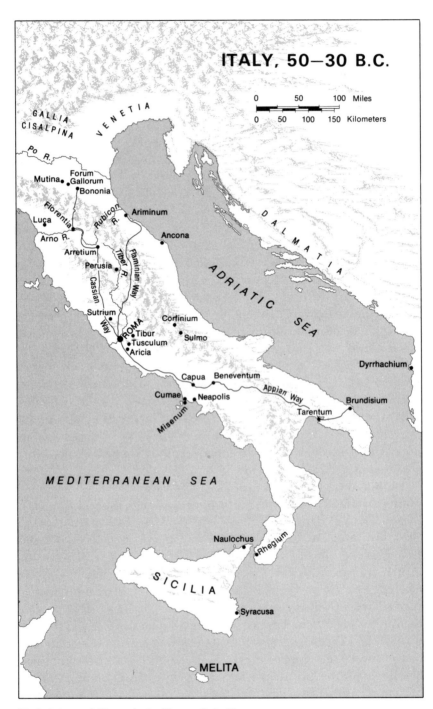

ITALY, 50–30 B.C.

0   50   100   Miles
0   50   100   150   Kilometers

GALLIA
CISALPINA

VENETIA

Po R.

Mutina
Forum
Gallorum
Bononia

Florentia
Luca
Arno R.
Arretium
Perusia

Rubicon R.
Ariminum

Ancona

Cassian Way
Flaminian Way
Tiber R.

Sutrium

ROMA
Tibur
Tusculum
Aricia

Corfinium
Sulmo

DALMATIA

ADRIATIC SEA

Dyrrhachium

Capua
Cumae
Neapolis
Misenum

Beneventum
Appian Way
Tarentum

Brundisium

MEDITERRANEAN SEA

Naulochus
Rhegium

SICILIA

Syracusa

MELITA

Mark Antony: A Biography by Eleanor Goltz Huzar
Copyright © 1978 by the University of Minnesota.

major offices were defeated. With the higher officials hostile, Antony's responsibilities as Caesar's tribune would correspondingly increase. Consistently, Caesar's domination of the Tribal Assembly was more effective than of the Senate. Antony was prepared to use his tribunician powers; the optimates schemed to bypass his authority, even illegally. The opposing plans soon clashed over the issue of Caesar's reelection as consul.[5]

In 56 B.C. the First Triumvirate had held its last meeting at Luca to apportion the governmental powers each leader wanted. Caesar had claimed a five-year renewal of his proconsulship in Gaul, which would extend his command until March, 50 B.C. However, the technicalities of the laws ensured that he would not be replaced by his successor until after the elections of 49 B.C. at which he was slated to win his second consulship for the year 48 B.C. Even his candidacy for the consulship would be allowed *in absentia* despite laws to the contrary. These arrangements would enable Caesar to go from the protection of the proconsular *imperium* in Gaul to the security of the consular *imperium*. This official power of the highest magistrates gave them command of armies and granted immunity from legal prosecution while they held office. In Rome's violent political arena, Caesar needed the support of his army even as a candidate for election, and he had no desire to justify in hostile courts of law his many patent illegalities as conqueror of Gaul.[6]

The five-year plans laid at Luca were not destined, however, to run their course. In 53 B.C. Crassus died in battle with the Parthians. Pompey and Caesar, though willing to make some concessions for mutual advantages, gradually drifted apart. The triumvirs had allied against the hostile optimates. Now the optimates were wooing Pompey, weakening their own power by granting him extraordinary commands, joining consular with proconsular *imperium* and permitting him to remain in Rome while he ruled his province Spain by legates. Increasingly, Pompey represented the Senate's positions whereas Caesar, distrusted by the respectable aristocrats and able to win patrician allies only among the insolvent and disreputable malcontents like Curio and Antony, posed as the champion of the people against the oligarchy. Since Caesar was not on the scene but in Gaul, he placed his henchmen primarily in the Comitia Tributa to support popular causes. Inevitably, both men were forced into increasingly hostile positions by their intransigent supporters and found it harder to make concessions which might suggest buckling under to a superior.[7]

By 52 B.C., Pompey was at the height of his power, appointed interrex and sole consul by the Senate. Caesar was hard pressed by Vercingetorix in Gaul, but his army was fanatically loyal to him and his reputation was formidable. As yet there was no overt break between the surviving triumvirs, only a jockeying for legal position through legislative measures. Early in 52 B.C. the ten tribunes, acting against the traditional senatorial control of provinces, united in a comitial law to confirm the agreement at Luca that enabled Caesar to continue as governor of Gaul, therefore to have immunity from prosecution until the end of 49 B.C. Pompey probably acquiesced in this law, but his optimate allies felt threatened enough to counter with their own legislation. The first of three new laws provided that the governors of the Gauls take office on March 1, 49 B.C., and required that candidates for office campaign personally in Rome. Both provisions were calculated to deprive Caesar of his *imperium* and his army before the consular elections, thus trapping him into his enemies' prosecutions from a position of weakness. The Caesarian protests that this denied the provisions of Luca led Pompey to stipulate that Caesar was an exception to the law. The second law, however, went further in providing governments for the provinces on January 1, thus potentially leaving Caesar a private citizen without *imperium* from January 1 to the election period in July, 49 B.C. The third law was designed to strengthen Pompey's hand by prolonging his proconsular command for Spain into 47 B.C., even though he remained in Rome. He would thus continue to hold the *imperium* and act from a position of strength after Caesar's *imperium* had lapsed.[8]

In the year 51 B.C. continued efforts were made, especially by the consul Marcellus, to set aside the Law of the Ten Tribunes, to take the province of Gaul from Caesar, and to buy off his veterans with pensions provided by the state instead of by Caesar. But vigilant tribunes vetoed all the measures. False rumors were spread that Caesar was mobilizing his forces. Yet neither Pompey nor Caesar wanted to resort to arms. And the optimates, fearing the proscriptions, confiscations, cancellations of debts, shortages of money, and other attacks on their position caused by civil war, seemed willing to compromise much for peace.[9]

By 50 B.C., however, the issue of Caesar's standing for the consulship of 48 B.C., with or without the immunity of his *imperium*, had to be resolved. Caesar and Pompey proposed and counter-proposed giving up power mutually, but their hypocrisy was patent. Senatorial legislation about Caesar's successor in Gaul was vetoed by Caesar's alert tribune Curio.[10]

On December 1, when a debate whether Pompey or Caesar should resign his force was threatening to jeopardize Caesar, Curio as tribune and Antony as tribune-elect proposed that both generals give up their armies, probably specifying March 1.[11] Amid resounding praise for Antony and Curio, the Senate approved the proposal 372–22. The anti-Caesarians, goaded by Cato, vetoed the measure, arguing that Pompey would give up four years of command to Caesar's four months and that the Senate had no right to limit Pompey's legal term. Cicero urged compromise. But the Pompeians had taken fright at the near success of Antony and Curio's measure. The consul-designate Marcellus reported rumors that Caesar was marching on Cisalpine Gaul and Italy, and in unconstitutional action he authorized Pompey to raise troops. Pompey accepted the commission, ignoring Curio's tribunician veto. It had been Pompey who had restored the tribunician rights after Sulla had limited their traditional powers of legislation and veto. Now he found the tool he had created for his personal use had become a weapon determining policies against him. His ignoring the veto was a critical step toward war. The tribunician obstruction of Curio and Antony had been Caesar's guarantee for holding his Gallic command. If legal action were no longer effective, Caesar would turn to his troops.[12]

Amid these threats to their constitutional powers, the new board of tribunes assumed office on December 10. Though Curio, out of office and again merely a member of the Senate, and other Caesarians like the tribune Quintus Cassius Longinus worked with him, Antony was Caesar's dominant spokesman. Indeed, he had probably gone to Caesar in Gaul for instructions before taking office. On December 18 the consuls proposed that Pompey declare Caesar a public enemy and take charge of the two legions that were mustered in Rome for a campaign against Parthia. Antony responded, using his maiden speech to attack Pompey: he criticized Pompey's life since childhood, damned his repression of civil rights in the Milo affair, and threatened armed intervention. Pompey's invective response belittled Antony as penniless and Caesar's "man of straw." More significant, Antony demanded that the two Parthian legions be sent to Syria and forbade Pompey's further recruiting. The altercation stalemated any action.[13]

On January 1, 49 B.C., Curio, who had traveled to Caesar in Cisalpine Gaul for instructions, attempted to read Caesar's dispatch to the Senate but was blocked. Antony and Quintus Cassius Longinus as tribunes then read Caesar's letter, listing his services to the state and demanding either that he be allowed to stand for the consulship *in absentia* according to the Law of the Ten Tribunes, or that, if he surrendered his command, Pompey do the same. The response of many senators judging the demands as reasonable was favorable. But the great majority, partly because they were intimidated by the troops Pompey had stationed near Rome, voted that Caesar had to dismiss his army, lose his *imperium* when he crossed the boundary of Italy, and stand for the consulship in Rome—though this meant he would be subject to prosecution for some months. During the course of the debate, Curio extended Caesar's offer to resign Transalpine Gaul with its eight legions at the end of his term of office if he could keep the *imperium* in Cisalpine Gaul with its two legions. On Cicero's urging, the demand was reduced to Caesar's holding Illyricum with one legion, the *imperium*, and the right to campaign *in absentia*. All the proposals were refused.[14]

Although Cicero was seeking to negotiate, the senatorial majority led by Pompey, Cato, and the consul Lentulus remained hostile and belligerent. The motion was made for the *Senatus Consultum Ultimum*: traditionally, the ultimate decree of the Senate, granting the consuls absolute powers to ensure that the state took no harm; in this instance it granted Pompey absolute dictatorial powers against Caesar. Antony and Cassius vetoed the Senate's motion. For a time the situation was bitterly debated in the Senate. The moderates like Cicero struggled to negotiate. But Pompey bragged that everything was ready for war, and the die-hard optimates would make no concessions. On January 7 the *Senatus Consultum*

Ultimum was proclaimed, declaring a state of war and regularizing Pompey's extraordinary authority to defend the state against its public enemy Caesar. It was a legal action with many precedents. More questionably legal were the insults and the threats of bodily harm with which the consul Lentulus attacked Antony and Cassius. Unable to impose their veto, probably in some real danger in an inflamed and frightened Rome, Antony and Cassius dramatically disguised themselves as slaves and fled north along the Flaminian Way to Caesar.[15]

With no further hindrance from the tribunes, the Senate mobilized the state for war. The distribution of the provinces had been obstructed since March. With Caesar now declared a private citizen, Lucius Domitius Ahenobarbus, who had felt blocked on what he considered a hereditary claim to the governorship of Gaul, was made governor of Transalpine Gaul. Marcus Considius Nonianus was named governor of Cisalpine Gaul, and the other provinces were given to safe Pompeians. Italy was divided into districts, each under an important senator responsible for its defense—a policy calculated to satisfy political ambitions more effectively than military readiness, if one judges by the uncertain policies in Campania, where Cicero was in charge. Under Pompey's overall command, a general military levy was ordered, and the treasury was placed at Pompey's disposition.[16]

The Senate action was reported to Caesar in Gaul by January 10. More than Pompey, Caesar had anticipated this outcome and had already begun to place his troops strategically and to secure critical positions. Although only one legion was stationed with him, he judged that he had to seize the initiative swiftly, and, on January 11, he led his troops from Gaul into Italy at the Rubicon River. Here Antony and his associates reached Caesar at Ariminum, still in the guise of slaves. Appearing so before the soldiers, in well-staged drama, they cried out that a small faction of aristocrats had illegally deprived the people's tribunes of their rights and endangered their lives and had robbed Caesar of the powers given him by the laws of the people. With these claims, Antony provided Caesar with his rallying cry to rouse the troops and the Italian peoples. Caesar henceforth played the champion of tribunes and claimed that all measures passed by the Senate after Antony and Cassius had fled were invalid. It was a hollow pretense. Later in 49 B.C. Caesar in turn was to threaten and push aside the hostile tribunes barricading the treasury door in Rome, and in 44 B.C. to attack tribunes who opposed him. But now his cry of tribunician rights for Antony and Cassius backed his claim to save, not destroy, the republic and gave righteousness to his march on Italy.[17]

Antony at once assumed a major role in military strategy. While still negotiating with Pompey, Caesar moved swiftly south along the Flaminian Way, the Adriatic coast road, and Antony crossed the Apennines to control the Cassian Way, the other major north-south route. With about 2,000 infantry and some Gallic cavalry, Antony easily occupied the major city of Arretium by January 15. With Caesar's flank thus secured, Antony rejoined Caesar on the coast at Ancona, and together they pushed steadily south, gaining towns and volunteers for the army. The civilian population, profoundly indifferent to the competitions of their betters, looked only to their own security. Caesar's control of his motley army and clemency to the conquered brought the people flocking to his side. There were a few challenges to the triumphant progress. His successor as governor of Gaul, Lucius Domitius Ahenobarbus, ignoring Pompey's orders to retreat, tried to hold the important city of Corfinium in the mountains east of Rome. Caesar laid siege to it for seven days until the people within opened the gates to him. While the siege continued, word came that the people of Sulmo, seven miles away, wanted to go over to Caesar's side but were prevented by a Pompeian senator commanding seven cohorts. Antony, with five cohorts, was dispatched to Sulmo. No struggle was necessary. The people opened the gates to Antony, though the senator hurled himself from the walls in honorable suicide. Antony brought the seven cohorts to join Caesar's army. From Corfinium (on January 17–18), Caesar followed Pompey south to the port of Brundisium, to which Pompey and most of the senators had fled. Here both sides skirmished, and fortified camps, and attempted to negotiate while Pompey maneuvered to transport his troops across the Adriatic to Dyrrhachium.[18]

Pompey was unquestionably in retreat and losing the initial advantage of his military position. Nevertheless, his retreat was strategic. Before the *Senatus Consultum Ultimum* he had assured the

Senate that the army was ready against Caesar. But he had failed to assess accurately the speed with which Caesar would attack, the steady loyalty of Caesar's army, and the readiness of the Italians generally to follow the commander who bid fair to be the victor and to be heedful of their grievances. Caesar had had only one legion when he crossed the Rubicon; but he was backed by the legions in Gaul, and his marching force had steadily grown with enlistments, many of them experienced veterans. However, some of his officers had defected, notably his senior officer and ablest tactician, Titus Labienus, who had been left in command of Cisalpine Gaul. Among Labienus's several justifications for switching to Pompey may have been his jealousy of Antony's rapid advancement in Caesar's favor. Nevertheless, on balance, far more of Pompey's adherents had gone to Caesar's side. When Caesar marched, Pompey had only the two legions ready for Parthia under arms. Three more were hastily mobilized before Pompey had to flee. Others could be marshaled, although they would be inexperienced soldiers of uncertain loyalties. But Pompey's real strength lay in the east where over fifteen loyal legions were being collected. It was for these legions and for the control of the Mediterranean Sea which he could command against Caesar's negligible navy that Pompey sensibly overrode the dismay of his followers and left Italy for the east. In his train reluctantly rode almost all the senators of Rome, giving prestige to Pompey's cause but also exhaustingly intruding divided and jealous counsels. Pompey himself grew more vitriolic with failure, threatening proscriptions and executions, to the horror of his more moderate followers.[19]

Both sides ostentatiously offered negotiations and compromises for peace, but probably only to gain time and keep the semblances of goodwill. Both issued patriotic claims of loyalty to the state and its forms, Pompey stressing the authority of the Senate, Caesar demanding the rights of the tribunes. But their followers, like Antony, well knew that the generals fought for their own ambitions and that the soldiers sought their own rewards of booty and power under whichever general could provide more liberally.[20]

Pompey's command of the sea was decisive. His troops and senatorial following were safely transported from Italy to Epirus with the loss of only two ships. Caesar, lacking the fleet to follow promptly, turned back to Rome. With a minimum of bloodshed he had taken all Italy in sixty-five days. Now his ambitions were to secure recognition as the legitimate head of state, to enlarge his war chest, and to organize a stable and loyal administration for Italy while continuing his campaigns against Pompey. Rome waited nervously for the arrival of Caesar, who for nine years had been absent from the city, represented only by agents like Antony.[21]

The great majority of patricians had followed Pompey to Epirus, and the consuls had set up a government in exile in Epirus. Still, a number of senators, led by three to five praetors, remained in Italy. Antony and Cassius, resuming their tribunician roles, placarded the towns with notices of a meeting of the Senate on April 1. Some senators, like Cicero, refused to attend the rump parliament, but enough responded to the pressure of the tribunician summons to constitute the appearance of the Senate. Antony and Cassius convoked the meeting beyond the boundary of Rome, so that Caesar need not illegally cross the *pomerium* (city limits) under arms.[22] For three days Caesar spoke of his claims and sought the support of the Senate for his governmental and financial settlements. But the Senate gave only tepid support to the policies imposed upon it, and in his anger at the body Caesar became more arbitrary in setting policies.[23]

The Comitia Tributa, more pliant under Antony and Cassius's leadership, quickly granted citizenship to all the Cisalpine Gauls. The right had been long promised, but now the area was opened more effectively to Caesar's recruiting. Moreover, on Antony's proposal, the Sullan law that prohibited descendants of the proscribed men from holding office was abolished. Many of the men attached to Caesar were malcontents: desperadoes, bankrupts, and men barred from public office by the crimes of their families. Now Caesar could subsequently use them at his discretion to fill the public offices and the Senate, which in 44 B.C. he enlarged from 600 to 900 members.[24]

His would-be pose as defender of the constitutional state had to be discarded in the face of his financial needs. It was an unsettled time financially for all Italy. Fears of confiscations and debt cancellations sapped confidence, prices soared, and money supplies from the east were blocked. The loyalty of Caesar's troops depended in part on his personal dynamism, but more on his frequent and generous donatives. The pay and bounty costs, demanded in bullion, had to grow with his army. Moreover, to allay the fears and suspicions of Rome, Caesar had provided a distribution of grain and had promised seventy-five denarii to each citizen. To fill his war chest, he was taking property as he needed it, claiming his right as dictator. He had not had to resort to the dread proscription lists but had confiscated and sold the property of those killed in the fighting and of those who had fled Rome. Since men willing to buy such estates would be few, the absurdly low prices for Caesar's henchmen would tempt even the bankrupts. Antony bought Pompey's Tusculan estate with its furnishings, although he already had a home in the luxurious Carinae section of Rome and a villa at Misenum which he had inherited from his grandfather and father.[25] With a poet friend, he bought Pompey's town house. Later he also purchased the villa of Pompey's father-in-law, Metellus Scipio, at Tibur; and he took one of the estates of Varro, who in 49 B.C. had been a Pompeian legate in Spain and then went east to Dyrrhachium. But even for these war-priced estates Antony had bought beyond his means, and in 47 B.C. Caesar wrote from Alexandria that Antony had to return Varro's estate and pay his debts for the other properties.[26]

Still, the confiscated property did not bring Caesar enough revenue. In their flight the Pompeians had left in Rome the rich state treasury in the temple of Saturn. Caesar now arbitrarily took the funds. The tribune, Lucius Metellus, tried to bar the door. Caesar's threatening and thrusting aside of the tribune, whose office he was claiming to defend in the cases of Antony and Cassius, angered the people and left Caesar's policies generally unpopular. After six or seven troubled days in early April, 49 B.C., Caesar left Rome to wrest Spain from the Pompeians.[27]

For his lieutenants during his absence, Caesar looked to his loyal men who could also claim some traditional responsibility for official positions. The provinces were assigned new governors: Antony's brother Gaius became governor of Illyricum with responsibility for guarding Italy's northeastern frontier. Within Rome the praetor Lepidus was made senior magistrate. Because maintaining the pretense of legal government was critical, Lepidus was to hold elections to replace the consuls who had fled with Pompey. Technically, the praetor was not empowered to create an official of higher rank; but Caesar counted on Antony as augur to back this breach of augural lore. Lepidus's failure to carry out this irregular measure, however, lay behind Caesar's later assuming the dictatorship for eleven days in September to hold consular elections. Antony, although continuing as tribune, was also to hold the irregular power of propraetor with *imperium* in command of Italy and its army—in fact, Caesar's second in command.[28]

Antony's responsibilities were grave. Severe economic disruptions were inherent in the civil war. The labor force, even of slaves, was drained by army recruitment and seizure. Money, already in lessened supply with the cutting off of eastern taxes, was being secretly hoarded by wealthy men against the fears of confiscations and the debt cancellations demanded by so many of Caesar's bankrupt followers. Most critical was the demand for an adequate food supply. Pompey's control of the sea meant an effectual blockade of Italy, whose survival depended heavily on grain from abroad. Caesar had sent Curio to capture Sicily and Sardinia for their grain; he had tried also to stabilize prices, credits, and the bullion supply. But his measures had not been very popular and were certainly only the beginnings of complex policies which Antony was supposed to elaborate. Militarily, Italy required defense, and Caesar's armies and navies had to be built from Italian recruits. Politically, even Caesar had not been strikingly successful, and skillful pressures needed to be exerted on the Senate and Comitia to effect Caesar's policies under the guise of legality. In the military arena Antony was at his most competent, and he won the loyalty of the troops by living their life and rewarding them well.

Affairs went badly on the various fronts. In North Africa Curio was defeated and killed. Dolabella's Adriatic fleet was defeated by the Illyrians, and he appealed to Antony for reinforcements. Antony sent a fleet under Quintus Hortensius, the son of the orator, and the three legions that had been stationed to protect the Italian coast towns—one legion under Antony's brother Gaius. But Pompey was also adding eastern legions. Ironically, Lucius Antonius at this time was propraetor in Asia under a pro-Pompey governor and had to cooperate in raising two legions against his brothers. Pompey could also buy or requisition any number of warships and transports from the bustling eastern ports. Thus the enlarged Caesarian army and navy were again defeated. Gaius Antonius had to give up the island of Curicta and was taken prisoner with fifteen cohorts of his recruits, and part of the fleet was lost. Illyricum itself was not captured by Dolabella and Hortensius—a serious failure since thus the land route against Pompey's forces was not secured.[29]

The sphere of political policy making showed Antony's worst weaknesses. He did help Lepidus fill the depleted Senate with Caesar's allies. But on his own, perhaps uncertain of Caesar's wishes, he seemed unable to formulate long-range policies, and Caesar's prestige was lessened by the reckless mismanagement of his leading agent. Antony's enemies reported that he was under the influence of irresponsible cronies and that he played the rough buffoon in satisfying his passions. Caesar had been eager to garner all possible senatorial support. Now several previously neutral senators fled Italy in disgust at Antony's rule.[30]

Most prestigious and influential of the senators still in Italy was Cicero, and Caesar, at his busiest, took constant pains to woo his allegiance. As a substitute for Caesar in courting the old consular, Antony failed miserably. He and Cicero had only faintly pretended to like each other since Cicero's execution of the Catilinarians had included Antony's stepfather. Now Antony wrote to Cicero assuring him of real devotion despite their minor differences. He stressed that Caesar's favors to Cicero were more faithful and substantial than those of Pompey, then added a covert threat by reminding Cicero of his need to protect his beloved daughter Tullia and her Caesarian husband Dolabella. Finally, he stated that he was under orders from Caesar to allow no one to leave Italy. To support his letter, Antony sent his friend Calpurnius to urge that Cicero remain. Cicero's response to these overtures was to fend off Caesar and Antony's pressures with vague talk of retreating to some neutral place like Malta to wait out the civil war.[31]

On May 3, 49 B.C., Antony came to the area near Cicero's home at Cumae. Cicero anticipated a visit from Antony, though he viewed the prospect with dread and distaste. To Cicero's censorious eye, Antony was blatantly traveling in an open sedan with the actress

Volumnia Cytheris as if she were his second wife (Fadia was apparently dead and Antony was estranged from Antonia, having charged her with adultery), followed by seven sedans of actors and female friends. He judged this display the more gross because Antony's mother was present, taking second place to Cytheris. The whole company was billeted on respectable families, and Antony exceeded the proper forms for a tribune by being accompanied by lictors, using horses and carriages and other extravagant displays.[32] Business with conscientious burghers was shunted aside for drunken revelry or recovery. So too the meeting with Cicero. Antony did send him word through a friend Trebatius that Caesar had given express orders that Cicero was to remain in Italy. But Antony's only contact was a letter, received by Cicero after Antony had left for Capua on May 10, stating that he had not come because he feared that Cicero was angry with him.[33]

The half-hearted gesture hardly fulfilled Caesar's instructions to keep Cicero in Italy. Cicero was now more indignant with Caesar because men of Antony's stamp were his agents. Antony's careless avoidance seemed the final insult to turn the always proud Cicero from his role of mediator. Not enamoured with Pompey, he judged Caesar's allies worse. As soon as arrangements could be settled, Cicero fled to Pompey. His escape was a well-deserved blow to Antony, a failure in his responsibilities to Caesar.[34]

Caesar had undertaken the most critical operations. Spain, which was legally and traditionally Pompeian, threatened the greatest immediate danger to Caesar's control of Italy and would endanger his army's rear if he followed Pompey east. Caesar marched toward Spain with six legions in April, 49 B.C. A hostile Massilia lay in his path, and three Caesarian legions had to be detached for siege operations there. With his army thus reduced by half, Caesar ordered Antony to speed the march of the Eighth, Twelfth, and Thirteenth legions from their posts under Antony's command at Brundisium to Gaul, thence to Spain. The Spanish campaigners saw hard fighting, ambushes, hunger. But in forty days the Pompeians had surrendered, and Caesar held a pacified Spain. Only the leading Romans escaped to Pompey.[35]

Caesar promptly returned to Italy to face the results of the military disasters of Dolabella and Gaius Antonius in Illyricum and of

Curio in North Africa. He met, too, the problems unsolved by Antony's leadership; but, knowing his lieutenant's loyalty and military capacity, he continued to use Antony. In September, 49 B.C., Lepidus, with the support of Antony, had the compliant people make Caesar dictator. The office was needed for only eleven days while he could put forward legislation without tribunician veto. Then in the elections for 48 B.C. Caesar had himself elected consul. He recognized the economic plight, especially of debtors, and the issue of the restoration of political exiles. But his most urgent threat was military and, apparently taking Antony, he was off for Brundisium. The debt crises left in Rome steadily worsened until near civil war threatened Italy, endangering the success of the military action in the east.[36]

In Brundisium Caesar's troops were ready, but only with difficulty could Caesar gather a fleet to transport them across the Adriatic to Dyrrhachium in Illyricum. Pompey had taken the ships available in Italy and gathered more in the east, so that now his navy patrolled the Adriatic Sea under the command of Marcus Calpurnius Bibulus, a staunch republican who in 59 B.C. had served as Caesar's hostile colleague in the consulate. During the summer of 49 B.C. Caesar built or commandeered about 150 ships, plus some small fishing craft, enough to carry only about half of Caesar's army, if it moved without supplies. Caesar believed it imperative to defeat Pompey before further resources of the east were put at Pompey's disposal. So, during the relaxed guard of winter, he transported about 20,000 infantry and 600 cavalry through Bibulus's blockade and then sent the ships back to Brundisium to bring the other half of his army and supplies under Antony and his other lieutenants.[37]

Bibulus had failed in letting Caesar cross. Now, alerted, he sank the returning Caesarian ships and blockaded the army under Antony remaining at Brundisium. As the harsh winter wore on, Bibulus died as a result of his exhausting command, but several squadrons continued to patrol the Adriatic, and Libo with fifty ships blockaded Brundisium from a nearby island. While Antony was still not in fighting readiness, Libo raided the coast, damaged some of the merchantmen beached there, and hailed his victory. Antony's capacity to fight was limited, but he responded boldly. Taking about sixty rowboats from the larger ships, he manned them and strung them out along the coast under protective cover. He then sent two of the triremes he had had built to the very entrance of the harbor at Brundisium under the pretense of practicing rowing. When Libo sent five quadriremes to cut them off, the triremes retreated as the attacking ships pressed in. At Antony's signal, the rowboats swarmed out to attack from every side, and the quadriremes fled. Beyond this tour de force, Antony struggled steadily against the blockade by stationing horsemen along the shore to prevent Libo's men from docking to get water. Eventually, Libo was forced to give up his area of the blockade.[38]

Still, the main blockade held, and even when a few fair days broke the winter weather, the generals at Brundisium were afraid to run for the opposite coast. Caesar grew ever more anxious. His supplies were desperately short; his troops were too few for a major engagement; and reports from his generals at other posts were not favorable. When not even word reached him from Brundisium, he began to question the loyalty of his followers and tried to recross the Adriatic in a small craft, but he was driven back by the high seas. At last, after almost three months, his spokesman Fulvius Postumus reached Brundisium with orders which showed Caesar's suspicions of bad faith: Postumus was first to ask Gabinius, in command of the troops, to sail for Dyrrhachium; if Gabinius would not leave immediately, Antony was to receive the same order. If Antony refused, then the trusted officer Quintus Fufius Calenus. As the final resort, Postumus was to rally and bring the troops himself.[39]

The descending order was not needed. The winter storms were lessening, and Libo was not an overwhelming opponent. Antony took part of the army, 3 legions of veterans and 1 of recruits, plus about 800 cavalry, and ran the blockade. Pompey's admiral, Coponius, gave chase and ran two ships aground; in one the recruits surrendered and were executed; from the other the veterans fought their way overland to Caesar. The rest of the ships Antony raced against Coponius's Rhodian fleet. Near capture was turned to victory when the rising wind enabled Antony's sails to outrun the oared ships into Nymphaeum, then served to wreck the Pompeian ships. Antony, safely landed, completed his daring crossing by capturing many prisoners and much booty from the broken galleys. Antony then led his troops to Lissus where the corporation of Roman citizens in charge of the town helped Antony's army in every possible way. Most of the ships Antony sent back to Italy to bring the remaining troops and supplies. Thirty pontoon ships he kept as a fleet so that Caesar could follow if Pompey should now determine to return to Italy. The precaution was prudent; counselors around Pompey were urging that Italy was now open to Pompey's taking. But since Pompey decided to fight in the east, the ships were not used and were later burned by Pompey's son Gnaeus.[40]

Antony still had to fulfill his main objective by joining Caesar. He had sailed north, beyond both Caesar and Pompey's camps near Dyrrhachium, when running before Coponius, and he had been seen by both. Now he sent word to Caesar of where he had landed and with how many troops. He then marched toward Caesar, perhaps under orders with which Caesar had anticipated such a contingency. Both Pompey and Caesar were also marching. Pompey, with a shorter route, hoped to defeat Antony before Caesar could arrive, and almost succeeded. Only the warning of natives that Pompey was near and planning a surprise attack alerted Antony to make his men secure and wait for Caesar. When Caesar's hurried march brought him behind the enemy force, Pompey retreated south to avoid being trapped between the two armies. Antony could now deliver his troops to Caesar virtually unscathed by the daring crossing.[41]

With the reinforcements, Caesar was ready, indeed desperate, for new campaigns. Particularly, he hoped to force Pompey into a major battle before Pompey's force received even more additions from the east, his own meager supplies were consumed, and his men suffered further from deprivation and malaria. Some of his troops had to be sent to Thessaly, Macedonia and Greece to seek control of the areas and their critical food supplies. But Pompey knew his advantage well and refused to be lured into the battle Caesar wanted. Instead, he retreated toward his base of supplies on the sea coast at Dyrrhachium. Caesar anticipated him, cutting him off from Dyrrhachium to the south, and boldly set out to imprison Pompey between a line of fortifications and the sea. Pompey built counterfortifications. Basically, both were attempting to starve out the army of the other. As the weeks wore on, Caesar's soldiers, hard worked in building the vast earthworks seventeen miles long, were reduced to eating roots but swore they would eat bark before they gave in. Pompey's men were fed, but water was painfully scarce and the fodder for horses ran out.[42]

There were skirmishes between the armies, and Antony, who was in command of the Ninth Legion and the southern part of the defenses, was so prominently in the action that he was the most talked-about man in the camp after Caesar. In one engagement he rallied soldiers who were in flight and turned them back to the battle. Again, when Pompey was successfully attacking a weak area, Caesar had Antony order the signal for a charge. Antony's troops were halfway down a slope and had to attack uphill. Although there were losses on both sides, Antony's forces conquered. In the final battle his role was critical. Pompey learned from deserters that the weakest point in the defense, where the fortifications had not yet been completed, was in the south where Antony was stationed. With sixty cohorts on the land side and a strong fleet on the sea, Pompey attacked at dawn and drove into the Caesarian camp. Antony, about three miles away, signaled Caesar, rushed twelve cohorts forward, and stopped the advance until Caesar could bring up yet more fresh troops. Still, the damage was so severe that a Caesarian counteroffensive failed disastrously. Had Pompey pressed his advantage, the war might then have been over. As it was, Caesar withdrew his troops.[43]

Caesar then decided that he had to link himself with his lieutenant Domitius Calvinus who had been operating in Macedonia and that he had to move Pompey from his base of supplies. Both objectives were achieved as the army, which under the pressures of need and exasperation was plundering and scavenging ruthlessly from the now hostile natives, marched inland to the region of Pharsalus in Thessaly. Pompey's decision to follow was forced. He also wanted to join his lieutenant Scipio in Macedonia, and he realized that victory over Caesar's legions could come by waiting rather than by fighting. But his cautious reluctance to fight was beset by the carping of the senators around him who urged action in Thessaly or in Italy. The indecisive victory near Dyrrhachium had brought them to such overconfidence that they thought only of a quick conclusion and a return to Italy where their properties and careers were suffering. Pompey they judged a tool to be used, then discarded. Few, if any, stood as loyally beside Pompey in the rough days and in triumph as Antony stood by Caesar.[44]

Obliged by his colleagues to follow Caesar to Pharsalus, Pompey took a secure position on a hill and waited while Caesar daily attempted to induce him to fight. On August 9 (June 7, Julian calendar), 48 B.C., despairing of a battle, Caesar was breaking camp to go after supplies when he recognized that Pompey was forming his legions for a fight. Caesar at once stationed his men, half Pompey's in number, but veterans eager for action. On the left wing Antony commanded the Eighth and Ninth legions, now so battle scarred that together they formed only one full legion. He faced the First and Third legions (those which Caesar had sent from Gaul to Pompey on the Senate's order in 50 B.C.), which were well protected by a stream with difficult banks. Domitius Calvinus commanded Caesar's center. Caesar and Pompey faced each other on Caesar's right wing, opposite which Pompey had concentrated his strongly superior cavalry.[45]

The Caesarians attacked while the Pompeians held their order. Then as the centers met, Pompey threw his 7,000 cavalry into a a flanking movement. But Caesar, anticipating the tactic, had strengthened his right wing with infantry and cavalry drawn from the left and center. Antony, then, was fighting hard to stand his ground on Caesar's left wing with greatly outnumbered troops; and in ancient battles the able commander was regularly in the front ranks of his men. On the right, Pompey's troops, lacking the critical determination, broke and fled to camp, only to flee on to the hills when Caesar stormed the camp. The cavalry under Antony pursued, slaughtering the stragglers. Most reached the mountains, but Caesar, pressing on his battle-weary men, surrounded the fugitives and cut them off from their water supply. By the next morning the Pompeians surrendered. About 15,000 of Pompey's men had been killed, and 24,000 were now prisoners. Caesar's losses numbered about 200 men, although 30 of these were centurions. It was an overwhelming victory for Caesar's genius and Caesar's veterans.[46]

Antony, as officer, had once more served his commander exceptionally well, and Caesar trusted him accordingly. For Antony, the congenial battlefield years under Caesar now ended. While Caesar went east in pursuit of Pompey, he sent Antony to Italy, again to be his representative in charge there.

V

Henchman to the Dictator

Pompey, his two sons, and many of the Pompeian leaders had fled
Pharsalus. Their fleet still sailed unchallenged. Caesar's task, therefore, remained pursuit and final conquest. The government of Italy, however, could no longer be neglected. As the two vast camps
were broken up, Caesar sent Antony with the bulk of the Pompeian and many of the Caesarian legions back to Italy. In a troubled
time, Antony was to settle the veterans on allotments of land and
with bonuses and to secure, for twelve months, Caesar's post as
dictator and his own as magister equitum (Master of the Horse).[1]

For over a year Caesar's military campaigns abroad left Antony
as the ruling official in Rome. Pompey had fled from Pharsalus to
Egypt, there to be treacherously slain. Caesar, following, received
the dead Pompey's signet ring and sent it to Rome with the report
of Pompey's death. But Caesar then attempted to arbitrate the
family struggle being waged for the Egyptian throne. His motives
were practical. He wanted to dominate and keep passive the strategically important country, and he wanted to claim a share of its
fabled wealth. Soon he was also committed militarily and emotionally to Cleopatra's faction; for in the young queen he recognized the ability and determination to hold Egypt as an independent but cooperative ally of Rome. A prolonged and desperate
struggle ensued until the few troops that Caesar had brought with

him were reinforced by Rome's eastern allies and by a legion of former Pompeians. Even after the victory he lingered to sail up the Nile with Cleopatra. When he left the queen, she was expecting a child whom she was to call Caesarion and whom Antony later claimed Caesar had acknowledged as his child.[2] The Egyptian stay ended when Pharnaces, the son of Mithridates, threatened Rome's eastern provinces by invading Pontus and Macedonia. Caesar left four legions in Egypt and marched north. His campaign against Pharnaces took five days; later, in his triumph he celebrated his victory by claiming, "*Veni, vidi, vici*" (I came, I saw, I conquered). But the affairs of Asia, disturbed by the Pompeians and by Pharnaces, demanded his longer attention. Africa, too, now threatened; for the Pompeians had had time to rally there. So Caesar prepared his African invasion. But the problems in Italy under Antony's leadership had grown so pressing that in the summer of 47 B.C., eighteen months after his week in Rome during the campaign of 49 B.C., Caesar returned to the capital.[3]

Antony's one-year rule in Rome had mingled competence and recklessness. In October he had arrived with the prestige of victory, leading the legions Caesar could spare. The people had responded to his pressures by voting extraordinary honors for Caesar. These included the dictatorship he demanded for 47 B.C. as well as the rights of presiding alone at the elections of all magistrates, except those elected in the plebeian assembly, of distributing provinces among the praetors, and of holding tribunician powers. Antony, however, was not viewed with the awe and terror inspired by the conquering Caesar. Objection was raised to the sequence of the appointments. Antony had claimed rank as Master of the Horse when arranging Caesar's appointment as dictator.[4] Traditional senators argued that the dictator and his Master of the Horse could legally be nominated by Caesar's fellow consul; but only when dictator could Caesar name Antony Master of the Horse. With more authority, the augurs objected to Antony's appointment for a year instead of the legal six months; but since no one dared to challenge Caesar's irregular year appointment as dictator, Antony was carried into office by his precedent. Still, Antony's extended term was an unnecessary provocation, and later he was charged with its illegality. Moreover, his authority as Master of the Horse was not clearly defined.

The rank held the *imperium* although with less authority than the *imperium* of the praetors or consuls. But because Caesar was not present to preside over the elections, no magistrates except tribunes and aediles had been elected for 47 B.C., and Antony's powers were virtually unchecked. It was an inauspicious start for Antony in his dealings with Rome's senators, priests, and laws.[5]

These leading men were precisely the ones whose goodwill Caesar was seeking through Antony. As traditional leaders they were needed in rebuilding the peace and health of the empire. Antony's responsibility was to treat the Pompeians with clemency, yet to watch them warily. Although most Pompeian senators were now joining forces in Africa and Spain, the number of Pompeians returning to Rome steadily increased. Antony published an edict forbidding them to enter Italy without Caesar's permission; but Caesar readily pardoned any who asked, excepting only those previously pardoned who had again fought against him. Marcus Brutus and Gaius Cassius, later the tyrannicides of Caesar, were among those promptly returned to Caesar's favor. Cicero's position proved more awkward. After much soul-searching delay, he had reluctantly joined Pompey's camp in time for its defeat. After Pompey's death, Cato had correctly offered Cicero the command as the senior ex-consul, but Cicero saw no further responsibility to the Pompeians and returned to Italy. There he was stopped at the port town of Brundisium by Antony's order. Antony may have enjoyed harassing his old political foe, but, expressing regrets, he courteously sent him a copy of Caesar's letter stating that no Pompeian might come to Italy without Caesar's express permission. Cicero protested that Dolabella had spoken for Caesar in urging him to return. Antony then publicly announced Caesar's order, but exempted Cicero, thus paining the orator with the publicity of his recantation of the Pompeians.[6]

Regrettably, the other aspects of Antony's rule were far less popular than enforcing Caesar's clemency. He reverted to his reckless, spendthrift revelry. Cytheris was awaiting his return in Brundisium, and again the irresponsible carousing, drinking, and indifference to conventions made him too often an object of ridicule. Instead of wooing the support of leading senators to build a stable society, Antony had taken possession of Marcus Piso's house and was forcibly billeting his motley gang of actors and courtesans in the homes of sober citizens. Though he assumed a democratic mien with appropriate toga (*laticlavia*) dress and had only six lictors, he left the impression of dangerous, arbitrary power by carrying a sword and being surrounded by a throng of soldiers. Even when he presided at festivals in Caesar's stead, the terrified people felt obliged to appear happy. The pattern was all too characteristic of Antony. The wild good times of the hour were irresistible even though they damaged his reputation and left him heavy headed for the next day's business. Friends were bawdy buffoons rather than the calculated political allies of a senatorial *factio*. Antony gave no evidence of planning long-term policies. Even though troublesome rumors repeatedly reported Caesar dead, Antony was not a statesman but Caesar's lieutenant.[7]

In economic policies perhaps it was inevitable that Antony satisfy no one, but his carelessness aggravated the difficulties. From many of the rich there was substantial confiscation of gold and silver. Perhaps this wealth came mainly from Pompeian property. Or perhaps Antony was carrying out Caesar's reenactment of an old law which said that no one should have more than 15,000 denarii in his possession. Certainly, Caesar's programs required major expenditures. But Antony's high living permitted the scandal that Antony was looting to repay his own debts.[8]

Among the masses, too, Antony came back to disorderly demands which he was incapable of quieting. Caesar had tried to deal with the crises of widespread debts in Rome with sensible and moderate legislation which satisfied the conservatives and provided hope for long-term amelioration. But debt legislation had been the basis of popular appeals for a century, and new demagogues now promised cancellation of all debts and remission of rents. In early 47 B.C. the tribune Publius Cornelius Dolabella, Cicero's son-in-law, proposed these policies against the embattled opposition of another tribune, Lucius Trebellius, who sought power also but with more moderate changes. Antony's initial response was favorable to Dolabella. The masses in Caesar's popularis party were clamoring for change, and the tribunes were divided. The wealthier classes, however, forcibly argued the dangers of the policies and the rejection of Caesar's legislation which such policies involved;

and Antony swung over to the opposition. From this time Antony appeared rather as a conservative than as a radical leader of the popularis faction.[9]

Probably personal animosities contributed to the shift. Dolabella was garnering the plaudits from the masses for the proposals. Worse, though married to Cicero's daughter Tullia, Dolabella was the acknowledged lover of Antony's second wife, his cousin Antonia. Despite the bond of their daughter Antonia, his wife's marital infidelity gave Antony grounds for a divorce.[10]

The economic turbulence was not so easily dispatched. Antony had ordered that no one carry weapons in Rome, yet armed gangs roamed the streets in the names of the tribunes. The Senate unwillingly granted Antony the right to keep troops within the city as a guard. Nominally he remained neutral, but covertly he aided Trebellius's faction with troops and encouragement.[11]

While Rome seethed with this disorder, Antony was summoned to Campania where the veteran legions were encamped awaiting discharge with bonuses from Caesar. The months had worn on with virtually no news of Caesar; indeed, persistent rumors circulated of his death. Now the troops were mutinous in demanding discharge. Antony could not quiet their hostility without pay and discharge, so that he had to leave the mutiny still rampant.[12]

While absent from Rome, without precedent for such an appointment by the Master of the Horse, Antony had named his uncle Lucius Caesar governor of the city (praefectus urbi), on the grounds that no other curule magistrates had been elected. But conditions in Rome had merely worsened, for the street gangs despised Lucius Caesar as old and incompetent. Antony on his return continued to pose as a neutral while encouraging Trebellius. At last the terrified flight of the Vestal Virgins with their sacred objects from the Temple of Vesta induced the Senate to urge that Antony increase his troop strength and keep order.[13]

Dolabella, despairing of victory against the soldiers, made the ultimate gamble by announcing that on a certain day he would enact his debt and rent laws and barricade the Forum. At dawn Antony ordered his troops into the Forum, destroyed the placards announcing the laws, and killed about 800 plebeians. In climax, the last holdouts were dashed to death from the Tarpeian Rock.

The brutal and bloody attack had not even success to argue for it; the deaths increased the violence, and Antony could not restrain the tumult.[14]

The report of Antony's crises had reached Caesar and impelled him to come to Rome before beginning his planned war in Africa. Moving with his usual celerity, he appeared suddenly in Rome in October, 47 B.C., and, with equal swiftness, stilled the riots that had grown under Antony. His retribution was turned rather on Antony than against Dolabella; for the tribune was now the popular favorite, and Caesar needed to capitalize on this popularity to win back the flagging support of the people. Dolabella was forgiven, indeed his power was increased; and Caesar made some economic concessions to the debtors and renters, following the lines of Dolabella's promises, although stopping short of cancelling all debts and rents. Antony, Caesar treated with greater severity, censuring his wild living so severely that Antony was chastened and even proposed a new marriage, to Clodius's widow Fulvia, as the token of a reformed man.[15]

In the course of his stay Caesar was under pressure to fill his coffers to satisfy the veterans and to wage war in Africa. He encouraged lavish gifts and used the term "borrowing" for levies that would never be repaid. Antony, who had bought Pompey's property with the cool assumption that he need never pay for it, now found himself with the painful obligation to pay in full to Caesar's treasury. The debt was just; but Caesar, ever lavish with the confiscated property of other men, would easily have set it aside had Antony been in high favor. Antony was chagrined and angry. An assassin found at Caesar's house was believed sent by Antony. Caesar denounced him in the Senate, and Antony was deposed from his position of authority. Two consuls were elected for the remaining months of the year. For 46 B.C., when Caesar would be consul for the third time, not Antony but Lepidus was named his fellow consul.[16]

The mutiny of the soldiers in Campania, which Antony had been ineffectual in quieting, had gained such momentum that the spokesman Caesar sent was driven out, two praetorians and other civilians were killed, and the legions marched on Rome. Caesar permitted them to enter the Campus Martius but stationed Antony's legions in Rome to protect Caesar's home and the exits of the city. Then he boldly faced the legions, satisfied some of their demands, promised more, and so won their loyalty that, forgetting their demands for discharge, they begged to be kept in his army. Caesar's mastery was therefore complete. Within two months he settled the crises which had arisen and worsened during Antony's rule. In part, Caesar had the prestige, power, and wealth to resolve the issues; in part, Caesar had the respect and confidence of the people and the soldiers which Antony had failed fully to win. Perhaps no one could compete with Caesar's brilliance. Certainly no other man did while Caesar lived.[17]

In November (September, Julian calendar), 47 B.C., Caesar led six legions to Africa where the Pompeians (allied with King Juba of Numidia) had had time to collect a formidable force. The difficult fighting culminated, in April (February, Julian calendar), 46 B.C., in Caesar's great victory at Thapsus. Beyond the slaughter in the battle, some of the Pompeians, like Cato, committed suicide; others, like the two sons of Pompey, fled to Spain. Caesar granted amnesty to almost all who asked for it, as he had done after the battle at Pharsalus. One whom he did kill, Lucius Caesar, was a kinsman to himself and Antony, and the son of the ineffectual man whom Antony had put temporarily in charge of the city after leaving for the legionary camps in Campania.[18] The younger Lucius Caesar was accused of atrocities too grave for Caesar to ignore. But such cases were rare. Roman senatorial ranks were again filling with former Pompeians who had fought against and been forgiven by Caesar.[19]

Caesar's return to Rome in late July, 46 B.C., brought a flurry of honors and exceptional powers voted by the Senate and the Comitia Centuriata which he increasingly controlled. Four triumphs of unprecedented extravagance were celebrated for conquests in Gaul, Egypt, Pontus, and Africa. After the paralysis of action in Rome during Caesar's absence in Africa, a wide range of new legislation was passed: to provide for the veterans, to improve Rome's economy, to limit the tenure of governors in the provinces, and even to reform the calendar.[20]

As Caesar prepared for the inevitable campaign against the remaining Pompeians mobilizing in Spain under Pompey's sons, he named Marcus Aemilius Lepidus his colleague in the consulship for 46 B.C., then Master of the Horse. Antony, who received no appointment, deeply felt the displacement by Lepidus, who now appeared as Caesar's right-hand man and apparently aspired to be Caesar's political heir. Antony did not accompany Caesar on either the African or Spanish campaigns; clearly, Caesar had not urged him to come. Discontented, Antony blustered that Caesar's demanding payment for Pompey's property meant that he had had no recompense for his previous successes. While Caesar fought to victory over the Pompeians at Munda, and while Lepidus ruled in Rome, we hear of Antony only as a bridegroom.[21]

Antony's third wife, Fulvia, was to be a major factor in his political life until her death in 40 B.C. Fulvia was a manager, and Antony was manageable. She had been twice married: to Publius Clodius and to Gaius Scribonius Curio, both at one time close friends of Antony. By Clodius, she had had a son and a daughter; yet there is a suggestion of a liaison with Antony, perhaps from about 58 B.C. When Clodius was killed, she married his friend Curio, by whom she had another son.[22] It seems likely that her tie with Antony was renewed after Curio's death and Antony's return from Pharsalus. Certainly, marriage in 47 or 46 B.C. closely followed Antony's divorce from Antonia and may have helped hurry the divorce—although it was also said that marriage represented Antony's new sobriety. By the standards of the day, the marriage was suitable. Now thirty-seven or thirty-eight, Fulvia appears attractive in her portraits. Her substantial wealth was a boon for the always spendthrift Antony. Her family, like Antony's, was of plebeian nobility, though more prominent in early than in recent times. And Antony loved his new wife so well that he even gave up Cytheris for her. Fulvia bore Antony two sons, probably his first legitimate male heirs, Marcus Antonius Antyllus and Iullus Antonius.[23]

Apparently, Fulvia's dominant characteristic was her drive for and manipulation of political power. She probably encouraged both her previous husbands' politically active careers. Antony's career, although temporarily shadowed by Caesar's disapproval, was certainly worth managing. She was consistently allied with pro-Caesarian men, and perhaps she had correctly assessed the oncoming reign of powerful men over the Roman Republic. Later Cicero labeled her cruel and greedy; but her early spirit appeared only as unduly sober, so that Antony sportively sought to lighten it. During the years of their marriage Antony was at his peak of political astuteness and ambition. Throughout his career Antony appears to have been an able lieutenant to strong leadership, and the leadership could come from a woman as well as a man. Led by Cytheris, he had been reckless and wanton. Living with Fulvia, he almost won control of the Roman world.[24]

Antony's most urgent political need (once marriage had reformed his personal life and rallied his ambitions for office) was to recapture the goodwill of Caesar. After victory over the Pompeians in March, 45 B.C., Caesar remained in Spain until June, settling the troubled affairs of the province and taking its tribute. In Rome the Senate and Comitia were heaping ever more honors on Caesar, and when it was learned that he would return in June, the leading senators hastened to Narbo to welcome the conqueror. Among them was the reformed Antony, showing his willingness to meet Caesar more than halfway. There, too, was Gaius Trebonius, in disgrace for his misgovernment of Farther Gaul. Cicero, in his later invective against Antony, charged that Trebonius was now plotting to murder Caesar in Narbo. Trebonius, who shared Antony's tent, sounded out Antony as an ally. Antony made no response to the overtures, and Trebonius gave up his attempt. But Antony never revealed the plot to Caesar. If Cicero's charges were true, Antony's silence might have reflected typical loyalty to the friendship of Trebonius or coolness in loyalty to Caesar. Demotion from office must have hurt, but Antony, in the broader context, may well have been puzzling the wisdom of being loyal to a leader whose conquests and stay in the Hellenistic east, especially in Egypt, had made him more authoritarian and more dangerous to Roman republican traditions.[25]

Now Caesar gave Antony every reason for renewed loyalty. Among the many senators fawning on him at Narbo, he singled out Antony to ride in his carriage while his grandnephew Octavian and friend Brutus Albinus rode in the following carriage. The honor was obvious, and during the long ride the reconciliation must have been complete. When Caesar became consul for the fifth time on January 1, 44 B.C., Antony was his colleague. Moreover, Antony's brother Gaius became praetor, and Lucius tribune. At a time when a whole generation of young patricians lacked normal opportunities to be elected to the offices which they deemed to be their birthright, the three Antonii were attaining an extraordinary concentration of official power. After this reconciliation, Antony seems to have been Caesar's most trusted and well-used ally.[26]

Quite possibly, Antony was thinking of himself as Caesar's heir, to fortune as well as political power; and Caesar may have been willing to hold his loyalty with this hope. But in September, 45 B.C., Caesar consigned a new and secret will to the Vestal Virgins, naming wholly different heirs. Although Caesar still hoped to father a son, he now named his grandnephew Octavian his adopted son, to carry his name and receive three-fourths of Caesar's vast estate. Two other grandnephews, Lucius Pinarius and Quintus Pedius, would receive the other quarter. In default of these three, a number of other people were named heirs, including Caesar's remote relative Antony, a third cousin once removed on his mother's side. Antony's unwarranted hopes in the inheritance were to create grave discords after Caesar's death. More important ultimately, however, Caesar did continue to set precedents in concentrations of powers and in legislative policies during the remaining nine months of his life, precedents to which Antony would fall heir.[27]

Although, or perhaps because, he had been out of Rome almost continuously for fifteen years, Caesar's lightning mind recognized a multitude of Rome's problems and undertook possible solutions. Most of the solutions were not highly original, but Caesar knew the wisdom of working from established Roman pattern. Some reforms, like the adjusting of the calendar and the recalling of such exiles as Antony's uncle Gaius,[28] were widely approved. However, major issues faced opposition which Caesar chose to ignore. The many war-mobilized legions of both Pompey and Caesar had to be discharged; the rewards that Caesar had promised his men had to be paid; and enough land or other security had to be provided them to defuse the dangers of discontented, armed soldiers. Other dictators before Caesar had established precedents of land grants and discharge bonuses. Caesar, like Antony and Octavian after him, had to meet these expectations without having available the extensive public lands which earlier generals had distributed among veterans. Caesar's solution lay partly in utilizing Pompeian wealth and land in Italy, more in colonizing the provinces, with land grants for those trained to farm and urban colonies for many of the other veterans and for the unemployed in Rome who were willing to emigrate. Although thirty-five legions were still under arms when Caesar was murdered, the number of such colonists had reached 80,000.[29]

Relief of unemployment by emigration was only one of Caesar's policies for easing the economic tensions within Rome which festered in the disrupting conditions of prolonged civil wars, monetary instability, confiscation of property, and slave labor competition. A rigorous census reduced the number of those on state relief from 320,000 to 150,000. Employment for the able-bodied was secured by ordering that free labor replace one-third of the slave laborers in herding and by greatly enlarging the public works program. Caesar's new Forum Julium and Basilica Julia, his library and theater were to be in Rome. But his proposed harbors, canals, roads, and drainage of marshes extended even beyond Italy as long-term economic improvements. Few projects were completed or even advanced beyond the planning stage, however, and the decisions about completing them would rest with Caesar's successors.[30]

The area in which Caesar was most ahead of his contemporaries lay in his relations with the provinces. His long years in Gaul had taught him the abilities and potentials of the provincial peoples and that talent should be utilized wherever found. In practical terms, he worked to decentralize the state and to integrate the provincial and Roman worlds, granting citizenship and even offices widely to provincials and founding colonies in the western provinces. His carefulness for the colonies was reflected in his Law for Provincial Charters (*Lex Julia Municipalis*), which became the standard political pattern for urban development in the west. On another plane, his travels in the east had shown him the wealth and organization of the Hellenistic states and had probably contributed to his increasingly arbitrary rule. Moreover, Cleopatra and Caesarion followed Caesar to Rome in 45 B.C. and were installed with a retinue of servants in one of Caesar's villas, to stay until April, 44 B.C. Even Cicero knew the arrogant queen, and no doubt Antony saw her often. Her influence was probably minimal, but Caesar did order the building of a new temple to Isis, and any suggestion of eastern interference scandalized the traditional Romans. It was rumored that Caesar intended to move his capital from Rome to the east and to be titled king outside Italy. Although probably ill-founded, such speculation about Caesar cleared the way for Antony's later basing his center of power in Egypt.[31]

Certainly Caesar was treating the Senate and even the Comitia, which had brought him much of his power, merely as his tools. He was capable of determining issues in the name of the Senate without any consultation with this body. The Senate and Comitia were themselves to blame in large part; they seemed paralyzed by the inadequacies of the old republican system to cope with the changing problems. Moreover, in terror of Caesar's military power and capacity for revenge, they fawned on him, voted him extravagant and unprecedented powers, and let him dictate the legislation which they rubber stamped. The fact that Caesar had made the Senate and Comitia truly ineffectual lies behind the helplessness of these bodies when, after Caesar's death, they let Antony take over the rule.[32]

To carry out his various measures, Caesar needed cooperative officials. As he had arranged Antony's offices, so now he placed other men in important posts. When useful, he arbitrarily increased the number of officials or, as in the case of the praetorship of Antony's brother Gaius, granted the offices to men younger than the required age. Indeed, in December, 45 B.C., Lucius Antonius, newly elected tribune by Caesar's dispensation, pushed through legislation giving Caesar the right to recommend half the candidates for the elections of all magistrates, except that both the consuls were to be nominated by Caesar. Granting that elections had always been rigged by the powerful senatorial families, this new legislation was·a callous pronouncement that only Caesar's men could aspire to the offices that were traditionally senatorial privilege.[33]

Because he was organizing a war against the Parthians and would be in the east for two or three years, Caesar made his selection of officials for this period in advance. Among his appointments, Dolabella was named to complete Caesar's consulship from March to the end of 44 B.C. Antony, Caesar's fellow consul, was roused to such fury that he defied Caesar's choice. His old jealousy of Dolabella had not abated, and he had hoped to be sole consul in Caesar's absence. First he denounced Dolabella in the Senate. Then, as presiding consul and as augur, Antony threatened to use religious prohibition (*obnuntiatio*) to stop the election; and, indeed, he dissolved the Comitia Centuriata electing the consul when the voting was supporting Dolabella. Caesar proved surprisingly acquiescent to this defiance and compromised by changing Dolabella's title to deputy consul. He did, however, specify that Dolabella would receive Syria, strategically important for an invasion of Parthia, as a proconsulship, whereas Antony's province would be Macedonia—also a critical military post, since the province had lately been harassed by raiding barbarians. Antony, accordingly, was to be out of Rome for two years while Caesar was in Parthia.[34] Other Caesarians were named consuls for these years: Aulus Hirtius and Gaius Vibius Pansa for 43 B.C., Decimus Brutus and Lucius Munatius Plancus for 42 B.C. Caesar's wide-ranging policies, then, set a number of precedents, of sound imperial rule and of high-handed one-man domination, to which Antony could aspire as the bases for his own control.[35]

The senators, frightened, subservient, yet bitterly resentful, constantly loaded Caesar with still more extravagant titles never before conceived of in the republic. Each of Caesar's victories had brought a fresh rush of honors and offices: dictatorship for ten years, then for life, consulship, censorial powers, tribunician powers, the entire management of army and finance; all were concentrated in his hands for prolonged tenures. These at least wore a pseudo-republican guise. But the external trappings of Hellenistic monarchy and even divinity which Caesar permitted to be voted for him shocked the traditional Romans more urgently and dramatically than the realities of his military and ruling power. Seventy-two lictors, with fasces wreathed in laurel, attended Caesar's triumphal procession; he was always to wear the triumphal dress and laurel wreath; he sat on a gilded chair with purple cloth and spoke first at Senate meetings. Imperator and then liberator were added as hereditary names, and the title Parent of His Country (parens patriae). His decrees were automatically binding, and all magistrates taking office were to swear not to overthrow his decisions. As for an eastern king, Caesar's well-being seemed the essence of the well-being of the state, and the Senate took an oath to protect Caesar—an oath which his murderers were to break. Thanks were given to the gods for Caesar; temples were built; a month of the calendar was named in his honor; games were celebrated; and an extra day to honor Caesar was added, according to a law carried by Antony. Steadily, the adulation turned toward deification. His descent from Venus was stressed. The statue of Caesar was added to that of the gods in processions, games, and temples. And a priestly brotherhood of Luperci Julii (Julian Luperci)[36] like that of Rome's founder Romulus, was established to honor Caesar, the divus Julius, as the founder of a new state. Caesar, then, was to be an important god.[37]

Antony was the trusted follower selected by Caesar, acting as pontifex maximus, to be inaugurated at the appropriate time as the priest (flamen Dialis) of the cult of Caesar as well as the leader of the Luperci Julii. The Luperci ritual was so primitive and rough[38] that the popularity of the cult had been declining; still, it was the fourth major priesthood in Rome, and by ancient traditions had elaborate qualifications and restrictions as well as special privileges. Only a patrician born of free parents properly married by the ancient rite (*confarreatio*) and so married himself could be chosen by the pontifex maximus. Antony, a plebeian noble, married to a plebeian without the ancient marriage rites, could not have qualified save that Caesar made his family patrician and waived the requirements for his parents.[39] The privileges: the wearing of the conspicuous dress (*toga praetexta*), the lictor bodyguard, the seat in the Senate, the royal curule chair (*sella curulis*), Antony would use. The clumsy restrictions on his life, prescribed for both the Lupercii and the flamen Dialis, he would ignore; priests in Rome were chosen not for morality but for politics. In fact, Caesar was dead before Antony was inaugurated into the priesthood of the Caesar cult; but the choice of Antony had been public, and the honor was indisputably his. Antony could not have believed in the divinity of Caesar, any more than Caesar did. But both men had seen enough of the east to know the advantages of a theocratic monarchy. The sophisticated men of a cosmopolitan age would shrug at the concept familiar in the east. The multinational masses of the empire's population, already long accustomed to divine monarchy in the east, would be more easily governed, by the god's high priest as well as by the god.[40]

It was the Senate and the people who thrust the reality of one-man rule on Caesar; yet they found the names king and god intolerable. Caesar apparently judged the titles useful and flattering enough to accept and even to seek them. Perhaps, as other lesser men have done, he also came to think the titles his due, and perhaps even half believed them true. Consequently, as he became increasingly feared and hated by the senatorial class, he grew more demanding of the tokens of power. On December 31, 45 B.C., the senators, led by Antony, consul-elect,[41] came to present Caesar with a new range of honors which they had voted. Caesar, seated on his golden throne, conducting business about the construction of his new Forum, barely acknowledged the honors and failed even to stand to receive the senators. The calculated discourtesy cut deeply and must have embarrassed Antony. Somehow Caesar, so jealous of his own dignity, was forgetful of the cherished ancient dignity of the senatorial families. Though Caesar tried later to explain his rudeness as illness, the senatorial bitterness had hardened.[42]

Caesar's power had been built on popular support led by the tribunes. Now Caesar heedlessly alienated much of this popular support. The title of king, with which Caesar was flirting, still had ancient evil connotations. When Caesar's statues on the Rostra were found crowned with diadems of monarchy, and two of the tribunes had them removed, Caesar was angry. When the same tribunes arrested people demonstrating for and hailing Caesar king, Caesar swiftly had another tribune depose them from office and expel them from the Senate. After a brief time, Caesar restored them to the Senate, but the actions blotted the record of the popular leader who had crossed the Rubicon as defender of the tribunes.[43]

Antony's role was central to the final drama of the kingship claim. During the annual celebration of an ancient primitive festival of purification, the Lupercalian priests, each clad only with a goat-skin, ran through the city striking the women they met with a thong of animal skin.[44] On February 15, 44 B.C., Antony ran as consul and also as priest of the Julian Luperci, newly instituted to honor Caesar. In the stage setting, Caesar sat on a golden throne, with his golden crown and purple cloak, high on the Rostra—which he had recently had rebuilt but on which he had Antony's name inscribed as the one responsible for the work. In the sight of the festival crowd, Antony ran down the Sacred Way and, lifted up by his associates, attempted to crown Caesar with a white headband wreathed with laurel, the diadem of monarchy. A claque of Antony's followers cheered. But when Caesar pushed the diadem away, the cheering of the people swelled. Several times the offer was made; each time the crowd's delight at Caesar's refusal grew. At last convinced of the popular attitude, Caesar ordered that the diadem be carried to the Temple of Jupiter Capitoline to hang there as a trophy, with the notation in the records of state that at the Lupercalia the people had offered Caesar a diadem, but he had refused it.[45]

Antony's reasons for proffering the diadem must remain conjecture. Perhaps he wished to discredit Caesar in the eyes of the people by a public display of Caesar's greed for monarchy. Cicero later charged that the public reaction to the scene was so antagonistic that Antony thereby became Caesar's real murderer. Perhaps he hoped to prove to Caesar once and for all that the public would not tolerate the title king. The most realistic explanation seems to be that Antony was acting not as an independent agent maneuvering Caesar but as Caesar's agent. Caesar may have wanted a public disavowal of monarchy. More probable, he was testing whether the title king could now be his. Whatever the cause of the charade, it proved again that Rome was not ready for a king and intensified the fear of Caesar's drive for power and the determination to eliminate the despot.[46]

Brutus and Cassius were now drawing together over sixty senators to plot tyrannicide. There must have been earlier plans for assassination. Later Cicero charged that Antony led such a plot as early as 47 B.C. and that Trebonius had found Antony's silence more loyal to him than to Caesar when Trebonius hinted death for the dictator at Narbo. Indeed, Caesar was well aware of disaffection among his closest associates. Past conspiracies he handsomely forgave. Future ones he defied, dismissing even the bodyguard which could have protected him. Antony's capacity for murder he scoffed at, saying that Antony and Dolabella were too fat and long-haired to be dangerous. He did acknowledge the dangerous potential of men like Brutus and Cassius, "thin, pale," and intense; but he counted on his generosity in forgiving their past Pompeian loyalties and in loading them with offices and honors to keep them faithful. Perhaps Caesar's ultimate failure appears in his having no friends whom he could trust fully.[47]

Even Antony, his loyal henchman for all the army years, now perhaps stirred by Fulvia, resented Caesar's cool manipulation of his political career and found Caesar's growing megalomania burdening. But no overt break occurred between the men, and when the more than sixty conspirators discussed Antony, they debated whether to include him not among the murderers but among the murdered. The majority favored killing Antony with Caesar: he had worked too long and closely with Caesar; he was powerful as consul and popular with the troops; he was able and personally ambitious; though a lesser man, he was enough in Caesar's mold and training to seize Caesar's role as his own. Against the majority, two spoke for Antony and won his life. Trebonius reported Antony's collusion in Narbo and assured the conspirators that Antony would not oppose this assassination plot. Brutus, who, among men of varied motives of fear, hatred, and ambition, had assumed the moral leadership of acting on committed patriotic principle and family antecedents, carried the argument. For him, Caesar alone was the tyrant, and moral Greek precedents of tyrannicides included no deaths of friends or underlings. The purpose of the murder was to reactivate the republic. Antony as second consul was needed to carry on constitutional processes. In practical terms Caesar's legions still under arms were dangerous, and Antony might control them where no other man could. Once the blows were struck, Antony could be counted on to look rather to his own ambitions than to loyalty to the dead dictator.[48]

Antony's safety, then, depended on mixed motives of principle and utility; so too did Caesar's death. On March 15, 44 B.C., was held the last meeting of the Senate before Caesar's departure for the Parthian campaign. Important on the agenda was the settlement that Caesar as pontifex maximus would make of Antony's pretended augural objections to the election of Dolabella as consul. The conspirators chose this meeting as their best and last opportunity to strike. But on the morning of the Ides Caesar felt unwell, his wife begged him not to venture out, and the religious omens were unfavorable. Even for Caesar the adverse arguments were prevailing, and he was about to send Antony to dismiss the meeting when the conspirator Decimus Brutus, a distant relative of Marcus Junius Brutus, persuaded him of the need to make an appearance. Antony accompanied Caesar to the hall of the portico next to Pompey's theater. But when Caesar entered, Trebonius, as plotted, detained Antony outside. Within, the tyrannicides struck. Antony made no futile effort to save Caesar. Knowing his own danger, he fled.[49]

Surely no one beyond his family had influenced Antony's life more than Caesar. For a decade he had been Caesar's lieutenant; for much of this time he was Caesar's most trusted second in command. The aura of Caesar was dazzling: a multisided genius, wholly free from restraints of traditions, except as he chose to observe them, driven by boundless vision, a man born to command. Aristocratic in taste and style, he dominated men at every level, and his contemporaries all viewed him as a giant. Antony said that he had "inbred goodness." But, though capable of great charm in society, great perception and forgiveness of other men's opposition, and great leadership to make his soldiers follow him through every hardship, he lacked the warmth to bind men closely in real friendships and the generosity to welcome them as equals. Cicero called him a gracious and stimulating dinner guest—whom one would not be eager to invite again. Antony followed him, learned from him, was generally loyal to him; but there is no evidence of a deep personal loss at his death. Caesar's arrogant ambition was for his own dignity. His death left Antony, consul and general, Rome's strongest political and military man. The tyrannicides had judged that Antony lacked the genius, the self control, the ambition, and the ruthlessness to be another Caesar. But with the Ides of March, the possibility lay open to Antony.[50]

VI

Caesar's Successor

Within hours after Caesar's murder Antony grasped the control of power and thus determined the next stage of Rome's history. On Pompey's porch the initiative had lain with the assassins. With other Caesarian and neutral senators, Antony had fled, disguised in the dress of a commoner, and had barricaded himself in his home in the Carinae district. The troubled populace watched bewildered, shattered by the death of their established leader, uncertain whether to commit themselves to the Liberty which the conspirators now proclaimed.[1]

The assassins raised their bloody daggers and called on Cicero who, although not privy to the plot, was now the leading consular to sanction it. To symbolize saving the state, the liberators marched to the Capitoline to dedicate their weapons. Marcus Brutus spoke to the crowds, but in the face of their chill response, the Capitoline seemed the assassins' haven. With this appeal to republican tradition, the conspirators' program of action was exhausted. Incredibly, they had not laid plans even for a temporary seizure of power. With political naiveté, they were deluded by the existence of hallowed republican forms into believing that the motley populace of Rome yearned for the traditional aristocracy and that with the tyrant dead, the republic would function again. And though the murderers talked only of principles, their long-range objectives were murky with private ambitions and hostilities.[2]

For Antony, as for Caesar, the reality of power lay with the army. While the assassins vainly waited for public acclamation of their service, Antony regained confidence in his immediate safety and sought the allegiance of other Caesarians. Most critical as an ally, and first to commit himself, was Marcus Aemilius Lepidus, who, as Caesar's Master of the Horse, commanded the only regular troops stationed in Rome. His small civil patrol had been stationed on the island in the Tiber. Lepidus had marched them to the Campus Martius and could easily have overwhelmed the few gladiators who were the only armed support of the conspirators. But before taking any action, Lepidus came to consult Antony as consul and Caesar's closer friend. Thus the army, fanatically loyal to Caesar, began to shift its loyalty to Antony. Lepidus, who might have used the army to compete with Antony, was soon bought off with the position of pontifex maximus, left vacant by Caesar's death. The office was legally an elective one, but Antony manipulated the appointment, and in the chaotic moment Lepidus assumed the position unchallenged. Only later was Antony attacked for his arbitrary appointment.[3]

Throughout his life Antony's greatest assets were coolness and boldness under stress, a sane daring much like that of Caesar. Less acute in appraisal and less tenacious in execution of long-term planning than Caesar, Antony probably was not yet reaching for the dictator's role. But his first astute decisions set him on his course as Caesar's successor. During the night he obtained, from Caesar's widow Calpurnia and secretary Faberius, Caesar's state papers and a rich, special fund of 700 million sesterces (approximately $30 million) from the state treasury in the temple of Ops. The money was critical for many needs, since Antony was chronically insolvent, but particularly it could satisfy Caesar's veterans with monetary and land settlements, and thus keep them loyal. The secret papers were potent weapons which Antony could use at will for his own ends.[4]

The day after the murder urgent meetings were held by both sides, while the people threatened rioting and the army was mutinous about the murder of their general. Antony conferred with various factions. He restrained the Caesarians Lepidus and Balbus who talked of vengeance. He negotiated with Decimus Brutus, one of the murderers, whom Caesar had appointed governor of Cisal-pine Gaul. Perhaps Antony hoped to secure the province for him-self, a province critical for its strength, strategic location, and large army. But Decimus Brutus, though intimidated, held his post. In the evening Antony summoned a council of his friends. Advice ranged from Lepidus's demand for violence to Hirtius's plea for co-operation with the conspirators. Meanwhile, the assassins' confer-ence seemed dominated by Servilia and Porcia, the mother and wife of Marcus Brutus, whose prime concern was for his safety. De-spite Cicero's pressuring, no plans were drawn for further action.[5]

On March 17 Antony as consul called a meeting of the Senate at the Temple of Tellus. The unusual meeting place was near Antony's home; so that he ran fewer risks in the disordered city. The mur-derers remained on the Capitoline. Despite the republican senti-ments of most senators, Antony boldly took charge, and with this assumption of control rendered the republican murder of Caesar futile. But Antony was moderate, showing knowledge and political acumen in manipulating the senators to his position. He praised Caesar as a peacemaker. When demands were made that all Cae-sar's acts be treated as invalid, he shrewdly noted that among the acts were the appointments of a number of senators to state of-fices. New elections would have to be held whose outcome was very unsure. The senators hesitated. They, or their kinsmen or friends, had counted on the prestige and the remuneration of of-fices. Moreover, they feared the reaction of the army if it expected that Caesar's generous promises to it should be ignored. Cicero, who was active throughout the meeting, spoke of concord and amnesty, citing Greek precedents. The cynical or relieved com-promise that all acts of Caesar be held valid was seized on gladly.[6]

Thus the proposal of honors for the conspirators was blocked, but so too were the Caesarian demands for punishment. With this settlement the murderer Decimus Brutus retained the province of Cisalpine Gaul and Trebonius kept Asia. Dolabella also received Caesar's consulship, already assigned to him once Caesar left for Parthia. Antony had earlier fought the nomination of the unscru-pulous opportunist and had been bitter when, after the Ides, Dola-bella, declaring himself in favor of the murder, appeared in consular dress. But in the spirit of senatorial amity, he now permitted Dolabella to preside as consul when the people demanded that he come to the Forum to reassure them of his safety. Even such Caesarian measures as the building of the temple to the Egyptian goddess Isis were reaffirmed. Thus the Senate meeting seemed to leave Caesar master of the state. But Antony held Caesar's official papers, to issue as he found useful, and Antony's domination as consul was now unchallenged.[7]

The conspirators descended from their defensive position on the Capitoline after receiving the sons of Antony and Lepidus as hostages for their safety; on the insistence of the crowd, Caesarians and murderers shook hands. Cassius dined with Antony, Marcus Brutus with Lepidus. The question of Caesar's burial had not yet been faced. The conspirators had intended to throw the body into the Tiber in calculated disrespect. Now the Senate had acknowledged his acts as valid. When Caesar's father-in-law, Calpurnius Piso, proposed at a hastily called second meeting of the Senate on March 18 that Caesar receive an honorific consular funeral at public expense, the measure was passed. The senatorial decisions were announced to the popular assembly.[8]

Before the funeral, Calpurnius Piso, as executor, had agreed to open Caesar's will. It was read in Antony's home and at Antony's urging. Caesar had had no legitimate sons or grandsons and, as Caesar's first lieutenant, Antony could hope to be named heir. The settlement, however, surprised everyone: three grandsons of his sisters received his estate, with three-quarters going to Gaius Octavian, who was also adopted by Caesar and thus given his name. Antony, with Decimus Brutus and some of the other assassins, was an alternate heir. Caesar's gardens were to become public, and every citizen would receive 300 sesterces (about two and a half months' wages). Antony's secondary position must have disappointed him. He was, in fact, asserting himself as Caesar's heir, and his seizure of power would be more difficult now that another had inherited Caesar's name and wealth. Perhaps Antony's reluctance to press for vengeance on the assassins or for deification of Caesar derived from his awareness that Caesar's glorification profited Caesar's heir but that Antony, as his own man, could accommodate himself to any useful allies.[9]

For the moment Antony could turn the will against the republi-

84

cans. Caesar's funeral was probably held March 20. Magistrates and ex-magistrates carried the funeral couch to the Forum. Since Caesar had no close male relative in Rome, Marcus Brutus as praetor had agreed that Antony should deliver the traditional funeral address for his fellow consul and kinsman. Antony shrewdly calculated the content to win the emotional allegiance of the people without alienating the republican senators, whom he had been so carefully conciliating since the murder for his own protection and his own ambitions. A model of Caesar's new temple of Venus Genetrix, his ancestress, was placed before the Rostra. Within were the funeral couch and a trophy with the bloodstained robe in which Caesar had been slain. Actors recalled Caesar's triumphs, and in scenes from Pacuvius and Atilius, players sang of the slaying of the man who had saved his murderers. In Antony's address he let the Senate pronounce its treachery by reading its decrees of honors and its oath to defend Caesar. The will was read, with its gifts of gardens and money to the citizens. Antony's eulogy could be brief; the throng was already inflamed.[10]

The cremation had been prepared in the Campus Martius, but the grieving crowd spontaneously ransacked the Forum to build a funeral pyre in the Forum. From it they carried brands to burn the houses of the conspirators, which were saved only by the resistance of servants and neighbors. The Curia in which Caesar had been slain was destroyed; and the poet Cinna, mistaken for a tyrannicide, died in the mob violence. Antony, unwilling to alienate the people by using troops to restore order, allowed the passions to subside. The conspirators fled from the city. Antony had deftly manipulated the funeral to increase his mastery in Rome.[11]

Nevertheless, during the weeks after the funeral Antony needed skillful juggling to retain control among the demands of the extremists and the fears of the moderates. When the people erected an inscribed column to Caesar in the Forum, Antony approved. But further excesses he was willing to block, even by the use of force. In early April, one Gaius Amatius reappeared from an exile imposed by Caesar. A demagogue, he had earlier stirred up popular demands by claiming to be the grandson of Gaius Marius, thus a relative of Caesar. Now he accused Antony of compromising with the assassins and pledged to avenge Caesar. The altar he set up in the Forum honored Caesar as a god. Within a week Antony, ignoring legal procedures, had him killed as a danger to the state.[12]

The infuriated populace demanded that Caesar worship be made official by having magistrates dedicate and sacrifice on Amatius's altar. Even when this was conceded, disorders ensued. This time Antony and Dolabella, as consuls, had to send troops. Rioting slaves were crucified; freemen were hurled to death from the Tarpeian Rock. Order was restored, but the people resented Antony. He had killed Amatius; he had used troops against the people as he had done in 46 B.C.; and he opposed the worship of Caesar as a god. Antony, therefore, was not finding his strength as a popular demagogue.[13]

Like Caesar, Antony found his strongest and most congenial supporters in the army. There his aura as Caesar's trusted lieutenant was untarnished, and his bold, careless immorality was merely comradely. From Caesar he had learned the value of a small committed force as a core of a larger army. It could be turned even against the civilian population. From Caesar he knew too that loyalty won in battle needed constant underpropping with money or lands. By late April Antony had parlayed the disorders in Rome into his need for a bodyguard and had summoned 6,000 veterans from Campania. By mid-May his leadership of a larger army was growing firmer. Caesar's money, now willed to Octavian, flowed freely to secure the military's loyalty to Antony.[14]

Antony still had little desire, and probably doubted his strength, to accomplish his ends by force. Therefore, he used the republican forms and offices and courtesies in dealings with his senatorial colleagues. Most of the senators had followed Pompey, reluctantly endured Caesar, and cheered the assassination. These men Antony sought to immobilize by a pose of moderation and conciliation.

Some of the senators were always part of the Caesarian faction. This group, indispensable to Antony's political effectiveness, inevitably now adjusted membership and leaders. Antony's brothers remained loyal to him; Lucius especially played the demagogue to woo the mob for Antony. Lepidus, whose appointment as pontifex maximus Antony had effected arbitrarily, was further tied to him by a betrothal between Antony's young daughter and Lepidus's son. Under Antony's moderating control, Lepidus discarded vengeance for Caesar's murder for the important military appointment to Spain, where Sextus Pompey, the surviving younger son of Pompey, had gathered the remaining Pompeians and now commanded six legions. Dolabella, whom Antony had finally acknowledged as fellow consul, looked to his own advantage but was won by Antony's gold. In his vacillations he had stopped the cult and taken down the altar of Caesar when it was revived after Amatius's death, then had the altar put up again. The republicans, especially Dolabella's father-in-law, Cicero, swung accordingly from early praise to final detestation for his ties to Antony and his misappropriation of public funds. Other Caesarian friends like Hirtius, Pansa, and Balbus criticized Antony's use of Caesar's money and soldiers but judged that only Antony gave hope of peace and perpetuation of Caesar's policies. Thus some of these senators joined the equestrians and soldiers in swearing duty and loyalty to Antony in a military type oath, much as the people had earlier sworn to Caesar.[15]

Marcus Brutus and Cassius left Rome in fear of the rioting, but they lingered safely in Italy where the sympathies of the country people were generally republican. For a time they appealed to young men of the upper classes to act as a bodyguard and troop for a march on Rome; but when Antony demanded the dissolution of the guard in late April, they meekly obeyed, saying that they were lesser officials under orders to the consul. Cicero, too, left Rome, as did many others of the conspirators, some to take the provinces Caesar had scheduled for them. Cicero continued to think of Antony as too concerned with the pleasures of wine and women to represent a major threat. But Quintus Cicero, nephew of the orator, was typical of some of the young nobility when he broke with his father and uncle on the grounds that previously he had prospered under Caesar and now he expected to receive his only advantage from Antony.[16]

Abiding by the amnesty decree of March 17, Antony remained overtly cordial to all, and so formal courtesy prevailed for months despite increasing strains. Antony's most threatening enemy was Sextus Pompey with his six legions in Spain. Even him Antony hoped to win by ending his exile from Rome and by compensating him for his confiscated property—though Antony had no intention of handing back his own share of the property. Lepidus's negotiations with Pompey, begun in April, by November did bring a truce, though not close amity. Other parts of the empire, especially Gaul, where powerful armies were posted, though restless, did not revolt. Antony's major opposition, therefore, undercut by his politic pronouncements and compromises, and suffering from its own vacillations of purpose and reluctance to fight, let Antony increasingly dominate developments.[17]

Antony's ambition was to secure enough power so that he could protect himself, ensure his control of the state, and run the empire effectively. He had learned much from Caesar about means as well as ends. Like Caesar, he saw autocracy as the inevitable new form of Rome's government, but, more than Caesar, he acknowledged the need for a republican facade for the one-man rule. On March 19 he won warm plaudits from the senators, though not from the people, by proposing the abolition of the dictatorship. It was the calculated gesture of dropping the hated name while retaining the reality of absolute power. To gain and hold the rule, attractive means like Caesar's clemency were preferable, but if realistic politics demanded force and manipulation of others, swiftness in striking, and calculated daring, these too were Caesar's heritage.[18]

The Senate decree of March 17, confirmed by an Antonian law on June 3, had been to abide by Caesar's arrangements for office holding and, therefore, for all affairs of state. Antony thus had bases for any popular or useful measures. Moreover, Antony's prompt securing of Caesar's papers from Caesar's widow and secretary enabled him to announce that any project which he deemed useful had already been provided for in Caesar's notes. On March 17 he had agreed with the Senate that no new decisions of Caesar should be published after March 15; but by April he felt strong enough to add new items or ignore known ones at will.[19]

Caesar's promises to the veterans had to be met promptly if Antony were to hold the loyalty of Caesar's army as his prime weapon. Extending the program of Caesar, therefore, he acted as patron for colonies of veterans, establishing some colonies, enlarging some of the old ones. Probably he utilized much of the money he had taken from the Temple of Ops for this. Perhaps, indeed, such had been Caesar's intention when storing the unusual treasure there. In April, bearded as a sign of mourning, Antony went to

Campania to help in land distribution for the veterans but also to be visible to the army as Caesar's successor and to summon picked veterans to Rome as his personal military force. In late May he returned to Rome with a large guard of Roman veterans and of Arab Ituraeans from Lebanon. Caesar had already settled about fifteen veteran legions, but about thirty-seven legions were still enlisted. These Antony, with an eye to his defense, encouraged to remain in camp under arms. Brutus and Cassius complained bitterly that while Antony built his army, he was ordering them to disband theirs.[20]

During this time Antony's tribune brother Lucius carried two agrarian laws setting up a commission of seven headed by Lucius and Antony for further land allotments in Italy. The commission roused protests. Religious prohibitions were pronounced against it but ignored. Antony was accused of providing land for his actor friends and other unworthies. After a year the commission was annulled on the grounds that the measure had been passed violently; but during the year it had helped gain veteran support for Antony.[21]

Useful, also, to Antony and to Rome, were colonies for the urban poor, which Antony, like Caesar, founded or refounded throughout the empire. Urso in Spain, for example, had received its regulations from Caesar, but Antony supervised the actual settling of the colonists. Such colonies provided an outlet for some of the distressed population of Rome. They also provided Antony with a widespread network of grateful clients, many of them freedmen, newly prosperous and holding office in their municipalities. But land was needed for the colonies. Antony continued Caesar's project of draining the Pontine marshes for new lands, distributing the remaining public lands, and buying more private land. Nevertheless, some land had to be expropriated from its owners. The struggle Cicero and Atticus waged to save the land of the Buthrotians in Epirus from Antony's confiscations must often have been repeated by less prominent and successful champions. Certainly, Antony, like all the other colonizers, gained enemies by these arbitrary land seizures.[22]

Although the spendthrift Antony now had enormous pressures for military pay and political patronage, he still worked within legal limits and republican practices. With Calpurnia's concurrence he had used much of Caesar's wealth. He had also taken from the Temple of Ops the special fund of 700 million sesterces probably intended as pay for the soldiers in Caesar's Parthian campaign. But, beyond some land for colonists, Antony did not expropriate private property, and such restraint muted hostility to his taking public treasure.[23]

Money was also traditionally obtained in the republic by selling offices and rights to provincials and satellite states; Antony seems to have used this practice no more nor less than others. In February Caesar had dictated to the Senate that Hyrcanus be installed as high priest in Jerusalem. In April, on the motion of Antony and Dolabella, the appointment was put in the public records. Deiotarus, an important vassal king of Galatia, for what was reputed to be a bribe of ten million sesterces, perhaps engineered by Fulvia, received formal recognition for his illegal seizure of territory. Crete paid for grants of special privileges.[24] And to the Sicilians, whom Caesar had given Latin status, Antony now granted full citizenship in exchange for substantial payments. The grant was not effective: Sextus Pompey controlled the island for a time, and Octavian later revoked the law; but Antony had the advantages of the bribes and Sicilian goodwill. Cicero was to charge Antony with recalling exiles for a price, but the only known exile recalled was a relative of Cicero's old foe Clodius; even in this instance Antony courteously sought Cicero's acquiescence.[25]

Other legislation (like municipal legislation on qualifications for holding office and census regulations) continued Caesar's plans; but some laws were introduced by Antony for selfish purposes, some for the ongoing needs of the state. Unfortunately, we hear of his programs chiefly from his critics. When a judiciary law extended eligibility for jury duty to men of centurion and even legionary rank and transferred the hearing of final appeals from the courts to the people, Cicero charged that Antony was packing the courts and fostering mob violence. The democratic measures were never given a fair trial, for, with Antony's other measures, they were canceled in 43 B.C. When Antony failed to hold the scheduled election of the censors, but did issue an edict on sumptuary laws, it became the object of ridicule because of his reputation. Nevertheless, that Rome remained calm during these days of transition indicates a strength and stability in Antony's administration of the state.[26]

The major arena of combat for leadership remained the control of the provinces and their armies. The approval of Caesar's legislation (on March 17) had been won when the republicans succumbed to the temptation of holding the Roman and provincial offices Caesar had assigned. Three conspirators who had received assignments to provinces in Asia, Bithynia, and Cisalpine Gaul went to hold them by early April. But of the three, only Decimus Brutus had received a military command of two legions in strategic Cisalpine Gaul. Caesarians held the other provinces: Lepidus, Narbonese Gaul and Hither Spain; Plancus, Comata Gaul; Pollio, Farther Spain; and Dolabella, Syria. Antony had been assigned Macedonia for two years, a rich and important province, manned by the four legions mobilized for Caesar's Parthian War and against the local tribes.[27]

Antony needed the proconsular *imperium* and the army. He also wanted to be closer to the power in Rome and to be protected by the proconsular *imperium* for longer than the two years stipulated in Caesar's legislation. Therefore, he worked to change Caesar's settlement of the provinces. On June 1 the Senate was summoned, but, intimidated by a guard of troops surrounding the meeting, the republican senators refused to attend. Antony then pushed a tribunician law through the Comitia Tributa to change Caesar's assignment of provinces.[28] Antony now received Cisalpine Gaul for six years, while retaining the four legions stationed in Macedonia plus a personal bodyguard. The conspirator Decimus Brutus, who lost Cisalpine Gaul, was now assigned Macedonia but without any troops. The demotion was patent, the loss of army too critical for the republicans to accept; and, because Decimus Brutus had a fortune to spend on securing soldiers, civil war overhung the decision. Dolabella's military command in Syria against the Parthians was lengthened to six years, with Antony's cooperation. The republicans tried to block Dolabella's appointment by religious omens, believing that Antony as augur would use the omens against his old rival; but Antony, like other Roman leaders, let political considerations determine his religious orthodoxy. On June 5 Marcus Brutus and Cassius were assigned the negligible, nonmilitary provinces of Crete and Cyrene respectively for the next year,[29] with an interim appointment to a special commission to collect grain in Sicily and Asia. The tyrannicides judged the trivial appointments insulting. Nevertheless, in a group consultation at Antium on June 8 they found no alternative to remaining outside Rome, where an increasingly hostile population threatened them. Antony had provided the urban praetor Brutus with special dispensation for being absent from Rome. After a friendly interview with Antony, both Brutus and Cassius had left Rome for the more congenial country area in early April. Now they sailed east, ostensibly on a government mission, but actually determined to raise badly needed money and to seize Macedonia and Syria as military bases.[30]

Though senior statesman, Cicero also despaired of the immediate situation and decided to go to Greece until Hirtius and Pansa should replace Antony and Dolabella as consuls. In May he had publicly praised Antony as his great friend, and even to his secretary Tiro he still declared that he was eager to keep his long friendship with Antony. Yet in private correspondence he was describing Antony as dangerous, careless, riotous, and dishonorable. Working politics admits many compromises! The conspirators and Antony appeared carefully courteous toward one another; but the republicans continued their retreat into the more sympathetic Italian country and provincial areas. Ever more clearly, the conspirators had lost the initiative, and, instead of directing the state, they were in disordered retreat, feebly responding to Antony's increasing control and military force.[31]

VII

Challenged by Octavian

The challenge to Antony's security and dominance appeared from an unanticipated source. Caesar's grandnephew and heir, the eighteen-year-old Gaius Octavius, arrived in Rome in mid-May, 44 B.C., to claim his inheritance. Antony must have known him previously through Caesar, for the boy had been in Caesar's entourage for several months and had been given a role in Caesar's triumphal processions. Although Octavius was the grandson of Caesar's sister, his father's family was equestrian; so that Antony later taunted him that his grandfathers were a provincial baker and a money changer. More accurate, his father had won nobility of office, his stepfather was an ex-consul; Octavius was now a patrician and already a pontifex by Caesar's appointment.[1]

Expecting to go with Caesar's army against Parthia, Octavius was at Apollonia on the Illyrian coast when the report of Caesar's murder reached him. With the encouragement of Caesar's officers, he at once crossed to Brundisium, where he learned of his adoption by Caesar and where a number of the troops declared for him. Against the urging of his parents, he determined to dare the risks of accepting Caesar's inheritance and name. Thereafter he called himself G. Julius C. f. Caesar, or Gaius Julius Caesar Octavianus.[2] His close friends called him Caesar. We commonly use the name Octavian, as did Cicero.[3] Perhaps he felt family loyalties. Certainly, he inherited Caesar's ambition, determination, abilities, and ruthlessness; for the sickly, inexperienced eighteen-year-old became at once a power to be reckoned with in Rome.[4]

For a time Antony underestimated Octavian and tried to ignore him; but Octavian boldly forced Antony's attention. After spending April in Campania conferring with other Caesarians and calling on Cicero, who pitied him when he should confront Antony, Octavian appeared in Rome during early May, announcing himself Caesar's son and winning popular support. Antony, who was at the army camps in Campania, hastily returned to Rome when he heard of Octavian's triumphs. Octavian, declaring that he would accept Caesar's inheritance, demanded Caesar's money to pay the various other legacies of Caesar's will. Antony had taken the fortune from Calpurnia the night of the Ides of March. He had mixed it with state moneys, not to pay Caesar's legacies but to buy the loyalty of the troops and veterans. By May the money was greatly depleted, and the two funds were indistinguishable. Antony's response to Octavian's demand was a calculated rudeness: keeping Octavian waiting, calling him too young for the inheritance, blocking Octavian's underage candidacy for the tribunate.[5]

Antony's stakes were high. If Octavian were intimidated enough to give up the inheritance, Antony, as second heir, had a major claim on the legacy. But Octavian, holding firm against Antony's bluster, succeeded so well in undermining Antony with the veterans that Antony had to compete for veteran support even at cost of the senatorial goodwill he had been cultivating so carefully. A brief reconciliation, effected by the tribunes, meant that Octavian supported Antony's claim to Cisalpine Gaul, but cooperation was soon shattered by conflicting ambitions.[6]

Subtly, the initiative passed to Octavian, while Antony, frustrated by his inability to attack Caesar's legitimate heir, futilely hurled invective. Though Octavian had been adopted in Caesar's will, formal ratification of the adoption by the Comitia Curiata was required. For five months Antony prevented the meeting of the Comitia. Then his brother Lucius, as tribune, was obliged to introduce Octavian at a public meeting, and his brother Gaius was the praetor to whom Octavian declared that he would accept the inheritance. Octavian had not waited to use Caesar's name, and now he was popularly called Caesar. As heir, he promised to pay his adoptive father's legacies of 300 sesterces (15 drachmae) to all the citizens and to hold games in honor of Caesar at his own expense. Since Antony would return nothing, Octavian sold everything still available from Caesar's estate, sent for the funds Caesar had left in Asia to pay for the Parthian campaign, supplemented by some of the annual tribute from the provinces, and solicited aid from Caesar's financial supporters, both the millionaires and the middle-class "new men" who had profited under Caesar and now turned to his heir.[7]

Octavian, indeed, was beginning to have a real party of followers. In June even Cicero, who had pitied Octavian and thought that Antony was indisputably in control, judged that he had to join Octavian to prevent Octavian's seeking an ally in Antony. Other senators agreed with Cicero, as Octavian cultivated their favor against Antony and offered the Senate the protection of his army. Antony, in dismay, saw that he was losing his carefully built compromise with the Senate as Octavian became its champion.[8]

Antony was being forced to pursue a policy of openly wooing supporters. He had to match Octavian in granting concessions to please and hold the Senate, while also retaining the role of Caesar's successor in the eyes of the army and the people. As propaganda, he issued coins, showing the Temple of Caesar's Clemency, with the portraits of Caesar and of a mourning, bearded Antony. In May the Games which had been held a year earlier in Caesar's honor were held again as mourning for Caesar. Octavian claimed the right to show Caesar's gilded chair at the Games as a symbol of his divinity. Antony, using cooperative tribunes, blocked the action because it was done on Octavian's initiative. In compensation Antony needed to placate the Caesarians. The recent naming of the month Quinctilis, "Julius," to honor Caesar, had been ignored after the Ides. Now, despite republican opposition, Antony revived it when he announced that the Games honoring Apollo would be given on the ninth of July.[9]

These Games would normally have been given by Marcus Brutus as urban praetor, and Brutus had wanted elaborate Games to win popular support from the Caesarians. Indeed, hearing that Octavian was planning Games in Caesar's honor, he undertook to buy up all the wild animals in Italy. But, by July, Brutus dared not return to Rome, and the praetor Gaius Antonius was in charge in his stead. Antony's effort to capitalize on the Games for his own popularity was diluted when Octavian used Caesar's birthday, which fell during the games, to distribute wealth to the people. At the end of July fresh Games honoring Caesar and his patron goddess Venus were held. Again Antony blocked Octavian's showing Caesar's emblems as those of a divinity.[10]

But when, on the last day, a comet appeared over Rome, the people, previously uncertain about Caesar's deification, passionately hailed him as a martyr and a god among the stars. The comet was henceforth to appear on Caesar's statues and coins, and Antony's credit suffered for having opposed showing Caesar's other trappings of divinity. Antony again sought public and veteran approval by honoring Caesar when he ostentatiously added a fifth day to Games held in September honoring Caesar as a god and giving thanks for the victories of the state. And, despite tribunician opposition from Tiberius Cannutius, he set up a statue to Caesar on the Rostra, inscribed *Parenti Optimo Maximo* (To the best and greatest Parent for his services), intentionally suggesting both that Caesar's murder was parricide and that he was himself the son and heir of Caesar.[11]

The propaganda victories, therefore, alternated between Antony and Octavian. Yet Antony's early Caesarian supremacy was being eroded, and Antony had let slip the possibility of giving guidance to the young Octavian. Such direction had gone, by default, to Cicero. This, indeed, was Cicero's last great year of leadership. He had not been among Caesar's murderers, though he had rejoiced loudly at the deed, regretting only that Antony had not been killed too. Like the murderers, he had left Rome to escape Antony's control, although he and Antony maintained surface courtesies. As the conspirators increasingly showed themselves helpless, Cicero planned a further retreat into Greece. But as he lingered in south Italy, Octavian sought him out for counsel and protested that he would be guided wholly by Cicero. At first Cicero was skeptical of Octavian's capacity to act against Antony. But, as Octavian's skill appeared in wooing popular and army support and, indeed, Cicero's too, Cicero came to dream, not of leading the state directly, but of playing wise Nestor to the young Agamemnon who would control the state. Under Cicero a true concord of the senatorial and equestrian orders could give peace and direction to the republic. It was a dangerous dream. Cicero had no expectation that Octavian would willingly reestablish the republic, any more than Antony would. Yet he underestimated the ambitions and abilities of Octavian and the other agents whom he wanted to manipulate.[12]

Nor did Cicero or the other republicans lay any long-term plans about building up republican armies or reasserting republican controls. While Antony had acted and Octavian had planned, the conspirators had dissipated the spring and summer with self-congratulation, frustration, and unrealistic hopes which had deadened the zeal of their followers. From March 17 until September 1, Cicero had not attended the Senate, and other senatorial leaders had equally given over the reins to Antony.[13]

In late August, however, Cicero turned back from his enforced literary retirement and his projected eastern travels. He had heard that Antony's policies were more conciliatory as the threat from Octavian increased. He judged that Antony's supporters were less loyal than Octavian's and that Octavian would be compliant to his counsel. The hope of gaining control was faint but still flickered. Cicero's return was warmly welcomed by the people. But the facade of friendship with Antony was shattered at once. On September 1 Antony summoned the Senate to propose special honors for Caesar and particularly notified Cicero. Cicero absented himself on the pretext that he was too fatigued from his trip to attend. Antony was enraged by his refusal to cooperate and threatened to have Cicero brought by force. Violence against the aged and honored consular was, of course, intolerable. Antony was readily dissuaded; but now the rift between the men was open. Cicero lacked Antony's boldness and courage; but he had written that the ideal leader must be a civil not a military leader and that the good man must do his public duty even though he anticipates defeat. Now Cicero was willing to expend every last resource of strength and ability to destroy Antony.[14]

By September 2 Antony had already left Rome. The Senate meeting was conducted by Dolabella. Cicero rose to deliver the first of fourteen diatribes against Antony which he and posterity have called the *Philippic Orations*. Cicero had declared that the times demanded the thunderbolts of a Demosthenes; and now he was claiming the role of a Roman Demosthenes, in politics against the tyrant as fully as in oratorical style. He claimed to be fighting for principles and traditions, though others also saw Cicero's hatred of Antony in the denunciations. This first attack, though firm, was still moderate and restrained, for the politician Cicero was not eager for a total rupture in relations with Antony. He spoke of Antony's good deeds, like the abolition of the dictatorship. But far more, he emphasized the evil deeds which he said followed a fundamental shift of policy since June 1. Antony had plundered the treasury and sold state privileges; he had seized Caesar's papers, then had manipulated decisions of Caesar which he had sworn to uphold; he had tampered with the judicial system to weight it in his favor; and he had used armed force at will. Every power of Antony that was illegal or contrary to republican usage was criticized, with appeals to Antony's traditional honor and duty. Ultimately, Cicero pleaded for Antony's turning back to the compromise settlement of March 17.[15]

Antony was fully aware of the propaganda power of Cicero's oratory for mobilizing the opposition, and he drew up his reply while at his country house at Tibur, amid drink and debauchery, if one may believe Cicero. The furious, abusive attack was delivered in the Senate on September 19, at a meeting which he had ordered Cicero to attend and around which Antony had stationed armed men. Among other charges against Cicero's public life, Cicero was blamed for knowing no gratitude to Antony for saving his life in 48 B.C. or to Caesar for many favors and benefits. He was even damned for having been largely responsible for Caesar's death. Antony did not scruple to read aloud some of Cicero's private correspondence with him in which Cicero had fawned before his power and claimed him as a friend. The attack was brutal; it also showed Antony's keen awareness of Cicero's painful vanity and his basic blend of timidity and courage. Cicero's fears kept him away. Later he claimed that Antony had forces present to murder him if he had dared a rebuttal. It was a charge which Antony disdained. But that no other senator rose to defend Cicero and that other opponents of Antony also feared to attend the meetings give weight to the charge of terror.[16]

Cicero again, in fear, withdrew from Rome to his country estate. During October he composed the second *Philippic*, not delivered as an oration but circulated widely as a pamphlet. Cicero's prudent friend Atticus warned Cicero, and probably the *Philippic* was not published until after Cicero's death. The statement was a lampoon, wildly exaggerated, rebutting the accusations in Antony's speech and filled with unsubstantiated, irrelevant, emotional charges against Antony's public and private life. He was called drunkard, gladiator, ruffian, debauchee, homosexual, even coward. His wives were pilloried. Politically, he was termed a tyrant, with all the implications of illegality, corruption, brutality, and pride; and Cicero urged his murder as a tyrant. Even in an age of extravagant political invective and character assassination, Cicero's charges gave evidence of his deep personal hatred, and—taken all too literally—they have blackened Antony's reputation for later generations. With the circulation of the pamphlet, no reconciliation was possible. As subsequent *Philippics* pushed on the same vitriolic personal and political attacks, Antony responded in rabid invective, spoken through his friends. Antony and Cicero were never to meet again.[17]

These Ciceronian attacks made Antony ever more aware that Octavian was a serious threat. Despite mutual efforts to disguise their hostilities, animosity was so apparent that in August the Caesarian troops had haled Antony and Octavian to the Capitoline and demanded a reconciliation between their two leaders. The army-enforced cordiality was soon broken, however. In October Antony publicly accused Octavian of hiring men for an assassination attempt. Octavian vehemently protested his innocence. The case was dropped, and the truth can only be surmised. It would seem that Octavian still needed Antony alive as support against their common enemy, the republicans. Yet Octavian was steadily showing ruthless daring in his ambition, and even a hostile contemporary like Cicero believed Antony's accusation. Octavian, indeed, was frightening sober citizens. Cicero might charge, rhetorically, that only the lawless derelicts were following Antony, but, in actuality, more nobles were trusting Antony than Octavian.[18]

Now Octavian showed his hand more clearly. In October and November Antony went to Brundisium to take command of the Macedonian troops assembling there. His preparations were for possible action against Decimus Brutus in Cisalpine Gaul, but also to hold Rome firmly; for he had declared that he would keep his army in Rome even after his consulship had ended and would come and go at will. However, in leaving Rome he underestimated the danger of turning his back on Octavian. The young Caesar at once went to the army camps in Campania where he used his name and liberal bribes of 500 denarii (c. $80) to win the loyalty of 3,000 legionnaires. The troops, indifferent to claims of theoretical right, responded to the payments, though many of the officers and some of the men remained loyal to Antony.[19]

Next Octavian suborned Antony's fresh Macedonian legions, half of whom defected from Antony. When the troops jeered at Antony's modest bribe of 100 denarii, Antony, backed by Fulvia, responded strongly, executing seditious ringleaders of the restless troops. But he had to pay as well, to counter Octavian's bribes. The dangerous precedent was thereby set: the troops could and must be bought. The practice had been used by Caesar. Now begun again, the bribery continued through the civil wars and drained ever more of Antony's personal and the state's wealth until Antony would have to devalue the coinage by minting denarii of low silver content.[20]

With the defection to his camp of so many of Antony's troops, plus widespread popular support, Octavian's ambitions swelled unrealistically. On November 10, with his new-won troops, he occupied the Forum. He hoped that his flattering and cultivating of Cicero and other senatorial leaders would induce the Senate to approve his military coup. When the Senate opposed him, he turned to the Comitia. There he used his tribune supporter Tiberius Cannutius to denounce Antony and praise Caesar. The coup, however, failed. The soldiers had defected from Antony for a price; yet they had counted on cooperating with him against the tyrannicides. When Octavian's attack was turned on Antony, the bulk of the troops found excuses for deserting. Octavian, left with an attenuated force facing the oncoming army of Antony, retreated into Cisalpine Gaul to regroup and rally new forces.[21]

An angry, frustrated Antony rapidly occupied Rome with a military guard. He called a Senate meeting for November 24 to declare Octavian a public enemy. But even now, one of Antony's Macedonian legions marching up the Adriatic coast transferred allegiance to Octavian, then another followed. Antony pushed through a resolution honoring Lepidus for negotiating peace with Sextus Pompey. Then he rushed to the legionary camp, hoping to hold the legions with bribes. Again he failed.[22]

Hurriedly returning to Rome, Antony summoned an illegal evening meeting of the Senate on November 28. Insults were hurled, though no action was taken against Octavian, whose loyal tribunes could veto any condemnation. But thirteen provinces were reassigned to governors, thus breaking the Caesarian settlements accepted on March 16. Technically the assignments were done by lot; actually the lots were manipulated to secure the provinces for Antony's allies. Most important, Gaius Antonius received Macedonia. Marcus Brutus's and Cassius's provinces were not among those adjusted, though they must have regarded the whole settlement as dangerous. Only the praetor Marcus Piso, hostile to Antony since Antony had seized his house in 47 B.C., dared to oppose the high-handed measures at the time, though some of the governors later resigned their commands as illegal. Antony had neither patience nor time for negotiations. With the Senate adjourned, he left promptly for the army camp. There he was honored by delegations of senators, equestrians, and plebeian leaders who swore loyalty to him; and many of the soldiers, though not the two defecting legions, were swayed to follow suit.[23]

A fresh and surprising alignment of allies was clearly emerging. Republicans had murdered Caesar but had compromised to a *modus operandi* with Antony as leader of the Caesarians. Octavian's claims against Antony had, however, split the Caesarians. Octavian, with a few noble supporters of his own, had been playing up to the republicans, especially to Cicero.[24] The elder statesman, though judging him untrustworthy and potentially dangerous, had hopes of controlling a man so young and inexperienced, of using him to republican advantage, then setting him aside. Not all the republicans agreed. Marcus Brutus warned Cicero that Octavian was more dangerous than Antony. Many senators and consulares allied

101

with Antony over Octavian or played both sides.[25] In measuring forces, the weak republican leadership seemed unable to cope with Antony or hold the legions unaided. Nor could Octavian win his illegal claims without allies. Negotiations between Cicero and Octavian, begun in April, grew more cordial. By December Caesar's heir had become the military champion of Caesar's assassins against Antony.

Both sides cloaked illegality with appeals to the traditional Roman *mos maiorum* (customs), *libertas* (liberty), *auctoritas* (authority) of the Senate or tribunician rights within the Comitia. Octavian claimed to be freeing Rome from the consul Antony's tyranny. But principles had no weight against the claims of ambition and mutual self-interests in friendship; and laws were defended with complete disregard for legality. Even Cicero and other senators argued that in crises so drastic, solutions could go outside the laws—the ends justified the means. The argument was suicidal for the state; but in actuality, theory followed the fact; for both sides were scrambling for advantages and allied by any expedients.[26]

In December, 44 B.C., Antony led his army to take possession of Cisalpine Gaul as his province. He had the sworn loyalty of most of the Senate, four legions, and hopes of reinforcements enlisted by his agents, especially his brother Lucius and Caesar's old army contractor Publius Ventidius. Moreover, he was offering substantial bounties to any troops who would join him.[27]

In opposition to his claim stood Decimus Brutus, Caesar's friend and second heir, who had, nevertheless, been one of his murderers. Decimus was governor of the province by Caesar's assignment. Though he had early complained that Antony would not let him go into his province, by April he had taken over his position, backed by two legions, and had subsequently been raising troops within the province and sustaining the army by exactions from the area and by spending his entire fortune of ten million denarii and borrowing widely.[28]

The region was always of great value precisely for its wealth and as a recruiting ground for legionnaires. Moreover, it lay across the route to the north and west, where the Caesarians Lepidus, Plancus, and Pollio held Gaul and Spain. These leaders were all ambitious and able and were solicited by both camps. Plancus in Comata Gaul was consul-designate for 42 B.C. and, looking after his own career, was willing to follow the victor. Lepidus, in Narbonese Gaul and Hither Spain, urged help for Antony. Pollio in Farther Spain, though skillful and ambitious, sincerely sought peace. All were too remote from Italy to participate actively. Yet Antony could hope for cooperation with old allies. Indeed, he may have hoped that if he held Cisalpine Gaul, Plancus as consul-designate would turn over Comata Gaul to him.[29]

When Antony ordered him to resign his governorship of Cisalpine Gaul, Decimus Brutus responded that he would hold the province as instructed by the Senate. Antony moved forward with troops and appealed to the towns to follow him. Only three are known to have done so. Some, traditionally republican, remained so; most sought to avoid any involvement. But Antony's power was effective. Decimus Brutus laid in supplies to stand a prolonged siege with his three legions behind the walls of Mutina.[30]

The republicans, led by Cicero, were committed to raising the siege and balking Antony's claims to Cisalpine Gaul. Marcus Brutus and Cassius had been levying troops in the east but could not yet send soldiers to Mutina. The consuls-elect, Aulus Hirtius and Gaius Vibius Pansa, would take office on January 1. They had been friends of Caesar, who had designated them consuls, but, wanting peace and order in an increasingly tumultuous state, they were so hostile to an armed Antony that they were willing to lead republican forces against him. Their military *imperium* to command armies would be valid with the consulship on January 1.[31]

On December 20 Cicero, who had kept away from Rome for three months after his bitter exchanges with Antony, returned to the Senate to ready the preparations for the consuls' marching promptly against Antony. On the twentieth he delivered his third *Philippic* in the Senate, which had been summoned by the tribunes in the absence of the consuls. Then he went to the Forum to persuade the people, by the fourth *Philippic*, to take action against Antony. Again Cicero used personal invective, castigating Antony as a drunken villain. But his significant attacks were on Antony's political position. He derided Antony as no true consul if his troops were mutinying against him. As a man who had disgraced his office, Antony should be declared a rebel, a *hostis* (enemy) of the state. Cicero ignored Antony's claim to the governorship of Cisalpine Gaul, a claim established by the plebiscite of June 1, but spoke of Decimus Brutus as the legitimate governor and carried his proposal that all the provinces be kept by those who held them until successors were appointed by a decree of the Senate. Because the legions that Octavian controlled were needed against Antony, Cicero publicly allied himself with Octavian, commended his winning an army by bribery, and urged that the Senate honor him and Decimus Brutus. This alliance of Octavian with Decimus Brutus, one of the most treacherous of Caesar's assassins, is explicable only because the young Caesar was determined to destroy Antony, as the greatest threat to his power, before turning against the republicans.[32]

January 1, 43 B.C., brought the new consuls, Hirtius and Pansa, into firm control. Under the consuls new levies could be raised. For days the Senate meetings hotly debated whether to take action against Antony. Lucius Calpurnius Piso and Quintus Fufius Calenus spoke in his defense; in response, Cicero attacked Antony's career and plans and lauded Octavian in his fifth *Philippic*.[33] The Senate, divided, could vote only to send an embassy to Antony, ordering him, at risk of war, to submit to the consuls, the Senate, and the People, to cease his attack on Decimus Brutus, to leave Cisalpine Gaul, and to hold his forces at least 200 miles from Rome. The embassy was also to confer with Decimus Brutus, to thank him for holding and encourage his retaining Gaul, since the Senate ignored the plebiscite giving Antony the province. Cicero's declaration that Antony should be outlawed as a public enemy was almost carried; but Piso and Antony's uncle, Lucius Julius Caesar, argued that Antony had the right to a hearing before being condemned, and Antony's mother, wife, and son appealed as suppliants to the various senators at their homes or en route to the Senate. Ultimately, the formal condemnation was vetoed by a tribune.[34]

Cicero's pushing forward of Octavian as the savior of the state gave the young man extraordinary and extralegal honors and powers. A statue was to be erected in his honor. Although the Senate had no right to grant him office unless he was elected by the people, he was made a member of the Senate and given dispensation to stand for the consulship when ten years younger than the legal age. Again there was support of the illegal armies of Decimus Brutus and Octavian, with promises to pay the liberal land allotments, money, and privileges with which Octavian had bribed the veterans, although the new recruits and provincial armies would not receive the same bribes. Octavian was given the military *imperium* of a propraetor as a disguise of legality for the army he had privately recruited. He was to cooperate with the consuls in military action: Hirtius was to go to Mutina, Pansa was to hold levies of troops throughout Italy.[35]

For war expenses, special taxes were levied, and the generals were advised to levy forced loans in the provinces. The returns did fatten the coffers. The middle class, especially, contributed substantial sums, hoping for a restoration of order in the state. Cicero thus carried most of his program; though in his sixth *Philippic*, addressed to the people in the Forum on January 4, he still cried for sending legions against, not embassies to, Antony. In his seventh *Philippic* delivered to the Senate during late January, he again stressed the futility of the embassy and of any possible peace with Antony. Action was needed, and the consuls had to lead.[36]

Meanwhile the embassy of three senators proceeded to Mutina. Tragically, the consular Servius Sulpicius Rufus, who headed the embassy, had accepted the responsibility to seek peace despite his critical illness, and he died on the mission. (Cicero's ninth *Philippic*, delivered in early February, successfully urged the Senate to vote Sulpicius Rufus a statue and the public funeral and burial plot awarded one who had died for his country.) Antony, however, far from acceding to the embassy's orders, refused to let the envoys reach Decimus Brutus and returned demands of his own: the Senate had to confirm Caesar's and Antony's laws, legally grant Antony the money he had arbitrarily taken from the Temple of Ops, recall Marcus Brutus and Cassius from their eastern mobilization of forces (though they could be consuls as designated), give the promised moneys and lands to Antony's soldiers, grant Antony his first imperatorship, and award Antony the governorship of Transalpine Gaul with six legions for five years. If these measures were fulfilled, Antony would disband his army and give up Cisalpine Gaul, in return for Transalpine Gaul.[37]

The demands must have seemed to the Senate tantamount to surrender, while to Antony they must have appeared the minimum needed to fulfill his past promises yet let him withdraw from control in Rome to a secure provincial command. Antony sent his quaestor and close companion, Lucius Varius Cotyla, to urge acceptance of the demands. The Senate responded by passing a *Tumultus* (State of Commotion) decree, declaring a sudden and dangerous war near Italy, then a *Senatus Consultum Ultimum* (Last Decree of the Senate), which imposed martial law and ordered the consuls and Octavian to protect the state by any means necessary. Only the intervention of Antony's uncle, Lucius Julius Caesar, carried the motion naming Antony an adversary of the state rather than a public enemy. To weaken Antony further, it was announced that soldiers who should desert to the senatorial side by March 15 would not be held liable for their previous service under Antony.[38]

Troops were being levied and the consuls readied for war even as the embassy was underway. Cicero continued as the chief agitator for keeping the state under arms, since few senior statesmen had survived the civil wars to lead the Senate, and Quintus Fufius Calenus, who was Antony's strongest supporter in the Senate, could moderate but not block Cicero's demands. Cicero also led in promoting the authority of Octavian. Generally, it was acknowledged that Octavian was needed, for already he commanded five legions, whereas Cicero's Senate had few troops.[39]

Though Cicero was prudent in conciliating and even proposing honors for Caesarians like Lepidus, his personal hatred for Antony knew no compromise. In late January, in the eighth *Philippic*, Cicero reproached Antony's supporters and warned against softening the attack on them under the false delusion of peace and security. No man and no property would be safe if Antony were victorious. Cicero demanded full military action. For Antony's followers, Cicero proposed granting an amnesty to anyone who laid down his arms and joined the consuls or Octavian, but viewing as a traitor anyone (except Antony's spokesman in Rome, Cotyla) who should now set out to join Antony. The proposal, in early November, that a second embassy be sent was lost through Cicero's unwillingness to be a member of it or to conciliate Antony. Perhaps, also, he feared facing Antony.[40]

106

When, in February, Marcus Brutus reported that he had, on senatorial instructions, taken Illyricum, Greece, and Macedonia from Gaius Antonius who had held the provinces by Caesar's assignment, Antony's supporter Calenus tried to return the command to Gaius Antonius; but Cicero's tenth *Philippic* gloated over the victory and secured legalization of the command for Brutus. When Marcus Brutus, winning over the Caesarian legions, took Gaius Antonius prisoner in Macedonia and asked the Senate to decide his fate, Cicero urged that all the Antonii should be eliminated. Lucius Antonius he charged, *inter alia*, with fighting as a gladiator in Asia Minor and cutting his opponent's throat. The eleventh *Philippic* then urged that Cassius take command of the eastern provinces against the claims of Dolabella, who in seizing the province of Asia had brutally murdered the republican governor Gaius Trebonius.[41]

The laws passed by Antony or his tribune agents in 44 B.C. were now annulled on the charge of being passed by force, illegally, and—most important—contrary to religious auspices. Some of the measures, like Antony's popular elimination of the dictatorship and his approval of Caesar's laws, were too valuable to discard; so the laws that were judged useful were passed again. Antony's land laws followed this path. They were repealed, then most were passed again, though new provisions took some of the land from Antony's men to give it to republican veterans and deserters from Antony's army. A commission of ten men, led by the consul Pansa and including Cicero, was established for the fresh land distributions.[42]

Probably behind the vitriolic attacks was fear that the tenuous alliances of the Senate, Decimus Brutus, and Octavian against Antony would not survive any jolts. Decimus Brutus and Antony had been comrades of old and had even shared the favors of Volumnia Cytheris; a realliance was surely possible. Hints of collusion between Octavian and Antony were also surfacing. In actuality, the Macedonian settlement was unwise; for strengthening Marcus Brutus was bound to alienate Octavian and drive him toward Antony. But Cicero failed to realize these implications.[43]

By late March or early April, after Cicero in the twelfth *Philippic* had opposed sending another embassy to Antony at Mutina, Antony had played into Cicero's political hands by writing to Hirtius and Octavian an intemperate letter which Cicero could use

against him. Antony damned the decree of the Senate against Dolabella and supported Dolabella's execution of Trebonius. He attacked Cicero, Octavian, and the Senate as still Pompeian, whereas
he was determined to lead the Caesarians to vengeance for Caesar's
murder. In reality, the trimmers were sensing defeat for Antony
and deserting him. Lepidus, governor of Hither Spain, advocated
peace. Plancus, governor of Comata Gaul, wrote to the Senate of
his loyal readiness to lead patriotic legions in support of the Senate. The Fathers voted Plancus thanks and added that senatorial
terms of peace required that Antony give up his armies. Cicero vehemently supported this position and worked to divide the Caesarians by making Antony's letter public. For Cicero no peace with
Antony or his supporters was possible. In the thirteenth *Philippic*
Cicero praised Plancus, Lepidus, and Sextus Pompey and struck at
Antony: "I am determined to overwhelm him with invective and
give him dishonored to the contempt of posterity."[44]

While Cicero fulminated and the Senate passed its resolutions
against the political rights and military powers of the Antonii, the
battleground at Mutina was being lost by Antony. Early in 43 B.C.
Hirtius as consul, joined by Octavian with four veteran legions,
had marched toward Mutina to relieve Decimus Brutus. Antony
gave up an outpost at Bononia but invested Mutina all the more
closely. With the two sides in close contact, soldiers could cross
sides, and Antony's cavalry especially was strengthened. But knowing that relief was at hand, Decimus Brutus held firm.[45]

In mid-April Antony, hearing that Pansa was approaching with
four legions of recruits as reinforcements for Hirtius, left his brother Lucius in charge of the blockade while he advanced with two legions and two praetorian cohorts against Pansa. Hirtius and Octavian in turn sent Pansa two praetorian cohorts and the veteran
Martian legion which had defected from Antony and which hated
him for the decimation with which he had earlier disciplined the
legion. Antony's ambush attack in a forest and marsh near Forum
Gallorum was masterly. While the veterans of both sides fought
splendidly, Antony himself led the center. Pansa's forces were
routed, though his camp could not be taken, and he himself was so
gravely wounded that he soon died. But while Antony's troops
celebrated and collected the booty of victory, Hirtius led twenty

crack cohorts from Mutina, about eight miles distant. Catching Antony's troops weary and disordered, Hirtius's army wreaked a heavy toll. Only nightfall and merciful help by Antony's strong cavalry kept his losses down to about half his men; the living found sanctuary in Antony's camp.[46]

Two eagles and sixty standards of Antony's troops had been captured. Hirtius, Pansa, and Octavian were all saluted as *imperatores* by their troops. In Rome the initial report of Antony's victory, then of his defeat, brought disorders, threats against Cicero, and finally a personal ovation for Cicero. In the last of Cicero's great orations which is intact for us, the fourteenth *Philippic*, he advocated a public funeral for the fallen and a public thanksgiving for an unprecedented fifty days because Antony, whom Cicero denounced as a public enemy, had been defeated.[47]

Antony, although battered, still held his camp, and Decimus Brutus remained under siege. To avoid a major battle, Antony held the enemy under control by his superior cavalry. But the fact that Decimus Brutus's army was in danger of starvation induced Hirtius and Octavian to force an action on April 27 while Antony was at a disadvantage. Octavian's army was victorious. Hirtius broke into Antony's camp, but he fell fighting there. Although Octavian alone could not hold Antony's camp, the action enabled Decimus Brutus to break through the siege works at Mutina. Both sides suffered serious losses.[48]

Antony could, perhaps, have retained his camp and resumed the siege, but he feared encirclement and defeat. Better to retreat to Transalpine Gaul, joining the three legions that Caesar's old ally Publius Ventidius had mustered for him and hoping to gain the allegiance of Lepidus and Plancus. He broke camp and, tricking Decimus Brutus, he retreated toward the Alps with a small force of badly armed infantry, augmented by the impressment of civilians and even criminals, and fed by plunder as he marched. It was a hard march, beset even by famine. But, as always, Antony was at his best when under pressure and was a model of endurance for his men.[49]

Decimus Brutus had to lick the wounds of his long siege before he could pursue Antony. By May he was marching with seven legions, which increased to ten as recruits came in and some of Antony's troops defected to the winning side. This was, indeed, a time of constant building and regrouping of armies as all the commanders offered recruiting bribes. After Mutina about forty-five legions were serving in the west, eleven under Octavian, ten under Decimus Brutus, seven under Lepidus, thirteen under Pollio, Plancus, and other generals, and only four under Antony. Such vast armies (over a quarter million men) inevitably dictated policies. Octavian failed to join Decimus Brutus to destroy Antony's weakened force. Partly he was reluctant to cooperate with Caesar's murderer; partly he was suffering from the propaganda rumors that he had effected the deaths of Hirtius and Pansa to hold all the power himself.[50] But, most important, he seems not wholly to have controlled his army, whose veteran legions were unreliable about supporting the Senate and Caesar's foe against Caesar's friend Antony. Whatever the causes of the ineffectual pursuit, Antony reached Transalpine Gaul, a strong position for regrouping his resources, with an enlarged army and confident still of victory.[51]

In Rome, while Fulvia was protected by Cicero's apolitical friend Atticus, Antony and his other followers were formally pronounced enemies of the state. For some vacillating men and divided towns, the condemnation brought firm adherence to the senatorial cause. But the condemnation, added to the news that Decimus Brutus, in seeking land for the veterans of four legions, was reclaiming the lands already allotted to Antony's veterans, solidified the opposition of Antony's outlawed associates and troops.[52]

VIII

Avenger of Caesar

Antony's active strength when he reached Transalpine Gaul had been badly battered, yet his prompt success in building legions and negotiating strategic alliances meant that he remained a commanding power in the state. His original legions, reinforced with one legion composed of all possible recruits, even slaves, were joined, in a swift march, by the three legions under Ventidius, Caesar's former quartermaster. Decimus Brutus had ordered Octavian to block Ventidius, but Octavian had not acted, perhaps was not strong enough to act. Antony now commanded eight legions.[1]

In Narbonese Gaul Caesar's former Master of the Horse, Lepidus, commanded seven legions, and Antony began negotiating for an alliance with his old comrade. In Comata Gaul the former Caesarian Lucius Munatius Plancus had three legions; in Spain Gaius Asinius Pollio had two. Among them, the experienced generals could well win over Antony's hastily assembled army. Cicero and other republicans wrote asking for their support, and they replied with assurances of loyalty to the republic. Plancus did, indeed, send 4,000 cavalry against Lucius Antonius who led Antony's advance troops into Gaul, though Lepidus had already assured Plancus that he needed no help to defeat Antony. Pollio also came from Spain at the command of the Senate to help Decimus Brutus; so Antony's forces were threatened with attacks from front and rear. Antony, however, coolly deceived Decimus Brutus, who sent his republican troops on a false chase while Antony led the main body of his troops safely into Lepidus's province.[2]

The armies of Lepidus and Plancus were encamped on the bank of the Argenteus River. Antony placed his men on the opposite shore, so confident of Lepidus's real loyalties that he disdained even to fortify his camp. He had judged the situation well. The Caesarian veterans under Lepidus and Plancus wanted to join Antony. Lepidus let Antony openly appeal to the troops and cross the river to his camp. On May 29, 43 B.C., Lepidus's army led their general to Antony's command. The shift was announced to the Senate in a letter. Cicero raged in his sixteenth *Philippic*; and on June 20 the Senate declared Lepidus, like Antony's other followers, a public enemy.[3]

Plancus, too weak to stand alone, soon followed Lepidus. Decimus Brutus, endangered by Antony's increasing strength and Octavian's refusal to help, had fled to Plancus. They had tried to hold out, had asked for more troops, and had faced Antony with fourteen legions. But ten of the legions were raw recruits, unready for a fight against the veterans. When Plancus and his army joined Antony and Lepidus, Decimus Brutus fled east toward Macedonia. En route, probably in October, 43 B.C., he was murdered by a Celtic chieftain on Antony's orders. Antony's brother Gaius, already captive in Macedonia, was executed on the orders of Marcus Brutus in reprisal for his kinsman. The able and honorable Pollio had encouraged resistance to Antony and had come from Spain to fight. Now admitting that Antony's agents had tampered with the loyalty of his troops and that the odds were with Antony, he changed sides. Within weeks and without a battle, Antony had regained a great army of twenty-three legions in Gaul (c. 156,000 men). By October, leaving six legions under a trusted associate, he was invading Italy with seventeen legions (c. 90,000 men).[4]

In Italy the main force against Antony was led by Octavian. But during the six months since Mutina, while Antony had been securing allies in Gaul, Octavian's position in Italy had changed radically. With Hirtius and Pansa dead, he was the only surviving general of the forces that had relieved the siege of Decimus Brutus at Mutina, and he expected to dominate the state. But the Senate, which had used him reluctantly on Cicero's urging at a time of emergency, now thought itself safe and ostentatiously set him aside. For the victory at Mutina, Decimus Brutus was awarded the prestigious military triumph, while Octavian, over considerable protest from the republicans, received the lesser ovation (*ovatio*). The Senate, ignoring Octavian's claim—though the pro-Caesarian legions balked at serving under the tyrannicide—commissioned Decimus Brutus general of the forces that Hirtius and Pansa had commanded. Generals like Brutus and Cassius who were hostile to Octavian and whom he could not accept as allies were strengthened to oppose him. Cicero, claiming that he could control his protégé, still urged a coalition with him. But Cicero's suggestion that Octavian and he be named consuls to fill the vacancies left by Hirtius and Pansa was ignored, even though much state business like elections was at a standstill. When, probably in May, 43 B.C., the Senate appointed ten commissioners to review the legality of the acts of Antony's consulship, Octavian was not on the commission.[5]

This slight had serious repercussions. The army feared that Antony's provisions for the veterans would be dropped. Already the bounties promised to Octavian's troops had been decreased on the plea that the absence of revenues from the troubled east made full pay impossible. Moreover, the colony for veterans which the Senate had instructed Lepidus and Plancus to establish at Lugdunum was endangered by their defection to Antony. The soldiers therefore turned to Octavian, who still paid them well, and they sent a deputation to Rome to demand their benefits and the consulship for Octavian.[6]

Octavian, thus, was building his military forces. His political party also grew around a core of exceptionally able and loyal young friends: Marcus Vipsanius Agrippa, straightforward and honest, an able general, a reliable statesman and shrewd politician; Gaius Maecenas, a dexterous diplomat and manipulator; and Quintus Salvidienus Rufus, a resolute military leader. Caesarians from all ranks watched Caesar's heir with sympathy and sometimes open support.

Octavian was playing a game of clever duplicity. He flattered Cicero. He seemed to work for cooperation with the Senate. He assured Plancus that he would join him for a campaign against Antony. Meanwhile he was negotiating with Antony and aiding his allies. He could never have expected a sincere alliance with any of these factions, but he calculated their usefulness while playing his lone hand.[7]

From the Senate Octavian demanded the consulship, a military triumph, and rewards for his troops. The Senate refused the proposals, although they offered the sop of a praetorship. The alliance with the Senate effected by Cicero clearly was unnatural. Now, counting too soon on the control of the eastern armies by Brutus and Cassius, the senators were ready to discard Octavian.[8]

Antony, however, was offering Octavian cooperation. With his backing, Octavian dared to let an army of eight Gallic legions plus auxiliaries cross the Rubicon River and march on Rome. As they advanced, the legions increased to eleven, then to seventeen (c. 100,000 men). Cicero's desperate appeal to provincial governors brought two legions from Africa. With these and the one stationed in Rome, the Senate, initially terrified, prepared to fight. No fight was possible. The Gallic army advanced in good order. Octavian had only to appear; the senatorial legions defected to the heir of Caesar. By August Octavian had taken Rome. Cicero fled the city, deeming the republic dead when an army ran the state and the Senate sat helpless.[9]

The army did, indeed, determine that Octavian's measures would pass. On August 19 Octavian had himself elected consul with his kinsman Quintus Pedius. He seized the state treasury to pay at least an installment of the promised soldiers' benefits. He also minted money for the pay, utilizing the coin types to portray Caesar's empty throne and other symbols of divinity. It was part of his calculated propaganda campaign to take Caesar's role. In late August the Comita Curiata was instructed to ratify Octavian's adoption by Caesar, so that Octavian became legally Gaius Julius Caesar Octavianus. In a specially established court, Octavian had a law passed decreeing the death penalty and outlawry for the murderers of his adoptive father and for Sextus Pompey, who was collaborating with them. Octavian, as general of an army, consul, Caesar, and avenger of his "father," was a potent force, far removed from Cicero's recent protégé. He now prepared to face Antony as an equal.[10]

The coalition of Antony, Octavian, and the other Caesarians against the republicans was so reasonable that only the personal ambitions of the leading men had delayed it so long. Antony had continued his role as Caesar's successor. He had even named his son born in 43 B.C. Iullus Antonius[11] in familial reverence to Caesar. But he recognized that the legions were loyal to Octavian as the bearer of Caesar's name and was now willing to use Octavian as his lieutenant. His error lay in not recognizing fully Octavian's ambitions and ruthlessness. Octavian, with an army only one-third the size of Antony and Lepidus's force, also needed Antony's cooperation and had grown confident that he could manipulate the less devious and calculating Antony. Both saw Lepidus and his army as needed allies.

Octavian in Rome made the first overtures. Led by his fellow consul Pedius, the Senate annulled its previous condemnation of Antony and Lepidus as outlaws and proclaimed its intention of seeking peace for all. Then late in October Octavian marched north to meet Antony and Lepidus at Bononia in the Po Valley. For two days the generals isolated themselves on an island in the river while their troops waited on the banks, eager for an agreement. All three acknowledged the need for a compromise that would ensure the loyalty of the troops, avoid suicidal strife among the Caesarians, and combine their legions against the republicans. Lepidus acted as ·mediator. The result was a signed, sealed compact creating the Second Triumvirate (*Tresviri reipublicae constituendae*).[12]

Antony, Lepidus, and Octavian had devised an unconstitutional alliance to run the state on the pattern of the First Triumvirate of Caesar, Pompey, and Crassus. This Second Triumvirate, to run for five years from January 1, 42 B.C., to January 1, 37 B.C., was made technically legal by the *Lex Titia* proposed by the tribune Publius Titius and voted by the Comitia Tributa on November 27, 43 B.C. The action was pro forma. The three had the consular *imperium*, with full and equal power at all times, with all legislative and executive functions under their control. Their acts were valid without senatorial approval, nor was a veto provided. The responsibilities of the Comitia were virtually abolished, though the people were still allowed to vote honors for the triumvirs! All the offices, the patriciate, the priesthoods were filled with their followers and at their command. Loyal officeholders could be promoted to important provincial commands. Typical of their appointments was that of Antony's uncle, Gaius Antonius. In 59 B.C. he had been condemned to exile for a wretched record as governor of Macedonia, but after a comfortable exile on a Greek island, he had been recalled by Caesar.[13] Now he was made censor. In like manner Octavian arbitrarily transferred his own consulship to his supporter Ventidius. The Senate, which Caesar had enlarged to 900, now grew to 1,000 members to give rank to new men supporting the triumvirs in Italy and the provinces.[14]

After the initial despotic changes, the relationship of the triumvirs to these appointed officials and screened Senate is shadowy and probably was never defined. The customary duties were performed usually without interference; the triumvirs would even request favors of the officials. It seems that the triumvirs wanted the stated right to rule at will, to grant petitions, issue edicts, raise armies, and deal with important foreign affairs. But they did not intrude into or even want to be bothered with the day-to-day operations of government. Moreover, each hoped, despite the presence of the armed guards, to retain the pretenses that he represented traditional government and that the triumvirate was a temporary aberration from republican ways.[15]

The program of the triumvirs was to defeat the republican assassins of Caesar and to "restore the republic." Their real goal was to rule the state unchallenged. For this they needed the emotional loyalty of the people. Caesar, who was their common bond and the ultimate basis of their popular support, was ostentatiously honored. In 44 B.C. an attempt to name Caesar a god had been abortive. On January 1, 42 B.C., a Senate decree confirmed by the Comitia officially recognized Caesar as god; and with the triumvirs and magistrates, the senators swore to uphold his acts. His image was placed on coins. The right of asylum was granted to his statues and to his new temples in the Forum and in some cities of Italy. Octavian bore the title divi filius (Son of the God) and derived the greatest benefit from the deification; but Antony and Lepidus were also strengthened by their former ties to the divinity.

The western provinces and armies were distributed despotically among the triumvirs, who put legati (legates) as governors under themselves and arbitrarily granted them proconsular *imperium* even though some of them had never held consular or praetorian rank. Lepidus kept Spain and Narbonese Gaul. Octavian, still the weakest of the three, was probably suffering from Antony's domineering arrangements when he received Africa, Sicily, and Sardinia —important provinces, but Sicily and Sardinia were almost entirely controlled by Sextus Pompey, and in Africa a pro-Antony general was dominant. Antony held all Gaul except Narbonese Gaul. His province included Cisalpine Gaul, which provided mastery of Italy. The control of Italy was divided among the three, as were the sixty legions.[16]

The armies' demands had to be met at any cost. About 80,000 veterans expected promised benefits, especially land. Eighteen of the richest Italian towns were seized for land allotments to the veterans; later sixteen more towns were added. Perhaps 50,000 of the veterans thus received their land. But about sixty legions (c. 360,000 men) were still under arms. With them Antony and Octavian were to carry the war against the republicans, while Lepidus remained as consul to govern Italy.[17]

Before the campaign began, Rome had to see the triumvirs' might. They entered Rome individually on three successive days of parade and panoply. Coins were issued by each, bearing their likenesses and the symbols of their families. For Antony, the reverse of the coin showed the hero Anton, as founder of the family. The young Octavian was formally betrothed to Claudia, Antony's stepdaughter by Fulvia, a dynastic tie which the ambitious Fulvia may well have engineered.[18]

Behind the triumphs and festivities ultimately lay fear. The republicans were strong, with armies that Brutus and Cassius were mobilizing in the east, and with many civilian supporters, especially among Rome's ruling class. The triumvirs also needed vast moneys to pay their armies and supporters. The prices of the armies were soaring ever higher as generals bid against each other for experienced soldiers to supplement the conscripts. The soldiers knew they could demand increased rewards and could plunder virtually at will. The eastern provinces sent almost nothing to Rome because they were dominated by Brutus and Cassius, and even from the western provinces much of the revenue was drained off by occupying generals. Two hundred million denarii, the shortage for actual needs, had to be supplied.[19]

The triumvirs added special taxes on the propertied classes, the first taxes on citizens of Rome in 120 years. So heavy were the exactions that it was proposed that people surrender all their property in lieu of taxes, then reclaim one-third; but in practice the one-third rarely was returned. One year's rental on houses was claimed, and one-half year's return on proceeds of the land. A forced loan of one year's income was demanded, and a 2 percent capital tax on everyone's property valued over 100,000 denarii. Heavy fines were exacted for false returns. Intimidation was so intense that effective protest was stifled, until the property of 1,400 rich women was taken. The victims appealed to the women of the triumvirs. Octavian's sister and Antony's mother received them sympathetically; but Fulvia expelled them roughly from the house. Hortensia, who had inherited eloquence from her orator father, then boldly pleaded their case to the triumvirs themselves in the Forum. The people gathered there were so sympathetic that the triumvirs were obliged to reduce the number of victims to 400. Yet still more money was needed. The confiscation of the property of wealthy enemies and forced sales of their goods promised relief. But the confiscated property found few buyers, and too much of the return was drained off to informers and agents.[20]

The greed of the triumvirs, therefore, led to unscrupulous, desperate measures. In their first agreements at Bononia, they had marked for death men whose political power was worth eliminating or whose property was valuable enough for expropriation. Publicly they justified their brutality: by telling of the wrongs they had suffered from their victims; by citing the evidence that Caesar's clemency to his enemies had ended in their murdering him; by asserting that since they had to go east to fight, they could not leave foes behind who would threaten a stab in the back. But their private motives showed the blacker side of their own and their associates' vengeance and greed. Their precedents were the proscriptions of Sulla and Marius, laws to themselves for murders and retributions. The first proscription lists of victims were published even before the triumvirs reached Rome.[21]

The guilt for the bloodletting lay upon all three, though the greatest, perhaps, on Antony. Lepidus was more follower than leader. Octavian had already liquidated enemies when he had marched on Rome and showed no compunction until he was in absolute control. But, as a younger man, he had fewer scores to settle than his older colleagues. Antony, bluff, hearty, honest in an army camp way, could also be coarse and ruthless; and the proscriptions revealed him at his worst. In savage inhumanity the triumvirs decreed that whoever sheltered a proscribed man should be proscribed too. Though most of the killings were done by soldiers, any free man who brought the head of a proscribed man to the triumvirs received 100,000 sesterces; a slave won 40,000 sesterces and his freedom. The same rewards went to those who informed against the proscribed.[22]

Though each triumvir could name victims at will, the first lists which carried names of their own family members and friends had been drawn up in common, with concessions to the bitter animosities and bloodthirstiness of each. Lepidus's brother, Antony's uncle, Octavian's close kinsmen were all proscribed. Over 300 senators and 2,000 equestrians, political and economic leaders of the state, were eventually listed. The consul Pedius, who worked to mitigate the violence and lessen the numbers of the proscribed, died of exhaustion and despair. The times of terror and pursuit, hiding and deception brought out the blackest treachery and the noblest heroism at every level. Some family members, slaves, and friends killed or informed and seized the rewards of their perfidy; others sacrificed their own safety, property, and lives for the ones they loved. Lucius Caesar, Antony's uncle who had been Caesar's legate and held office with Antony in 47 B.C., had shifted from a position of neutrality to the republican side after Mutina and had proposed that Antony's agrarian law be repealed. After Antony's defeat, he had endorsed the denunciation of his nephew as an "enemy of the state." When he was proscribed, he fled to his sister Julia, Antony's mother, who courageously won pardon for him.[23]

Less fortunate was Cicero. For years he and Antony had maintained a correct but calculated friendship with a pragmatic awareness of self-interest. But Cicero, whose effectiveness had always been checked by his lack of military force, had ended his worried vacillations. His public denunciations in the *Philippics* had so enraged Antony that Antony had insisted—even to the extent of trading the death of his own uncle to Octavian—that Cicero be on the first list of those proscribed. It was a contemptible murder of an old man of dignity, honor, and learning, who had served the state well. Antony's reputation has suffered the censure of the ages for the brutality, while Cicero's has risen proportionately. Yet Cicero's policies, so violent in denunciation and attack, had forced Antony to extremes he had not intended. And Cicero's support of Octavian, even to the point of illegality and war, had determined Antony's turning to the legions with all the resultant dangers of renewed civil wars. Cicero, though vacillating and not personally courageous, apparently never dared hope for an appeal to Antony. Their enmity was personal; but the two men also knew that they stood for totally different ideals of the state. The murder itself was accompanied by unbridled barbarity. Soldiers decapitated Cicero as he fled Italy. His body may have been claimed and buried by Lucius Aelius Lamia, who had been Cicero's spokesman to Antony. But his head and right hand were delivered to Antony and Fulvia who treated them contemptibly, then had them nailed to the Rostra in the Forum from which Cicero had delivered his denunciations of Antony.[24]

Cicero's family also suffered. His son Marcus had joined Brutus after the Ides, was a good commander, and was on the list of the proscribed. However, because he was studying in Athens, he escaped death. Cicero's nephew Quintus had favored Caesar, joined Antony for the money which the spendthrift boy always needed, and bragged that he was Antony's right hand. But in June, 43 B.C., he turned to Brutus and Cassius and claimed that he would call Antony publicly to account for his seizure of the public moneys. Cicero had not trusted his claims nor his conversion. But when his father was proscribed, the young Quintus supported him courageously, and the two died together.[25]

Cicero's closest friend, Titus Pomponius Atticus, though proscribed, was more skillful in saving himself. A rich equestrian, he had avoided public office and had a genius for cultivating friendships in all political camps. He was devoted to Cicero and had loaned 400,000 sesterces to Brutus when visiting Greece. Yet he had also maintained a steady correspondence with Antony and had supported Fulvia in legal problems and loaned her interest-free money to settle debts when Antony had been branded a public enemy. Now he kept the friendship of the men who had proscribed him. Antony personally looked out for him, and he survived with even his fortune intact, so that he was able to succor others who had been proscribed.[26]

Another survivor was the learned Marcus Terentius Varro, who had supported Pompey but had been forgiven and made librarian by Caesar. Now Antony proscribed him; though he escaped to lead a life of peaceful scholarship, his libraries were plundered and his villa taken by Antony. Others also escaped by flight to Brutus, Cassius, or Sextus Pompey, who aided their escape and welcomed their support. Thus the crimes of the proscription were sometimes, though too rarely, mitigated. With abject irony, the cowed Senate presented each triumvir with the wreath symbolic of saving lives— because they had limited the numbers of their victims.[27]

The proscriptions, though damning the reputations of the triumvirs for all time, did fill their war chest and eliminate, cow into submission, or put to flight the leaders who could have rallied opposition. Now Italy submissively accepted their ordering of affairs, even naming magistrates (for several years ahead) who would hew to triumvir policies. Lepidus was left nominally in charge of Italy, although Antony's lieutenant Calenus, commanding two legions there, was also powerful. To crush the republican assassins, Antony and Octavian led their armies to the east.[28]

In the eastern provinces, Brutus and Cassius had been struggling to assert supremacy and now could face the Caesarians with a large, well-financed army. Their retreat to the east had been forced when Antony seized the initiative at Caesar's funeral and changed the liberators' role to that of assassins. They had lingered in south Italy until late August, conferring about their uncertain policies, issuing proclamations justifying their acts as patriotic and as virtuous by a "higher authority" than the law, but afraid to enter Rome even to fulfill duties of the state offices they held. They had not wanted, they perhaps had feared civil war against Antony, who kept them off balance by mingling gestures of friendship with his threats. At last they had sailed east to take, not the important provinces of Macedonia and Syria to which Caesar had appointed them, but the

121

humiliating posts Antony had approved for them: to collect grain in Sicily and Asia, then on January 1 to assume office as governors of Crete and Cyrene.[29]

The republicans had left Italy with hopes of rallying supporters, even armed forces in the rich eastern provinces. Certainly, when Brutus, docking in Athens in August, 44 B.C., was hailed as a liberator and found statues erected to honor the tyrannicides, his ambitions for republican leadership revived. Though posing as a student of philosophy, he was recruiting an army—the youthful poet Horace and Cicero's son Marcus joined him—and receiving legions from Illyricum. His first objective was control of Macedonia, the province which Gaius Antonius had been assigned to govern on January 1. Brutus's uncle Hortensius and other agents worked there to win over the loyalty of the legions and to secure the supplies gathered at Demetrias for Caesar's planned Parthian campaign as well as the funds due to go to Rome from the province. In February, 43 B.C., Brutus assumed command of the entire Balkan area, accepting the authority from his uncle, who willingly placed himself and his province under Brutus's control. Gaius Antonius was too weak to control his province. Though he struggled for a time, he had to surrender to Brutus, who kept him in honorable captivity until he attempted revolts and became a retaliatory victim, executed in reprisal for the murders of Decimus Brutus and Cicero. The official vote of the Senate giving Brutus the command came only after the *fait accompli* and the passionate urgings of Cicero in his tenth and eleventh *Philippics*. The practical result was the existence of a republican army in the east.[30]

From Greece Brutus went east. Cicero and other republican leaders were summoning him to Cisalpine Gaul to help Decimus Brutus; but Marcus Brutus had disapproved of Cicero's support of Octavian and his urging that the leading tyrannicides be reconciled with Octavian. In Brutus's judgment, the desirable and possible reconciliation was that between Antony and the Senate. Octavian was a far more dangerous political threat than Antony. The rift caused by this disagreement closed slowly. Thus Brutus looked first to his own army and the money he needed for it. Marching east in the late summer of 43 B.C., he fought some tribes in Thrace, for which his troops hailed him as imperator. He then took western Asia

Minor, where, as in other lands he controlled, he solicited or forced major contributions. His successes, even though technically illegal, meant power for Brutus and an increased conviction of his destiny as the savior of the republic. Like Cassius, he was issuing coins showing the dagger of the liberators but also his own portrait—an extraordinary assumption of privilege for a living man. Even more than Cassius, Brutus was becoming the rallying point for the republicans, his righteous and inflexible Stoicism giving him the aura of a prophet of ancient virtues.[31]

In practical terms Cassius was operating with even greater speed and success in Syria than Brutus in the Balkans. He was also facing a determined opponent, Publius Cornelius Dolabella. Antony had reluctantly acknowledged Dolabella as fellow consul after Caesar's death; when Antony effected a redistribution of the provinces, Dolabella was governor of Syria in place of Cassius. In January, 43 B.C., Dolabella seized Asia Minor by force from the republican governor Trebonius, whom he slew brutally. For this he was declared an enemy (*hostis*) by the Senate. But he continued to hold the territory and exact men, money, and ships from the provinces of southern Asia Minor despite the grant of *imperium* to Cassius and Brutus. In Rome Cicero urged in vain that the Senate recognize Cassius as the legitimate governor of Syria and commander of the eastern armies so that he could legally requisition men and supplies and prosecute the war against Dolabella. The Senate would not grant Cassius rank over other governors or a coordinated command which would again give a general extraordinary powers. Independently, then, as various Caesarians defected to him, Cassius built a force of twelve legions, financed by 700 talents. In response, Dolabella crossed to Syria, but he was helpless against Cassius's forces and authority. Defeated in battle, Dolabella committed suicide. His troops defected to Cassius.[32]

Cassius also looked toward intervention in Egypt. When the four Roman legions that Caesar had stationed at Alexandria mutinied, some soldiers had joined Cassius and some had urged the republicans to take over Egypt. Justifications for an attack were there: Cassius had bid for the queen Cleopatra's support; but Cleopatra's ties had been to Caesar, and she claimed that he had fathered her son, Caesarion. She could, therefore, hope for little from Cassius

123

or the other republicans and had negotiated with Dolabella, promising to send him troops in return for his recognition of Caesarion as her coruler. Perhaps she was also corresponding with Antony. Legions, ships, and money were reported sent to Dolabella; but the aid had never reached him. Cleopatra claimed that the troops had been intercepted by Cassius and that the fleet had been prevented from setting out by a storm. It seems unlikely that the crafty Cleopatra had actually committed her forces; she was more likely to husband her resources to bargain with the sure victor for her own advantage. Still, when Dolabella died, Cleopatra demanded recognition of Caesarion from the triumvirs on the claim that she had sent aid to Dolabella. Antony backed her, perhaps hiding her failure actually to send help in order to set up Caesarion as Caesar's son and counterclaimant to his adopted son. Octavian, of course, resented any increase in Caesarion's power but had to concede the recognition lest Cleopatra, the only remaining Caesarian ally in the east, turn strategic Egypt over to the republicans. Cassius's plan, then, to attack and occupy Egypt could be justified. But Brutus demurred, arguing that other goals were more urgent.[33]

It was time for a meeting of the two republican leaders who independently had been seizing control of the eastern provinces. In November, 43 B.C., after the formation of the triumvirate had been announced, Brutus and Cassius met at Smyrna for a strategy conference. By now both held proconsular rank, the title imperator, large armies and navies, and commands that gave them domination over all the provinces and armies from the Ionian Sea to Syria. The eastern provinces paid fifty million denarii tribute each year, and for two years this revenue money had not reached Italy but had supported the republican legions. The ultimate struggle had to be against the triumvirs. But in preparation, to secure their holdings and to increase their treasuries, they agreed that Cassius would reduce a hostile but rich Rhodes, while Brutus would attack Lycia.[34]

Cassius effected his conquests uncompromisingly. Capturing Rhodes, he drained its great wealth. The rich city of Tarsus provided 1,500 talents. Other cities of Asia were forced to pay in one year the tribute normally assessed for the next ten years. Local dynasts like Ariobarzanes of Cappadocia who failed to help or threatened opposition were executed. The exactions were ruthless, but the republican war chest had precedence over justice or mercy. Beyond needed supplies and supplementary gifts, pay was now 1,500 denarii per man—more for officers—to about 70,000 soldiers who, knowing little patriotism to Rome, were loyal only to their paymasters. Brutus, for his part, took Lycia after brutal fighting. And he allied with Deiotarus, ruler in Armenia Minor and Galatia to whom Antony had given his throne for a price of ten million sesterces. But Brutus's monetary returns were far fewer than Cassius's. Brutus still strove, though often futilely, to stand on legality and win by kindness; for Cassius, desperate crises justified any means in getting money and allies.[35]

In January, 42 B.C., another meeting, at Sardis, was needed to thresh out their disagreements. Though Brutus and Cassius were different and their policies contrasted, they deeply respected each other and their common goal of victory to restore the republic. Both were hailed as *imperatores*. Both agreed on readying for war. Together, commanding nineteen legions, and with aid promised by the Parthian king Orodes, they reached the Hellespont in September, 42 B.C., and marched west against the triumvirs.[36]

The battle site for the armies marching from the east and the west was at Philippi, north of the Aegean Sea in Thrace. When the troops from Italy set sail from Brundisium under Antony's command, sixty galleys under Murcus, Cassius's man, blocked the harbor. Antony's forces took so many casualties trying to force the blockade that he asked Octavian for help. Octavian had been in Sicilian waters trying to check the proscribed Sextus Pompey, whose role in providing haven for the triumvirs' victims steadily increased his power. Pompey erred in failing to keep Octavian tied up in the west or to support Murcus and Gnaeus Domitius Ahenobarbus, the republican admirals. With the additional help of Octavian's fleet, Antony transported his troops through Murcus's lines, though he suffered losses of perhaps three legions and faced a strong continuing blockade of his supplies from Italy.[37]

Forty legions had been readied by the triumvirs for the campaign, but they may not have been up to full strength and not more than half of them actually saw battle. Forty legions were too many to maintain in the hostile, impoverished land of Thrace; and Lepidus needed perhaps eleven legions to protect Italy. In Macedonia probably one legion remained at Amphipolis to guard the naval base. When the battle lines were drawn, about nineteen legions (c. 100,000 men) were committed on each side. The numbers were about equal or were weighted slightly in favor of the Caesarians.[38]

Brutus and Cassius arrived with their eastern legions before Antony. They drove back Antony's small advance force and took a strong position across the Egnatian Way in mountainous terrain at Philippi. Their flanks were protected by the mountains and marshes; their supply lines by sea were nearby and secure. Octavian had fallen ill at Dyrrhachium, and though he followed as soon as possible to forestall Antony's domination, Antony arrived first. Antony placed his camp opposite Cassius's; Octavian's faced Brutus's. The Caesarian supply lines were inferior and near no running water; Antony even had to dig wells. Clearly it was to his advantage to precipitate a battle since his supplies were short, and his men were experienced veterans; but it was equally to the republican advantage to delay.[39]

For ten days Antony's troops worked to cut Cassius's camp off from the supply road by stealthily building a dyke through the swamp. Cassius countered by building an opposing dyke. But as the republican troops were so engaged, Antony attacked their construction and then, in high mettle, stormed into Cassius's camp. The salient into the camp was too extended. After plundering the camp, Antony withdrew his troops. Brutus retaliated by capturing Octavian's camp and wreaking havoc while the ill Octavian fled to safety. Brutus, overextended, also fell back. This seizure and loss of the camps on October 23, called the first battle of Philippi, was costly in lives but merely tentative and inconclusive except for an extraordinary result. When Cassius's camp was occupied, he mistook action in Brutus's camp to mean that the republicans everywhere were overrun. In ill-founded despair, Cassius committed suicide.[40]

The loss of their best general was a grave blow for the republicans. Even with Brutus's strong moral prestige, supplemented by additional donatives to the troops, his army knew that he was not an outstanding soldier; and they feared that he was inferior to Antony. All the republican advantage depended on delay. The Caesarian supplies, always short, were now running out. The ships conveying men and supplies across the Adriatic were being captured by the republicans. Antony again tried to cut off Brutus's supplies or force him into battle. Unwisely, the worried soldiers pressured Brutus to fight.[41]

In mid-November the republicans attacked. While Octavian, sick again, held the camp, Antony routed Brutus's men, and his cavalry effectively slaughtered or captured the fleeing. When his few remaining troops lost courage to counterattack, Brutus—though saved once by a loyal officer, Lucilius, whom Antony honored for his act—followed Cassius in suicide. Antony, despite bitterness about Brutus's execution of his brother, covered Brutus's body with his own purple cloak, honoring the man who had struggled to his death for the ideal of a republic which other men had already discarded. Later, a more vindictive Octavian decapitated the corpse, intending to throw the head at the base of Caesar's statue in Rome. A kindlier fate caused it to be lost at sea. Brutus's wife, Porcia, also suicided. And men of rank, like Cato's son, died fighting or committed suicide. Perhaps as many as 50,000 died at Philippi and in the concurrent naval actions.[42]

With their leaders lost, few in the vast republican armies could still dream of a patriotic cause more compelling than their own safety. Some fled to Sextus Pompey, who again gave sanctuary to republicans. Others, like Murcus and Ahenobarbus, joined the triumvirs. Most of those captured who had been proscribed were now executed. A few, like Marcus Valerius Corvinus, who surrendered to Antony were saved by him. Some, like Cicero's son and the poet Horace, were later pardoned. The rank and file of the defeated soldiers marched before Antony and Octavian, clearly demonstrating their respect for Antony, their contempt for Octavian as generals. Many of the captives taken during the battles had been slain by both sides. The survivors now were soldiers for pay, not patriots, and about 14,000 willingly took service under the triumvirs as their new paymasters and donors of the promised veteran benefits which Brutus and Cassius could no longer provide. The Caesarian victory ended with a magnificent sacrifice and rewards or penalties to their armies by Antony and Octavian.[43]

Philippi destroyed the final glimmers of republican hopes. Petty conspiracies but no great civil wars would again rally under the

127

banner of a restored republic.[44] Sextus Pompey was gathering the republicans, but he did not talk of a republican government. In the longer view, however, the battle was only the last struggle in a deteriorating political pattern whose outcome had been determined by the changed conditions within the empire which had built vast armies under ambitious generals and which had given evidence of the inadequacy of the conservative, senatorial government to cope with the changed problems of an extended empire. Brutus and Cassius had been quick to use violence and expropriation in their turn. And in place of a program of government reform, they seemed inflexibly determined merely to resume the old patterns, however ineffectual. If there were hints of change, these appeared rather in their issuing coins imprinted with their own portraits and in their claiming powers not unlike those of the dictators whom they attacked. At least Antony and Octavian, illegal by traditional forms, were proving competent to mobilize military forces. But they still had shown little evidence of long-term constructive policies beyond those initiated by Caesar. Now the opportunity was theirs to rebuild the prostrate state. The triumvirate, with Antony dominant, had worked together for military victory. The oncoming cooperation should be effective in solving the problems of a world at peace.[45]

IX

Relinquishing the West

A pattern ominous for the future emerged at once in the distribution of responsibilities and powers after the battle of Philippi. Ignoring Lepidus, Antony and Octavian divided forces and looked for ways of increasing their real strength vis-à-vis each other. Nothing was said of the eastern provinces; but probably they had been unquestioningly assigned to Antony, who foresaw their usefulness. A signed compact distributed the western provinces. Octavian received Spain, Numidia, Sardinia, and Sicily—though Sardinia and Sicily he would have to wrestle from Sextus Pompey. Antony took Africa and all Gaul, save that Cisalpine Gaul was changed from a province to a part of Italy proper. Italy remained common ground for administration and for recruiting legions. Lepidus had lost his authority. His troops were now integrated into the common army, and he was even suspected of collusion with Sextus. Essentially he was now discarded from the triumvirate. He was allotted no provinces, although, because he had ties with Sextus and influence in the Senate, the possibility of his receiving Africa remained as an inducement for cooperation.[1]

Of the legions at Philippi only 11 remained in service, with 14,000 cavalry. Other soldiers who had completed their tour of duty were discharged, and from these only 8,000 reenlisted. Antony took 6 of the 11 legions and 10,000 cavalry. Then, because he was going to remain in the east while Octavian returned west, Antony exchanged 2 of the legions that he had stationed in Gaul for 2 of the 5 Philippi legions that Octavian had received.[2]

Financing the legions to hold their calculated loyalty to a pay-master general and rewarding the veterans to dissolve potentially dangerous gangs of malcontents remained the most urgent problems. The triumvirs had promised land and 5,000 denarii to the troops fighting at Philippi. Accordingly, Antony undertook to raise the moneys needed for promised discharge benefits from the richer east. Sailing to Asia, he began the reorganization and domination of the east which was to occupy the rest of his life. Octavian had to find the farmlands in Italy that the veterans demanded. Land had been taken in the proscriptions, but most of it had been sold for cash or given to partisans. Expropriating land from established owners was an ugly job, calculated to alienate the farmers as much as it satisfied the veterans. But the farmers' resistance was disorganized; part of the needed land could come from property of the proscribed; and Octavian had probably already recognized the political strength of holding Italy with grateful landowners.[3]

Octavian founded his first veteran colony at Philippi, one of the strategically placed semi-military colonies with which the triumvirs hoped to secure their position. Then Octavian turned west. As an auspicious beginning in Rome, he performed the religious rites in the thanksgiving celebration that the Senate had voted to honor the victory of the triumvirs. Statues to Concord were set up. But the times were bad and growing worse; Octavian faced real danger from the discontented people. Sextus Pompey dominated the western seas and radically reduced needed imports to Italy. Internally, the food supply had suffered the ravages of the civil wars: trees had been felled, houses burned, cattle slaughtered, crops leveled, and reserves plundered. Little had been planted under the threats of destruction and expropriation. Now the granting of the fields of skilled farmers to inexperienced veterans further decreased production. Desperate robbers prowled the roads. In 42 B.C. even the Vestal Virgins had to be protected by lictors. Additional taxes on slaves and inheritances diluted the loyalty of rich supporters.[4]

The land distributions pleased no one. The displaced farmers were miserable and argued for compensation for their losses. Even the soldiers realized that their own families could be dispossessed. Among those evicted, but later protected, were the poets Horace, who had served under Brutus at Philippi, and Vergil, whose appeal to Octavian brought back the Mantuan property which had been given to Antony's veterans; but few fared as well. The agricultural lands and other property held by eighteen of the richest cities were assigned for confiscation without recompense; eventually over forty cities suffered. Some of the dispossessed stayed on as tenants of the new owners or were scattered as colonists among the veterans, but many migrated to the cities or became armed marauders. For years to come, Antony and Octavian would work to settle these dispossessed folk. Even the veterans were rebellious. They claimed that the triumvirs had promised them the best land of Italy. In a number of instances, officers or others with special claims seized lands by violence. Apparently, Antony and Octavian had agreed that veterans settled in strategic colonies would stabilize their control. Yet Antony's adherents accused Octavian of favoring his own men and using proscribed lands for Octavian's advantage.[5]

Somehow Octavian emerged from the crises stronger than he had entered them. He was showing the political acumen that would so effectively make him the savior of the state in later years. He pushed ruthlessly when he could, made concessions when he must. However taken, land was granted to veterans of twenty-eight legions; and six more legions were otherwise rewarded to win their favor. A propaganda machine convinced many of the veterans that Octavian, not Antony in the remote east, was their special protector and benefactor. He was loyal in patronage to his friends, more so than Antony; and Octavian's men were the ones holding high offices in Rome and critical commands in the provinces. Even his physical health, so disordered in the battle camp, recovered in the more peaceful setting. Increasingly, he was extending his grasp over Italy.[6]

Antony's followers recognized the threat to Antony's primacy in Octavian's successes. It was not Antony, absorbed in his eastern activities, but his agent Manius and the Antonine family in Italy who protested Octavian's western settlements. Lucius Antonius, powerful, popular, and loyal to his older brother, was consul for

131

41 B.C. Antony's wife, Fulvia, appears to have been even more dominant and determined. Later Augustan writers portrayed her as cruel, vengeful, greedy, and already jealous of Cleopatra and Antony's other paramours in the east.[7] Even if the worst character traits are dismissed as propaganda, Fulvia still emerges as the driving force in the events of 41–40 B.C. In recognition of her role as a commander-in-chief, her portrait appeared on the coinage—the first Roman woman to be so recognized. To her credit, she saw the dangers from Octavian as Antony did not seem to, and promptly sought to discredit Octavian. Mark Antony in 41 B.C. was issuing coins with the figure of Pietas, to claim the title of heir to Caesar. Now Lucius took the cognomen Pietas to represent his fidelity to his brother.[8]

With a complex of disorders to manipulate in Italy, Lucius Antonius shrewdly came forward as the republican consul championing the senatorial, middle, and farmer classes even against the triumvirate and the army. It was a strained and inconsistent posture; Lucius was claiming, indeed, that he would persuade Mark Antony to resign his extraordinary command as triumvir to resume constitutional office and keep the propertied classes secure.[9] Yet the Senate declared Lucius an enemy (*hostis*). In the hard times of confiscated properties, disordered government, bitter hostilities, and threatening famine, much of Italy, especially in the areas north of Rome, rallied behind Lucius against Octavian and his veterans.[10]

The goodwill of the indispensable army and veterans had to be cultivated too; and Lucius stressed that the Antonii were the influence behind veteran legislation and the founding of colonies. Fulvia bribed Octavian's army to mutiny; then, early in 41 B.C., Fulvia with her children, Lucius Antonius, and Manius came before the troops, reminding them that Antony as well as Octavian had granted them land and urging them not to forget Antony as their patron. Antony's reputation with the troops far exceeded Octavian's. Yet the pull and tug between commanders worried the troops, who lacked a clear understanding of the issues. Twice the legions brought the leaders to negotiations and even agreements for peace, but the arrangements were promptly ignored, and both sides appealed to the troops for military support.[11]

The response from Antony's officers and men was muted. His

reputation with the troops was unquestioned, but they were not sure if he commanded these new conflicts. Though both sides had written to Antony, and he had replied vaguely about preserving his dignity, he had sent no orders for a campaign. His loyal generals in the west, Calenus and Ventidius in Gaul with eleven legions, Pollio in the Po Valley with seven legions, Plancus in south Italy with the three legions that Fulvia had raised—all moved their troops forward but awaited Antony's orders to fight. Fulvia and Lucius raised six legions on their own and supplemented them with two won from Octavian's legions in Rome. It was with these eight legions that they prepared to fight.[12]

Octavian, with four legions free from defense against Sextus Pompey, also summoned his generals and recruited large levies especially from among the veterans. Salvidienus Rufus marched six legions from Spain, closely followed but not blocked by Pollio and Ventidius. Agrippa took Sutrium north of Rome, threatening Lucius's position. Lepidus was given two legions for the defense of Rome but lost the city and the army to the eight Antonian legions. In Africa Fulvia ordered the pro-Antonian general Sextius to regain control of the province for Antony. Bogud of Mauretania, once allied with Caesar, and now Antony's man, invaded Spain for Antony, but he was recalled by a revolt in Mauretania headed by his brother, Bocchus, who supported Octavian.[13]

The fighting was desultory and widespread over troubled Italy, but the main front was north of Rome. Octavian and his generals blocked off Lucius, who had marched north of Rome to meet the Gallic generals, then forced him into the hill town of Perusia. The city was skillfully blockaded. Lucius, a second-rate commander, had not supplied the town for a siege but counted on rescue by the other Antonian generals. They came—their watchfires could be seen by the besieged—but without orders from Mark Antony, they never fully committed their troops to relieve the siege. By early spring, 40 B.C., ineffectual attempts to break out and grizzly starvation forced the capitulation of the city. Octavian was welcomed back in triumph to a rejoicing Rome.[14]

Mark Antony later attributed his silence to distance and unawareness of the crisis; and, certainly, winter communication with the eastern provinces was unreliable and slow. But other news of

Antony in Cappadocia and with Cleopatra had reached Rome. Although busy with many eastern responsibilities, Antony apparently was avoiding intervention. He had not stirred up the campaign that Lucius and Fulvia were waging. He was reluctant to alienate the veterans whom Lucius and Fulvia were attacking or the upper classes whom they were supporting. He still preferred to work with rather than against Octavian, who was fulfilling the responsibilities agreed to after Philippi. Yet he could not openly repudiate his wife and brother, though they never involved him in responsibility for their actions. So he feigned ignorance and claimed innocence though this meant victory for Octavian.[15]

Octavian's terms after the surrender were carefully calculated to his own advantage. Those he judged his personal enemies, like Bogud of Mauretania who lost his kingdom, suffered special vengeance. But to maintain a form of cooperation, he took no reprisals on Antony's family beyond divorcing Fulvia's daughter Claudia. Antony's mother, with many others, fled to Sextus Pompey. Fulvia, with Plancus and 3,000 troops, escaped to Greece. Lucius Antonius was not only spared but made governor of Spain. Pollio with seven legions escaped northeast to hold Venetia for Antony and to win over (for Antony) the staunch republican Gnaeus Domitius Ahenobarbus, Cato's nephew, and his Adriatic fleet. The other Antonian legions were incorporated into Octavian's army but dispersed to Africa, Gaul, and Spain. The civilians, however, especially the upper classes of Perusia, suffered grievously from slaughter and rapine. The very city, rich and ancient, was promised to the soldiers for pillage, though the flames of an uncontrollable fire destroyed the city before the men could.[16]

For his supporters, Octavian had rewards. There was booty for his generals like Agrippa. The two legions he was able to win over from Plancus were well rewarded. And, over the protests of the people who resented losing food to the army, loyal veterans were again granted confiscated lands. The faithful though ineffectual Lepidus received Africa, a province seriously torn by the struggles between Octavian and Antonian followers. Salvidienus received the command in Gaul, where Antony's loyal lieutenant Fufius Calenus had died. The death was providential for Octavian, and he hurried there to take command from Calenus's son.[17]

134

Powerful Gaul with its huge army was now under Octavian's control. The arrangements made after Philippi had been arbitrarily upset. Although Antony still had loyal troops in Italy, and forty legions under his control, he had to decide to what lengths he was willing to go to regain his massive western power.

Antony was in Asia Minor preparing for a campaign against the Parthians when news reached him of the fall of Perusia. Despite the threat of the Parthians, he felt obliged to go west instead of east. At Athens he met Fulvia, Plancus, and some of their supporters in flight from Perusia, still bitter about their failure and laying new plans to ally with Sextus Pompey against Octavian. Agents of Sextus were present too, arguing that Octavian was a dangerous and unscrupulous ally and that Antony's fortune now lay with the Pompeians and republicans who had gathered around Sextus. Antony saw the perils on both sides. But his promise of cooperation had been given to Octavian, and, as he did consistently if imprudently, Antony determined to keep his trust to Octavian unless Octavian failed him.[18]

Bitter reproaches passed between Fulvia and Antony over their differing political stands. Antony left her in anger, and, already ill, Fulvia soon died in Sicyon. Rumor said that she died of a spirit broken by Antony's indifference. Certainly he regretted that he was at least partly responsible for her death. She had been a strong woman, passionately committed to her political and even military activities. Some of Antony's ambition since 45 B.C., much of his brutality, and even part of his steel had been drawn from the force of this wife.[19]

Antony had deserted her to settle troubled affairs in Italy and Gaul. At Corcyra, as he sailed west, came the grim news of the death of Calenus and of the appropriation of powerful Gaul and its eleven Antonian legions by Octavian.[20] Antony, who had just determined to maintain the terms of his pact with Octavian, now looked more favorably at the alliance that Sextus Pompey was offering.[21]

Sextus was a factor in Mediterranean power politics with which Antony had to come to terms. Since his father's death after Pharsalus, Sextus had seemed a pirate; yet he was so strong that he controlled Sicily, Sardinia, parts of North Africa, and Farther Spain—

as Antony had learned when he tried to found the colony that had earlier been planned by Caesar at Urso in Spain. Sextus had become the refuge for heterogeneous malcontents from all classes—provincials, slaves, even criminals—but especially for the republicans who had fled the defeats at Pharsalus, Philippi, or Perusia or had survived the triumvirs' proscriptions and confiscations. He had, therefore, a considerable army of probably 18 legions, although it was not powerful enough to compete with those of the triumvirs. In addition, Murcus and Ahenobarbus supported him with such sizable fleets that Sextus, manning some 350 ships with 50,000 rowers, could at will blockade Italy's grain supply, terrifying the whole peninsula with the threat of famine.[22]

Although Sextus played a childish role as Neptune's son and agent, his reputation in the lands he ruled was that of benevolence; and the areas prospered economically. A sympathetic Senate at the time of Mutina had recalled him, indemnified him for the loss of his father's property, and assigned him an extraordinary naval command. But the triumvirate had proscribed him, and he had returned to his outlaw rule. Here he hesitated uncertainly, lacking a sure goal and planned policy. His power was great enough to win the big stakes, not alone, but in alliance with another powerful leader. Thus, had he joined the Antonians against Octavian in the battle of Perusia, they might well have won.[23]

When Lucius Scribonius Libo and Sentius Saturninus came to Antony as Sextus's agents, Antony was fully aware of the advantages of this ally against Octavian and that Sextus was warning him against Octavian. He was also grateful for the protection that Sextus had granted his mother, Julia, after Perusia. Accordingly, Antony expressed his friendship and received his mother back from Sextus. But whereas Antony and Sextus reached only a friendly understanding, Octavian snatched the victory of Sextus's support and a guarantee that Sextus would not starve Italy by blockading the coast with his superior fleet; for Octavian took Scribonia, Sextus's aunt by marriage, as his elderly but politically useful wife.[24]

In response, Antony's ally Pollio now conferred with Gnaeus Domitius Ahenobarbus, a sympathizer with Caesar's assassination. Ahenobarbus had been outlawed by the triumvirs but had independently gathered a substantial fleet. Pollio brought the two leaders together in the Adriatic. Antony sailed forward with only five war-ships in the face of Ahenobarbus's entire fleet. It was a challenge of trust which Ahenobarbus met gallantly. After a frightening pause, he lowered his flag and ran his ship broadside to Antony's murderous ram. The leaders issued coins for 40 B.C., marking their reconciliation, and together they sailed to Brundisium.[25]

To Antony's indignation and dismay, the gates of Brundisium were locked against them. The city, like the rest of Italy, must have been uncertain about the shifting alignments of the generals. Aheno-barbus had been an outlaw and had attacked Brundisium the pre-vious year; now he appeared with Antony, who had outlawed him. Antony assumed that Octavian had ordered him excluded from the port, despite Octavian's protests of innocence. The triumvirs had agreed that Italy and its capital should be equally the property of and recruiting ground for all of them. Therefore, Antony laid siege to Brundisium, turned back hostile cavalry attacks, and be-gan seizing territory in south Italy. Sextus and other republicans eagerly allied with Antony and Ahenobarbus and took control of Sardinia from Octavian. Gathering his forces, Octavian marched to besieged Brundisium. Both sides struggled for propaganda as well as military victories. Antony lived up to his reputation of invincible general by capturing an oncoming force of 1,500 cavalry with 400 of his own. Yet another fratricidal civil war seemed under way.[26]

Peace could still be forced upon the generals. The troops and even the officers, reluctant to choose between the two Caesarian leaders, urged compromise and openly fraternized. Octavian was willing. Though he had the greater army, he was unsure of the loy-alty of his troops. Antony agreed. He knew that his main battles belonged in the east, where the Parthians had destroyed the eight legions Antony had left in Syria and carried off their eagles to add to those taken from Crassus. No alliance with Sextus Pompey would be as valuable for Antony as cooperation with Octavian. Even Fulvia's death made concessions between Antony and Octa-vian easier. Mediation was conducted by their mutual friend Lucius Cocceius Nerva, by Octavian's skillful diplomat Gaius Maecenas, and by Antony's able ally Asinius Pollio. Antony's mother, Julia, related also to Octavian, was appealed to as intermediary. To aid the peace, Antony sent Sextus to Sicily and Ahenobarbus to

137

Bithynia. The outcome of their efforts was the Pact of Brundisium, in the early fall of 40 B.C.[27]

The new agreement inevitably augmented Octavian's power at Antony's expense. What Octavian won were the western provinces of Transalpine and Narbonese Gaul and Dalmatia to add to his holding of Spain. Antony still held the east beyond the River Drin, the boundary between Macedonia and Illyricum. That Antony agreed at all to the diminution of the western lands under his control was probably due to his concern about returning east to wage the Parthian war and to his honest, if naive, willingness to cooperate with Octavian, whose promises he believed as honorable as his own. Content with half the world, he had not yet realized that Octavian would settle only for the whole. Antony never totally lost his ties with the west; some towns and some individuals remained loyal to him, whether through traditional bonds or through calculated appraisal of his dominance and usefulness for enfranchisement. The former agreement that Antony and Octavian would share equally in levying Italian troops continued, though Octavian later proved faithless to the pact. For the moment, there was an effort to equalize the two armies. Octavian was to send Antony five Gallic legions that had served under Calenus and were now under Salvidienus but whose loyalty to Octavian was questionable. Indeed, most of the troops in the Caesarian armies, aggrieved at not having received the bounties promised for their fight at Philippi, could be held in check only with difficulty. Antony's army now probably numbered twenty-four legions.[28]

Other careers also had to be settled at Brundisium. Lepidus again retained control of Africa. Ahenobarbus's condemnation as outlaw was lifted, and he was made proconsul of Bithynia, an assignment favorable to Antony, who could utilize his fleet. Sextus still controlled Sicily and had regained Sardinia from Octavian's general; but his position was ambiguous. Despite his recent alliances with Antony and Octavian, he was expanding his power. Now Octavian was to try to arrange a peace with Sextus; but if he was unsuccessful, as seemed likely from the bloody forays of their armies, Antony would support Octavian in any war against Sextus. To reward friends, the triumvirs nominated consuls for several years ahead. The general Ventidius was assigned command of the army against the Parthians for 39-38 B.C. And Pollio, as proconsul with probably eleven legions, was assigned the Macedonian province under Antony's control, where the Parthini tribe was disrupting the peace.[29]

Enemies, in turn, paid their penalties, as friends had received their rewards: Manius, for example, died for his part in the War of Perusia. As a token of good faith to Octavian, Antony revealed that Salvidienus Rufus, Octavian's lifelong friend to whom Octavian had entrusted Gaul after Calenus's death, was proposing a startling collaboration with Antony against Octavian in this powerful province. Apparently, Salvidienus was calculating Antony's superior strength; but he was also responding to the Gallic troops' unwavering loyalty to Antony, which not even Octavian's land grants to them could shake. Octavian promptly summoned Salvidienus to Rome and had him executed for treason. Antony had again, as at Perusia, been honorably faithful to his pact with Octavian, even at a dangerous cost. Octavian's scruples about the alliance stopped exactly at the point of his own advantage.[30]

Octavian's ambitions now led him to offer his own sister as wife to the widower Antony. Octavia was young, beautiful, virtuous, and recently widowed; and Antony recognized the advantages of the match. Octavian was counting on her loyalty to him and hoped for an agent in Antony's home. But Octavia was capable of loves and loyalties to both brother and husband, and she undertook the role of mediator between the rivals. A dispensation was demanded from the complaisant Senate to permit Octavia to marry within the established ten-month mourning period after her husband's death.[31]

Together Antony and Octavian traveled to Rome in November, 40 B.C., to announce the treaty of peace, to reward friends with state offices, and to consummate the marriage with Octavia. The people, in their yearning for peace, rejoiced at the reprieve from the civil war they had dreaded and committed the care of the city to the triumvirs. Statues were erected to Concord as they had been in 42 B.C., and coins were imprinted with a caduceus and clasped hands and with two opposed cornucopiae on a globe. The victory, although in a civil war, was hailed as a triumph. Octavian began to call himself officially the son of a god. Antony was inaugurated into the role of priest of the divus Julius. Vergil wrote the *Fourth Eclogue* celebrating the world at peace and, perhaps, hailing the child to be born to Antony and Octavia as descended from lines of gods. And so the celebrations for the peace and marriage waxed gala, Octavian entertaining in traditional Roman military fashion, Antony introducing Asiatic and Egyptian fashions.[32]

Bad times checked the revels. Disappointed at not being a partner to the Pact of Brundisium, Sextus Pompey grew more daring, raiding the Italian coast. His blockades raised prices, lessened Italy's food supplies to near famine levels, and forced harsh financial measures. More taxes, too, were collected to pay the standing armies. Latent popular hostility toward the triumvirs was inflamed to riots and even the stoning of Octavian until Antony called out the army to rescue his rival and to restore order by slaughtering the insurgents. Clearly, the triumvirs had to come to terms with Sextus, if Italy were to eat and their control were to last.[33]

The agent between Antony and Sextus was Scribonius Libo, father-in-law to Sextus, brother-in-law to Octavian. In the spring of 39 B.C., conceding to the entreaties of the people, the three leaders, with their forces, met at Misenum, on the neutral territory of platforms set on piles driven into the sea bottom. Their own and their followers' differing ambitions and expectations made compromise difficult. But Antony patched together the motley array of terms that each demanded for peace. Sextus conceded his control over the food supply in Italy by sending the grain of Sicily and Sardinia to Rome, by quieting the pirates, and by withdrawing his troops from Italy. In compensation, he was allowed to keep his control and naval bases in Sicily, Sardinia, Corsica, and Achaia in Greece for five years. Sextus had ambitions for a Roman political career; he had hoped to replace Lepidus as triumvir but settled for a compromise. He was to be augur and to hold the consulship in 37 B.C. Meanwhile, the triumvirs ensured the latter office for themselves or their allies: for 38 B.C., Antony and Libo were to be consuls, though Antony could substitute whomever he wished; next Octavian and Pompey; Gaius Sosius and Gnaeus Domitius Ahenobarbus were consuls-designate for 36 B.C. (though by 36 B.C. their war service in the east kept them from taking office); Antony and Octavian were named consuls for 35 B.C.; and Antony was designated consul for 31 B.C. Sextus was to be compensated for his father's property which had been confiscated; and his baby daughter was engaged to Octavian's three-year-old nephew, now also Antony's stepson.[34]

Pompey's camp had been the refuge for a great range of malcontents from high-principled republican patricians to runaway slaves. Now every refugee under his protection was pardoned except Caesar's murderers; and every runaway slave was freed. Eligible men could again hold office. One quarter of the property of those proscribed was returned, and others recovered their real property—all the restitution the spendthrift triumvirs could afford. Discharged veterans of Sextus, even if freedmen, were to receive the same bounties as those of Antony and Octavian.[35]

The terms of the agreement were widely hailed. The hungry masses hoped for plentiful food. The exiles and refugees, including nobles like the young son of Cicero, left Sextus to return home, grateful and loyal, especially to Antony, though gradually they were to come into the sphere of Octavian's influence. Sextus, Antony, and Octavian themselves celebrated. The tale is told that when all three dined on Pompey's ship, his lieutenant Menodorus proposed to Sextus that he cut the cables mooring the ship, thus leaving the rulers of the Roman world at Pompey's mercy.[36] Sextus's reply was that the plot would have been sound if done without Pompey's knowledge; but that once he knew, he had to forbid the treachery. The story may be apocryphal, but it does reflect the mixing of honor, treachery, ruthless ambition, and bonhomie in the relations of the three men. This latest attempt to compromise among the three leaders would prove futile. Octavian and Sextus were unwilling to live up to the agreed terms, and Octavian seemed determined or destined always to outdo Antony. But, for the moment, hopes ran high. During the summer Octavia bore Antony the first of their two daughters named Antonia; and the family settled into Athens, which, for two years, Antony was to use as his headquarters for reorganizing the east and preparing for war against the Parthians.[37]

Sextus and Octavian were soon exchanging charges of bad faith and building up their forces. Sextus's piratical raids again disrupted shipping, and only part of the promised grain arrived in Italian ports. Had Sextus not been fundamentally weak, he could have followed up his victories. On his side, Octavian for once let emotion take precedence over policy. In 38 B.C., the day after Scribonia had given birth to Octavian's daughter Julia, he divorced her to marry Livia, the wife of Tiberius Claudius Nero. It was a marriage of love, which lasted for life. But Octavian was also aware that it brought him political ties with powerful patrician factions, to counter the family prestige of Antony, Lepidus, and the now indignant Pompey.[38]

Antony, busy in Athens with the eastern provinces, with preparations for Parthia, and with Greek good times, wanted peace with Sextus. But Sextus accused him of not handing over the Greek province of Achaia, which had been awarded to Sextus at Misenum, until the debts owed to Antony by the various cities had been paid. Moreover, Antony's lieutenant, Sosius, held the strategic western island of Zacynthus. And Octavian repeatedly used real or contrived accusations against Sextus to rouse Antony's apprehensions. Under such pressures, and because Sextus's attacks were distressing the economy so that even Antony had to debase his coinage, Antony agreed to meet Octavian at Brundisium with naval aid. No doubt Antony had a price to exact for his help, the higher because he had opposed Octavian's breaking with Sextus. Other affairs needed settling as well. Octavian had not sent the Italian troops promised to Antony. And the *Lex Titia*, which had established the Second Triumvirate for five years, would expire at the end of the year 38 B.C.[39]

Antony therefore sailed to Brundisium with a large fleet of 300 ships. Perhaps the display of Antony's impressive power made Octavian reluctant to admit his need for help. Or perhaps Agrippa's recent victories in Gaul had raised Octavian's hopes. Octavian was not in Brundisium to meet Antony, and Antony would not wait for the younger man. He sailed with his fleet, leaving the advice that Octavian should make peace with Sextus. Octavian's response was further readying for war.[40]

The open break that threatened the triumvirate was closed by Octavia's mediation. By spring, 37 B.C., she had drawn her husband and brother to a conference at Tarentum. Antony's objectives included securing the Italian troops and keeping his prestige and faction alive in Rome. Perhaps he also hoped to share the glory of victory against Sextus. But chiefly, in the face of repeated provocations from Octavian, Antony still worked to be a faithful Caesarian ally.[41]

The Pact of Tarentum in 37 B.C. renewed the triumvirate for five years. It had expired on December 31, 38 B.C.; now it was extended through 33 B.C. No plans for the triumvirate were made for the period after 33 B.C.; but Sosius and Ahenobarbus were named consuls for 32 B.C., Antony and Octavian for 31 B.C. No evidence is extant that these agreements were ratified by the people, although the previous triumvirate had been established by a special law, and perhaps the extension was also legalized. Certainly, the army favored the arrangement, which would satisfy their promised land claims.[42]

The distribution of military units was the all-important element that had forced the renewal of the alliance. Both Lepidus and Antony agreed to send ships for a war against Sextus, who, as an enemy, now lost his augurate and promised consulship. Antony had had 200 ships built in the east in 40 B.C., then had increased the number to 300 by adding the fleets of Ahenobarbus and other adherents. Of these he would provide Octavian with 120 warships. In return, Octavian was to send Antony, 20,000 soldiers, 4 legions for Parthia, plus a bodyguard for Octavia of 1,000 picked men. These transfers would equalize the armies of Octavian and Antony at 26 legions each. The 4 legions in Africa under Lepidus would remain stationed there.[43]

The pact was a final attempt at Caesarian peace; but it would prove no more than an uneasy collaboration. Antony calculated that he had already fulfilled his obligations, whereas Octavian had not. In the outcome, Antony sent 120 ships yet never received the 4 promised legions from Octavian. But for the moment, the pact was hailed. Coins were issued to mark the harmony of Antony, Octavian, and Octavia. To seal the agreement, Antony's son Antyllus was betrothed to Octavian's infant daughter Julia.[44]

Antony now sailed east for action against the Parthians. Octavia, who had given birth to Antony's second daughter Antonia, parted from Antony at Corcyra to return to Rome under Octavian's protection. Octavian readied for his final settlement with Sextus.[45]

Marcus Vipsanius Agrippa, Octavian's loyal lieutenant and friend, provided the superior naval skill that Octavian lacked. In 37 B.C., as consul, he left victorious campaigns in Gaul to take command of building and training a fleet against Sextus. In the Bay of Misenum north of Naples (Neapolis), he joined Lakes Lucrinus and Avernus to each other and to the sea by canals and developed the port of Cumae. Then for a year in these protected naval stations, he trained 50,000 provincials, freedmen, and expropriated slaves as rowers for 300 ships.[46]

On July 1, 36 B.C., despite Octavian's losing part of the fleet, Agrippa defeated Sextus in battle, and the Caesarians could plan an invasion of Sicily as Sextus's final stronghold. Octavian pressured Lepidus to invade south Sicily with his African legions. Antony's urging may well have been necessary to persuade Lepidus to attack with fourteen legions and take Lilybaeum. Concurrently, Statilius Taurus sailed from Tarentum to eastern Sicily with 102 of the 120 ships sent by Antony.[47] Agrippa and Octavian, sailing from Misenum toward northern Sicily, lost half their ships in a storm, but, while Sextus recklessly ignored his chances of victory, they readied their fleet again. In mid-August Octavian lost more ships when landing his legions on the Sicilian shore. But Agrippa compensated for Octavian's blunders; and indecisive skirmishes by land and sea showed the combatants closely matched. At last, in the great naval battle of Naulochus, September 3, 36 B.C., Agrippa destroyed 160 of Sextus's fleet of 300 ships. Agrippa, Octavian, and Lepidus could then take command of Sicily and restore the slaves, who had been guaranteed their freedom by the Senate, to their masters.[48]

Counting on his once having sheltered Antony's mother, Sextus, with his few remaining ships, fled east to Antony. Other surviving Pompeians, like Gnaeus Cornelius Cinna, also sought refuge with Antony as more compassionate than Octavian. Sextus reached Lesbos, where his father's reputation ensured him a warm reception. There Sextus learned that Antony was suffering reverses in Parthia and that he had drawn all but a few effective troops out of Asia Minor and Syria. Sextus, therefore, changed from a suppliant to an aggressor. Calculating the most favorable terms, he sent envoys to Antony and to the rulers of Thrace, Pontus, and Parthia. Antony's agents captured his messengers and brought them to Alexandria;

144

but Antony still preferred to trust Sextus, who counted on Antony's goodwill despite repeated provocations. Without waiting for replies from the kings, Sextus refitted seventeen ships, mobilized three legions of infantry, and tried, without success, to seize Ahenobarbus as a valuable hostage. In the spring of 35 B.C. he attacked the ill-defended province of Asia and seized Lampsacus on the Hellespont. With enlarged land and sea forces, he attacked Cyzicus but failed—at least partly because of the struggle put up by a force guarding some gladiators belonging to Antony. An attempt to bribe the Italian cavalry sent by Octavia to Antony also failed. But, reaching the province of Bithynia, Sextus plundered Nicaea and captured Nicomedia.[49]

The attacks had to be met. Gaius Furnius, the governor of Asia, mobilized forces and sought help from Ahenobarbus—back from Antony's invasion of Parthia and now governor of Bithynia—and from the client king Amyntas of Galatia to the south. With opposition mounting to Sextus's reckless aggression, some of Sextus's recently recruited soldiers, and even his senatorial allies, began to desert. A fleet of 120 ships under Marcus Titius, sent from Syria by Antony, caught and burned the Pompeian ships in the Propontis. Sextus, forced to retreat overland toward Armenia, was captured at Midaeum by the Galatian king[50] and sent to Miletus. His three legions shifted allegiance to Antony. At Miletus, in 35 B.C., Sextus, now forty years of age, was killed by Antony's supporter, Marcus Titius, perhaps on Antony's direct orders. Octavian sponsored wild animal games in the Circus and set up a chariot at the Rostra in Rome honoring Antony for the death of their rival. And, as part of his efforts to quiet the mutinous troops demanding lands and money for their victories, Octavian now stationed at Tarentum on inactive service the fleet that Antony had sent to fight against Sextus.[51]

The death of Sextus eliminated one of the few remaining claimants to republican leadership. It is hard to know Sextus now through the hostile propaganda which remains. Evidently he was enough of a threat that the triumvirs mobilized their full force to destroy him. Yet Sextus must be judged rather as a name to rally the republican cause than as a real republican. The civil wars which had spanned his lifetime taught him self-serving one-man rule rather than republicanism; and many of the true republicans who had rallied to his side later left him in disappointment. Nor did he offer long-term plans for conquering, then stabilizing the state. Like a guerrilla leader, he could win local skirmishes but could not survive full-scale war. For Antony, he had been both an irritant and a very useful diversionary check on Octavian's power in the west.[52]

In Sicily Octavian's triumph over Sextus was challenged briefly by his fellow-triumvir Lepidus. Competition, even treachery between the allies had erupted during the campaign. Sextus's land army of eight legions had surrendered to Lepidus's fourteen legions and had been incorporated into a formidable force of twenty-two legions. With this backing and the sense of superiority drawn from Octavian's frequent defeats, Lepidus's ambitions soared. Confronting the younger man, he ordered Octavian to leave Sicily to his command. It was a hopeless challenge. Octavian had only to appeal with the magic name of Caesar and with the promise of pay to have the vast mass of the army desert Lepidus.

The general without an army meekly accepted Octavian's terms. Because he held the traditional religious office of pontifex maximus, which Octavian saw as a useful symbol of the republic, he could live. But he lived under surveillance in an Italian town, an exile from Rome. His army, his provinces, his wealth fell to Octavian. Only the now insignificant office of pontifex maximus remained his token of former glories during the twenty-three years he was still to live in obscurity. His title of triumvir was erased, although the "duumvirs," Antony and Octavian, continued to call themselves triumvirs. Antony was informed, not consulted, about the settlement; but Lepidus's deposition almost inevitably followed the failure of his power play. Indeed, only Octavian's confidence in his secure strength saved Lepidus's life.

Lepidus had always been the weakest triumvir: the poorest in war, the least skillful in political manipulations, the remotest from Caesar's legend. Yet he had provided a significant brake to the rivalry between Antony and Octavian. Without his balance, the split between Antony as leader in the eastern empire and Octavian in the western empire showed starkly and dangerously.[53]

With Antony now deeply involved in Parthian campaigns, Octavian could deal with the followers of Sextus and Lepidus at will.

The proscribed leaders were mostly pardoned; but many Sicilians were exiled, and captured slaves were returned to their masters or died by impalement. The Sicilian towns paid huge indemnities; and their political status was demoted from Roman citizenship to municipal status. Sixty thousand freeborn legionnaires were incorporated into Octavian's army, now swelled to over 45 legions, plus 25,000 cavalry and 40,000 light-armed troops. But such forces were no longer needed; and prolonged service was turning many soldiers mutinous. Octavian sent Antony's ships to Tarentum, discharged the 20,000 time-expired veterans of Mutina and Philippi, quieted the others with promised bonuses, and returned to Rome in triumph. Confidently he proclaimed the end of civil wars and promised that the discharge of the other troops and the restoration of constitutional government awaited only Antony's defeat of the Parthians.[54]

X

Reorganizing
Eastern Provinces and Allies

For Antony, the meetings with Octavian and struggles with Sextus and Lepidus had been troublesome interruptions to his prime responsibilities in the east. But, despite the time-consuming trips to Italy, Antony had been gradually settling the disordered affairs of a number of provinces and client kingdoms to the mutual benefit of the eastern states and of Rome.

Octavian's troubles and triumphs had derived from his responsibilities for settling the veterans on Italian land. Antony's eastern responsibility was to stabilize Roman relations with eastern states and to extract the monies needed for veteran benefits (500 drachmas promised to each soldier). The task demanded breadth of understanding of the peoples of the east, diplomatic acuity in wooing cooperation or enforcing settlement, and a grasp of the economic complexities of the Mediterranean world. Rich as the east was, it had been ravaged repeatedly by warring generals, most recently by the desperate Cassius. Antony had precedents for his decisions in the settlements imposed by Sulla, Pompey, Caesar, and, more recently, Brutus and Cassius; but a fresh overview and countless particular decisions were needed for the war-weary lands. Antony's settlements, though occasionally sullied by favoritism or carelessness, were temperate, sensible of new conditions, shrewd, and designed so well to fit the traditions of the past that many of the patterns he established were continued long into imperial times.[1]

Antony went into the east with every advantage of military power and the prestige of the victor of Philippi. He led 8 legions and 10,000 cavalry. The more distinguished republicans who survived Philippi had chosen surrender to Antony rather than to Octavian. A number of others came over to Antony at Thasos as he traveled east, so that his company included even such republican names as Cato's grandson, Lucius Calpurnius Bibulus. That he took firm control of the east is seen in the coinage now issued, commonly with his head on the obverse, no matter who issued it.[2]

During the winter of 42-41 B.C., Antony set up long-term headquarters in Athens. Though he relished the leisure and learning of the university city and the pose, if not genuine intellectual sophistication, of the philhellene, there were official deputations to receive and benefits to distribute. The states and rulers that, however reluctantly or unsympathetically, had felt obliged to aid Brutus and Cassius, now hurriedly sent apologies and protestations of friendship to Antony. For most, Antony's response was cordial but reserved, for financial exactions were still to be imposed as the price of triumviral friendship.[3]

In the spring of 41 B.C., he crossed to Ephesus to settle the affairs of Asia. There he sacrificed to the city's famous goddess Artemis, and in turn he was eagerly and elaborately hailed as the god Dionysus incarnate.[4] To Ephesus he summoned representatives of the various states and either formed an Assembly of Asian states or utilized an already existing one. In his address to the Assembly, his first demands were financial. He lauded Rome's generosity but claimed what he called the traditional tithe of the earlier Attalid rulers of Asia. The tithe he praised as sharing the better and worse years of the people. In actuality, the Romans continued the publican tax system whereby contracts for collection were let in Rome several years in advance, irrespective of the varying productivity of the seasons. To meet the veterans' benefits, he demanded money for twenty-eight legions, and the same equivalent to ten years' tribute that the eastern states had painfully provided Brutus and Cassius.[5]

The lamentations of the representatives at the Assembly were noisy and valid. The states had been desperately drained economi-

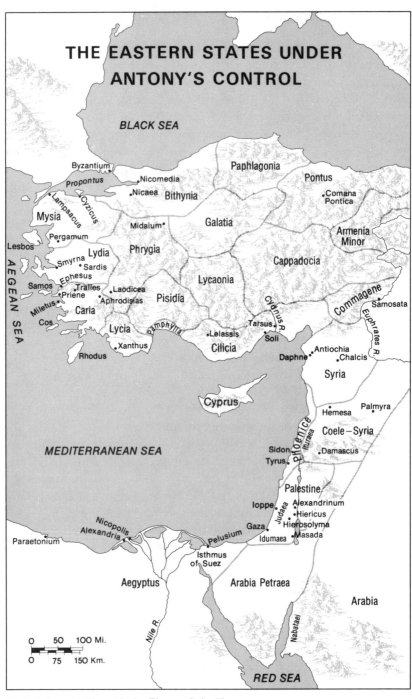

THE EASTERN STATES UNDER ANTONY'S CONTROL

BLACK SEA

Byzantium
Propontus
Lampsacus
Cyzicus
Mysia
Pergamum
Lesbos
Lydia
Smyrna
Sardis
Ephesus
Samos
Tralles
Priene
Laodicea
Aphrodisias
Miletus
Caria
Cos
Lycia
Xanthus
Rhodus

Nicomedia
Nicaea
Bithynia
Midaium
Phrygia
Galatia
Paphlagonia
Pontus
Comana Pontica
Armenia Minor
Cappadocia
Lycaonia
Pisidia
Pamphylia
Cilicia
Lelassis
Tarsus
Soli
Cydnus R.
Commagene
Samosata
Euphrates R.

AEGEAN SEA

Daphne
Antiochia
Chalcis
Syria

Cyprus

MEDITERRANEAN SEA

Hemesa
Palmyra
Coele–Syria
Ituraea
Damascus
Sidon
Tyrus
Phoenice
Palestine
Alexandrinum
Hiericus
Hierosolyma
Masada
Judaea
Ioppe
Gaza
Idumaea

Nicopolis
Alexandria
Paraetonium
Pelusium
Isthmus of Suez
Aegyptus
Arabia Petraea
Arabia

Nile R.
Nabataei

| 0 | 50 | 100 Mi. |
| 0 | 75 | 150 Km. |

RED SEA

Mark Antony: A Biography by Eleanor Goltz Huzar
Copyright © 1978 by the University of Minnesota.

Mark Antony, victorious triumvir (identification uncertain). Stylized bust found in 1830 at Tor Sapienza and dated to the Flavian period (late first century A.D.). Vatican Museum. Alinari photo. Reproduced with the permission of the museum. Yellowish marble, ht. .68m.

The information found for the sculptures is incomplete in some instances. Notably, without inscriptional evidence, the subjects of most ancient statuary can be only tentatively identified.

Julius Caesar, commander and dictator. Colossal head modeled after Caesar's death on an unknown sculpture of about 50 B.C. National Museum, Naples. Reproduced with the permission of the German Archaeological Institute, Rome. Marble.

Pompey the Great, defeated rival of Caesar. Probably a second-century A.D. copy of an official bronze sculpture dating from c. 53 B.C. Ny Carlsberg Glyptothek Museum, Copenhagen. Alinari photo. Reproduced with the permission of the Art Reference Bureau. Pentelic marble, ht. .44m.

Cicero, republican orator hostile to Antony. Augustan Age (first century A.D.) copy of a c. 40 B.C. bust showing Cicero in his mature years. Uffizi Gallery, Florence. Reproduced with the permission of the German Archaeological Institute, Rome. Marble, ht. .74m.

Marcus Brutus, republican champion and Antony's foe. First-century A.D. bust, portraying Brutus idealized as a man in his thirties. Capitoline Museum. Alinari photo. Reproduced with the permission of the Art Reference Bureau. Marble.

Agrippa, conquering admiral at Actium. Bust from the Claudian period (c. A.D. 50), copied from the official bust of c. 25 B.C. The style is Hellenistic. Louvre Museum. Reproduced with the permission of the German Archaeological Institute. Marble.

Lepidus, member of the Second Triumvirate (identification uncertain). Bust found in 1830 at Tor Sapienza and dated to the Trajanic period (early second century A.D.). Reproduced with the permission of the Vatican Museum. Yellowish marble, ht. .78m.

Cleopatra VII, queen of Egypt (identification uncertain). Bust dated to c. 35 B.C. The representation combines classical form and soft impressionism. Reproduced by courtesy of the Trustees of the British Museum. Fine-grained limestone, ht. .27m.

Octavia, wife of Antony, sister of Octavian (identification uncertain). Bust found at Lyons. The hairstyle and dignified idealization are typical of the late republican period. Louvre Museum. Alinari photo. Reproduced with the permission of the Art Reference Bureau. Basalt, ht. .27m.

Roman warship with Egyptian crocodile, celebrating victory at Actium. Stone relief from the ruins of the temple of Fortune at Praeneste, c. 25 B.C. Vatican Museum. Alinari photo. Reproduced with the permission of the Art Reference Bureau.

a. Antony. Silver denarius, 34 B.C. b. Antony and Octavia. Aureus, 39 B.C. c. Antony bearded in mourning for Caesar. Denarius, c. 44 B.C. d. Sextus Pompey. Aureus, 42-38 B.C. e. Fulvia. Silver coin from Eumenia, 41 B.C. f. Gnaeus Domitius Ahenobarbus. Aureus, 42-41 B.C. g. Antony as Dionysus. Aureus, c. 37 B.C. h. Cleopatra. Bronze coin issued at Alexandria, c. 34 B.C. Coins a, b, e, f, g, h reproduced by courtesy of the Trustees of the British Museum, and coins c and d the American Numismatic Society, New York.

Antonia, daughter of Antony, mother of the emperor Claudius (identification uncertain). Bust in an idealizing and decorative style. Reproduced by courtesy of the Trustees of the British Museum. Marble, ht. .68m.

Ptolemy, king of Mauretania, grandson of Antony and Cleopatra. Bust dated to the first century A.D. Louvre Museum. Alinari photo. Reproduced with the permission of the Art Reference Bureau. Yellowish marble, ht. .72m.

Octavian, the victor. Idealized bust of Octavian (emperor Augustus) as a priest sacrific-ing, late first century B.C. National Museum, Rome. Reproduced with the permission of the German Archaeological Institute, Rome. Marble.

cally by general after general during Rome's conquests and civil wars. Most recent, Brutus and Cassius in 43 B.C. had demanded that 50 percent of the annual produce of Asia be handed over for two years, with the unconvincing promise that the Senate would repay the amount. There had been billeting of troops, various personal services, other exceptional contributions such as grain; and many men of property, especially those who had backed the losers, had gone into bankruptcy.[6] Antony was obliged to acknowledge their plight and lowered his requisitions from ten years' tribute paid in one year to nine years' tribute paid over two years. Somehow, the sum was met, although Asia's economy showed the effects for a generation.

Antony's economic policies were fundamentally good. Trade between east and west was encouraged and increased both in quantity and in quality. Antony established a number of colonies to settle veterans and to encourage prosperity. They must have succeeded; for Octavian worked to destroy all records of them, and many are known only by the coins they issued under Antony's instructions. Several of these coins, issued from 39 B.C. on, pictured Octavia, subsequently other subjects. Most of the coins were minted to pay the armies and to wage the Parthian war. More were needed for active trading than were issued, but the policy was sound; and Octavian extended the same types of coinage later.[7]

Antony taxed every possible revenue on a thorough, although reasonable basis: tithe, custom duties, houses, slaves, agricultural production, rents of public lands and mines, fisheries. Moreover, he pressured for contributions from kings and other men of wealth. The policies were severe, and the east continued to suffer the impoverishment resulting from such war measures. But Antony was not vindictive, listened sympathetically to delegations with complaints, and encouraged whatever economic strength the states could muster. Financial responsibility was not his greatest talent, but the problems had intensified for a century, and only the prolonged *Pax Romana* could restore real prosperity to the area. But the requisitions, however diverted, did satisfy veteran needs; the eastern countries did recover; and Antony's control of the disordered east took hold firmly.[8]

Off setting these prudent policies, Antony hampered recovery by

his careless extravagances, especially for favorites, and by the demands of the army that he was mobilizing. Too often the wealth-
iest men were willing to collaborate with Antony to get special
exemptions. Some of Antony's friends, especially the artists, received extravagant gifts; some of Antony's cronies embezzled funds
and went unpunished. There were confiscations of the private
property of the rich as well, sometimes by Antony's orders, sometimes by his indifference to the illegal plundering of his followers.
And not all the money reached Antony from his subordinates or
the veterans from Antony. Antony delighted in living handsomely,
and he was openhanded to his congenial friends. When, for instance, his friend or freedman Marcus Antonius Artemidorus asked
him to give special privileges to an athletic corporation of victors
at sacred games, he granted them exemption from military service,
liturgies, or billeting, ensured their personal safety, and gave them
the right to wear purple. He also enlarged the vast, nonproductive
area of asylum at the temple of Artemis at Ephesus. He could even
give tax-collecting responsibilities backed by a military guard to an
inappropriate favorite like the lyre player Anaxenor. But such
prodigalities profited others; Antony remained always out of
purse.[9]

From Ephesus, Antony made an almost regal tour through Asia
Minor, Syria, and Palestine, arranging political and economic affairs. Pardons were granted to all but the guiltiest republicans; tyrants faithless to Rome were expelled; taxes and contributions
were levied; titles were sold. But also lands, like Athens, Lycia,
and Rhodes, that had held out against Brutus and Cassius and suffered for it were rewarded and their taxes lightened. Tarsus, as one
such city, was exempted from taxes, its tax debtors were freed
from imprisonment, and the city was given a gymnasium. Antony
appointed the demagogue Boethus, who had shrewdly composed a
poem honoring the triumvir's victory at Philippi, its gymnasiarch;
and Antony remained loyal for life to his choice even though Boethus proved a thief who did not scruple to steal even the oil of
the athletes for whom he was responsible. Recklessly, Antony
ordered a raid into Palmyra, hoping to gain wealth from this
trading city; but his men found that the fabled wealth had already
been hidden in the desert. Yet even with such carelessness and

favoritism, Antony was showing flexibility in varying his solutions to meet local problems. He had the real breadth of international understanding and sympathy that marked him as a new Roman, in the tradition of Caesarian imperialism, rather than a limited Roman leader.[10]

While at Tarsus, Antony sent his agent, Quintus Dellius, to summon Cleopatra VII, queen of Egypt, to justify her failure to aid the Caesarians against Brutus and Cassius. Although, nominally, Egypt was independent and Cleopatra free in charting Egypt's foreign policy, the Caesarians had counted on her help against the tyrannicides. When Caesar had come to Egypt pursuing Pompey after Pharsalus in 48 B.C., the young queen had recognized him as the conqueror of the Mediterranean and had become his mistress. She had borne a son whom she called his and named Caesarion. She had followed Caesar to Rome and was established in one of his villas, returning to Alexandria only after he was killed. Perhaps as early as Antony's first fighting in Egypt on behalf of her father, certainly during Caesar's associations with her, Antony must have known Cleopatra and realized the value of ties with Egypt and its queen. To satisfy her, he had declared to the Senate that Caesar had acknowledged the illegitimate Caesarion as his son. Octavian, the adopted son and heir of Caesar, was inevitably hostile to any legitimizing of Caesar's natural son. Yet, in 42 B.C., the triumvirs had acceded to Cleopatra's urging that Caesarion be acknowledged her consort and king of Egypt with the name Ptolemy, because Egypt's support against Brutus and Cassius had seemed critical. Still Cleopatra had remained out of the struggle, and Antony demanded to know why. The demand would have been calculated for political and personal ends. Antony must have been aware of Egypt's powers and problems, for Rome had been supervising the affairs of the client kingdom for a century. And Cleopatra was not a woman he would have forgotten. The meeting, then, was arranged to strengthen the hands of both.[11]

It was late summer when Cleopatra sailed her ornamented barge up the Cydnus River to Tarsus, magnificently playing the role of Aphrodite to Antony's Dionysus. Perhaps the stage directors for the elaborate and popular public show were Antony and Cleopatra themselves. From the first encounter, when Cleopatra declined

Antony's invitation but he accepted hers to a brilliantly elegant banquet, Cleopatra asserted her will, and Antony genially acquiesced. In return, she became his mistress. Antony must have been flattered to be the lover of a fascinating queen.[12]

The queen also had prizes to win from the triumvirs. Cleopatra's account that she had refused help to Cassius and Brutus and had tried to help the Caesarians at Philippi was accepted. But her sister Arsinoë, who had helped Cassius and whose supporters formed a faction of opposition to Cleopatra in Alexandria, was torn from religious sanctuary at the temple of Artemis in Ephesus and killed on Antony's orders. Arsinoë's supporter Serapion, the governor of Cyprus, was also executed, as was a man who posed as her dead brother, Ptolemy XIII. Cleopatra thus used Antony's power for her personal vendettas. Antony may have calculated the advantages of an Egyptian ally freed from factional struggles. But, basically, he seems to have been sacrificing expendable foreign lives to satisfy the queen. When she returned to Alexandria, he promised to follow her. Pausing in Syria to name governors, he reached Alexandria by the winter of 41-40 B.C.[13]

Antony arrived in Egypt as a private citizen, without the legions or lictors which the Alexandrians had resented in Caesar's retinue, though with his personal praetorian guard. He even wore Greek dress and spent his time in the temples and schools. Cleopatra's role was that of an independent queen, welcoming her Roman guest as equal, not as master. It was as equal that she refused to give him the money that he sought. Yet, combining political dexterity with feminine attractions, she studied to make herself indispensable to Antony. Part of her skill lay in satisfying Antony's boisterous zest for good times. A band of boon friends, led by Antony, took the title "Inimitable Livers" and indulged in every luxury. Cleopatra played her role superbly. Twins, Alexander Helios and Cleopatra Selene, born in 40 B.C., were the fruit of these months.[14]

Yet judgment must be suspended about whether Antony really loved the queen he so enjoyed. He had won and left many mistresses for casual pleasure. While Cleopatra calculated ways for Antony to strengthen Egypt, Antony was assessing the military defenses of Egypt and improving his own command. He supported his followers who were seizing control of north Africa but sent little of the booty that had been promised to Octavian. Recognizing his weakness at sea, he was enlarging his fleet by 200 ships. And shrewdly, he let Egypt provide the excuse for his failure to help his wife and brother in the Perusine war against Octavian of which he disapproved. His winter Egyptian visit, then, was profitable, if also pleasant.[15]

In February or March, 40 B.C., learning of Antony's relaxation, Labienus led the Parthian cavalry across the Euphrates, raided the provinces of Syria and Asia to the Aegean, and killed Lucius Decidius Saxa, Antony's governor. Antony at once went north from Alexandria with a fleet of 200 ships and did not see Cleopatra again for almost four years. Each was always informed about the other's activities; an Egyptian astrologer in Antony's camp is reputed to have been Cleopatra's spy and spokesman on her behalf, but more standard contacts were available too. Nevertheless, politically and militarily Antony needed Octavian now more than Cleopatra; and, despite the tales of illicit passion told by his detractors, Antony was ruled by his head, not his heart.[16]

Antony went directly to the port of Tyre, then to Cyprus, Rhodes, and Asia Minor, gathering his fleet and troops. But his planned action against Parthia was disrupted by reports of the fall of Perusia, Octavian's taking over powerful Gaul with its huge army, and the rising threat of Sextus Pompey. Antony's western stakes had to be secured. He returned to his established headquarters in Athens. Until 38 B.C. he used Athens as his base for settling Italian affairs with Octavian and Sextus Pompey, for planning campaigns against the Parthians, and for extending further his political and economic settlements for the eastern states.[17]

But however busy with his trips to Italy and his eastern tasks, Antony could relish living; and his new wife Octavia—so different from Fulvia and from Cleopatra—brought him the zest of unwonted domesticity. Like Caesar, Antony had sensitivity and adaptability to foreign peoples, without the dangerous sense of superiority that blighted the relations of so many Roman administrators with the provincials. To the Italians, his conduct sometimes seemed playing the buffoon; but the subject peoples appreciated his gestures toward their cults and practices.

Like Octavian in the west, Antony organized Caesar worship in the east. But his own honors increased as well. The deification of rulers was regular practice in the east, and other Roman conquerors had been so honored; yet it was an exciting novelty for Antony, and he recognized its political utility in marking him as Rome's eastern potentate. In Asia in 41 B.C., he had been hailed as Dionysus incarnate; in Egypt he was Osiris. Now, in late 39 and through 38 B.C., the Athenians continued his deification, and he relished the trappings of a Greek Dionysus. He wore Greek dress; he attended philosophical lectures; he acted as gymnasiarch for the Panathenaic Antoniea. The Athenians set up inscriptions honoring the New Dionysus, and he held banquets in a cave sacred to Dionysus. Such adulation, though heady, remained an amusing game for Antony. Octavia was hailed as Athena Polias; but when the people declared that Antony was betrothed also to the Athena of the Parthenon, Antony wryly demanded, and got, a dowry of 1,000 talents from the city. The Athenians, presumably, regretted this extravagant romanticism but not Antony's deification. The other eastern states competed in the divine honors extended: temples, priesthoods, coin portraits, and the claim of adoption by or descent from the divine founders of the states. Though the concept and titles were never used in the west, for the next ten years Antony was hailed as Dionysus in Asia and Greece, and as Osiris in Egypt.[18]

The role playing, however artificial on both sides, did confirm Antony's position as ruler of the eastern provinces and client states, making effective the many new appointments and divisions of lands and authority which were his serious responsibilities before he marched against Parthia. The problems, and therefore the settlements, were very complex. The states had a variety of traditions and laws, most of them Hellenistic, but some going back centuries before Alexander the Great. The Roman conquerors and succeeding governors had added new, often troublesome factors. The Roman civil wars had forced leaders to take sides and had drained the eastern wealth into the battlefields. The resolutions of these many and varied problems were harried by Antony's need for funds and hurried by Octavian's appeals from the west and the Parthian threats in the east.

Greece was always a special province: under Roman control for a century, passive militarily yet arrogant intellectually, realizing fully the Roman dependence on Greek ideas. It was also a poor land, whose meager resources had been ruthlessly exploited. Nevertheless, Antony scoured the Peloponnesus for remaining wealth before Sextus Pompey could claim the area after the Treaty of Misenum. Like Caesar, who had granted citizenship widely among the wealthy, Antony too sold Roman citizenship for a price or for enlistment in his legions against Parthia. Inevitably, he established political collaboration with the wealthy oligarchs, though he would also aid the careers of talented men from all ranks. The Greeks resented his generally oligarchic favoritism which tampered with their constitutions, but they still favored Antony's rule over that of Octavian.[19]

The other Aegean lands were soon under Antony's control. The Thracian leaders supported Antony. Macedonia had long been troubled by wild tribes along the Dalmatian coast. But in 39 B.C. Gaius Asinius Pollio defeated the Parthini and Dardani; and Antony secured the Adriatic coastline with a fleet and the land with a substantial garrison of perhaps seven legions. Like Caesar, Antony also established colonies in the Aegean and southern Black Sea areas, in part to increase Romanization, to settle legionary veterans, to encourage trade and other economic developments, but in large part also, to provide military defense of the area.[20]

For the Asiatic lands Antony sought policies and attitudes stabilizing the troubled states and setting down sensible, diplomatic policies which would continue for decades. Although he learned much from Caesar's program, these decisions were his own. He had supporters and clients whom he trusted and rewarded—like the rich Pythodorus of Tralles in Asia, who married Antony's eldest daughter Antonia and, by his distinguished progeny, continued Antony's blood in the ruling families of Pontus, Thrace, Armenia, and Cilicia. He could also lavish moneys, positions, and opportunities to perform on personal favorites among the actors and musicians. But the personal favoritism was incidental to Antony's overall carefulness and his conformity to the established proconsular powers. The widespread appearance of Antony's name in later days proves how many and varied men of ability were enfranchised by his grants during these years. And Antony was willing to entrust power to talented freedmen, like the Demetrius who was given charge of Cyprus.[21]

Of the Asiatic states, Rome had incorporated only Asia, Bithynia, and part of Cilicia. These had generally favored or at least been subject to the financial exactions of Brutus and Cassius. But they had veered to the victors after Philippi; and an inscription set up in Pergamum was already hailing Lucius Antonius as patron and savior. These provinces Antony could put into order with his proconsular *imperium*, knowing that although his settlements would be presented to the Senate, they had been ratified pro forma in advance. The other states were governed as satellites of Rome, under native rulers or oligarchies or leagues. Pompey had set Rome's pattern of preferring these client kings or aristocracies, rather than democracies, as easy, inexpensive means of keeping native people in order, guarding the frontiers, even paying tribute and providing soldiers and supplies for the legions. Loyal collaboration with Rome meant that the petty rulers would have Roman support against their internal and external enemies and could govern with fair security until Rome chose to annex the territory as a province. With these client states, Antony moved deliberately along the pattern Pompey had laid out, postponing changes until he knew the men and the problems well. The caution permitted settlements that would continue long after Antony; but with the urgent crises following the civil war, his enemies could criticize Antony's prudent delays as laziness. Yet gradually, sometimes by force, often for pay, occasionally as a reward for loyalty, kingdoms were created, or reliable kings were established in existing client states, until a strong system of vassal states reached from the Black Sea to Egypt.[22]

A brief survey indicates the kinds of settlements Antony arranged or sanctioned. Asia Minor, still staggering from the exactions of Brutus and Cassius, was granted further reliefs. Some of the old Greek cities, traditionally quite autonomous, like Aphrodisias, Tarsus, and Miletus, were given freedom, autonomy, and generous grants of Roman citizenship. Where leagues of cities had been formed, they were permitted to continue, although mainly for religious rather than political ends. A strong federation in Lycia had wavered between the republicans and Caesarians, and Antony threatened fines but settled moderately, by relieving the cities of the taxes levied for Brutus, but by demanding their contribution to the rebuilding of the ruined city of Xanthus. There were various petty native princelings or hereditary priesthoods, nominally free but actually so much under Rome's domination that Antony's orders would bring them to heel. King Antiochus I of Commagene, who had given refuge to fleeing Parthians and had killed Roman soldiers, was besieged in his capital Samosata until he paid 300 talents. The priest Lycomedes, installed by Caesar in Pontic Comana, gained territory under Antony. The priestly state of Soli in Cilicia was given to Queen Aba. The long list represents the complex divisions of the area.[23]

Of prime importance were the greater kings who held strategically valuable land. These Antony won to loyalty—to himself, perhaps, more than to Rome. North of the Black Sea, the Bosporan Kingdom (Bosporus Cimmericus), important to Rome for grain shipments, had been ruled by King Asander since Caesar settled the area in 47 B.C. Antony extended its boundaries north, fortifying the Black Sea trade routes against the wild Scythian tribes. South of the Black Sea, Antony first considered dividing into smaller countries the state now uniting Pontus and Bithynia. Instead, he extended it by the addition of more Black Sea coast because he counted on the loyalty of its kings: first in 39 B.C. Darius, then in 37 B.C. Polemo, the son of a trustworthy dynast and notable orator from Laodicea in Syria. Polemo's title was reward for his loyalty against the Parthians and compensation for the portion of his land that had been granted to Cleopatra. Armenia was a dependent state of Rome, controlled by Publius Canidius Crassus, Antony's general there. Armenia Minor was given to Artavasdes of Media, whose new allegiance to Antony was marked by the betrothal of his daughter Iotape to Alexander Helios, son of Antony and Cleopatra.[24]

In central Asia Minor Antony had confirmed Deiotarus as king of Galatia in 44 B.C. The king was not from the royal family; but after a dangerous allegiance to Cassius for a time, he had fought for the Caesarians at Philippi, and he offered the substantial payment of ten million sesterces for his crown. Antony divided the kingdom; but when Deiotarus died in 40 B.C., Amyntas, his major successor, remained under Antony's patronage and kept the hard-fighting tribesmen of central Asia Minor at peace. In 40 B.C. Antony joined Paphlagonia to Galatia; in 37 B.C. he divided these states again, but he did add parts of Pamphylia and Cilicia to Galatia and thus held Amyntas's loyalty.[25]

Cappadocia was ruled by Archelaus. Here Antony had set aside as disloyal the son of the king whom Caesar had named, and he has been blamed for elevating the son of Glaphyra, a lady (presumably a mistress) whom Antony greatly admired. But Archelaus was also of a priestly royal family claiming rightful succession to the throne, and he ruled Cappadocia well for a half-century. Thus Antony's major kings, with many of the minor rulers to whom Antony entrusted Asia Minor, served their states well and were continued in office under Octavian.[26]

South of Asia Minor, in the former Syrian holdings of the Seleucids, Antony claimed the rule from the tyrants who had seized control of the cities during the Roman civil wars. He also assumed the pose, which the Seleucids traditionally struck, that he was selected and protected by the gods.[27] When he went to Syria in early 37 B.C., he continued Seleucid policies, such as requiring a tithe of the produce as his tax, for fat year or lean; and the coins of the cities in Phoenicia were issued with his portrait. It was to a lively Syrian court that Antony summoned Cleopatra. From there he would launch his war against the Parthians and would continue the disposition of Asian thrones.[28]

To the south, he held Cyrene in North Africa firmly; and his allies struggled to hold the lands to the west. Malchus, king of the Nabataean Arabs, he deemed unreliable. The Roman general Ventidius had already fined Malchus for siding with the Parthians. Now Antony decreased his territory as penalty for supporting the Parthians and for hostility to Antony's friend, Herod of Judaea.[29]

Herod the Great's relations with his neighbors and with his own subjects were regularly tumultuous and involved Antony for a decade in settling bitter disputes. Because Herod was a master sycophant, he zealously did favors for whatever Romans were leaders for the moment and tried to make himself seem indispensable in the east Mediterranean theater. His family's career of political prominence had begun under Caesar. Herod's father, Antipater, a commoner from Idumaea, south of Judaea, served as regent, under strict Roman surveillance, for the high priest Hyrcanus II whom Pompey had made ruler of Judaea. (During Hyrcanus's reign, 57–55 B.C., the young Antony was winning a reputation as cavalry officer in Judaea and in Egypt under Pompey's proconsul Gabinius.) Antipater recognized that Rome would be the future ruler in the area. He sided with Gabinius, then Cassius against rebellious Jews and sent money and 3,000 Jewish soldiers to help Caesar in his Alexandrian campaign in 47 B.C. Caesar, indeed, virtually owed his life to these troops. For his aid Antipater was given Roman citizenship, made Roman procurator in Judaea, and won liberal terms for the Jews from Caesar. But the Jews hated him as an Idumaean and pro-Roman, who was willing to increase and collect the tribute for the Romans, as not many other client kings were obliged to do. He died by poison.[30]

Both Herod and his elder brother Phasael had assumed substantial political and military power as governors of Jerusalem and Galilee under their father and were backed by the Romans, so that the Jews were eager to depose them from the office of regent too. When Antony came to Asia Minor after Philippi, both camps sought audience with him, first in Bithynia, then near Antioch. A delegation of 100 Jews, claiming that the rights and the government of the high priest Hyrcanus had been usurped by Phasael and Herod, presented Antony with a golden crown and asked that territory taken by the Tyrians be restored to them and that the Jews sold as slaves by Cassius be freed. To this donation and to these requests Antony agreed. But their accusations against Phasael and Herod were futile. When Antony asked Hyrcanus, in the presence of Phasael and Herod, if they were good rulers, the old priest lacked the courage to levy charges. The brothers, in their turn, showed the courage and political dexterity Antony respected. Their father's and therefore their allegiance and monetary exactions had veered to Cassius when he seemed the likely winner. But this defection had ended with Philippi. The brothers spoke of Antipater's old ties with Gabinius and Antony and of Caesar's favor. They also offered money which Antony needed critically for his troops. Antony recognized that a Palestinian state was probably best run by a Jewish ruler and that Antipater's sons would be willing tools for Roman power. Therefore, he granted them together—perhaps as a prudent check on each other—the title tetrarchs, the administrators of sections of the province. They carefully treated Hyrcanus with great respect and kindness to try to win the loyalty of the Jews; and Herod was betrothed to Hyrcanus's granddaughter Mariamne.[31] But the priest's followers were irreconcilable to the presumptuous alien upstarts. A deputation of 1,000 came to Tyre, a city already troublesome to Antony because its ruler had allied with Cassius, to protest to Antony, but the Roman guard received orders to be rid of them before they could confront Antony. When they refused to disperse peaceably, the troops attacked. Several Jews were casualties, several prisoners taken, and these Antony later executed for sedition. As the Jewish sense of grievance increased, so did Antony's anger at their intransigence in the face of his fair settlements. His commitment to Herod, the younger but the abler of the two brothers, grew firm.[32]

The Parthians became an element in the struggle after 42 B.C., for they were capitalizing on all local discontent within Rome's eastern provinces to weaken Rome's holding. A great Parthian army under Pacorus, the son of the Parthian king, invaded Palestine, Syria, and Phoenicia, routing the Roman armies. The opportunity for the Hasmonean dynasty of Hyrcanus to reassert control was taken by Antigonus, nephew of the old priest, who bought Parthian support for his claims against Herod and Phasael with 1,000 talents and 500 women. Antigonus invaded, attracting many supporters; the Parthians followed. Jerusalem became the battleground. The Parthian commander proposed a parley between Hyrcanus and Phasael, then treacherously seized them both. Phasael committed suicide, and Hyrcanus was mutilated so that he could no longer serve as high priest. Antigonus was then named high priest and king.[33]

Herod, with his family and troops, fled to the citadel of Masada in Idumaea, which he had fortified and provisioned against any of his potential enemies. Leaving his followers secure, he sought help from the friendly king in Arabia, then in Egypt. Antony, whom he was seeking there, had already returned to Rome. Cleopatra had ambitions to regain Palestine for Egypt; but for the time being she was willing to cooperate with Antony's friend. She may have offered him a high command in her own army and perhaps was embittered when Herod was interested only in Judaea and braved the wintery Mediterranean to follow his patron west.[34]

In late 40 B.C. Herod appeared in Rome to recount his dangers and to ask Antony to appoint him regent for Hyrcanus and his line. Herod had been negotiating with Antony, and no doubt money had been given. But the outcome surpassed even Herod's ambitious claims. Antony, persuaded by friendship, pity, but especially by sound eastern policy and Herod's promises of money, introduced him to Octavian as an able, energetic ally of Caesar. Friends of Antony (Marcus Valerius Messalla Corvinus and Lucius Sempronius Atratinus) spoke in the Senate of Herod's usefulness. The Senate heard Herod guarantee his family loyalty to Rome. He lamented that he had been driven out of his land, not by the Jews but by the Parthians, Rome's enemies and his. Antony added assurances of Herod's value as an ally in Antony's projected war against Parthia and urged that Herod be made not tetrarch and regent but king.[35]

The Senate, reflecting on the turbulence in the critical Palestinian area into which the Hasmonean Antigonus had welcomed the Parthians, saw Herod as the best hope for order. Although he lacked family title to the monarchy and a strong kingship meant a division between monarchy and high priesthood, in 39 B.C. the Senate proclaimed him king but not high priest. With the consuls and magistrates leading the procession, Antony and Octavian escorted Herod from the Senate to the Capitol for sacrifices. Antony was host at a banquet of celebration for the first of the eastern kings he was to appoint. Within a few days Herod turned east again to conquer his country, at this early stage with the help of Antony's man Ventidius, governor of Syria and Cilicia. His reign would be tumultuous; but it was always closely dependent upon Antony, and he remained loyal to his patron so long as Antony could be useful.[36]

The fighting between Antigonus and Herod lasted about two years, with pitched battles and brutal guerrilla raids. Throughout, Herod received aid from the Romans under orders from Antony, although some of the Roman officers were venal enough to make untrustworthy allies. Once the Parthians had been driven out of Syria by Antony's legate Ventidius, 2 Roman legions and 1,000 cavalry were freed to fight under Herod, and even more troops were added when Antony arrived in Syria in 38 B.C. Antony had come to take Samosata by siege from Antiochus, king of Commagene, who had aided the Parthians. Herod fought his way through to Samosata, lending his troops to aid the Romans. Antony negotiated peace, finally, with Antiochus, but again Herod deserved Antony's gratitude and loan of more troops against Hasmonean armies. With these allies, Herod fought repeated actions and gradually conquered Judaea. In spring, 37 B.C., aided by Roman legions under Antony's governor of Syria, Sosius, he laid siege to Jerusalem, with 11 legions, 6,000 cavalry, and auxilia to support his own 30,000 troops. The long, hard-fought, bitterly nationalistic and religious siege ended in late summer, 37 B.C., in slaughter and carnage. Romans would have pillaged the Holy of Holies itself if Herod, fearing still greater religious hatred from the Jews, had not bribed their forbearance.[37]

During the siege, with real passion but also with zeal to be linked with the traditional royal line, Herod had married the last Hasmonean princess, Mariamne, granddaughter of Hyrcanus. Nevertheless, he could institute proscriptions against the leaders of the Hasmonean faction and urge Antony, to whom Antigonus had been taken as prisoner, to kill him as a dangerous rallying point for Jewish rebellions and a threat to Herod's kingship. Antony would have preferred to lead Antigonus in triumph in Rome, but he bowed to Herod's fears and to his substantial bribe, secured by melting down the royal plate. The fortress palace Herod now built for himself near the Temple in Jerusalem he called the Antonia.[38]

Herod was ruthless to his opponents, but Antony did not intervene as he settled bitter scores, especially with the Sadducees. The jealous dynastic competition between Herod and the remaining Hasmoneans continued to disorder his reign. Cleopatra became involved, and, inevitably, Antony acted as court of final appeal in the venomous turbulence. To weaken the Hasmoneans and subordinate the office of high priest to that of king, Herod passed over Mariamne's brother, Aristobulus III, the legitimate claimant to the high priesthood on Antigonus's death, and installed, rather than a Hasmonean, Ananel, from an ancient priestly family claiming descent from Aaron and willing to collaborate with Herod.[39]

The claims of the young Aristobulus and of Mariamne were fiercely sponsored by their mother, Alexandra, who hated Herod and deeply resented the close surveillance the king kept over her and her children. She therefore petitioned Cleopatra, already hostile to Herod for spurning her military command in 40 B.C. and for holding land she claimed as Egyptian, to urge Antony to depose Ananel and to make Aristobulus high priest. The decision was grave for the stability of the country. Herod's rule was challenged, and religious passion could flare over the sacrilege of deposing a consecrated high priest. Antony cautiously sent his representative Quintus Dellius to Jerusalem to investigate the growing discords and report to him. The handsomeness of the brother and sister must have been extraordinary. It impressed Dellius, as it did so many others, and he sent portraits of the two to Antony, always susceptible to beauty. Antony invited Aristobulus to Alexandria. Herod feared that Aristobulus in Antony's court would be a dangerous foe and promptly made him high priest as the lesser evil. But the jealousy remained, even increased by the extravagant joy with which the people welcomed the young priest from the hereditary line.[40]

Alexandra, driven by maternal watchfulness and ambition, wrote to Cleopatra that she feared for the lives of her children. Cleopatra, even more hostile to Herod, offered sanctuary in Alexandria, and the family accepted. Herod had them too well guarded. They were captured as they fled. The reprisals Herod would have wished to take on Alexandra and Aristobulus were balked by his fear of Cleopatra, and therefore, Antony. But in 35 B.C., Herod ordered an "accidental" drowning of Aristobulus, for which he could publicly express sorrow. The vengeful mother could not be deceived and reported to Cleopatra that murder had been done and that Antony should look into the boy's death. Antony was loathe to have trouble with his trusted client king, but Cleopatra pressured for retaliation against her increasingly hated neighbor.[41]

Upon Antony's return from a Parthian campaign in 35 B.C., he asked Herod to come to Laodicea to defend himself against the charge. Herod left his uncle Joseph as regent, with secret orders that if Herod did not return, Mariamne should be killed rather than given to another man. When rumors spread that Herod had

165

been executed by Antony, the Hasmonean party raised a rebellion which swept the country. The regent Joseph seemed helpless and was considering fleeing with the women to the Roman legions in hopes that Antony would succor them once he saw the beautiful Mariamne. But Herod reappeared and readily crushed the rebellion. Antony, since Cleopatra was not present and Herod's bribes and loyalty were valuable against Parthia, in essence had refused to hear the case against Herod, saying that the internal affairs of a client state were not his business. Probably the king's guilt was too clear-cut to disprove if brought to trial. Herod was left unquestionably in control, through Antony's favor, though surrounded by a bitter family, court, and nation.[42]

Herod, of course, was placing his agents in critical posts. One such was Nicolaus of Damascus, a councillor, diplomat, and agent who was also a learned philosopher and historian. He may have studied at Alexandria or he may have been singled out by Cleopatra and Antony in Damascus or Palestine; for he became the tutor of their children in Alexandria. His loyalty, however, lay with Herod. He was the first historian to deny that Caesarion was Caesar's son, as Cleopatra claimed. When Herod finally deserted Antony for Octavian, it was at the Jewish court that Nicolaus settled, and the adult Herod whom he tutored.[43]

Cleopatra's dreams of regaining the preeminence Egypt had held two centuries earlier under Ptolemy II Philadelphus involved retaking territory such as Judaea, long lost to Egypt. Her sole weapons of conquest were her influence with Antony and the fact that he needed her help against Parthia, but she wielded these with considerable success. Caesar had given her Cyprus; Antony confirmed her control of the island and added part of Cilicia, valuable for the timber needed in Egypt. She received Phoenicia, except for the strong ports of Tyre and Sidon, although much of this land had been part of Roman Syria. She persuaded Antony that the tetrarch of the Ituraeans had aided the Parthians and must die, and she then won his gentile or semi-gentile lands under her control.[44]

Next she sought the lands of Herod and the king of the Nabataeans by having them deposed; but Antony balked. His ally Herod had recently received some hard-won Nabataean land, and further conquests from the desert Arabs were simply too costly to be undertaken lightly. Yet the Nabataean Arabs had to hand over part of the coastline on the Red Sea. Jericho, with its valuable date palms and monopoly of balsam gardens, and the Dead Sea area, with its useful bitumen monopoly, were granted to Cleopatra in 34 B.C. A resentful Herod then had to rent the land from Cleopatra for 1,200 talents. The Arabs were to process the bitumen. But Herod scored by promising to act as middleman, in place of Antony or Cleopatra, collecting the government fees for the monopoly. The service pleased Antony, while giving Herod the right he wanted to intervene in Arab lands. From Judaea, Egypt regained almost the entire coastline. Cleopatra had not gained all she hoped from Antony; but from 37 B.C. on, the coins she issued with Caesarion were dated to a new era, marking her restoration of Egyptian territory, with a few exceptions, to the empire held by Ptolemy II. Egypt was still a vassal state, but Antony and Cleopatra were treating it almost as Rome's equal.[45]

Still disputed were Idumaea and Gaza where Herod's southern frontier and his ambitions for expansion conflicted with those of Egypt. He had appointed as governor one Costobar, a nobleman, but of an ancient non-Jewish priestly family. Costobar was committed more to reviving both his pagan religion and Idumaean state than to serving Herod; and for these ends he found an eager ally in Cleopatra. An independent Idumaea would weaken Herod's holdings and would be subject to Egyptian influence. Cleopatra urged Costobar's arguments to Antony. Again, Antony tried to stay loyal to Herod, although Gaza and Joppa (Ioppe) in 36 B.C. seem to have been lost to Herod as a result of Costobar's claims. Normally, the king would have demoted and perhaps executed Costobar. But Herod was walking a tightrope between Cleopatra's jealousy and Antony's loyalty; so he married Costobar to his sister Salome, to win him or at least to immobilize him. To Cleopatra, Herod was ostentatiously courteous, avoiding any rupture that would force Antony to choose between them. But the wariness and strain continued, and Antony's settlements in the east were weakened accordingly.[46]

Egypt itself remained an independent, albeit satellite monarchy under Cleopatra and her son-consort Caesarion. Egypt was the Mediterranean's richest land, and Antony needed its wealth to maintain his armies, to strengthen his navy, and to meet his political and personal expenses. Conquest, in itself easy enough, would have alienated the other client kings Antony was tying to himself in the east and would probably have brought repeated popular revolts which would require troops to forestall or to crush. Antony recognized a decidedly more agreeable alternative in a personal and political liaison with the alluring queen who was already the mother of his twins. In 37 B.C. he gave her the land grants. In 36 B.C., when Octavia with her two daughters by Antony and Antony's children by Fulvia had returned to Rome, Antony sent Fonteius Capito to conduct Cleopatra from Alexandria to his lively court at Antioch, where he was readying for the Parthian war. He required more gold, supplies, ships, troops than he could mobilize in the east or borrow from Octavian. He also needed a rear well secured as his troops attacked. Cleopatra knew Egypt's value and Egypt's need for Roman backing. She also knew her own attractions. Her price was land—Chalcis in Syria—and marriage. Early in 36 B.C. Antony married Cleopatra, according to Egyptian customs.[47]

Antony must have calculated all the personal and political implications. A marriage with eastern rites to a foreigner would not be considered valid in Rome, so there would be no charge of bigamy. But flaunting a mistress so ostentatiously would further break the ragged ties with Octavia and Octavian and would blacken his reputation among the Roman people. Nor was he king of Egypt in Roman eyes, although the Egyptians, with whom he was popular, hailed him so. Technically, Caesarion remained king, and Antony was loathe to challenge the son of Caesar, although Cleopatra's double-dated Egyptian coins after 37 B.C. marked her ties with both Antony and Caesarion. Cleopatra's twins, Alexander Helios and Cleopatra Selene, born in 40 B.C., Antony acknowledged as his children. Another son, Ptolemy Philadelphus, was born late in 36 B.C. All such Egyptian ties were bound to alienate the solid Roman sense of decency. But Antony's immediate end, for which these were the means, was victory over the Parthians. The conquest of Rome's greatest remaining foes, the glory of the greatest triumph, would leave Antony supreme in the empire, above any criticism of his personal peccadilloes.[48]

168

XI

Parthia Invicta

Republican Rome's military attitude seems epitomized by the demand that Antony eliminate the fear felt for the eastern boundary and by the assumption that an able Roman general could triumph over any oriental barbarians. The anticipation that he would be victorious had given charge of the east to Antony as the better general at Philippi, while Octavian was assigned the less military tasks of settling western provinces. Granted Antony's many responsibilities in reorganizing provinces and distributing client kingdoms, in stabilizing shattered economies and societies. Ultimately, he could remain Caesar's foremost successor only by military victory over the Parthians.

The threat from the eastern state had surfaced in Roman awareness only in the past three decades. Originally a satrapy of the Persian Empire lying east of the Caspian Sea, Parthia had fallen with the rest of the empire to Alexander the Great, then to his Hellenistic successors in Asia, the Seleucids. In the mid-third century B.C. the Parthians had revolted against the Seleucids. While Roman attacks had kept the Seleucids engaged, then conquered, Parthia had expanded, reaching east almost to India and west, through Mesopotamia and Armenia, to the boundaries of the Roman provinces and the Roman satellite states. Parthia was, therefore, a vast and rich state, whose trade routes brought Oriental luxuries as far west

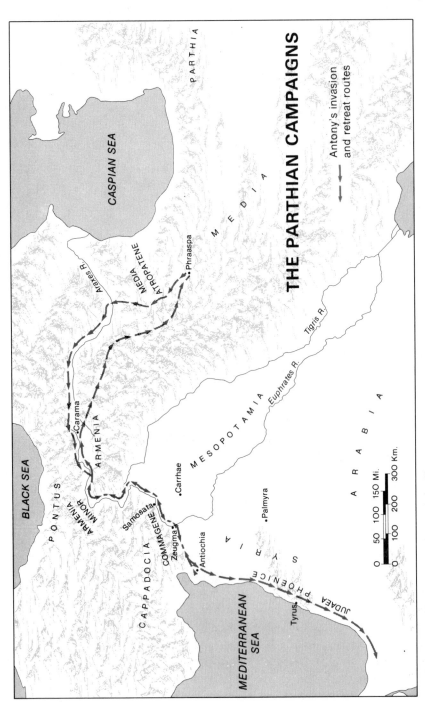

THE PARTHIAN CAMPAIGNS

Antony's invasion
and retreat routes

CASPIAN SEA

BLACK SEA

PONTUS

ARMENIA
MINOR

ARMENIA

CAPPADOCIA

COMMAGENE

Samosata

Zeugma

Antiochia

Carrhae

MESOPOTAMIA

Euphrates R.

Tigris R.

MEDIA

MEDIA
ATROPATENE

Phraaspa

Araxes R.

Carama

PARTHIA

SYRIA

Palmyra

A R A B I A

JUDAEA PHOENICE

Tyrus

MEDITERRANEAN
SEA

0   50   100 150 Mi.

0   100 200 300 Km.

Mark Antony: A Biography by Eleanor Goltz Huzar
Copyright © 1978 by the University of Minnesota.

as Rome. Its power was checked only by the need to defend a long frontier, subject to attack especially in the east, and by the recurring dynastic strife within the royal Arsacid clan.[1]

As Rome moved east and took Seleucid lands, thus impinging on the Parthian sphere of influence, the regions of dispute between Parthia and Rome were Armenia and the headwater lands of the Tigris and Euphrates rivers: rich areas, crossed by east-west trade routes, and lacking natural barriers to invasion. Lucullus threatened incursion of Parthia when fighting in Armenia in 69 B.C.; Pompey and Gabinius actually invaded Parthia in 66 B.C. But neither side saw the other's territory as a prime objective, and Armenia and Parthia agreed to accept the boundaries Rome established. Rome made some slight territorial gains; but Parthia won the important alliance with the buffer state Armenia. For the next decade both Roman and Parthian energies were directed chiefly to consolidation of territories taken and to internal struggles for power.

In 55 B.C. the cautious nonbelligerency was shattered by the triumvir Crassus, who, envying the military prestige won by Pompey in the east and Caesar in Gaul, determined on a campaign against Parthia. The unjustified attack was unpopular in Rome, but Crassus still marched with some 40,000 troops in 7 legions as well as some cavalry and reluctant allies. Crassus's errors were monumental. After provoking the Parthians with attacks and plunder, he gave them time to mobilize 10,000 cavalry. He ignored the advice of Armenian allies and wiser Roman heads to follow mountain or river roads; instead, in 53 B.C., he crossed the open plains to Carrhae. There his infantry was easily surrounded and cut down by the superb Parthian cavalry. The cataphract horses and men wore plate armor; the light-armed cavalry were equipped with compound bows discharging arrows which could outdistance the Roman bow shots and penetrate the Roman armor, and could outlast the Roman quivers by the supplies of arrows loaded on 1,000 camels. The result was massacre. The allies deserted; a quarter of the Romans escaped. But 20,000 Romans, including Crassus and his son, died, and 10,000 Romans with their legionary eagle insignia were captives of the Parthians.[2]

The foolhardy incompetence of Crassus had provided a Roman-Parthian rift that brought cries for revenge. Honor demanded the retaking of the captives and eagles. The eastern provinces, now rebellious, would come to heel only if Rome could prove again its invincible might. Struggles for power within both states delayed the war that Rome now believed had to be fought.

The Parthians were slow to follow up their advantage. In 51 B.C. Cicero, Bibulus, and Cassius, governors of the eastern provinces, girded for an expected attack which, when launched, merely raided for plunder but left Rome afraid. In 49 B.C., scouring the east for support in his civil war against Caesar, Pompey solicited Parthian aid. The minor help given the Pompeians further fueled Caesar's determination to overwhelm the Parthian threat and thus to win public approval, even for monarchy. When assassinated, Caesar had already mobilized a force of 16 legions and 1,000 cavalry and was prepared to march against Parthia. The very magnitude of his army and supply train indicates his recognition of Parthian power. His campaign died with him, and it is impossible to know what would have been the outcome. But Parthia was apprehensive and, for handsome pay, provided a small troop contingent to Caesar's assassins at Philippi. Parthia's concern was hardly for the republican cause; it hoped merely to keep Rome weak through factional strife. But in its gestures of help to the anti-Caesarians, it added causes for Antony's retaliation.[3]

Antony's responsibilities after Caesar's death were too complex for him to use the troops and organization Caesar had readied for a Parthian attack. The years of planning and the early initiative were therefore lost, and Antony had to watch his best opportunities be postponed because of Octavian's demands or provincial needs. Meanwhile, provocations for war multiplied on both sides. Some pro-Parthian leaders in Syria fled to Parthia in fear of Antony's provincial reorganization. When Antony, on a trumped-up charge of friendliness to Parthia but really with an eye to booty, sent some cavalry against the prosperous trading city of Palmyra, the enraged population fled with all their possessions to the Parthian court.[4]

Aiding these anti-Romans in their clamor for war was Quintus Labienus, a republican whom Brutus and Cassius had sent to negotiate for Parthian aid against the Caesarians. After Philippi he had feared to return to Rome and had remained as the king's trusted adviser. In early 40 B.C., when Antony was in Egypt, Labienus and the Parthian prince Pacorus attacked Syria, confident that the eastern provinces would join them in revolt against Antony's policies and taxes. The attack met with widespread success, especially winning over the many garrisons that had once served under Brutus and Cassius. Labienus, now calling himself imperator Parthicus in parody of Roman triumphal honors, turned north into Asia Minor, defeating and killing Antony's governor Saxa, seizing booty, and accepting the ready capitulation of many cities. Pacorus, swinging south, took all Syria except the island fortress of Tyre. It was to him that the Jewish pretender, Antigonus, offered money and women for help against Herod and Phasael, and by him was crowned King of the Jews. With one campaign the Parthians had taken most of the Roman territories in Asia, and the remaining cities, shakily defended by pro-Roman partisans, seemed destined to fall to Parthia.[5]

The campaign of revenge against the Parthians was thus resulting in aggression within Antony's own provinces. Simultaneously, the Perusine war was raging in Italy. Fulvia and Lucius Antonius were losing to Octavian, and although Mark Antony was trying to avoid involvement in a war of which he disapproved, his position in Italy had to be his first concern. Therefore, as he left Alexandria in early spring of 40 B.C., sailing north, he stopped only at loyal Tyre. Crossing to Athens, he met Fulvia, Sextus Pompey, and other adherents with tales of Octavian's perfidy and brutality. His enlarged fleet sailed to Brundisium to confront Octavian. There the earnest urging of the armies and the skill of the diplomats reconciled the generals. Antony was more willing to compromise because of the Parthian crisis. In the renewed agreements, Antony married Octavia, legions were reassigned, and confederates given new posts. Because Antony still needed time for settling Italian and other eastern affairs, his loyal lieutenant from Gaul, Publius Ventidius Bassus, was given command against the Parthians. It was almost two years before Antony could resume the eastern command. The threat of Sextus Pompey and the unstable ties with Octavian bound him to Italian affairs until 38 B.C.[6]

He had, however, chosen his lieutenant well. Ventidius outgeneraled and outfought Labienus in Syria. Labienus, captured in flight, was killed, and the surviving Roman troops fighting under him deserted to Ventidius. Cilicia was then retaken; and because Jerusalem was still in the hands of the pro-Parthian Hasmoneans, Ventidius, for a price, left troops there under his lieutenant Silo to aid Herod in its recapture. Pacorus had withdrawn from Syria late in 39 B.C., but early in 38 B.C. he attacked again, counting on catching Ventidius still in winter quarters and on stirring up the local people against the oppressive Roman occupation. As he had done with Labienus, Ventidius lured Pacorus into a disadvantageous position at Zeugma and, on the anniversary date of the battle at Carrhae, defeated the army and killed Pacorus. It was a significant victory. Pacorus had been able and trusted by Parthia's client kings. Parthia no longer seemed to have the superiority to Rome that it had shown at Carrhae. Antony, as Ventidius's superior, celebrated the victory at Athens, as he did the victory of Pollio against the attacking tribes of Illyricum. Among the lavish entertainments at Athens, he was master at an exhibition of gymnastic games and, probably, was again saluted as imperator.[7]

A number of cities as well as individuals in the eastern provinces had deserted the Romans for the Parthians. The victorious Ventidius made retaliatory raids and exactions as he brought the area back under Roman domination. The worst offender was the small state of Commagene on the upper Euphrates, a state which was accused of forming an alliance with Parthia and of giving sanctuary to the Parthians in flight from Ventidius. Whether for his treachery or for his great wealth or for his control of the strategic Euphrates region, King Antiochus of Commagene was besieged in his capital city of Samosata by Ventidius. The siege made little headway, and jealous carpers accused Ventidius of accepting the king's bribes of 1,000 talents. Perhaps Ventidius rather was awaiting instructions from Antony on whether to make peace on the king's generous terms.[8]

The decision could be Antony's because, freed temporarily from Italian entanglements, and perhaps eager to have a share in Ventidius's glory of victory, Antony arrived in the summer of 38 B.C. to take command at Samosata. He disdained the proffered 1,000 talents and settled into the siege. Like Ventidius, Antony found the siege stubborn and dangerous enough that he was grateful when

Herod brought a contingent of troops through Parthian lines to his aid. Eventually the surrender of the city was negotiated. The dynastic feuds and murders at the Parthian court had been renewed when the heir apparent, Pacorus, was killed; and when Phraates won the Parthian throne, Antiochus was hostile to him. Antiochus therefore was left on the throne of Commagene. Antony received a face-saving 300 talents.[9]

When Ventidius was awarded a triumph in Rome for his Parthian successes, Antony, too, was given the honor, although it would have to await his return to Italy. It had been an undistinguished campaign, yet the honors were well deserved. The Parthians had overrun nearly all the Asiatic provinces and the allies of Rome, and had held them for almost two years. But once they had been driven out and Pacorus killed, they never again took the offensive. Antony was free to reassert order in the reconquered lands and then to ready his attack.[10]

Again Italian crises took precedence. Fears of Sextus Pompey, the expiration of the triumviral five-year agreement, and various dissatisfactions with Octavian's living up to agreements about troop transfers took Antony back to Italy in late 38 B.C. for negotiations. By spring, 37 B.C., the Pact of Tarentum renewed the triumvirate for five years and provided for the exchange of military forces. Antony gave 120 warships to Octavian for the naval war against Sextus Pompey; Octavian would send 20,000 soldiers to Antony for action against Parthia. Only then could Antony return to Antioch to prepare for a campaign in 36 B.C.[11]

During his absence the eastern situation was shifting. He had left Gaius Sosius in command in Syria, and, among other settlements of the area, Sosius had aided in the conquest of Jerusalem in 37 B.C. Antigonus was dead; Herod was now King of the Jews, indebted to Antony for his throne. In the north Publius Canidius Crassus had forced an alliance on Armenia and made King Artavasdes provide cavalry for Antony; then he pacified the land north to the Caucasus so that no powerful state would threaten Antony's rear as he marched eastward. The weaknesses in these settlements proved to be that the forced alliances with pro-Parthian kings were unstable and that Antony lacked the troops to garrison Armenia and other states to hold them loyal. Meanwhile, in 37 B.C., the

175

revolutions in the Parthian court had caused the flight of many of the aristocrats who had opposed the victorious King Phraates IV. Among the exiles, the noble Monaeses came to Antony promising that the Parthians were ripe for revolt from the harsh king and that he would act as guide for the Roman safety. Antony was strongly influenced by the man and his assurances, which corresponded so closely to Antony's own hopes. He granted Monaeses control over and revenue from three Syrian cities during the course of the war, with a promise of the Parthian throne after Roman victory. When, despite these substantial incentives to Roman allegiance, Monaeses accepted Phraates's urging of loyalty, Antony merely sent him a request for the return of the Roman eagles and prisoners.[12]

The negotiations were the merest front, perhaps calculated to lure the Parthians away from war preparedness. After his return from Italy, Antony was mobilizing fully for a campaign to begin in the spring of 36 B.C. Octavian never sent the 20,000 soldiers promised, nor was Antony allowed to recruit in Italy. Despite these serious deficiencies, Antony's army, joined by the troops of Canidius Crassus, numbered 100,000 men. Sixteen legions of 60,000 Romans were the backbone of the army. The 10,000 cavalry came from Spain and Gaul. Thirty thousand allies, about half of them Armenians, provided other horsemen and light-armed troops. Able Romans, like Titius and Ahenobarbus, staffed the officer ranks.[13]

Such a force required supplies and money, which meant the draining of the already exploited eastern provinces. At a risk to romanticism, probably monetary needs helped precipitate Antony's marriage to Cleopatra in this spring. The army needed some of Egypt's wealth as well as a secure southern flank. Other considerations may have been more prominent in the marriage, but for Antony victory in Parthia would be the base from which his other ambitions could spring. Cleopatra, eager for the power a victory would give Antony, went as far as Zeugma when Antony led his army east; then she returned to Egypt. It is unknown how much Egyptian money actually traveled farther.[14]

In spring, 36 B.C., the army crossed the Euphrates. Because Caesar's earlier plan of attack is unknown, we cannot judge whether Antony now followed it. Clearly, Crassus's errors in crossing the deserts and open steppes at Carrhae had to be avoided and the whole region of the Euphrates had to be carefully guarded. During summer the northern route was the easier one. Artavasdes, client king of Armenia, counseled a northerly route through Armenia into Media Atropatene, a vassal state of Parthia whose king and troops were already with the Parthians. The northern route should be safe and well furnished with supplies, and it passed through lands from which allies could be drawn. Artavasdes soon deserted to the Parthians and may have been playing a game of duplicity throughout; but avoiding the plains of the Tigris-Euphrates valley, attacking weak allies, and taking major cities to force the Parthians to fight on Roman terms seems a defensible strategy.[15]

Nevertheless, the campaign was catastrophic. The winding roads through the mountains were 500 miles long and slower than Antony had planned. Particularly his baggage train, including 300 wagons carrying his heavy siege equipment, advanced with agonizing slowness as the summer came on. Finally Antony led his cavalry and most of his better infantry by a shorter road to his first objective, Phraaspa, capital of Media Atropatene. Two legions under Oppius Statianus were left to protect the baggage train as it struggled over the longer road which was fit for the lumbering wagons. King Polemo of Pontus and an escort from Artavasdes of Armenia further secured the siege train.[16]

At Phraaspa Antony was dismayed to find not an undefended capital but a hill city, strongly fortified for a siege. With his siege machinery still en route and a shortage of timber in the area for building some, Antony did his best with earthworks and mounds, but the city held secure. Now the Parthians attacked, cutting off his foraging parties and luring the Armenians into desertion. Most serious, Phraates attacked the baggage train, catching it ill-defended. The two legions guarding it were killed, the supplies and equipment looted or destroyed. Polemo was taken prisoner; Artavasdes deserted or fled. Couriers brought news of the attack to Antony, who promptly marched with reinforcements; but by the time he arrived, the carnage was complete, and he could only drive off the victors.[17]

No hope remained for the success of the siege or of using Phraaspa as a winter base from which a second season's campaign could be launched deeper into Parthia. One major effort to win in a set battle was foiled by the Parthian tactic of strategic retreat and harassment rather than battle. Roman morale plummeted. Foraging parties for needed food were picked off by Parthian archers. When the besieged themselves attacked, the Romans fled, and Antony had to resort to decimation of his ranks and substituting barley for wheat in the daily rations to restore discipline.[18]

The siege had lasted into October, but, clearly, neither side could maintain it through the severe mountain winter which was already setting in. Once again tempted by the promises of Parthian agents working to break Roman morale, Antony tried negotiating for the captives and eagles but received only assurances, of questionable reliability, that his retreat would be uncontested. He had no alternative to retreat. He abandoned the siege equipment he had constructed at Phraaspa, and started desperately short of provisions for the long march.[19]

Antony would have withdrawn by the same route he had marched in; but a pro-Roman Mardion native counseled him that the Parthians were reassuring him of the safety of the road to trap him in terrain favorable to Parthian cavalry tactics. Another hill road would be safer, shorter, and better provided with villages which could supply the army. The advice was sound and, although losses ran painfully high, the route probably saved the army from total annihilation. For two days the Romans retreated without harassment. On the third day they found the road flooded, and the guide warned that the Parthians had broken a dike to stop them. The Parthian attack came immediately and was sustained for the next twenty-five days of retreat. Antony formed his men into a defensive square around his supplies, using his remaining cavalry and light-armed troops to fend off the Parthian raids. But still stragglers were lost, and even in the square the Roman casualties mounted. When one Roman officer, Flavius Gallus, tried an ill-executed attack, only Antony's swift arrival with a crack legion saved the bulk of the troops. Nevertheless, 3,000 had been killed, 5,000 wounded in the abortive attempt. Forty thousand Parthians attacked the main force the next day, expecting that the Roman battle casualties, the near starvation of the men, and the widespread illness from bad water, unwholesome food, and biting cold would bring easy victory. But the Roman formations held firm.

Antony's finest qualities as a man and as a soldier were evident in this crisis, and only his leadership kept the retreat from becoming a rout. His generalship was prudent, his courage in fighting inspiring. He shared every deprivation and hardship with his men, comforted the wounded, and fended off despair with his own spirited determination as the men hailed him as their leader. Repeatedly he rejected Parthian blandishments, choosing the safer if harsher mountain routes, and thus staved off disaster. Only on the last night did the crumbling army break into disorder and loot Antony's baggage. Antony wavered enough to provide that a trusted freedman would kill him if Antony so ordered. But safety was reached just short of calamity. A river provided the boundary which the Parthians would not cross. Under Antony's orders, the cavalry defended the rear while the wounded and then the infantry crossed the river. The Parthians saluted the courage and hardihood of the Roman commander and army, and withdrew. Six more days' marching brought the legions to Armenia.[20]

Artavasdes had played the Roman alliance false and had withdrawn his 16,000 Armenian cavalry when Antony needed them most. There would be bitter scores to settle. But while his troops desperately needed sanctuary and supplies, Antony would smile and hail the Armenian alliance. For this he gained recovery time for his army. Still, he dared not let his troops disband for winter quarters in a treacherous country, nor could he count on Armenia to provide the army with needed supplies for months. Again the army marched through mountains and winter storms so harsh that 8,000 men died en route. At last Syria offered a safe haven. There Cleopatra, to whom he had dispatched an appeal for help, was waiting with clothing and food but without the money which Antony had requested. To disguise her unwillingness to help in what she judged a useless struggle, Antony added treasure from his own fortune and those of his friends and allies; and every Roman and allied soldier received a gift of money. As the troops settled into winter quarters, Antony and Cleopatra returned to Alexandria.[21]

The Parthian disaster marked a final turn in Antony's career. He had counted on this victory to reassert the military prestige he had garnered in his wars under Caesar and at Philippi, to ensure his supremacy over Octavian. Far from conquering the Parthians and recovering the captives and eagles, he had lost over 32,000 men, one-third of his vast army, to disease or in fighting eighteen defensive battles. More prisoners had joined the men of Carrhae; many of those dead or captured were Antony's trusted veterans. Phraates, the king of Parthia, now was striking over the captured coins of Antony and Cleopatra with Parthian coin markings. Border client kingdoms were discarding Roman ties for those of Parthia, and even Sextus Pompey, whose defeat Octavian was ostentatiously cele-brating in Italy, was offering his services to Parthia. Antony sent word to Rome that Parthia was defeated, and probably at this time he was saluted imperator for the third time. Some people rejoiced. But Octavian and other state leaders knew that the reports were fraudulent. For the moment they ignored Antony's disaster because Sextus Pompey still threatened in the west. Far from avenging the defeat at Carrhae, Antony had lost more men than Crassus. He had also lost his aura of invincibility and with it his secure dominion. Even in Cleopatra's Alexandrian court, Antony's winter must have been bitter.[22]

With resolution, but also with some desperation, Antony busied himself rebuilding his depleted army, stabilizing conditions in the east, and preparing a war of retaliation against the treacherous Ar-menian king and perhaps even the Parthians. His enemies were more helpful than his allies. The Parthians could have reasserted their recently lost control over Syria while Antony's army was still reeling from its losses. But instead, the kings of Parthia and Media Atropatene squabbled over the loot captured from the Romans. Trapped between the two hostile powers, the Medians now deserted the Parthians, allying themselves with Antony, who apparently was impressive and trusted even in defeat. Thus he won a base for an attack on Parthia or Armenia. The objectives of the desperate-ly hard campaign to and retreat from Phraaspa had been gained by bloodless diplomacy, but the main campaigns were still to be waged.[23]

Briefly in 35 B.C. Antony had to take time to settle the issue of Sextus Pompey, who, though in flight from Octavian, had been emboldened by Antony's failures in Parthia, to raise three legions in Asia Minor and then to offer them as mercenaries to both An-tony and Parthia. When Sextus's emissaries to Parthia were intercepted, Antony sent the Syrian legions under Titius against him, then ordered the captured Sextus slain and the remnant of his three under-strength legions incorporated into Antony's army.[24]

Rebuilding his depleted legions was Antony's greatest need, both to battle the Parthians and to counterweigh Octavian's increasing forces and prestige in the west. In all, he counted twenty-five legions, which, although they were not full strength, were a powerful force and one deeply loyal to Antony. Five more legions were raised, but with unusual composition. Because a Roman legionnaire had to be a Roman citizen, Antony and Octavian had agreed that Italy would be open recruiting ground for both their armies. However, Octavian had been blocking Antony's recruiting there since 36 B.C. It was critical for Antony that he not lose the Italian soldiers. If need be, he would fight for the recruiting grounds. But for now, Antony employed the fiction of a citizen army which Pompey had used and Octavian would use in the future: he granted citizenship to any one entering the army, then built legions of Asiatics and Greeks. The 20,000 soldiers Octavian had promised to send east in return for the 120 ships Antony sent west had never arrived. Now, as an insolent token of provocation, or perhaps because he wanted to force Antony's decision openly between Cleopatra in the east and Octavia in the west, Octavian sent 2,000 men and 70 of the ships that Antony had sent to aid Octavian's fight against Sextus Pompey, but these would do Antony no service against the land empires of Parthia and Armenia. It was Octavia who brought the 2,000 troops to Athens, adding cattle and money for her husband. Antony had already left Alexandria when he learned of Octavia's coming. He responded to her overture by turning back to Egypt and notifying her to send on the supplies and men but to return to her brother in Rome. The dutiful Octavia, always Octavian's pawn against Antony, set sail for Italy. Further disregarding Roman opinion, Antony this year married his elder daughter Antonia, now nineteen, the daughter of his wife Antonia, to Pythodorus, a rich Greek of Tralles.[25]

In the spring of 34 B.C., accompanied by his nine-year-old son Antyllus, and partway by Cleopatra and Herod, Antony marched into Armenia. Ostensibly he would use Armenia as a base against the Parthians; actually he intended to punish King Artavasdes for treachery at Phraaspa and for recent negotiations with Octavian against Antony. Antony had played the role of ally when he needed sanctuary in Armenia during his retreat. Subsequently, he had tried to lure Artavasdes into Egypt by sending Quintus Dellius with an offer of marriage between Antony's son by Cleopatra and an Armenian princess; but Artavasdes had not risen to the lure. Now Antony still feigned alliance by soliciting consultation with the king about the marriage. In the Armenian capital Artavasdes finally fell into the trap of entering the Roman camp. He was seized and sent to Egypt in chains. With his wife, children, and booty, he was given to Cleopatra, then, after the battle of Actium in 31 B.C., executed.[26]

The Armenians elected as the king's successor one of the king's sons, Artaxes, who fought Antony fiercely until he too was driven out of power. Antony then easily completed the conquest of Armenia and made it a Roman-occupied client state, with a Romanized son of Artavasdes as nominal ruler but with the real control determined by the Roman legions stationed there under Canidius Crassus. This was the only province that Antony added to the Roman Empire. Had the control been stable, it would have secured a large and strong buffer state against the Parthians and a region important for its resources and its trading links with eastern markets. But the Armenians for a century were to resent Antony's perfidy; and the "Armenian Question" remained an unresolved threat of antagonism on Rome's frontier.[27]

In Rome the conquest was ignored. But in the autumn of 34 B.C. Antony returned to Egypt in glory to celebrate a kind of triumph for his victories. For the first time, a "triumph" was held outside Rome. Although Antony was named imperator for the fourth time, he probably did not intend the celebration to serve as a Roman triumph. It was more of a Dionysiac religious revel. Antony himself was in a golden robe, holding the sacred wand of Dionysus. The Alexandrians were feasted and given gifts of money. The captives, including the Armenian king, and booty were marched through Alexandria, then presented, not to Jupiter on the Capitoline, but to Cleopatra seated on a golden throne on a silver platform, with her children on lower thrones. Resentful of her role as an eastern queen celebrating a western triumph, the prisoners would do her no obeisance. As part of the festival, Caesarion was formally named Caesar and Cleopatra's son, coruler of Egypt. Antony and Cleopatra's son Alexander Helios received the grandiose title "King of Armenia, Media and Parthia, from the Euphrates to India."[28]

Perhaps, had Antony continued his attacks beyond Armenia, taking advantage of the disorder and the element of surprise, he could have taken some of the eastern lands he was presenting to his son. But Antony was almost entirely immobilized by the challenge that Octavian was ever more clearly presenting in the west. Antony would have to fight in both the east and the west; his only question was the timing of the wars. His hope was an east stabilized and even helpful behind him as he turned west. Therefore, he postponed any major Parthian attack. Instead, in 33 B.C., he met the Median king Artavasdes in Armenia where an alliance was concluded, directed against the Parthians and against Octavian. The treaty was not aggressive; rather it was a defensive alliance calculated to keep the area quiet and secure as Antony faced west. Part of Armenia was granted to the Median king, and Antony and Cleopatra's young son Alexander Helios was betrothed to his daughter. The captives taken in the 36 B.C. campaign were exchanged, and the eagles captured from Statianus were returned to Roman hands. Polemo, a Median who had collaborated with Rome, was granted the rule of Lesser Armenia. Again the settlement by diplomacy seemed more effective than that by war, and Antony could hope for an ever more reliable ally in a critical area.[29]

The hope proved evanescent, however. One attack by the Parthians and revolting Armenians was turned back by the combined arms of the Medians and Romans. But then the threat from Octavian forced Antony to summon the legions in Armenia under Canidius Crassus. Without Roman support, King Artavasdes was defeated and fled to the Romans. Media was again allied with Parthia. Armenia, Antony's occupied client state for only two years, allied more closely to Parthia, declared itself independent, and massacred all the Romans remaining in the country. No attempt was made by either Antony or Octavian to retake the land; and Armenia continued to be an independent state. The usual dynastic disorders plagued Parthia. One claimant, Tiridates II, asked Octavian for aid; but the war against Antony deterred Octavian from helping.

Tiridates later fled Parthia to Rome, bringing with him the son of the king. This hostage Octavian in 20 B.C. was able to use as a pawn in negotiating an agreement with the Parthians, the compromise by which Octavian regained the eagles and prisoners lost by Crassus and Antony. Octavian had learned from Antony's defeats. He made no effort to invade Parthia, contenting himself with encouraging the dynastic struggles that kept Parthia and Media from becoming major threats.[30]

Antony, far from winning the fame of a Parthian victory, had had to settle for the hollow trumpery of an Alexandrian triumph, unstable allies and provinces, and heavy losses from his loyal legions. The losses in power and prestige were grave. Antony had never been free to throw his full forces against Parthia. Now even his defensive garrisons would have to be withdrawn to mobilize the east against Octavian's threat from the west.

XII

Breaking with Octavian

Step by step, Antony had been drawn into the role of the ruler of the east, divorced from Rome and the west. He had never planned or wanted such a break. On the contrary, like every Roman statesman, he looked to Rome as the focus of imperial power; like every Roman general, he drew his legions from Italian manpower. Antony judged himself a Roman triumvir, sharing with Octavian the rule of the whole Roman Empire. Yet, insensibly, he was being relegated to only half the empire and being criticized for giving precedence to the east over the west.

Several factors contributed to this shift. For some, Antony was responsible; of others, he was the victim. His duties to collect money for the veterans and to defeat the Parthians lay in the east. It was a vast area to administer, and its problems required his full attention. Fair enough! Nevertheless, knowing the importance of keeping a hold on the west, he should have made the time and exerted the effort to travel to Rome. He had been in Italy only three times since 42 B.C., twice only briefly. His last visit to Rome had been in 40 B.C., his last to Italy in 37 B.C. The usual time required for messengers to travel between Rome and Alexandria in summer was eighteen to nineteen days, and double that in winter; so reports seemed dulled or distorted by time as well as distance. Antony had, to be sure, agents in Rome who spoke for him and kept him informed;

but they could hardly match the dynamism of his presence. Meanwhile, Octavian's solid achievements and propaganda machine were emphasizing the preeminence of Caesar's heir in the west and Antony's remoteness in the east. From 43 to 37 B.C. Octavian had been dependent on Antony's strength, which could have destroyed him or let him be destroyed. But Antony, loyal to his compacts, sent troops and ships when Octavian needed them, and spurned offers like that of Sextus Pompey to cooperate in eliminating Octavian. By 36 B.C. Octavian was beginning to occupy the strong position. Antony, only partly aware of western affairs, made no strike against Octavian's growing power base.

Antony's preoccupation with eastern affairs, then, was politically imprudent. Yet behind it lay the broader vision of the Roman Empire which Julius Caesar had realized. The empire, to incorporate the whole Mediterranean, must equalize its peoples, must fuse the Hellenistic with the Latin and Gallic worlds. The intense Roman nationalism and sense of superiority over conquered lands must give way to a cultural integration. Antony seems not to have worked through all the implications of this conviction, but he was spontaneously living such a position. Like Caesar, Antony knew no disdain for the "barbarians" beyond Italy, whether in military camp, in government office, or in personal relations. Not so Octavian, who, with full calculation, was ostentatiously playing the role of old Roman and reviving Italian creeds and practices of an earlier day.

The bulk of Antony's followers, in the court and in the army, had not progressed as far as he in this realization and acceptance of eastern equality. Political dexterity required that Antony promote his policies cautiously and persuasively. But profound analysis and subtle manipulation were not Antony's long suits. He succeeded in understanding eastern forms and needs and in playing an eastern role; yet by doing so, he alienated many of his own followers, and, dangerously, he provided weapons for Octavian's propaganda war to discredit Antony and his eastern policies.

Cleopatra must be judged as destroying Antony's reputation more than almost any other factor in the east. Whether or not Cleopatra controlled Antony, people believed that she did, and Antony's policies had to function within the belief that Antony was letting a woman take precedence over his duty. The "infinite variety" that "age cannot wither . . . nor custom stale" reaches also to the range of interpretations with which people of her own time and later generations have tried to capture her.[1] Much we can never know accurately; for the hostile sources who worked to discredit Antony were even more virulent in attacking the woman whom they named the cause of his alienation from Octavian and the west.[2]

This Hellenistic queen, this *fatale monstrum* of the Orient,[3] was not Egyptian in blood but Macedonian-Greek. She was the last ruler of the dynasty established by Ptolemy, kinsman and general of Alexander the Great, when the death of the conqueror in 323 B.C. brought division of his empire among his ablest and most ambitious henchmen. Imperious, determined, courageous, ambitious, intensely alive, Cleopatra was a true heir of Alexander the Great. She could and did learn, work, organize for her ends. Yet her prime goal was to rule Egypt well.

Egypt's flood-fertile soil had made it the most productive land of the Mediterranean area for countless centuries. The pharaohs, with meticulous detail and growing bureaucracy, had organized the wealth of agriculture, trade, and manufacture for maximum economic return and political stability. By the last centuries of pharaonic rule, various conflicts and weaknesses were troubling the ancient, fixed policies. But the energetic early Ptolemies reasserted firm leadership and thorough regulation of the native population, using a ruling caste of Hellenic officials and the protection of Hellenic troops. For almost three hundred years the Ptolemies had continued this foreign domination and had been a power in the eastern Mediterranean. But problems had been weakening their rule. The Ptolemaic dynasty was interlocked in goodwill and bad with the other Hellenistic states that had been wrenched out of portions of Alexander's empire. They traded the goods of the entire Near East, intermarried within the ruling dynasties, and developed a Hellenistic culture blending the Greek of the ruling classes with the Oriental elements of the eastern subject peoples. The states also fought an exhausting succession of wars among themselves and by these bitter hostilities invited or provoked increasing Roman intervention in the eastern Mediterranean.

For a century before Cleopatra's reign, the Romans had been assuming ever more total control of Egyptian affairs. Straightforward conquest would have been easy for them. But Egypt, unlike the other Hellenistic states, passively collaborated with the Romans, so that there was no urgency about its conquest.[4] Jealous fears among Roman classes and leaders lest any political faction become dominant over the power and wealth of Egypt kept the land nominally independent and the Ptolemies nominally the rulers on the throne. In actuality, Egypt was a client state, obsequious to Rome's bidding. The Ptolemies repeatedly and lavishly had paid Roman generals, like Gabinius with his lieutenant Antony in 55 B.C. and Caesar with his lieutenant Antony in 48 B.C., to seize and hold the throne for them. All the Roman intervention resulted in drains on the Egyptian treasury. Repeatedly, taxes were levied to satisfy Roman greed. When greater financial burdens were accompanied by deteriorating competence within the Ptolemaic family, the native Egyptians were driven to desperate revolts. These triggered more appeals for help to Rome, more costly interventions, further disintegration in the economic patterns of the country.

This dangerous decline was reaching its nadir under Cleopatra's father, Ptolemy XI, who, after repeated humiliations and financial drains from the Romans, had hired Gabinius's legions to recapture his throne. Cleopatra VII was born, probably in late 70 B.C., into a court of intrigue and corruption. Even as a girl she struggled for survival and power, however won. She had Caesar kill her young brother-husband, Ptolemy XII, and Antony her sister Arsinoë, so that she could hold the throne uncontested. Lesser victims also knew her wrath. She had inherited an almost empty treasury from her father; her wealth, therefore, was dependent on annual revenues. The rich land had been gravely misused: the coinage depreciated, the inflexible bureaucracy extravagantly enlarged, the irrigation canals silted, the trade routes blocked. Famine and depopulation threatened. Cleopatra made only small gains in recovering from the abuses of the previous Ptolemies, and there is little evidence that she or Antony fully understood the agricultural difficulties or recognized Egypt's potential as a middleman for luxury trade from the east and the south. But her concern and efforts reached the native peoples, as did her ability to speak Egyptian, as no other of her dynasty had. For generations to come she would be revered as "The Queen."[5]

Cleopatra perceived Egypt's recovery as depending heavily on regaining foreign lands held under the early Ptolemies. Such lands had provided commodities like timber which Egypt needed and had served as recruiting grounds for the Greek troops which were the backbone of Egypt's army. For recovery, Cleopatra, like Antony, recognized the need to fuse Rome and the east in power and in culture. This ambitious queen conceived of a Mediterranean-wide state ruled from Alexandria; but she was also totally realistic and knew that her effective power, indeed existence itself, could come only through Roman help. The Roman Republic had deteriorated to the level of rule by one man; Cleopatra, therefore, calculated the probable victor in the Roman power struggle and sought his backing for Egypt. Dozens of hard-beset monarchs of weak states were making the same calculations and buying Roman support with money, troops, or favors. The reward for the successful was a client kingdom at least temporarily secure. So had the later Ptolemies held their throne.[6]

But Cleopatra was a woman. Glaphyra had used womanly wiles toward Antony to gain the Cappadocian crown for her family. Like other queens, Cleopatra made her company one of the rewards for which Roman leaders would pay. When Caesar had followed the fleeing Pompey to Egypt after Pharsalus, she had won his support for her throne by capturing his heart—granted also that she had paid her father's debts to him. She had borne his son Caesarion, followed the married dictator to Rome to live unabashedly in one of his villas, and let her statue be placed in Caesar's temple of Venus. Her goal was the reconfirmation of Egypt's alliance with Rome. But the Ides of March which killed Caesar destroyed also Cleopatra's hopes and plans for some joint rule of the Roman Empire with Caesar. She fled to Egypt with Caesarion and watched with apprehensive calculation the shifting power struggle among the tyrannicides and the triumvirs. Asked for aid by both sides, she claimed that she had sent the four legions that Caesar had stationed in Egypt to the aid of the Caesarians.[7]

Of the several leaders who might have dominated the east, Antony was probably the one most susceptible to Cleopatra's policies.

Four times married, endlessly involved with women, he was always ready for a fresh conquest. He had known Cleopatra in her youthful beauty and in the dazzling brilliance of her position as Caesar's mistress. Now Cleopatra was the highest and the most exotic prize he could win. Ancient descriptions and coin portraits do not stress her beauty; rather, they show her a mature, strong woman. As such, she was fascinating: charming, dramatic, skilled in all the arts of captivating men. Highly educated and cultured, she had readily matched wits with Caesar. Her understanding of Antony made her rather match camp jokes than philosophical subtleties; but Antony was well enough aware of her tastes that at Ephesus in 33-32 B.C. he gave her 200,000 scrolls from the great library at Pergamum as compensation for the 700,000 scrolls that had been burned when Caesar was fighting in Alexandria. Her court was luxurious but within the restraint of elegance. For Antony, from the simpler west, most of whose life had been spent in army camps, it was a marvelous wonder.[8]

Indeed, Alexandria as a whole was the most sophisticated city in the world, with its blend of ancient Egyptian and Greek cultures, its Great Harbor with the lighthouse which was one of the seven wonders of the ancient world, its learned Museum of sciences and arts, its Library, gymnasium, zoo, the great palace, and numberless temples to an Egyptian and Greek pantheon. Even Cleopatra was numbered among the gods, as were her ruling ancestors. She was the daughter of the Egyptian sun god, Ra, and she herself was the living manifestation of the mother fertility goddess, Isis for the Egyptians, Aphrodite for the Greeks.[9]

The woman, the court, the policies won Antony's wholehearted backing—as Cleopatra had intended. He understood Cleopatra's unscrupulous ambition, her fierce devotion to the Ptolemaic line, her courageous determination to do and have what she wanted, whatever the means or the cost. Antony willingly fell into line behind truly strong leaders like Caesar, even strong women like Fulvia. Cleopatra was of the same mold of dominance, and her intellect and imagination were her ultimate appeal beyond romantic love. There was passion between them for a decade. There was a family of two sons and a daughter. There was a lavish court life of banquets, frolics, and scandal, attuned to Antony's bluff tastes. But both Antony and Cleopatra were playing a mortal game for control of the Roman world, and ultimately, they were together because each deemed the other useful.[10]

At first the dependence was greater for Cleopatra. She wanted independence for Egypt, return of lands held earlier by Egypt, and —in her boldest dreams—rule over a Greco-Roman world with Antony. The troubled times had given rise to prophecies that Roman might would fail and that an Egyptian monarch would rule the world in tranquillity, prosperity, and generosity. But for Cleopatra to be this savior, she had to gain the rule through Antony. Policy did not exclude affection. Cleopatra was faithful to Antony for a decade, as she had been to Caesar while he lived. (The queen was not promiscuous, no matter how her detractors defamed her.) When she fought to keep Antony from going west to Rome and Octavia, foreign policy was mixed with feminine feelings.[11]

Antony had at first found the elegant queen useful while being attractive, then he came to be increasingly dependent upon her. Emotionally he came to love her, far more than he had loved before, deeply enough that he was willing to marry her at the cost of his Roman family and friends. But not deeply enough that he was willing to lose the world for her. He intended to have the supreme rule and have Cleopatra as his wife as well. Where he erred was in letting her influence his policies about Rome when she did not know Rome well enough to judge Roman attitudes accurately. She argued against his returning to Italy when he needed Italian associations, because she feared that Octavia would center his interests in the west. She sued for concessions of land which were bound to anger the Romans. Because Antony was too much at her court, he failed to realize the hatred being generated at Rome against the *fatale monstrum* whom the Romans were being conditioned to dread as their greatest threat since Hannibal. Ultimately, Antony had to adjust his policies to hers because he had broken alternative ties and had no other place to go except as an underling to Octavia and Octavian. Hate must have mingled with love, increasingly so as both realized their crossed purposes and the possibility of their mutual destruction. The world they wanted was slipping from their grasp.[12]

The lovers, notwithstanding, found consolations in their formal rule and in the extravagant court life shared with their friends. How reckless were their entertainments we can probably never know. Hostile propaganda from Octavian's camp has so colored the accounts that the reader could believe in perpetual debauchery. Republican Roman invective against political or personal opponents was unfettered by libel laws and traditionally went to wild excesses of character defamation for sexual indecency and financial bankruptcy. When the suspicious Roman view of eastern effeminacy and decadence and of an Egyptian queen's lasciviousness provided additional areas of censure, the gossips and propagandizers could blacken Antony's reputation so thoroughly that the tales still dominate the picture of Antony. He did not make much of an effort to refute the charges; such effort has proved futile over the ages. Rather, he attacked Octavian in the same fashion. But at best, he could not control Roman opinion from Alexandria; and it was Octavian's propaganda that was saved for the historians of the age.[13]

Not that Antony was a model of ancient Roman sobriety or ostentatious virtue. His tastes were bluff and hearty, and he saw no reason to disguise them. His amusements in court were much what they had been in military camp: bawdy tales, gambling, drinking, women. Cleopatra was wise enough or devoted enough to accommodate her pleasures to his, spicing even practical jokes with her wit and taste so that the entertainment never palled. A band of "Inimitable Livers," established in 40 B.C., included all their court friends who relished high living. Antony had always been prodigal, of others' fortunes and his own; and the luxurious, leisurely Alexandrian court life, and the delights of nearby pleasure resorts, led him to spend fortunes for trifles like dinners or gifts or specially trained slaves. In a rough Roman jest, he might also lead Cleopatra and his friends, as a rowdy gang in disguise, into the back alleys of Alexandria. The Alexandrians, who had idolized Antony since 55 B.C., when Gabinius's young lieutenant had been gallant to them, relished or forgave his buffoonery. Antony, in turn, took the widespread jokes about his behavior, especially his love affairs, with good spirit.[14]

At another level, Antony was a man of Greek philosophic and artistic interests; and although he did not pose as an intellectual, he

192

listened with interest to the studies of others and gave generous patronage to men of ability from all classes. With Roman arbitrary power, he transferred the Pergamene library and a number of Greek artistic masterpieces to Alexandria. For his Roman officers and men and the people in Alexandria, even those who hated the influence of Cleopatra, his fundamental artlessness, tolerance, trust, and integrity were far more important than his indiscretions, and a loyal following held firm among those who knew him best.[15]

The way in which Antony most clearly showed his acceptance of eastern ways and his determination to preside as ruler of the east was in his assumption of the role of god. Polytheism and syncretism had been almost universal for centuries; throughout the east, kings, queens, indeed any effective rulers, were automatically hailed as gods. For the Greeks, there had been since Homer's time a faint line between gods and more-than-human heroes. Roman conquerors like Sulla, Pompey, and Caesar had been worshiped as gods in the east, not because they were actually believed to be gods but because this was how political allegiance was invariably displayed. Such theocracy added stability to a rule and could be usefully exploited. Caesar, who recognized the importance of eastern control and who may even have planned to shift the capital of the empire east, was murdered in part because the republicans suspected that he would institute this Hellenistic kind of divine monarchy. And Antony knew more than most men about Caesar's hopes.[16]

Romans had long felt hostile about hailing their mortal ruler as divine or as the reincarnation of divinity, because they considered it a trapping of the monarchy which they had overthrown in 509 B.C. Granted that they, like the Greeks, traced the ancestry of the great patrician clans to gods or more-than-mortal heroes; the remote legends gave dignity, not divinity. Recently, however, a more ambiguous attitude had developed as the Romans met or conquered eastern peoples who hailed their generals as gods, and as their republic degenerated into one-man rule. No Roman official had yet demanded divine honors at Rome. But Caesar dead had been hailed as a god, complete with temple and priests. Octavian was calling himself the son of the god Caesar, and of the lineage of Venus from whom the Julian line claimed descent. He was also letting the poets under his patronage term him the son of Apollo, the god of rational wisdom and beneficence to men. Even more overtly, Sextus Pompey played the role of the son of Neptune, thus lord of the seas. Increasingly, the Romans seemed acquiescent to such claims, provided that they smoothed the path for political and economic affairs.[17]

Antony's deification developed quite spontaneously from both these traditions, then gradually enlarged as a calculated state policy for the east. In Rome his family claimed descent from Heracles, and the soldier Antony always stressed this heritage and sponsored this cult. Thus he issued coins for the Parthian campaign displaying the lion which was the emblem of Heracles but also of the Antonian gens. Then as the victorious conqueror of the east, he issued coins displaying the figure of the sun as symbol of the east. But his identification was primarily with the god Dionysus, who was often worshiped in close association with Heracles. The cult of this eastern god proved very popular in Hellenistic times. Even in Italy Dionysus was worshiped and sometimes identified with the native chthonic Pater Liber. But the god who in the east was considered not only a fertility god but also a benefactor to man, a protector and patron of artists and philosophers, a founder of civilization and of cities, even a god of the conquest of Asia, and a harmonizer of the Greek and Roman worlds, in Italy was associated chiefly with wine and orgiastic Bacchic rites: the ivy, satyrs, Pans, harps, and flutes. In 187–86 B.C. the *Senatus Consultum de Bacchanalibus* had forbidden the secret meetings of the worshipers, although not the god himself, in Rome. As Rome had grown more cosmopolitan, the cult had become more widespread; but traditional Romans still held it suspect. Antony, by adopting it, showed more clearly his preoccupation with eastern over Roman attitudes and was more subject to criticism at home.[18]

The cults of the Egyptian gods, especially Isis, followed a similar pattern. For forty years Isis was worshiped in Rome until the patricians' increasing fears about her strange rituals climaxed between 58 and 48 B.C. in repeated destructions of Isis temples in the city. The triumvirs reversed this hostility by decreeing, in 43 B.C., the construction of a new temple to Isis and Serapis; but although the cult had no political implications, the vast majority of Italians still viewed the worship as alien.[19]

194

The eastern peoples began the cult of Antony, the first of the triumvirs so honored. Without any illusions of divinity, Antony responded to the role as useful politically. Once involved, he was unable to disengage himself from the elaborating worship. It had begun when Antony first went to Ephesus as the victor at Philippi and was proclaimed the New Dionysus. When Cleopatra joined him at Tarsus, it was in the guise of Aphrodite to his Dionysus. The people hailed the union of these gods, and as Aphrodite and Dionysus they continued during their winter of 41–40 B.C. at Alexandria. The acclamations of divinity arose, however, from the people independent of Cleopatra. When Antony married Octavia and spent 39–38 B.C. with her in Athens, the people proclaimed them *theoi euergetai*, the Gods of Good Works. Antony was again the New Dionysus, and for the first time Dionysus appeared on his coins. Octavia was identified with Athena Polias. After Athens, it was only the next step that Antony had himself proclaimed Dionysus in all the cities of the east. He viewed divinity as a moral force of control, a skillful propaganda to organize the east. The people—from hopes, from fear, from flattery—responded fervently.[20]

The culmination of this deification came in Egypt when Antony returned to Cleopatra in 37 B.C. Here the role was so traditional and so appropriate for the rulers of Egypt that every political instinct demanded capitalizing on it. Antony, who always relished dramatic parts, played it to its full potential. Alexander the Great had claimed descent from Dionysus; since the Ptolemaic house was kin to Alexander, its rulers, too, carried the divinity of the god. So also did other Hellenistic houses like the Seleucids and Mithridates of Pontus. The later Ptolemies, like Cleopatra's father, called themselves New Dionysus. Antony's divinity, then, was natural to his position. For the queen, Aphrodite was the matching goddess; and Caesarion became Eros, the son of Cleopatra's Aphrodite. These Greek gods were appropriate to the Ptolemaic court at Alexandria. For the Egyptian people their equivalents had long before been found in Osiris, Isis, and Horus (the son of Isis), the all-important ancient Egyptian gods of fertility, rebirth, benevolence, and love. Throughout Egypt, therefore, Antony and Cleopatra were worshiped as gods. In Alexandria, painted and garbed as Egyptian divinities—Antony with the golden wand of Osiris or with the wreath and thyrsus of Dionysus—they were carried in religious processions. Cleopatra ordered the building of a temple to Antony in Alexandria. It was all practical politics in governing the east.[21]

It was also exhilarating to wear a diadem and purple cloak and to sit on a golden throne like an eastern emperor. Antony must have been tempted by the eastern luxuries and power, epitomized by his queenly mistress, to dream of being a second Alexander the Great. But his core of common sense tempered such grandiose illusions. Practical jokes on the court were played by the royal gods. Antony delighted in the orgiastic, bacchantic aspects of Dionysus. When Octavian played up Antony's weaknesses and fondness for drink by satirizing Antony as the god of wine, Antony's rejoinder was an essay: "On his Drunkenness" (*De sua Ebrietate*). Rude popular jest, which Antony would have heard, called him Dionysus Carnivorous for looting the eastern provinces. So, whatever the temptations, Antony kept his sense of proportion and capacity to laugh at himself.[22]

In late 34 B.C., a few days after the "triumph" Antony staged for the conquest of Armenia, a still more brilliant ceremony was performed in the great gymnasium of Alexandria, a city which apparently was now called New Rome. Antony and Cleopatra in their double role as rulers and as gods sat elevated on golden thrones placed on a silver platform. A little below them on lesser thrones sat their three children: the twins, Alexander Helios and Cleopatra Selene, aged six, little Ptolemy Philadelphus, aged two. Cleopatra was dressed in the garb of Isis; Antony may have played the role of Dionysus-Osiris, although he may instead have worn his Roman uniform: the sources do not say. Clearly, he was acting as Roman consul and triumvir in his proclamations that he was reorganizing Rome's provinces and client kingdoms in the east. This was his right as triumvir. His responsibilities in the east were to set up client kings loyal to Rome in states that Rome found more convenient not to rule itself. But the decisions announced at this ceremony were startling. In the so-called Donations of Alexandria, he apportioned the eastern states among Cleopatra and her children, granting them the lands not because they were proved able and loyal but because they were heirs of the Ptolemaic dynasty.[23]

Antony himself received no land. Despite his golden throne and

196

regal trappings, he still bore the titles triumvir and, briefly in 34 B.C., consul; and the powers he held and the titles he regularly used, as on coinage, were Roman. Moreover, Antony's aim was dominion over the whole Roman Empire, west as well as east; to mark off a private preserve in the east would have limited his greater claims. Significantly, he had already named his heir: his eldest son by Fulvia, Marcus Antonius—whom the Greek writers call Antyllus —now about eleven years old. In 34 B.C. he issued coinage stamped with the heads of both father and son. As Octavian was claiming the imperial inheritance of Caesar, so Antyllus seemed marked as Antony's successor in the control of all the empire. For him, as for Antony, no specific lands were assigned, only the suggested inheritance of the Roman Empire.[24]

It was Cleopatra, the heir of the Ptolemies, who triumphantly accepted the lands of the Donations of Alexandria, who gloried in the almost complete restoration of the extended empire Egypt had controlled under Ptolemy II Philadelphus. Only Palestine and part of Syria were still independent; but Egypt, Cyprus, Coele-Syria, Libya, and part of Cilicia were restored to Egyptian dominion. Her title was Queen of Kings, and the commemorative coinage she issued in Egypt showed her as the absolute Egyptian ruler, superior even to the nominal joint rule with her son Caesarion. She was not, however, free of Antony. Roman coins issued outside Egypt, e.g., at Antioch, portrayed Antony on the obverse, Cleopatra on the reverse. Granted that this coinage portrayal tied the Egyptian state to Rome; still Cleopatra received an unprecedented honor. Fulvia, then Octavia, had been the only living women pictured on Roman coins; Cleopatra was the first foreign woman. There were other evidences that Egypt was still a client state, ruling at Rome's sufferance. Cyprus, for example, had been given to Cleopatra by Caesar and was included in her royal claims. Yet here, and elsewhere, Roman officials were really in charge, and under the duress of preparations for Actium, the coins issued showed Antony as imperator. Still, for this day, no such limitations surfaced to dim the grandeur of Cleopatra's honors.[25]

Caesarion, now aged thirteen, as Ptolemy XIV was the nearest claimant to his mother's honors, and he was associated with Cleopatra in the rule of the Egyptian Empire. Even more significant,

Antony affirmed him as Caesar's son, the claim which depreciated the preeminence of Octavian, Caesar's adopted son, as heir. Since her son's birth, probably in 47 B.C., Cleopatra had asserted Caesar's paternity and called him Caesarion, although Caesar had not acknowledged him. In 42 B.C., when Dolabella was seeking Egyptian help for the Caesarians against Brutus and Cassius, the triumvirs acceded to Cleopatra's demands and named the child king of Egypt. Since then, he had been Cleopatra's passive consort, officially portrayed as a baby held by Cleopatra. Now Antony was again proclaiming that Caesarion was Caesar's son, indicating a kind of legitimacy to the birth, possibly on the special plane that Caesar and Cleopatra, like Antony and Cleopatra, were gods, not bound by human laws of monogamy. The boy was nominal ruler of Egyptian lands; but probably he was dressed as a Roman, and he may have been called King of Kings, over even Antony's sons by Cleopatra. His potency was as a propaganda tool for Antony: the symbol of unity of east and west, evidence that Caesar before him had united with the Egyptian queen, so that Antony was Caesar's heir in policies. Above all, it symbolized that Octavian was a usurper of the Caesarian name and program.[26]

The three young children of Antony and Cleopatra were each proclaimed ruler of a part of the east. They all bore names symbolizing the regal and divine missions to which they were born. Alexander Helios represented the world conquests of the great Alexander but also the world unity, peace, and salvation which the popular worship of the sun god promised to the peoples throughout the east. The six-year-old boy wore Median dress and was attended by an Armenian bodyguard; for he was now called King of Kings over Armenia, Media, and Parthia as far east as India. It was a grandiose claim: the Armenian king had been taken captive, and the royal prince had fled to the Parthians when Antony had made Armenia a province of Rome; the Median king was presumably allied with Antony, and the little Alexander was briefly betrothed to the king's daughter; Parthia was still completely independent. At best, Alexander's claim was of a client kingship of Armenia and of potential control over willing client kings in the vast eastern area. His twin, Cleopatra Selene, signified in her names not only her mother but also the moon goddess identified with Isis in Egypt, twin of the sun god and like him worshiped throughout the east. To her was assigned Cyrenaica, the North African coast west of Egypt, which had been willed to Rome in 96 B.C. and then united with Crete to form a Roman province. Therefore, Crete, too, may have been donated to Cleopatra Selene. The baby Ptolemy Philadelphus, named for Ptolemy II whose vast empire Cleopatra was striving to reconstitute, wore Macedonian dress and received a Macedonian honor guard. His donations included parts of Syria, Phoenicia, Cilicia, and Asia Minor west of the Euphrates as far as the Hellespont. These were territories held by client kings loyal to Antony: Archelaus of Cappadocia, Polemo of Pontus, Amyntas of Galatia. Ptolemy Philadelphus, who was also called King of Kings, was to rule the lands as lord over the client kings, with Asia Minor thus subject to Egypt.[27]

The Donations as they are described in the sources hostile to Antony seem an astonishingly high-handed, untraditional partition of the lands of Rome and of Rome's client kings. Antony was subordinating Roman interests and power to the imperial demands of Cleopatra. The states were being presented to children with concern for the Ptolemaic dynasty rather than for able leadership of the states. The eastern provinces would be irretrievably broken off from the west.[28]

But less hostile sources pass over the Donations so incidentally that Antony's actions cannot have been highly irregular. Roman generals in the east for a century had been making and unmaking client kings, and the Roman government had accepted the military and economic advantages of having loyal native rulers handle remote areas and different cultures. The organization of the east had shifted repeatedly. Caesar, especially, sought an integration of native with Roman rule. Now Antony was elevating the trustworthy house of Ptolemy into Rome's special powers, to make the region economically valuable and particularly to protect, efficiently and inexpensively, the east against a resurgent Parthia. For the present, Roman officials continued to take charge of various responsibilities in the area.

Antony's fatal miscalculation was less in his granting of land to the Ptolemies than in his failing to realize the hardening temper of the Roman people and the hostility that Octavian's propaganda had been rousing against Cleopatra during the five years since Antony had been in Rome. In a letter to the Senate, Antony reported the Donations, asking for senatorial confirmation of his arrangements. His supporters, aware of the resentment such donations would raise, tried to block the reading of this section of the letter and did not publish the Donations. But Octavian had the weapons he could use against Antony. He blocked the announcement of Antony's Armenian successes; and when Antony sent the Senate an offer to give up the power of the triumvirate and to return the state into Senatorial hands, i.e., to restore the republic, Octavian brought the offer to naught.[29]

Octavian had been assigned the consulship for 33 B.C. He held the office for one day, January 1; then, as Antony had done for his assigned consulship the previous year, he resigned the office to a friend and returned to Dalmatia to complete his campaign there. But on January 1 as consul, he levied his first public attack on Antony. It was the opening volley of an intense campaign of propaganda and scurrilous vilification on both sides. Possibly Octavian also wrote privately to Antony, criticizing especially his marriage to Cleopatra and his acceptance of Caesarion as Caesar's son. Antony replied, either to such a letter or to general public accusations, coarsely asking how his liaison with Cleopatra differed from Octavian's many extramarital affairs. He accused Octavian of illfaith: in not sending east the legions he had guaranteed, in not opening Italy to Antony's recruiting officers, in giving inferior land grants to Antony's veterans, and in deposing Lepidus and taking his territories without consultation or sharing. Antony again stressed the legitimacy of Caesarion and called Cleopatra his wife.[30]

Although Roman politics traditionally used crude invective and character assassination, in this final struggle for control of the Roman Empire, vituperation knew no limits. As a result, it is hard to distinguish fact from fiction, especially about Antony, since Octavian as military victor also won the propaganda war for the historians. As the year wore on, Octavian accused Antony of every immorality, of throwing away Rome's welfare for the eastern harlot queen, of adopting eastern religion and customs. For the past century a semi-religious, prophetic literature had circulated, promising an eastern savior (sometimes identified as a woman) who would draw Greece and Rome into harmony, or even crush and enslave Rome. Now every appeal was made to Roman xenophobia and fears of the east to break down Antony's heroic reputation. Antony evened the accusations: Octavian had been born of an undistinguished father; he had been cowardly and incompetent in the wars won by his associates; he had broken every pledge; he too lived in rampant immorality and played the role of Apollo. In the verbal barrages Octavian had the one great advantage: he was present in Rome, attuned to and able to manipulate the hopes and fears of the people.[31]

Antony's popularity, notwithstanding, continued little diminished, particularly among the upper classes. The wars and proscriptions had decimated the ranks of the old families; natural mortality ended the careers of men like Ventidius, and some leaders like Pollio refused further political involvement; the Senate, enlarged by Caesar, had to be replenished with still more new families without traditional ties to the republican past. But, despite the changes, those who had been politically aware during the years since Caesar's assassination judged Antony as less Caesarian, more compatible with ancient liberties than Octavian. Many such men remained in Rome; a surprising number were with Antony in the east. Some had held civil or military office in the east; some had been Pompeians who sought sanctuary with Antony against the vindictive Octavian.

A list of a few representative names is instructive. Gnaeus Domitius Ahenobarbus, staunch republican nephew of Cato, who had brought his fleet to Antony outside Brundisium, remained Antony's close confidant, so intimate that his son was betrothed to Antony's elder daughter by Octavia. Grandson of Cato and intensely republican was Lucius Calpurnius Bibulus, who was serving Antony as governor of Syria when he died there in 32 B.C. The close relatives of Sextus Pompey—Lucius Scribonius, Marcus Aemilius Scaurus, and Gnaeus Cornelius Cinna (who all bore distinguished patrician names)—joined Antony. From the triumviral camp, Gaius Furnius, who had commanded the army against Sextus, was Antony's governor in Asia in 35 B.C. Especially close to Antony were Quintus Dellius, dextrous as Antony's confidential agent in delicate missions, Marcus Titius, proconsul and consul-designate, and his uncle Lucius Munatius Plancus, governor of Syria, in charge of Antony's seal ring and correspondence, and with hopes of assuming power after Antony. Few patrician clans were not represented at Alexandria—although family prudence sometimes placed sons under both Antony and Octavian for protection against either victor. Admittedly, the various factions and the selfish calculations diluted the loyalty of some, leaving uncertain the cohesiveness of Antony's camp when real challenge threatened.[32]

Among the plebeians, personal loyalty was more likely to count than political affiliations. Thousands of veterans who had fought under Antony swore by him even after they were settled on veteran land holdings in Italy. The many clients of the Antonian house were mindful of their traditional obligations. And widely over Italy, Antony could still count on sympathy and support. It was typical of his secure position that a loyal correspondent over the years was Atticus, devoted to Cicero but a prudent friend to all in power, and that when Atticus's daughter married Agrippa, Antony served as *conciliator*.[33]

For the decade since Philippi, Octavian had been shrewdly appraising every weakness in his own position and utilizing every means to strengthen it. His early seizures of powers and the proscriptions, in which Octavian had seemed the most vindictive of the triumvirs, had engendered fear, especially in Rome. The upper classes, in particular, recognized that Octavian was more unscrupulous and dangerous than Antony, whom they trusted as an aristocrat of known ability and integrity. The settling of 100,000 impatient veterans of Philippi onto Italian lands had often caused severe hardships for the farmers whose lands were arbitrarily expropriated. Soldiers, whose hopes exceeded realities, were dissatisfied enough to be restless, and even to mutiny in 36 and 35 B.C.; Octavian had to balance judiciously between severity and generosity to try to keep their loyalty. The ready solution of sending some of the unreliable legions east to Antony he had to reject lest Antony's power increase. So Octavian faced a formidable array of hostilities and dangers from the army and the people.[34]

Yet Octavian was successful. The veterans gradually settled into civilian life, and the legions increasingly looked to Octavian for securities and bounties. The battles against Sextus Pompey had been won only after major setbacks and only through the skill of Agrippa and other subordinates. But they had been won, and the subordinates had dutifully stood aside to give Octavian credit for the victory. In 35–33 B.C. Octavian had launched border wars against Illyrian tribes that had been ravaging the Adriatic coast. His attack was trumpeted as a campaign to safeguard Italy and Macedonia from raids and to regain border lands lost during the civil wars. Octavian's real goals were furbishing his undistinguished military record, keeping his legions active so that they would be in fighting trim and discipline, and having an excuse not to send east the 20,000 troops he owed Antony. Octavian had calculated well. The action was hard but not major. Supported by able friends, Octavian led the army himself and even was wounded several times so that he could take full credit and receive a triumph for the campaign. The fighting was a cleaning-up operation rather than a conquest. Antony's threat in the east kept Octavian from committing himself wholly against the barbarians. Still, the troubled frontier was stabilized, and the legionary eagles lost to the tribes during Gabinius's dismal campaign in 48 B.C. were recovered. The contrast with Antony's failure to regain the eagles from the Parthians was noted.[35]

The civilians needed other assurances than more military action. After the violence of Perusia was quieted, Octavian assumed within Italy a pose of gravity and constitutionality. The bloody retaliations and rapacity toward opponents of the civil wars were discreetly covered over. Octavian's personal life with Livia in a modest home became decorous. He cultivated the aristocrats who favored Antony, so that a number of leaders turned to him or shrewdly placed relatives into both camps as a guarantee of backing the winner. Meanwhile, Octavian built up an enlarged Senate of new men dependent on him for their sudden patrician status. The common citizens were grateful for the sure supply of bread when Sextus Pompey's piracy on grain ships had been halted. The petty brigandage which terrified travelers and property owners was quieted by an efficient police force. Taxes decreased; some debts of private individuals to the state were even canceled. Agriculture and business flourished in the order Octavian had restored after the civil wars. Public works like baths, theaters, and temples relieved some of the unemployment of the veterans and displaced farmers who had drifted to Rome. His friends like Maecenas contributed to these public works. Agrippa, who had already been consul and spent time settling affairs in Gaul, generously acted as aedile in 33 B.C., repairing public buildings, water pipes, and other needs of the city. Although Octavian was the master of the state, he was creating the illusion of being the solicitous head of a vast family.[36]

Octavian's pose, much like Antony's pose in the east, indeed influenced by it, was that of both a traditional republican official and the more-than-human son of the divine Julius. In the one role he spoke of Roman and Italian rule over the Mediterranean. He held regular political offices like the consulship for 33 B.C. Admittedly, he was granted exceptional powers like the sacrosanctity of a tribune without holding the office; but Caesar had already set the precedents, and the powers were couched in republican terms. He played up traditional Roman practices, like the triumphs in Rome, which Antony seemed to be flouting. He encouraged all aspects of the traditional Italian religion and rites, filled the traditional priesthoods, and acted as augur. He himself accepted their Greek counterparts. But the Asiatic and Egyptian religions in which Antony was taking part were ostentatiously banned as hostile and licentious. Through Agrippa's acts, he won popular support by expelling from Rome the eastern astrologers and magicians who told strange prophecies of Rome's downfall and the dominion of the east under a promised Messiah. Octavian patronized the historians and poets who heralded ancient Roman virtues and glories. His catchword was "liberty," and he spoke of reestablishing the republic once the Parthian menace had been overcome. He built or beautified state buildings and temples. However illusory the freedom and security, Italy seemed to be consolidating and stabilizing in patterns that little offended ancestral ways.

At the same time, partly to counter Antony's deification in the east, Octavian also stressed his sonship to the god Caesar. He constructed the temple to Caesar which the people had voted in 42 B.C. By 40 B.C. he was using the title Son of the God, and the coins issued to celebrate his victories and honors bore the legend "*Impe-*

rator Caesar divi filius." More, he was now taking the praenomen imperator, a title name which an obsequious Senate had, in 45 B.C., voted to Caesar and his heirs. Simultaneously, Octavian encouraged the belief that he was Apollo's son and under his patronage. In 36 B.C. he dedicated a temple to Apollo on the Palatine. The duality of his claims troubled no one in a polytheistic age. Indeed, Antony was likewise playing the dual role of Dionysus and Heracles; and Octavian was pointedly contrasting the pure and intellectual Apollo with the primitive, orgiastic aspects of Dionysus. The statue of Octavian, like that of Caesar, was set up with the city gods in local shrines. And although Octavian stopped short of acting the part of a god himself, as Antony did in the east, he abstained only because western peoples were more reluctant than eastern peoples to hail men as gods.[37]

Real freedom, then, was gone in Italy; but security seemed more precious than freedom. Octavian ruled benignly and was surrounded by able, loyal men who served the state well. Maecenas, his diplomat, remained an equestrian, thus winning the support of the wealthy trading classes, and contributed munificently to the beautification of Rome. Agrippa, Octavian's superb general, could defeat Sextus Pompey, serve as a competent governor stabilizing Gaul, and be elected aedile in 34-33 B.C. to take responsibilities for repairing Rome's reservoirs, aqueducts, and baths. Such men and their followers were handsomely rewarded with honors, booty, prestigious marriage alliances. But other Romans also were prospering with offices and land and business ventures. Fears, pressures, inequalities, and illegalities were still widespread; but people generally came to accept the system that promised peace and order under Octavian and looked with increasing dread at the threat from Antony's eastern forces.[38]

Until 33 B.C., then, the match between Antony and Octavian seemed drawn; and astute men were found in both camps. In actuality, Octavian's scale was steadily being weighted by his skills in administration and in propaganda, while Antony's image and effectiveness were lessening. By January 1, 33 B.C., Octavian was confident enough to make an overt attack on Antony in the Senate. By the end of 33 B.C., he was cutting all ties with Antony.

The triumvirate, which had been renewed in Tarentum in 37 B.C., was due to expire December 31, 33 B.C. Octavian declared the alliance over and ceased to use the title triumvir. Antony, who had regularly issued coins in the name of the triumvirate and had been more faithful to their agreements than Octavian, continued to use the title. He did, however, propose in a letter to the Senate that he was willing to disband the triumvirate if the traditional constitution were restored. In practice, the discarding of the triumvirate was not of great consequence. Antony had the *imperium* in the east. Octavian had no office for 32 B.C. but would be consul in 31 B.C., and although he tried to maintain republican forms to win public favor, he was strong enough to assume a proconsular *imperium* at will.[39]

For 32 B.C., Antony's adherents, Gnaeus Domitius Ahenobarbus and Gaius Sosius, entered into the consulate to which the triumvirs had assigned them in the 37 B.C. distribution of offices. Antony counted on them as his spokesmen to explain his conquests, donations, and other policies to the Senate. Ahenobarbus, who was in charge in January, read the temper of the city as so hostile that Antony's case would not have a fair hearing, and remained silent. In February the more impetuous Sosius was in charge and attacked Octavian vehemently in a Senate speech. Octavian had anticipated the attack and absented himself from Rome; but a tribune, playing the role for Octavian that Antony had played for Caesar before the Rubicon, vetoed proposed legislation against Octavian.[40]

A few days later, without pretense of legality, Octavian surrounded the Senate with an armed guard and denounced Antony. The Senate was helpless in the face of the military threat. The 2 consuls and 300 senators fled Rome to join Antony in the east. It was a striking declaration of Octavian's illegality and of the Senate's commitment to the more moderate Antony. Granted that Octavian could claim to represent the republic because 700 senators remained; still, these included the neutral, the undecided, the trimmers, and the frightened. The senators in Alexandria met under the legitimate consuls Sosius and Ahenobarbus and claimed to be the true Senate. The claim would be hard to disprove—although it was a serious question whether the Senate could sit anywhere except in Rome. At Rome, Octavian handpicked two friends as the new consuls.[41]

206

A casualty of Octavian's diatribe against Antony and the hostilities between them was Antony's marriage to Octavia. It had been a dynastic marriage from the start, and Octavia's forebearance had made it serve this function miraculously well. Time after time she had mediated between her brother and her husband to lead them to a compromise. In the face of Octavian's disapproval, Octavia had remained loyal and faithful to Antony. She had borne him two daughters in their happier days in Athens. Even when Antony's liaison, then bigamous marriage, with Cleopatra was public scandal, Octavia, disregarding her brother's urging, had remained in Antony's house in Rome, welcoming his friends and caring for his two sons by Fulvia as devotedly as for her own two daughters by him. To her, as to Livia, Octavian granted many honors, such as the sacrosanctity of the Vestal Virgins and tribunes. Her unquestioned and uncomplaining virtue won the sympathy of the people and therefore their censure for Antony.[42]

In early summer 32 B.C., as preparations accelerated for war against Octavian, Antony formally divorced Octavia, and she left Antony's house. She took all of Antony's children with her, except his eldest son, Antyllus, who was with his father. Octavia's plight provided her brother with a propaganda weapon in the west. Even in the east, the Romans who had gathered around Antony were dismayed, for Octavia's sake and because Cleopatra's influence was so greatly enhanced. For some senators, the divorce was the decisive factor that made them desert the camp of Antony.[43]

Two long-term adherents who now left Antony were the consulars Lucius Munatius Plancus and his nephew Marcus Titius. Plancus, especially, was known to be obsequious at the Alexandrian court, but his financial manipulations had recently lost Antony's esteem. Now, eager to buy favor with Octavian, they told of Antony's will, for which they had served as witnesses and which had been placed in the safekeeping of the Vestal Virgins at Rome. Octavian seized the will from the Virgins—forcibly, illegally, even sacrilegiously. Only Octavian saw the original will—assuming that there was such a will. What Rome saw was what Octavian chose to publish, and it should be held suspect. According to Octavian's account, Antony willed much of his property to Cleopatra and to his children by her. He also asked to be buried beside Cleopatra in

Alexandria. It is doubtful that the Donations of Alexandria were included, since they had already been granted. The legal problem was that because Cleopatra and her children were not Roman citizens, not only was the marriage invalid and the births illegitimate, but they could not inherit Roman property. Antony knew Roman law too well to have blundered so clumsily, particularly when he was placing the will in the Roman custody of the Vestal Virgins. A possible explanation is that Antony made some provision for his Egyptian children in a will which gave at least his Italian property to his children by his Roman wives.[44]

Despite Octavian's inveighing, the people seem generally to have been incredulous or indifferent to most of the provisions of the will. What distressed them most was Antony's desire to be buried in Alexandria. Beyond representing Antony's dereliction in patriotism, the choice of Egyptian soil seemed to threaten the very shift of the center of empire to the east. The baleful influence of Cleopatra, which had thus distorted Antony's loyalty, challenged the well-being of all Rome.[45]

Octavian judged that public sentiments and fears were sufficiently roused against Cleopatra, but not against the still popular Antony. In late 32 B.C. war was formally declared against Cleopatra. The Senate was reluctant to endanger the patricians in Antony's camp; and Octavian did not trust his popularity enough to include Antony in the declaration. Rather than a threat to Rome (which the people would not believe), Antony was treated as a mere tool of Cleopatra. His *imperium* was recalled; his assured election to the consulate in 31 B.C. was annulled. Any power that Antony had granted Cleopatra was to be withdrawn as the product of an irrational act. Thus Octavian adroitly avoided forcing the people's choice between himself and his rival or appearing to revive the dreaded civil wars. But it was against Antony's generalship that the military strategy had to be drawn.[46]

XIII

The Lion at Bay

The declaration of war against Cleopatra merely formalized a readying for battle which had been under way for over a year. The preparations had included the mobilizing of armies, the organizing of supplies, and the winning of supporters, both Roman and foreign. Whatever the pretense of war against Cleopatra, and Octavian's claim that he was championing the west against the east, this was again a civil war of Romans, aided by foreign supporters.

Octavian held no regular public office in 32 B.C. What he did orchestrate, however, was an unprecedented and even unconstitutional oath of allegiance, not to the state but to himself personally. Agents circulated through the army, through the towns of Italy, through the western provinces, accepting an oath akin to the one that soldiers normally swore to their commanders. Allegiance swelled when whole towns or regiments pledged a common oath. Clearly, Octavian had won widespread loyalty by good administration and by settling the veterans peacefully. He had also succeeded in his propaganda campaign: that the wanton Egyptian queen sought to enslave all Rome as she had Antony. Particularly the wealthy classes judged Octavian the better hope for stability and security and perhaps for more lucrative contracts in the east than Antony had provided. Some senators, like Titius, Plancus, and Lucius Pinarius Scarpus, the nephew of Caesar, were shifting from

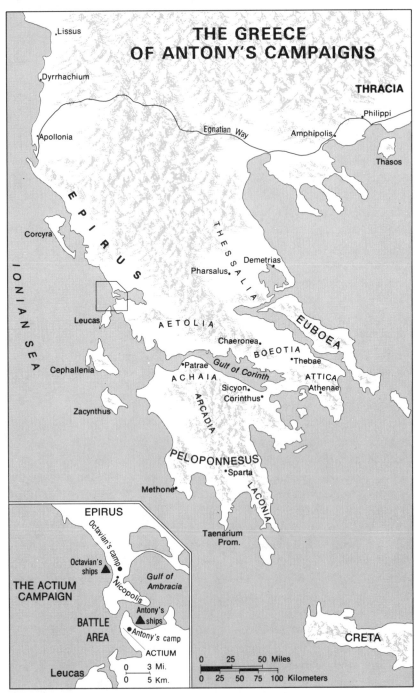

THE GREECE
OF ANTONY'S CAMPAIGNS

Lissus

Dyrrhachium

THRACIA

Philippi

Apollonia

Egnatian Way

Amphipolis

Thasos

E P I R U S

Corcyra

T H E S S A L I A

Demetrias

Pharsalus

I O N I A N   S E A

Leucas

A E T O L I A

EUBOEA

Chaeronea

BOEOTIA

Cephallenia

Patrae   Gulf of Corinth

Thebae

A C H A I A

ATTICA

Sicyon

Athenae

Corinthus

Zacynthus

ARCADIA

PELOPONNESUS

Sparta

Methone

LACONIA

Taenarium
Prom.

THE ACTIUM CAMPAIGN

EPIRUS

Octavian's camp

Octavian's
ships

Gulf of
Ambracia

Nicopolis

THE ACTIUM
CAMPAIGN

Antony's
ships

BATTLE
AREA

Antony's camp

ACTIUM

CRETA

Leucas

| 0 | 3 Mi. |
| 0 | 5 Km. |

| 0 | 25 | 50 Miles |
| 0 | 25 | 50 | 75 | 100 Kilometers |

Antony's camp. And some of the eastern rulers, like the kings of Paphlagonia and Galatia, and the lord of Mysia, were also defecting to Octavian as probable victor. When Octavian joined the army mobilizing at Brundisium, he was accompanied by an impressive retinue of the well-born and wealthy.[1]

Western allegiance to Octavian was far from unanimous, however. Antony had friends, clients, veterans who remained loyal. To counter Octavian's literary propagandists and agents with bribes, he subsidized his own spokesmen; and, for whatever inducements, many swore their oaths of allegiance to Antony. Bononia's people were hereditary clients of Antony, so Octavian had exempted them from his oath. But later they, as well as the people of a number of other towns who swore to Antony, were punished for such loyalty. The chief opposition to Octavian, however, arose from resentment at taxes now increased for the war preparations. Oaths of allegiance rarely opened purses. Romans were not accustomed to being taxed; provincials usually supplied the monies needed. Now Octavian had to impose a 25 percent income tax on free men. Additionally, prosperous freedmen worth 50,000 denarii (roughly equivalent to $15,000) had to pay a 12½ percent capital levy (c. $2,000). Revolts resulted, involving even arson and murders, until the army was called out to restore order.[2]

Octavian had been mobilizing a major army for the war. Ancient sources, as usual, do not make clear precisely how large it was or who composed it. But Octavian reportedly had commanded forty-five legions (c. 270,000 men) in 36 B.C. and had been recruiting steadily since, even among Antony's veterans in Italy. The trusted Maecenas was left with some troops to keep order in Rome and Italy, and to defend the Italian coastline. Other soldiers were stationed under leaders loyal to Octavian in the western provinces, so that no revolts would harass Octavian's rear. But perhaps 80,000 infantry gathered at Brundisium and Tarentum, prepared to cross the Adriatic to the Greek shore. In 31 B.C. Octavian commanded as consul for the third time.[3]

At Ephesus Antony and Cleopatra spent the winter of 33–32 B.C. gathering and stationing forces throughout the east. The navy needed to be enlarged since Octavian's forces had to cross the Adriatic, and all the eastern Mediterranean might prove to be the battle area. Cleopatra supplied about a quarter of the 800 ships needed, as well as their rowers. Others were being brought from various eastern ports. Nevertheless, a building program was undertaken, so vast and urgent that by 32 B.C. Antony's admiral had to order the Coan cyprus groves sacred to Asclepius cut down for the timber needed to build ships. In keeping with Hellenistic navies, Antony had some ships larger than usual Italian craft and had them bound with iron to prevent damage by ramming.[4]

The main army, which had fought under Antony against the Parthians and Armenians, had been stationed under Canidius Crassus in Armenia to control the area. In November, 33 B.C., despite the dangers of revolt within the new province, Antony ordered the sixteen legions to march to Ephesus, leaving the client king Polemo of Pontus to guard the Armenian frontier. Seven legions were also called from Macedonia. Still more legions and auxilia were being recruited.[5]

Italian troops were the regular bases for the Roman legions, indeed, were judged indispensable. But because Octavian had blocked Antony's recruiting in Italy since 39 B.C., fresh recruits could come only from the east. Some of these were of Italian origins: veterans and sons of veterans or traders who had settled in the east; but most had to be non-Italians. Many came from client kingdoms loyal to Antony. Despite imprecision in the ancient sources, it seems reasonable to estimate that about 60,000 Italians, 50,000 non-Italians were mobilized by Antony. Since about a third of the troops, the less battle-worthy legions, had to remain guarding Egypt, Syria, Macedonia, and Cyrenaica, Antony's active command was probably nineteen legions plus auxilia from the client kings.[6]

Despite the usual Roman sense of superiority to other peoples, these native troops were certainly as able fighters as the Italians, though they had to be drilled thoroughly in Roman fighting techniques. Less sure was the depth of their loyalty to a Roman general in intra-Roman power struggles, especially when the generals with military priorities commandeered men, supplies, and monies, and disrupted normal economic production and trade until the provinces, already exhausted by exactions for the Parthian wars, staggered under the economic distress. Antony therefore had to make careful readjustments in the eastern client states. Some kings,

such as Polemo of Pontus and Mithridates of Commagene, sent troops and were rated as loyal allies. Others, like the Dacian king Cotiso, although courted by both sides, joined Antony. Some, like the Median king, were loyal to Octavian. Herod of Judaea, Antony's most loyal ally since his reign depended so totally on Roman support, was unwillingly removed from Antony's councils. He did send money and supplies and was prepared to lead his troops for Antony; but Cleopatra, still jealous and hostile over Palestinian lands, persuaded Antony to send Herod and his troops south against the Nabataean Arabs, who were delinquent in their payments to her. It was a foolish disposition of critically needed forces. But Cleopatra's enmity ultimately saved her foe. Herod was still in remote Arabia when the final battles with Octavian were fought; so he could subsequently appeal to Octavian for clemency as a client king who had not warred against him.[7]

The opposition between Cleopatra and Herod was representative of the stresses and strains troubling Antony's camp. The various factions among his followers were gradually coalescing into two main positions: opposing or supporting Cleopatra. The 2 consuls and the 300 senators who had fled to Antony after Octavian's armed intimidation of the Senate were the ardent republicans, the heirs of Cato, Pompey, and the tyrannicides, who viewed Antony as the last hope for replacing Rome's repeated dictatorships with constitutional government. Their concern was in the west, their means the traditional Roman legions. Gnaeus Domitius Ahenobarbus, loyal counselor to Antony since his fleet had joined Antony's at Brundisium, disdained even to call Cleopatra queen. The other faction, including such Romans as Canidius Crassus and Munatius Plancus, acknowledged her indispensable power and her ability, flattered her, and took seriously her policy of securing a strong eastern empire based in Egypt. Her enemies charged her supporters with being bribed and advised Antony to be rid of her. Herod bluntly urged her murder and the annexation of Egypt. But Antony was growing steadily more dependent on Cleopatra, militarily and emotionally. Cleopatra, who was supplying much of the wealth and naval force for the expedition, was determined to protect her Egyptian lands and sustain Antony's unsteady ambitions to rule the Roman world. Although she remained with Antony to

the end, her presence was always a storm center, which even Antony must often have wished away.[8]

In spring, 32 B.C., Antony and his supporters began to move west, gathering resources and choosing the final battleground. April was spent on the island of Samos. There was business to transact, but the sources tell us chiefly of the magnificent festivals over which Antony and Cleopatra presided. Artists, especially those dedicated to Dionysus, came from all over the Greek world to participate in Bacchanalian revelry and music, which brightened Antony's boisterous spirits but which were also religious appeals to the god he represented. In the same spirit of license and devotion, he presented the city of Priene to the artists of Dionysus as their official residence; he gave grants of citizenship and freedom from military service to chosen individuals; and he gave three great statues of Zeus, Athena, and Heracles done by Myron, in the temple of Hera at Samos, to Cleopatra. The fetes were luxurious and extravagant, the more so because the coins minted for the legions were now being debased.[9]

In May Antony's retinue crossed the Ionian Sea to Athens. It was from Athens that Antony sent Octavia notice of divorce, testimony to the overt break with her brother, but evidence, too, of Cleopatra's triumph over her marital rival. Athens had greatly honored Octavia as Athena Polias when Antony had brought her there as his bride. Now Cleopatra demanded similar distinctions. After the war the Athenians would lose territory for supporting Antony, but now the pliant Athenians welcomed the goddess Isis into their city. Not everyone could adapt so readily. Plancus and Titius, increasingly hostile to Cleopatra and calculating the dangers of Antony's defeat, now defected to Octavian, winning his forgiveness by revealing the will that Antony had deposited with the Vestal Virgins. For every accusation that Octavian made on the basis of the will, Antony lashed back with ugly charges. The propaganda war raged on, using harshest invective and producing prodigies and other religious signs to terrify the credulous. For both camps, the struggle could win the support of loyal troops as well as the civilian population.[10]

In Antony's headquarters a different, more urgent struggle was under way. Councils about the strategy of the war and the role of

Cleopatra in it were ever more bitterly divided. The consuls and senators who had fled to Antony and acted as a Senate to give Antony the aura of respectability expected to be heard; but even they proffered conflicting advice. The republicans urged a swift invasion of Italy while Octavian was unprepared and while widespread support for Antony could be won among the people, since Antony still claimed the consulship which Octavian had refused him and he had used bribes widely to win support. Antony's legions would fight best when their homes and Italian lands were the prizes. Antony's preeminence as an army general would have full play in Italy.[11]

The obstacle to this plan was Cleopatra. If the queen of Egypt, the goddess Isis, the eastern paramour of Antony, landed on Italian shores with Antony, all Italy would rally against them. The republicans urged that Antony be rid of her. But he would not; and he reasoned that he could not. It would be hard to attack Italy from Greece since its eastern coast had few adequate harbors. Cleopatra's 200 manned ships were needed for any invasion of Italy. Equally critical were her reserve wealth of 20,000 talents and the supplies that she had brought. Some of the Roman generals, like Canidius Crassus, argued that her contributions were indispensable. But most of the Romans were so hostile that Cleopatra feared that if Antony returned to Italy without her, she would lose not only her lover but also the plans for an Egyptian Empire which had been launched with the Donations of Alexandria. For her hopes, even victory over Octavian would be defeat if Antony's focus of interest shifted from Alexandria to Rome. Therefore, Cleopatra maneuvered to keep Antony surrounded by Egyptians, cut off from his Roman advisers. Her machinations drove an increasing number of leaders and even the troops to desertion: Romans such as Sallustius Crispus, grandnephew of the historian Sallust, left. Even some of the client kings were defecting. Most of these men had made prudent shifts of loyalty before; their departure signaled loss of faith in Antony's victory.[12]

Cleopatra succeeded; the Italian invasion plans were discarded. Then western Greece was judged to have advantages as the battleground. The battles of Pharsalus and Philippi had been fought there chiefly because Greece represented the break between the resources and forces of the west and the east. It was, indeed, Antony's westernmost area of command, where he could legitimately station an army and against which Octavian's attack would constitute illegality. Pompey and Brutus and Cassius had fought in Macedonia in the north, where control over the Egnatian Way, the main overland route, meant access to supply areas. Allies, like King Cotiso of the Dacians who could aid from the north, urged this position now. Antony, however, pitched his winter camp in the Peloponnesus. His critical supply routes were by sea to Egypt. Well supplied by Egypt's granaries, he could wait out Octavian's attack, for which men and materiel had to be brought across a longer passage on the often turbulent Adriatic.

From Athens, Antony had brought his army to the western Greek island of Corcyra. In September or October, 32 B.C., the men established winter quarters at Patrae on the Gulf of Corinth. In the spring they moved to Actium, the south shore of the entrance to the Gulf of Ambracia, a superb harbor for the fleet. Strategy included cutting off Octavian's attack and keeping supply lines open to Egypt. Therefore, ships and men were stationed on the islands and coastline of western Greece, from Corcyra south to Methone, the westernmost point of the southern Peloponnesus, which controlled the passage around it. Crete and Cyrenaica completed the supply line secured to Egypt. The land army now included 19 legions of approximately 60,000 Italians, 15,000 light-armed Asiatics, plus 12,000 cavalry. The navy had over 500 manned warships. Antony, imperator for the fourth time, claiming the consulship for the third time—although Octavian's other consuls were actually in office—seemed strongly positioned.[13]

Octavian, however, had some critical advantages and the daring to use them. His army and navy were slightly stronger than Antony's: a likely estimate is 75,000 legionnaires, 25,000 light-armed, 12,000 cavalry, over 400 warships. His officers were united behind him. His admiral was Agrippa, who had already proved his naval genius against Sextus Pompey. While Antony prepared his defense, Octavian initiated the offensive.[14]

In early spring, 31 B.C., Agrippa, with half Octavian's fleet, broke Antony's lifeline to Egyptian supplies by capturing Methone, Antony's southernmost harbor in Greece. Octavian then crossed the Adriatic to the north, landing his army in Epirus but marching south swiftly in an attempt to catch Antony unprepared. Failing in that hope, Octavian fortified a high position and secured for his fleet an adequate harbor north of the entrance to the Gulf of Ambracia and opposite Antony's camp at Actium on the southern point.[15]

While Octavian thus immobilized Antony's main army and locked his navy into the gulf, Agrippa seized critical positions along Antony's supply line. The island of Leucas, which was southwest of Actium and along which Antony's ships bound for Egypt had to sail, was seized. Then Corcyra, Patrae, and Corinth, which secured the Gulf of Corinth and access to the Peloponnesus, were taken. Octavian dominated the Egnatian roadway to the north. With startling swiftness, Antony had lost the whole superiority of Egyptian granaries and had been reduced to foraging supplies from impoverished northern Greece for his vast host. Plutarch recounts his great-grandfather's tale how the people of Chaeronea in Boeotia, goaded by whips, were forced to carry their meager supplies to Antony's camp. Antony crossed to the northern shore, trying to provoke Octavian to fight, but Octavian would not be lured from his safe heights. Next Antony tried twice to encircle Octavian and cut off his limited water sources. When these efforts failed, Antony withdrew again to Actium, essentially besieged.[16]

The distresses of siege beset the camp. Widespread disease, malaria or dysentery, resulted from the brackish water. Food grew scarcer. The coinage issued to pay the troops—portraying Antony as consul for 31 B.C. and Cleopatra as goddess, *Cleopatra Thea neotera*—was increasingly debased. By August, Antony tried to break the blockade by sending an army north under the joint command of Dellius and Amyntas, king of Galatia, which he followed with another contingent, while the fleet tried to break out of the Gulf of Ambracia. The effort was disastrously aborted. Amyntas, now free of Actium and in command of 2,000 crack Galatian cavalry, deserted to Octavian. So, too, did Dellius, the courtier and historian who had written an account of the Median invasion and who had in former years acted as diplomatic agent between Antony and Cleopatra. He brought as his pledge to Octavian a full account of Antony's problems and plans.[17]

Desertions were now so common that the legions and ships were undermanned, and sailors had to be impressed throughout Greece. Antony was driven to execute as examples the king of Emesa (Hemesa) and a Roman senator who were caught while fleeing. The most painful desertion for Antony was that of Domitius Ahenobarbus, for years his most trusted counselor. Ahenobarbus had opposed Cleopatra's influence so intractably that the republicans had even offered to follow him in place of Antony; but Ahenobarbus had refused the command. Now, critically ill but despairing of Antony as a republican leader, he left for Octavian's camp. Antony sneered that he had changed sides to be with his mistress; then, with a typical gesture of bravado but also of generous friendship, Antony sent his possessions, servants, and friends to the dying man.[18]

Escape from the rapidly worsening situation was imperative. Disagreements were only over means. The Romans, trusting the legions and Antony as general, argued that their army could cut its way overland into Macedonia, thence to Asia, Syria, and Egypt. Cleopatra still trusted the sea and was unwilling to desert her rowers and burn her fleet. She argued that if Egypt were secured, new legions could be raised throughout the east. Let Octavian hold the west, provided they were secure in the east. Antony, no longer trusting either the army or the navy or, perhaps, his own leadership, accepted the Egyptian plan, realizing that the fight by sea was needed to enable the land forces to escape.

Canidius Crassus, who had brought the legions out of Armenia, was given charge of about 50,000 men to march inland to Macedonia, thence to Asia and Egypt, if the sea battle were lost. Antony took charge of the fleet, realizing fully his inexperience at sea and the attrition his navy had suffered from disease and desertion. Indeed, despite the impressment of Greek sailors, he had more ships than rowers and burned the craft he could not man. He was left with about 230 ships to Octavian's 400 ships, although Antony's ships on the average were larger and well reinforced with metal braces against ramming. In the face of the odds, Antony's objective was not a fight to victory but successful flight. Sails and tackle were added to the ships, awkward for naval maneuver but appropriate for swift flight. To the dismayed crews they were explained as needed to pursue retreating ships. The treasure, necessary for any future struggle, was loaded on Cleopatra's flagship, the *Antonia*, which commanded a squadron of sixty warships. The sailors and the 20,000 legionnaires and 2,000 archers and slingers manning the ships were exhorted to fight. They read the preparations as those for flight and lost all heart for the battle.[19]

The morning of September 2, 31 B.C., was fine. Antony's fleet sailed from its harbor and stretched in a long north-south line. The strongest squadrons were on the wings; Antony was in charge of the best three squadrons on the right. The center of the line was weaker, but behind it lay Cleopatra and her squadron of sixty ships. Octavian's fleet formed an opposing line. Its left wing, under the admiral Agrippa, faced Antony. Octavian did not command a sector; but on a swift Liburnian ship, he was visible to his men as a focus of morale. The two land armies, drawn up along the shores, waited and watched. For some hours the ships delayed. In the afternoon the regular northwest wind rose. Now Antony moved out, lengthening his line, drawing Agrippa into a matching movement, so that both lines grew longer and the centers thinner and weaker.[20]

Two explanations are proposed for the maneuver. If Antony intended to fight for victory by outflanking Agrippa's ships, he could turn the line, forcing it back to land where Octavian would be besieged by Antony's ships holding the waterways; thus Octavian would have to fight by land and at a disadvantage. The other explanation is that Antony's prime objective was always flight. He waited for the favoring afternoon breeze from the northwest to take him south beyond the island of Leucas. Once in the open sea, he could use the sails to speed the fleet toward Egypt. Still more important, Antony was pulling the already weak centers even thinner so that Cleopatra and her squadron of sixty ships placed behind the center could break free and run toward Egypt. Perhaps Antony was alert for the opportunities of turning Agrippa's flank. But his conduct indicates that his main objective was to enable Cleopatra with her treasure to escape the blockade, then to follow her with the maximum number of his ships. Not unlike his land retreat from Phraaspa, this was a sea retreat from an untenable position undertaken to minimize losses.[21]

In the action, Antony's right wing was unable to outflank Agrippa's line. Rather, Agrippa broke and scattered Antony's line; as the individual ships rammed and grappled, Agrippa's greater numbers prevailed. Twelve Antonian ships were captured, including Antony's huge flagship. He himself escaped on a lighter ship. While Antony's right wing fought valiantly against the odds, although getting the worse of it, the center and left wing were also engaged. About mid-afternoon, when the northwest breeze was at its strongest, Cleopatra's sixty ships, which had waited passively behind the line of action, sailed through the weakened center and fled toward Egypt. Antony was now free to follow with what ships he could save. About forty of his right wing escaped with him.[22]

The other ships were trapped, fought savagely for a time, then, turning toward shore, surrendered to Octavian. Notwithstanding, fragments of battle persisted until dark, and Octavian remained on board all night, patrolling to cut off any remaining ships still fleeing to join Antony. Surrender lessened the casualties. Fifteen ships and 5,000 of Antony's men were lost. Agrippa used part of the surrendered fleet as a naval police force; but Octavian burned most of the ships, saving only the metal beaks to display on Caesar's temple at Rome.[23]

The battle of Actium, then, although decisive politically in determining that Octavian would rule the Roman Empire, was not a major military action. Only in the later accounts written to glorify the victor Octavian was the tale colored and magnified to heroic stature. In these accounts Cleopatra, then Antony under her baleful influence, deserted their men, casting aside honor for selfishness and lust. A less emotional analysis argues that Octavian's victories occurred earlier when Agrippa cut Antony's supply lines to Egypt and put Antony under a virtual siege. At Actium Antony had broken out and, against considerable odds, had saved the Egyptian queen and her treasure, a hundred of their ships, and perhaps 20,000 of his better soldiers. Thus they could mobilize fresh forces and initiate new strategies to control the east.[24]

Such renewed ambitions had to be based on resolute determination, however. Cleopatra was planning the next steps for dominion of the east; but Antony watched with despair the disintegration of his forces. The swift ships with which he had escaped caught up with Cleopatra's squadron, and he got aboard Cleopatra's flagship. A few of Octavian's ships had followed, but only a contingent under Gaius Julius Eurycles, a Spartan, dared actual combat. Eurycles wanted vengeance on Antony, who had executed his father on a charge of robbery, which Eurycles believed to have been a pretense for confiscating his wealth. Antony turned his ships to face the threat. Eurycles captured two vessels, then escaped to safety. Thereafter Antony's fleet sailed unchallenged to Taenarum on the southern tip of the Peloponnesus. During the three days' sail, Antony sat alone at the prow of his ship, brooding about the losses of his men, his ships, his reputation, his career as Caesar's successor to the Roman Empire. As general, he knew the magnitude of his defeat; as man, he was shattered by the disaster. Only while the fleet waited at Taenarum for any stragglers who could still break free from Octavian bringing news of Actium could Cleopatra induce Antony to rejoin her and to plan their next move.[25]

The reports from Actium justified Antony's despair. The land army, intact and powerful, left under the command of Canidius Crassus, had not followed Antony's orders to march north through Greece to Macedonia, thence to Asia and Syria. Instead, the army had marched only a short distance, then spent seven days negotiating a favorable peace settlement with Octavian. The veterans had lost their general and paymaster when Antony sailed south, and they had no reasons of their own to fight. Experienced in the civil wars of the past fifteen years, they knew that Octavian would grant generous concessions to avoid bloody carnage between two massive Roman armies, and even possible defeat. Octavian met their terms: humane treatment, later, veterans' benefits equal to his own army's for all but the special enemies who would be punished.[26]

Most of the legionnaires were then returned to Italy to await Octavian's settlements and donatives. Only Canidius Crassus and the other officers feared Octavian's reprisals and escaped to inform Antony of the army's surrender. Some of the client kings also defected to Octavian. Polemo, Archelaus, Mithridates remained loyal to Antony. Even they, and others already with Antony, could probably win clemency in time. Caesar had set the precedent of generosity to his opponents, and Octavian would profit by a like reputation and by the quieting of hostilities within his state. Therefore,

Antony released any who wished from their promises of loyalty, enriched them generously, and arranged secure hiding for them in Greece until they could safely petition mercy from Octavian.[27]

Octavian, hailed imperator for the sixth time, was playing his role of clement victor well. In Rome the doors of the Temple of Janus—the symbol of peace in the empire—were closed for the third time in Rome's history. Near Actium, Octavian began the establishment of a city, Nicopolis, to commemorate his victory. He thanked Apollo, Neptune, and Mars for his triumph, dedicated ten of Antony's ships to the gods, and in 27 B.C. established a quinquennial festival to honor his patron god Apollo at the new city. Other local Actian games were founded by eager rulers.[28]

In the autumn, after a visit to Athens, Octavian sailed to Samos, until January making it his headquarters to settle the affairs of the east. In less critical states he could afford the luxury of political patronage for his supporters as well as taxes and punishments for his opponents; but generally he was moderate, and in the major states of Cappadocia, Pontus, and Galatia he continued the settlements Antony had made. Most of the eastern leaders, led by the adaptable Herod, hastily assured him of their allegiance. Only a troop of gladiators in training at Cyzicus dared to announce loyalty to Antony and marched across Asia Minor toward Egypt. Amyntas of Galatia, Philopator in Syria, Herod of Judaea, the recent converts to Octavian among the kings, tried to block their passage; but the gladiators got safely to Daphne, near Antioch, where Octavian's governor dared not oppose them. Their determined loyalty was in vain. When they sent word to Antony that they were waiting his leadership to fight for him, Antony, despairing in Egypt, made no reply. With the kings and soldiers, the gladiators gave up their loyalty to Antony.[29]

Still Octavian was not free to follow Antony to Egypt, for troubles had flared in Italy. Maecenas had been in charge in Italy and had succeeded in controlling the troubled land and in suppressing a revolutionary conspiracy under Marcus Lepidus, the son of the triumvir. But, as the discharged veterans began to return home, restless for promised bonuses and land allotments, disorders increased until Octavian sent the general Agrippa to quiet the veterans. In late January Octavian himself had to go to Brundisium, where the carefully staged hero's welcome was disrupted by ugly demonstrations. The soldiers wanted land and money which Octavian did not have. He could expropriate the lands of his enemies, as he and others had done before; but the memories of earlier riots and the Perusine war made him reluctant. He needed Egypt's wealth to compensate owners for lands taken and to pay bounties promised to his troops. Until he held the Ptolemaic treasure, he had to temporize. Lands of communities and individuals who had been overtly loyal to Antony were confiscated and given to Octavian's longest-term veterans. Thus they remained loyal to him; and other soldiers were reassured that their time would come. One-quarter of the exceptional taxes he had levied on freedmen were removed as a token of more tax relief in the future. Such aids were possible because of various expropriations and exactions throughout the east. But the Egyptian treasury remained the full solution to his economic problems. In the spring Octavian returned to Samos and began his march through Asia to Egypt.[30]

Antony knew the reality of Octavian's victory. But for Cleopatra there was still the security of Egypt's frontiers and the glory of Egypt's crown. Taking her treasure and garlanding her ships in a bold pretense of victory, she had sailed to Alexandria. There, before her enemies could learn the truth, she seized the initiative, killed those deemed dangerous to her and those whose wealth was more valuable than their lives, and confiscated their property. Even the wealth of ancient Egyptian temples was seized to finance her resistance or escape. She worked at readying her frightened land for defense but simultaneously planned new bases of operation abroad. Spain with its rich silver mines had been a refuge for defeated Marians and Pompeians for decades. But Antony had few adherents there, and Spaniards, like Italians, would not follow an Egyptian queen. The east was her sphere. She had trade contacts in India. There a new kingdom could be established. She had ships hauled over the Isthmus of Suez, readying a fleet to carry her supporters down the Red Sea to the east. The bold attempt foundered; for Malchus and his Nabataean Arabs, whom Cleopatra had opposed and exploited, now burned the ships. Cleopatra therefore looked not to flight but to defense. Yet she knew that her only real hope was negotiating with Octavian to exchange her wealth for the right to the Ptolemaic throne. There were precedents. Rome had left other rebellious kings or their sons on their thrones. But the messengers she sent to Octavian with this offer replied that Octavian would treat with Cleopatra only when she discarded or destroyed Antony.[31]

Antony was not sharing Cleopatra's planning. He had sailed from Taenarum south to Cyrene, where five legions had been stationed under Lucius Pinarius Scarpus, Caesar's nephew and Antony's legate at Philippi, to protect northeast Africa. The soldiers had turned against Scarpus and were now under Cornelius Gallus, Octavian's man. Like the other legions, they recognized Octavian as the real ruler, even in the east. Their hope of veteran land allotments in Italy lay with the winner. And their loyalty did not lie with Egypt against Rome. Even eastern auxiliaries were reluctant to fight against Rome. Only those who feared for their personal safety under Octavian and those who felt a rare loyalty in friendship remained with Antony. As Antony took stock in the Egyptian port of Paraetonium, his despair was so great that he tried suicide but was balked by two loyal followers. It was a small contingent that sailed with him to Alexandria.[32]

At Alexandria, Antony found Cleopatra feverishly preparing her defenses. More realistic about the magnitude of the defeat at Actium than she, Antony could tolerate no pretenses of hope. Rather, he needed time to face the despair of all his hopes. Covering his need for solitude with a swagger of playing the role of Timon, the ancient Athenian misanthrope, Antony secluded himself in his Timonium, a small house on a mole projecting from the south shore of the Great Harbor, near the lighthouse. For weeks he refused company and comforts. Then his grim desperation shifted to grim abandon. He left the Timonium for the court and Cleopatra. "The Order of Inimitable Livers," renamed "The Diers Together," wined and dined in unprecedented splendor and caroused with the wantonness of despair. With special pomp Caesarion and Antyllus, who had been with his father in Asia and Egypt, were declared adults. Caesarion, aged sixteen, entered the Greek Ephebia, the training corps of young citizens; Antyllus, aged fourteen, received the Roman *toga virilis*. The boys were already condemned by their birth. The title of adult could not increase their danger.[33]

In the spring and summer of 30 B.C., Octavian inexorably advanced on Alexandria. Antony took a fleet of forty ships to Paraetonium in westernmost Egypt to block an attack from Cyrene by Cornelius Gallus. When Gallus trapped most of the fleet, Antony's troops defected. The story is told that Gallus, with trumpet blasts, drowned out Antony's exhortations of loyalty to his troops. But it could have mattered little. The troops knew that Antony had no hopes of victory, and their loyalty was to their own safety.[34]

Octavian came overland through Syria and Judaea where the obsequious Herod had provided his army with supplies. Other client rulers also collaborated. The eastern Egyptian port city of Pelusium fell so easily that there were accusations of treachery against Cleopatra and retaliations against the family of the commander of the city. On July 30 Octavian reached the suburbs of Alexandria. Antony had made no efforts to fortify the city; but on July 31 he challenged Octavian with forty ships and about twenty-three legions of Roman and eastern troops, and waged a propaganda campaign of leaflets promising money to defectors. Antony's ships and many of the infantry deserted after a minor battle; but the cavalry attacked and dispersed Octavian's cavalry. Antony boldly announced and celebrated his last victory.[35]

Legend, based on Octavian's propaganda, has it that during the night the sweet sounds of Bacchanalian revel, beginning at the palace, went through Alexandria and left the city. The god Dionysus had deserted Antony; men need no longer revere him as sacred. On August 1 even the eastern soldiers were hailing Octavian. Antony offered Octavian single combat. Octavian refused to face the aging lion.[36] Nor did he accept the proposal Antony sent by his son Antyllus that if Octavian would spare Cleopatra, Antony would kill himself; nor the several offers of money in return for safety, which Cleopatra sent. Octavian had no need for such concessions. The armies and the day were his. Antony knew it and dreaded to endanger more lives for his own glory. On August 1, for the last time, Antony drew up his infantry and sent out his fleet in a desperate hope. There was no battle. The fleet hailed Octavian and joined his ships. The cavalry followed. An infantry skirmish was lost. In the blackness of his despair, Antony accused even Cleopatra of treachery.[37]

Within Alexandria the resolute Cleopatra was still fighting for the throne of Egypt, for her children if not for herself. Caesarion she now sent with a guard across the desert toward the Red Sea.[38] She was trying to slow the fighting against Octavian and was sending messages to Octavian promising cooperation; his replies were noncommittal but courteous. She knew that her remaining trump card was the wealth of the Ptolemies in precious metals, jewels, ebony, ivory, and spices, since Octavian needed resources to settle his veterans in Italy. Accordingly, she enclosed herself with two handmaidens and a eunuch and all possible portable wealth in a stone mausoleum which she had almost finished building for herself near the tombs of the other Ptolemies. With the wealth she also placed highly inflammable materials, so that Octavian would have to make concessions to gain the wealth intact.[39]

Perhaps her choice of the mausoleum as a refuge made rumor report her death to Antony. Perhaps, as some unkinder sources record, she intentionally deceived him because he was now a liability to her. Antony had already lost his troops and honors. Now he heard that Cleopatra was dead. He ordered his servant Eros to kill him with his sword. The faithful Eros chose to slay himself rather than his master. Shamed that his servant was more ready than he to commit suicide, Antony plunged his sword into his bowels.[40]

The thrust, although mortal, had not yet killed Antony when word came from Cleopatra that he should come to her in the mausoleum. His servants bore him on a stretcher to its barred door. From a window, Cleopatra and her women let down a sling and, straining, drew up the dying Antony. Briefly he counseled Cleopatra to trust only the equestrian Gaius Proculeius in her dealing with Octavian. With sympathetic imagination, Plutarch reports that as he lay dying, Antony told Cleopatra "not to lament him for his last reverses, but to count him happy for the good things that had been his, since he had become the most illustrious of men, had won greatest power, and now had been not ignobly conquered, a Roman by a Roman." Then, to shorten his agony, he asked for wine, and died in Cleopatra's arms. It was the evening of August 1, 30 B.C.[41]

Octavian's men arrived as Antony lay dying. A guard had carried Antony's bloody sword to Octavian, and even while asserting his

innocence to his associates, Octavian ordered the capture of Cleopatra and her treasures. By a ruse of Gaius Proculeius whom Antony had trusted, Octavian's soldiers gained entrance through the
window, seized Cleopatra and her treasure, and restrained her
from following Antony in suicide. On August 3, under guard, she
was allowed to leave the mausoleum to bury Antony with rich
pomp and honors.[42]

Cleopatra had not wholly lost her courageous ambitions. When
Octavian visited her on August 8, she reminded him of her love for
Caesar; she offered to buy the throne for her son with her fortune;
hostile propaganda later added that she even tried to woo the virtuous conqueror. Octavian was courteous and reassuring; but he
had already seized the wealth that was Cleopatra's one hope for
mercy, and he was rapidly gaining control of all Egypt.[43]

On August 9 Cornelius Dolabella sent word to Cleopatra that
Octavian planned to take her to Rome to march in his public triumph. Octavian was behind Dolabella's message, for he needed
Cleopatra's suicide. A woman marched in triumph was more taw-
dry than even the propaganda accounts of the evil eastern menace
would make acceptable. More, this woman had been his adoptive
father's mistress, and her statue stood where Caesar had placed it
in Rome. Even a permanent, remote exile seemed dangerous when
the prisoner was Cleopatra. Octavian carefully lessened the guard
around Cleopatra and instructed them to avoid seeing any suicide
attempts.[44]

Cleopatra had lost all hope of rule, or even of freedom. Her pride
would not let her go to Rome as a prisoner. She visited Antony's
tomb in a final lament and voiced her hope that she might be buried
beside him. Then the queen, with regal courage, took poison or
suffered the bites of poisonous snakes smuggled into her chamber
in a basket of fruit. Her handmaidens followed her in death. Octavian feigned courteous regret and stressed that the suicides were
voluntary. According to their expressed wish, he ordered that Cleopatra be buried beside Antony in the royal tomb that they had
planned.[45]

For eighteen days Cleopatra's children appear in the records as
nominal rulers. On August 29, the Egyptian new year, Octavian
was proclaimed ruler of Egypt, with all the ancient titles and hon-

ors, including divinity. He treated Cleopatra's memory with respect in Egypt where her cult was deeply reverenced, and for centuries her reign was viewed as great. Antony's reputation, however, was designedly debased and his memory formally eradicated. In Alexandria his statues were overthrown. Throughout the Greek cities of the east, the decrees honoring Antony were removed. In Rome Octavian had chosen the son of Cicero the consul suffectus of 30 B.C. as another propaganda blow against Antony. Now the young Cicero had his vengeance for his father's murder by announcing Antony's death. Antony's name had already been erased from the Fasti of Rome, and the Senate decreed that no one should ever again bear the name Marcus Antonius. The dates of the victories at Actium and at Alexandria were recorded as memorable on the state calendar, Antony's birthday as a sinister day, perhaps on the grounds that it had been celebrated in Alexandria. Coins were issued commemorating the victory and peace. And the temple of Apollo on the Palatine, which Octavian had planned after defeating Sextus Pompey, was now completed, honoring the victory at Actium as well.[46]

Octavian proclaimed a policy of clemency toward the supporters of Antony and Cleopatra, but it proved valid only for those whom Octavian saw as no threat. Canidius Crassus, who had been Antony's loyal general in so many campaigns and had been put in charge of Caesarion when Antony died, led the list of the several Antonians killed. Caesarion was slain as he fled toward Arabia. Antyllus, Antony's eldest son, once betrothed to Octavian's daughter, sought sanctuary in the temple of the divine Julius in Alexandria, but the executioners sent by Octavian dragged him from the temple and killed him. The twins and Ptolemy Philadelphus were judged too young to be dangerous and lived to walk with the statue of Cleopatra in Octavian's Roman triumph.[47]

Despite these killings, the policy of clemency brought most of the Antonians to Octavian's camp, and any regrets they felt were duly disguised. A few, chiefly in the east, remained loyal to the memory of Antony. But the Cocceii, the Dellii, Sallustius Crispus, and other patricians became close associates of Octavian. To his camp also came Antony's many eastern clients, officials, and soldiers. Octavian's settlement of the east, therefore, was enormously eased. However harshly his propaganda had condemned conditions in the east before Actium, he now acknowledged the good sense and stability of Antony's eastern arrangements and left all Antony's appointees in power except for a few minor dynasts and officials, whose posts Octavian's supporters could readily fill. The governors of the Roman provinces inevitably rotated to proconsuls named by Octavian. The last of Antony's troops also declared for Octavian and were incorporated into his army and treated with almost equal generosity. With the confiscated Ptolemaic wealth as backing, Octavian was able to provide land for about 75,000 veterans, thus reducing his active army from 70 to 26 legions. Some land was confiscated from Antony's followers in Italy; much of the land was in the provinces. But, despite hardships for a number of individuals, the allotments as a whole were effected with remarkable efficiency and order. Octavian was also able to distribute 1,000 sesterces each to 120,000 men in the colonies. Thus he confirmed the loyalty of the veterans to their new paymaster, who could fulfill at least some of the promises Antony had made.[48]

In Egypt, too, whatever the changes in nomenclature, Octavian was the heir to the governmental policies of Antony and Cleopatra. With the Ptolemies deposed, Octavian was an eastern king in all but title. Although he called Egypt part of the Roman Empire, essentially it was wholly under his control. He alone headed the government, with all the powers, rights, and properties of the Ptolemies. He confiscated the vast palace treasures immediately and took extensive property from individuals. For the remainder of his forty-five-year rule, his enormous wealth and the power derived from it would be drawn in substantial part from Egypt. His tendance was careful. He worked to restore prosperity, which had been neglected during the war preparations: e.g., cleaning the choked canals, repairing roads, and stabilizing the currency. Alexandria was now the second greatest city of the empire, and he governed it generously. He did, however, return to their original owners the art treasures that Antony had drawn from the temples and palaces of the east to enrich the Ptolemaic museum and palace. In his turn, Octavian carried some of the treasures of Egypt to Rome. Near Alexandria he founded another Nicopolis, with quinquennial games to celebrate his victory. There were some restorations of territory.

Cilicia, Crete, Syria, Cyprus, and Cyrene, the lands that Antony had given to Cleopatra, were all again Roman provinces; and Herod received back the Palestinian lands which Cleopatra had gained.[49]

In 29 B.C., after two years in the east, Octavian returned in glory and with the wealth of Egyptian treasure to Rome, declaring that the Roman world at last knew peace, prosperity, and order. The Romans honored him fulsomely. On August 13 through 15 he celebrated three successive triumphs: for Illyricum, for Actium, for Alexandria. Popular enthusiasm, even for victories over Romans, was ensured when he gave 400 sesterces to each Roman citizen. Antony's twins walked with the effigy of Cleopatra in the triumph over the Egyptian queen. Antony's tragic part was carefully overlooked. Octavian had declared war only on Cleopatra because he feared the extent of Antony's popular support. Even now, with universal surface loyalty to the new regime, the Romans mourned rather than gloried in the loss of Antony.[50]

The fate of Antony's family is known, at least partly, for another three generations until A.D. 131. It is even known that his houses on the Palatine and the Esquiline were taken by Agrippa and by Octavian's stepson Tiberius. Alexander Helios and Ptolemy Philadelphus, his young sons by Cleopatra, have no recorded history after Octavian's triumph. Like Antony's other children, they were reared by Octavia in Rome. Probably they died young, of natural causes, in the strange land. Cleopatra Selene, who married the scholarly King Juba II of Numidia and Mauretania, had two known children. Her daughter, Drusilla, was married to Marcus Antonius Felix, a powerful freedman of the emperor Claudius. Her son, Ptolemy, reigned over the lands of King Juba from A.D. 23 to 40, when he was killed by his cousin in the Antonian house, the emperor Caligula. With the death of this grandson of Antony and Cleopatra, the main line of the great Ptolemaic house was ended.[51]

Antony's children by his earlier wives were protected through Octavia's kindness and lived the patterns of the leading patrician families. His eldest child, Antonia, daughter of his wife Antonia, in keeping with Antony's remarkably cosmopolitan sympathies, had been married to a rich Greek, Pythodorus of Tralles. She may have died before Antony, but her daughter, Pythodoris, was married to two Asian kings appointed by Antony, Polemo of Pontus and Archelaus of Cappadocia, and ruled over a small eastern kingdom along the southeast coast of the Black Sea for thirty-one years. Pythodoris's son by Polemo (Antony's great-grandson) reigned as king of Armenia. Her daughter, queen of Thrace, had three sons and two daughters (Antony's great-great-grandchildren) who were rulers of Lesser Armenia, parts of Arabia, Pontus, East Thrace, the Bosporan kingdom, and the Cilician principality of Alba, Cennatis, and Lelassis.[52]

Antony's younger son by Fulvia, Iullus Antonius, was not killed with his brother Antyllus because, rather than joining Antony in Egypt, he had remained under Octavia's care in Rome. He was highly cultured and able; and Octavian arranged for him to receive monies owed by Antony's freedmen. He must have gained Octavian's approval as well; for he became priest, praetor, then consul in 10 B.C., and the governor of provinces. He also married Marcella, the daughter of Octavia and Marcellus. His fortunes plummeted in 2 B.C., however. He was alleged to be the lover of Octavian's notoriously adulterous daughter Julia. The tragedy is shadowy; the personal license may have been part of a conspiracy to overthrow Octavian's rule. In the end, Iullus either committed suicide or was executed on Octavian's orders. His son, last of the Antonii, lived in exile, a scholar teaching in Massilia.[53]

Antony and Octavia's two daughters, both named Antonia, received money from Antony's estate and continued the social preeminence of their mother. Through them Antony's heirs were part of the Julio-Claudian dynasty, and three descendants ruled as emperors of Rome. Antonia the Elder married Lucius Domitius Ahenobarbus, son of Antony's close supporter, himself the winner of a triumph for German wars. Their daughter's daughter (Antony's great-granddaughter) Messallina married Claudius, her cousin, and was empress of Rome. Their son, Gnaeus Domitius Ahenobarbus, married his cousin Agrippina (Antony's great-granddaughter) and won the consulship in A.D. 32. The son of this couple, Nero, was emperor of Rome (A.D. 54–68). Antonia the Younger married the younger stepson of Octavian, Nero Claudius Drusus, and remained the center of a powerful dissident faction after her husband's death. One of her sons (Antony's grandson) reigned as the

231

emperor Claudius (A.D. 41–54) and honored Antony by restoring his birthday to favor. Her other son, Germanicus, was consul in A.D. 12; his son (Antony's great-grandson) was the emperor Caligula (A.D. 37–41); his daughter Agrippina was the mother of Nero, the second wife of Claudius. Thus, like Banquo, Antony's ghost could find content; his heirs would wear the Roman crown: "Thou shalt get kings, tho thou be none."[54]

XIV

"My Fame
is Shrewdly Gored"[1]

Antony still remains an enigmatic, contradictory figure, defying a final appraisal. For centuries he has been condemned as the brutal murderer of Cicero or dismissed as the drinking, carousing captive of the queen of Egypt, losing an empire for his passions. Joseph Ernest Renan called him "a colossal child." Yet the records also reveal a man who served Caesar so well in Gaul that Caesar trusted him as his spokesman and administrator in Italy while Caesar fought abroad; who, seizing control of the state after the Ides, defeated the forces of the republicans, apparently with the concurrence of most of the citizens; who ruled much of the Roman Empire for a decade; and who was conquered only by one of the most calculating and able men in history. The contradictions center in the ancient sources through which we know Antony. For critical judgment one must ask: What sources are extant? Where did the ancient writers get their information? How unbiased were they in presentation and interpretation? A typical instance—one among many possible—illustrates how variously a tale can be told.

After Caesar's death, Antony won control of the state from the republicans who lost their initiative and retreated east. In Rome, Octavian became Antony's competitor for power, although for a time they maintained appearances of Caesarian loyalty. But on October 5 or 6, 44 B.C., this surface cordiality was broken when

Antony accused Octavian of hiring men to murder him. The ancient authors give these differing reports:

Nicolaus of Damascus (*Life of Augustus*, 30-31): "[Antony] became provoked again at seeing the good will of all the soldiers inclining very much toward Octavian . . . he spread a report that he was being plotted against, and seizing some soldiers, he threw them into chains, on the pretext that they had been sent for this very purpose of killing him. He hinted at Octavian but did not definitely name him. The report quickly ran through the city that the consul had been plotted against, but had seized the men who had come to attack him. Then his friends gathered at his house, and soldiers under arms were summoned. In the late afternoon the report reached Octavian also that Antonius had been in danger of being assassinated, and that he was sending for troops to guard him that night. Immediately Octavian sent word to him that he was ready to stand beside his bed with his own retinue to keep him safe, for he thought that the plot had been laid by some of the party of Brutus and Cassius. He was thus in readiness to do an act of kindness entirely unsuspicious of the rumor Antonius had started or of the plot. Antonius, however, did not even permit the messenger to be received indoors, but dismissed him discourteously. The messenger returned after hearing fuller reports and announced to Octavian that his name was being mentioned among the men about Antonius' door as being himself the man who had despatched the assassins against Antonius, who now were in prison. Octavian when he heard this at first did not believe it because of its improbable sound, but soon perceived that the whole plan had been directed against himself, so he considered with his friends as to what he should do. . . . On the following morning he sat as usual with his friends and gave orders that the doors be opened to those of his townsmen, guests, and soldiers who were accustomed to visit him and greet him, and he conversed with them all in his usual way, in no wise changing his daily routine. But Antonius called an assembly of his friends and said in their presence that he was aware that Octavian had even earlier been plotting against him, . . . that one of the men sent to accomplish the crime had, by means of substantial bribes, turned informer in the matter; and hence he had seized the others; and he had now called his friends together to hear their opinions as to what should be done in the light of the recent events. When Antonius had spoken the members of his council asked to be shown where the men were who had been seized, so that they might find out something from them. Then Antony pretended that this had nothing to do with the present business, since, forsooth, it had already been confessed to; and he turned the discourse into other channels, watching eagerly for someone to propose that they ought to take vengeance on Octavian and not submit quietly. However, they all sat in silent thought, since no apparent proof lay before them, until someone said that Antony would do well to dismiss the assembly."[2]

Appian (*BCiv.* 3.39): "Antony announced to his friends that some of his body guard had been tampered with by Octavian, who had formed a plot against him. This he said either as a slander, or because he believed it to be true, or because he had heard of the emissaries of Octavian in his camp, and turned the plot to checkmate his actions into a plot against his life. When this story was noised about, there was a general tumult forthwith and great indignation . . . seeing what Octavian suffered daily from the indignities and the losses inflicted on him, [many] considered the accusation not incredible, yet held it to be impious and intolerable that a conspiracy should be formed against Antony's life while he was consul. Octavian ran with mad fury even to those who held this opinion of him, exclaiming that it was Antony who had conspired against him to alienate from him the friendship of the people, which was the only thing left to him. He ran to Antony's door and repeated the same things, calling the gods to witness, taking all kinds of oaths, and inviting Antony to a judicial investigation. . . . He attempted to enter the [Antony's] house. Being prevented from doing so he again cried out and railed at Antony and vented his wrath against the doorkeepers who prevented Antony from being brought to book. Then he went away and called the people to witness that if anything should happen to him his death would be due to Antony's plots."[3]

Cicero to Cornificius, governor in Syria, mid-October, 44 B.C. (*Fam.* 12.23): "I should myself write you . . . especially of the attempt made by Caesar Octavian [on Antony's life]. As to that, the rank and file think it was a charge trumped up by Antony as an excuse for raiding the young man's property; men of penetration and patriots, however, not only believe it is true but give it their approval. In short, there is much to hope for in him [Octavian]. There is nothing he is not expected to do for the sake of honor and glory. Our 'dear friend' Antony, on the other hand, knows himself to be so cordially detested that, though he caught the murderers in his own house, he does not dare to make the matter public."[4]

Velleius Paterculus (2.60.3): "Antony began wickedly to insinuate that an attempt had been made upon his life through plots fostered by Octavian. In this matter, however, the untrustworthiness of the character of Antony was disclosed to his discredit."[5]

Suetonius (*Aug.* 10.3): "At the advice of certain men he [Octavian] hired assassins to kill Antony, and when the plot was discovered, fearing retaliation he mustered veterans by the use of all the money he could command."[6]

Plutarch (*Ant.* 16.4): "Afterwards, as he lay asleep that night, Antony had a strange vision. He thought, namely, that his right hand was smitten by a thunder-bolt. And after a few days a report fell upon his ears that the young Caesar was plotting against him. Caesar tried to make explanations, but did not succeed in convincing Antony. So once more their hatred was in full career."[7]

How can these widely divergent accounts in the primary sources be reconciled? It is a problem of *Quellenforschung* which must be faced for every detail in Antony's biography.[8]

Authors contemporary with Antony should provide the most reliable evidence; but, though best informed, these writers had the least political and personal detachment in this age of murderous civil wars. Later writers drew from them or from other authors no longer extant; but since ancient writers rarely cited their sources except to criticize their errors, the line of dependence is often hard to trace.

Ancient Romans knew as well as we the potency of propaganda, either favorable or adverse. And no libel laws restrained the insults, slanders, and invective used so universally and brutally. Even in lesser political competitions, opponents were termed cowardly, cruel, and corrupt, their families and friends ignominious. In the life and death struggles of Antony's age, involving Octavian, Cicero, Fulvia, Lucius Antonius, Sextus Pompey, Antony, and others, *Fama* flew through pamphlets, lampoons, graffiti, whispering cam-

236

paigns, even comments on arrows, slingshots, or projectiles as generals sought to win over opposing troops.[9]

Thus Cicero (*Phil.* 3.15) declaims: "How insulting he [Antony] is in his edicts! how boorish! how ignorant! First of all he has heaped on Caesar [Octavian] abuse culled from the recollection of his own indecency and licentiousness. For who is chaster than this young man? who more modest? What brighter example among youth have we of old-world purity? Who, on the contrary, is more unchaste than the calumniator?"[10]

And Suetonius (*Aug.* 2.3–4.2) records: "Marcus Antonius taunts him with his great-grandfather, saying that he was a freedman and rope-maker from the country about Thurii, while his grandfather was a money-changer. . . . Antonius again, trying to disparage the maternal ancestors of Augustus as well, twits him with having a great-grandfather of African birth, who kept first a perfumery shop and then a bakery at Aricia."[11] Besides low ancestry, Antony leveled charges against Octavian of immorality, cowardice, duplicity, and cruelty—charges which must have won hearts in that age and which have remained, at least in fragments, to darken Octavian's reputation to this day.[12]

By the late 30s B.C., the propaganda war had been effectively won in the west by Octavian, who played up his republican and peace-loving role in the Senate and discredited Antony as the slave of Cleopatra, drunken, playing the part of Dionysus, parceling out the Roman Empire to Cleopatra's children, receiving omens that portended the anger of gods.[13] Above all, Octavian's propaganda declared Antony responsible for the split between the Caesarians. The outcome was Actium, fought as a crusade against Cleopatra, "plotting ruin 'gainst the capital and destruction to the empire with her polluted crew of creatures foul with lust" (Hor. *Car.* 1.37.7–10).[14] Republicans, like Cato, Cicero, Pompey, and Brutus, were returned to public favor as Augustus stressed the restoration of the republic; but Antony's reputation was never rehabilitated. Even after Antony's death, the Senate passed a series of decrees against him. The manuscripts and inscriptions honoring Antony were destroyed, and his name was erased from general inscriptions. The temple begun by Cleopatra in honor of Antony was completed honoring Octavian.[15]

Most of this propaganda has been lost in its original form, though an occasional sling pellet still gives evidence of the larger picture. But the extravagant accusations and laudations have been incorporated into contemporary and later writings, and a modern historian must beware the character distortions in every source. In broad generalization, three major political "camps" during the late republic and early empire were coloring the record about Antony: the republicans, the adherents of Octavian, and Antony's supporters.

The republicans included the former Pompeians, the followers of Brutus and Cassius, and the other foes of the Caesarians. As their heroes died, most surviving republicans had to shift adherence to either Antony or Octavian, and their propaganda was adjusted accordingly. Almost all this literature was lost—some intentionally destroyed. Still, a few writers can be identified.

The republican Cicero has been the most important single influence on later judgments of Antony. So much of his work has always been extant and studied, and the presentation of his position is so effective that he has swayed every generation. Even under Augustus his work became respectable, as presenting the formulation of the laws, the rights of property, and the peaceful consensus of the classes (*concordia ordinum*). Antony's reputation has suffered accordingly. The two men were never personally or politically congenial, and the generally frank picture in Cicero's letters is one of distaste. Antony's amiable stepfather had died by Cicero's order with other Catilinarians. Antony supported Caesar, about whom Cicero had mixed feelings despite his careful surface courtesies. Moreover, Antony lived riotously and clearly enjoyed his good times—to Cicero's dismay if not jealousy. Yet Cicero disliked many men with whom he worked politically; and for several years he was politically associated with Antony. Especially after the Ides, they cooperated for peace; and Antony in power was courteous to Cicero, as Caesar had been. Cicero's letters to and from Lepidus, Pollio, Plancus, Brutus, Cassius, and especially Atticus reveal this dichotomy.

It was Octavian's arrival in Rome, his fawning over the old orator, and Cicero's naive hopes of using him and any other legal or extralegal means to restore the republic that changed the relations with Antony to open denunciation. The fourteen *Philippic Ora-*

tions are models of eloquence, rancor, and misrepresentation. Cicero charges Antony with every unnatural vice, and even flagrant cowardice because he was lurking in Rome while Caesar was fighting in Spain! Antony, by showing public affection to his own wife, made mock of Roman decorum and decency.[16] As Cicero (*Phil.* 13.40) proclaimed: "I will brand him with the truest marks of infamy, and will hand him down to the everlasting memory of man."[17] The *Philippics*, like Cicero's other speeches and letters, are enormously important for the history of the age, but clearly must be used with the greatest caution to retain historical perspective. Still, Cicero's death stopped almost the only contemporary comment extant, and leaves the following decade distressingly obscure. Inevitably, later writers laudatory of Cicero—with Augustus's approval—damned Antony as his enemy and responsible for his death.

The other republican writings are known only in fragments. Cicero's freedman secretary, Marcus Tullius Tiro, composed a laudatory biography of his master. Marcus Brutus's letters in Greek are now suspected of having been written in the first century A.D. when the myth was growing that he was a Stoic saint whose death was caused by Antony. Lucius Calpurnius Bibulus, Brutus's stepson by Porcia, wrote about Brutus—though after the republican defeat at Philippi Bibulus became a follower of Antony. His account of Brutus and the biography by Publius Volumnius, another adherent of the tyrannicide, were used by Plutarch in his *Life of Brutus*. Varro, a Pompeian who became state librarian under Caesar, lost his property to Antony during the proscriptions. When Octavian allowed him to retire to a life of scholarship, he wrote a huge quantity, though more with erudition than with passion. Messalla Corvinus represents the changing commitments of the changing times. A follower of Brutus and Cassius, he went to Antony after Philippi, then to Octavian. He always called himself a republican and kept some degree of political independence; but it was he who proposed the title *Pater Patriae* (Father of his Country) for Augustus, and he was part of the literary circle of the imperial court under Augustus's patronage. Other republican writers are more shadowy, as mere names or sources of quotations—in the school boy's phrase, "Those dim men writing fragments."[18]

POLITICAL SYMPATHIES OF THE PRIMARY ANTONY SOURCES

REPUBLICANS: BRUTUS, CATO	OCTAVIAN	ANTONY
(M. BRUTUS, 85-42 B.C., LETTERS) (L. CALPURNIUS BIBULUS, d. 32 B.C.) (P. VOLUMNIUS, 1st c. B.C.) PROPAGANDA FRAGMENTS	*AUGUSTUS, 63 B.C.-A.D. 14, RES GESTAE, (MEMOIRS) (M. AGRIPPA, 63-12 B.C.) (G. MAECENAS, d. 8 B.C.) (G. OPPIUS, 1st c. B.C.) (L. CORNELIUS BALBUS, 1st c. B.C.) PROPAGANDA FRAGMENTS	*(M. ANTONY, 83- or 82-30 B.C., SPEECHES, DE EBRIETATE SUA) J. CAESAR, 100-44 B.C.) (OLYMPUS, 1st c. B.C.) PROPAGANDA FRAGMENTS
	*CICERO, 106-43 B.C. (TIRO, 1st c. B.C., LIFE OF CICERO) VARRO, 116-27 B.C. (MESSALLA CORVINUS, 64 B.C.-A.D. 8)	*(ASINIUS POLLIO, 76 B.C.-A.D. 4) (Q. DELLIUS, 1st c. B.C.) (MUNATIUS PLANCUS, 1st c. B.C.) (M. FADIUS GALLUS, 1st c. B.C.)

(TITUS LABIENUS, Augustan Age)
(TIMAGENES OF ALEXANDRIA, Augustan Age)
	VERGIL, 70-19 B.C.
	HORACE, 65-8 B.C.
	PROPERTIUS, 50-16 B.C.
	NICOLAUS OF DAMASCUS, 64-1 B.C.
	  Caesar
	  Augustus
	*LIVY, 59 B.C.-A.D. 17
	  Cicero
	  Caesar
	  Augustus	

(CREMUTIUS CORDA, d. A.D. 25)
(CASSIUS SEVERUS, d. A.D. 35)
	VALERIUS MAXIMUS, d. c. A.D. 30
	  Varro
	  Cicero
	  Livy
	VELLEIUS PATERCULUS, 19 B.C.-A.D. 31
	  Varro
	  Cicero
	  (Asinius Pollio)
	  (Messalla Corvinus)
	  Augustus
	  Livy	

(THRASEA PAETUS, d. A.D. 66)	SENECA, 5. B.C.-A.D. 65 LUCAN, A.D. 39-65 JOSEPHUS, A.D. 37-100 Nicolaus of Damascus	

Varro
Cicero
Caesar
(Asinius Pollio)
(Q. Dellius)
(Plutarch's grandfather and
great-grandfather)
Augustus
Livy
Valerius Maximus

*SUETONIUS, A.D. 69-140
Cicero
(M. Brutus)
(M. Antony)
(Messalla Corvinus)
(M. Agrippa)
Augustus
(G. Maecenas)
(Cremutius Corda)

*APPIAN, A.D. 90-165
Varro
Caesar
(Asinius Pollio)
(P. Volumnius)
(Munatius Plancus)
(Messalla Corvinus)
Augustus

*CASSIUS DIO, A.D. c. 160-230
Cicero
Caesar
(M. Antony)
(Asinius Pollio)
Augustus
Livy
Nicolaus of Damascus
(Messalla Corvinus)
(Timagenes of Alexandria?)
(Cremutius Corda)
Plutarch?

FLORUS, 2nd c. A.D.
Augustus
Livy
AURELIUS VICTOR, 4th c. A.D.
Livy
Suetonius
EUTROPIUS, 4th c. A.D.
Livy
Suetonius
FESTUS, 4th c. A.D.
Livy
OROSIUS, A.D. 380-420

* Especially influential authors.
( ) Extant only in fragments or not at all.
Primary authors in capital letters.
Sources used by authors in lower case.

Octavian was his own best propagandist, and his works lasted long enough to influence later writers. In a scurrilous vein, he wrote indecent verses against Antony, Fulvia, and Pollio.[19] In his formal, brief *Res Gestae*, the most authentic autobiography surviving from antiquity, he does not refer to Antony by name but speaks of the "tyranny of a faction"[20] and of "my antagonist": "I replaced in the temples of all the cities of the province of Asia the ornaments which my antagonist in the war, when he despoiled the temples, had appropriated to his private use."[21] Much fuller was the thirteen-volume *Memoirs of Augustus*, covering the years until 24 B.C. It provided the official account of the conflict between Octavian and Antony and was one of the greater factors in the development of the "Antony-Octavian myth." The few surviving fragments show that it carefully promoted Augustus's fame and republican image. Despite its pseudo-republicanism, it was much used by succeeding authors, like Livy, Appian, Cassius Dio, Nicolaus of Damascus, Plutarch, and Suetonius, but especially by those laudatory of Augustus, like Florus and Velleius Paterculus.[22]

Agrippa, Octavian's friend, admiral, and son-in-law, wrote a biography praising Octavian. Gaius Maecenas recorded a journal of Octavian's career. Oppius and Balbus wrote, rather, biographies of Julius Caesar but used them to favor Octavian, including Octavian's claims against Caesarion. The bulk of the pro-Octavian literature was written after the battle of Actium, when the identity of the victor was clear to the trimmers and when court patronage favored the "party liners"—although historians, grateful for Augustan order and peace, could also be perfectly honest in approving the principate.

Of literature sympathetic to Antony, a good deal was written, but the extant primary sources are now negligible, and only traces can be ferreted out in later criticisms of Octavian.[23] Antony himself left letters and speeches. Octavian reportedly read Antony's letters to his friends to justify himself, and some were read by later authors.[24] But these letters must have been censored by Augustus since they were used to denigrate Antony. For instance, Antony's essay *De Ebrietate Sua* ("On His Drunkenness"), a satiric defense against charges of his drunkenness, was twisted to prove the charges.[25]

Julius Caesar (or Hirtius for the last campaigns) should be a prime spokesman for his lieutenant. Granted that his work is invaluable in tracing the military action and political involvement in which Antony participated, Caesar's vanity was such that he did not play up his subordinate in these accounts, which he intended rather as propaganda for himself and his policies or as attacks on his foes. It is evident that Caesar trusted Antony and used him in critical military and political roles. But his preeminence has to be inferred from a meager dozen mentions in the *Gallic Wars* and *Civil Wars*.

Olympus's memoirs should be added because, as Cleopatra's physician, he provided Plutarch a few kindly words about a much abused lady. But for Antony, a few papyri, inscriptions, and coins are all that can be added further. Throughout, the evidence is clear that material favorable to Antony was destroyed in calculated policy.

The most significant source representing a balanced position between Octavian and Antony was Asinius Pollio (c. 75 B.C.-A.D. 4). A consular, Pollio was a man of great abilities, prestige, and political independence. For a time he favored Caesar. After the siege of Mutina he sided with Antony against Octavian and served him well militarily and diplomatically. But by 39 B.C. he was neutral and strong enough to remain so during Actium. His yearning was for the old Italy, not the new one-man rule. Under the principate he remained a "privileged nuisance" because, although he talked of liberty, he did not advocate assassination or civil war.[26] His history was a full eyewitness treatment of the period from 60 to 42 B.C., moderate in tone, evidently judging that the war between Antony and Octavian was only a contest to see who should be master. Unlike most ancient authors, he was hostile to Cicero, partly because he disapproved of his literary style, but also because Cicero was unjust to Antony. Pollio's history was probably the most important source on Antony's career independent of the official tradition imposed by Octavian. Although the loss of this acute first-hand account is most regrettable, happily Pollio's work was extensively used by later historians, especially Appian. Whenever a moderate note toward Antony is sounded, modern historians assume the influence of Pollio.[27]

Valerius Messalla Corvinus, Quintus Dellius, Lucius Munatius

Plancus, and Marcus Titius, like Pollio, were once allied with Antony. But they deserted him for Octavian, then became leading apologists for Octavian, and their writings were used by later authors. Dellius, the best known of the four, accompanied Antony on the Parthian campaign and is probably our chief source for this period. The sections of Plutarch's *Life* favorable to Antony but hostile to Cleopatra seem to have been based on Dellius's account.[28]

Actium represented a break in historical writing, as in so many other aspects of the Roman world. Subsequent writers appear dominated by the Julio-Claudian principate. The well-patronized poets and historians praised the Augustan peace and order, shuddering at the near danger of the eastern harlot and lauding Augustus's victory over Antony.[29]

One of the writers greatly influenced by Augustus's *Memoirs* who helped establish the pro-Octavian tradition was Nicolaus of Damascus (born c. 64 B.C.). As adviser and court historian to every ruler's friend, Herod the Great of Judaea, he came to Rome and wrote a panegyrical biography of Augustus (part of which survives) and a universal history of Rome from earliest times to the death of Herod. With obvious bias, he stresses the evils of Cleopatra, the failures of Antony to keep faith, and Octavian's legitimate rights, justice, and courage in destroying Antony. His most direct influence was on the later Jewish historian Flavius Josephus (A.D. 37–100).[30]

Valerius Maximus (fl. early first century A.D.) and Velleius Paterculus (c. 19 B.C.–after A.D. 31) uncritically followed pro-Augustan writers and wrote their summaries of Roman history in the same strain of eulogy. Belonging to the equestrian class that supported the emperors and the empire, they felt no regrets for the lost republic or sympathy with Antony. Although they used Livy, Cicero, and Varro, they represented the "official line" of their day, while being perfectly honest in their ardent, unquestioning approval of the principate.[31]

More complex and infinitely more tantalizing is Livy's (59 B.C.–A.D. 17) view. No loss of ancient historical writing is greater than that of Livy's detailed history of this period, for which only the epitomes remain. It is said that Augustus called him a Pompeian; but although Livy tempered his enthusiasm for the principate, at least he accepted it. However, there was no known compromise in

Livy's hostility to Antony. For Livy, Antony carried laws by cruelty and violence and was indifferent to constitutional forms; he treated Caesar shabbily; he wantoned with Cleopatra and subjected Romans to an eastern queen; he lacked judgment in his Parthian invasion. Livy remains one of the greatest influences on later historiography; although we have only his epitomes, his nearer successors had his complete history. Writers from the second to the fifth centuries A.D., like Florus, Cassius Dio, Aurelius Victor, Eutropius, Festus, Orosius, Cassiodorus, Julius Obsequens, not wholly but to a great degree were writing their own condensations of Livy.[32]

Livy and the poets associated themselves with the new regime chiefly because Augustus's propaganda portrayed his rule as a direct continuation of the republic. This role playing went so far as to include lauding the inflexible republican martyr Cato and downgrading the dictator Caesar. Since even Caesar was officially overlooked by his "son" and heir who had climbed to power on his name, certainly Antony could be wholly discredited.

Beyond this propaganda effort to win people's minds, Augustus and his successors increasingly resented opposition and controlled free expression. As early as 36 B.C., when Lepidus was deposed, Octavian destroyed evidence about their struggle, and this "editing" of the historical records enlarged with time. Not all adverse criticism was suppressed; but some ugly cases of thought control and book burning mar the favorable image of freedom proclaimed by the Julio-Claudians. The books of Cassius Severus, Titus Labienus, and Timagenes of Alexandria, all critical of Augustus, were officially burned. Their authors, like the censorious Cremutius Cordus in the time of Tiberius and Thrasea Paetus under Nero, were exiled or forced to suicide. A brief attempt under Caligula, the great-grandson of Antony, and under Claudius, his grandson, to recover these condemned works soon failed.[33] Book burning seemed merely a peccadillo to survivors of the proscriptions and civil wars. Indeed, in a people grateful for peace and prosperity, historical writing and even thinking readily conformed when power, prestige, propaganda, religious omens, and divine manifestations all supported the principate and when imperial patronage generously rewarded loyal spokesmen. The official view of Antony was voiced by Nero's adviser Seneca (*Epist. Mor.* 83.25): "A great man, a man of distinguished ability; but what ruined him and drove him into foreign habits and un-Roman vices, if it was not drunkenness and—no less potent than wine—love of Cleopatra?"[34]

When the Julio-Claudian dynasty ended in A.D. 68, a century had passed since Actium. Talk of the republic was now antiquarian, stirring curiosity not passion. The new ruling dynasties felt no compulsion to honor Augustus, and more balanced history and biography could be written. Moreover, national and family archives, which had prudently been closed, now provided fresh materials. Still, historians (a number of them non-Italians, such as Josephus) were now writing secondhand, often from the official propaganda of the Augustan age. Though many sources were used, so rarely are they identified that the modern historian is hard pressed to determine their reliability. But even the questionable scraps look good to hungry historians! The contributions and distortions of these later writers on whom modern interpretations depend require careful analysis.

Because Shakespeare used it, Plutarch's *Life of Antony* has probably been the most influential account molding modern judgments. Plutarch is unique in making Antony the focus of his study, although his *Lives* of contemporaries like Brutus, Caesar, and Cicero also include material on Antony. In many ways Plutarch (c. A.D. 47-120) is reliable. His grandfather and great-grandfather had told firsthand tales of Antony's career in Greece.[35] Plutarch himself had read extensively in the available sources. But such sources included Cicero's writings and Augustus's personal accounts and were generally weighted so that, although Augustus is criticized for having been a harsh youth, Plutarch accepts the common presentation of his growing to a generous maturity.[36] Plutarch praises some of the last republicans, but in the second century of the empire, he never questions the need for a monarch.

Beyond the partiality of his sources and his limited familiarity with Roman institutions and ways, Plutarch's purposes in writing distorted his appraisals. His *Lives* were written to provide noble examples on which others might model their characters. History, chronology, geography are subordinated to actions that can be judged moral. Such noble men, whose virtuous qualities are the only ones stressed, can be effectively contrasted with ignoble men, who use high position for selfish and unjust actions. In an extreme example of moral simplification, the Roman Antony and the Greek Demetrius Poliorcetes are compared as "men who bore most ample testimony to the truth of Plato's saying that great natures exhibit great vices as well as great virtues. Both alike were amorous, bibulous, warlike, munificent, extravagant, and domineering."[37] Antony is pictured as becoming insolent in prosperity, abandoning himself and his responsibilities to oriental luxuries in Cleopatra's court.

Other attitudes also color Plutarch's interpretation. Drama sometimes dominates history: "Now that the Macedonian play has been performed, let us introduce the Roman" (*Dem.* 53.4).[38] Plutarch attributes to Fortune or Providence developments which to the modern historian appear the responsibility of the participants. Thus Antony seems the victim when Plutarch says that a partial Fortune contributed to Antony's excesses for the very purpose that they profited Octavian; or, again, that Antony was destroyed by his evil genius Cleopatra. The modern historian can discard Plutarch's capricious Fortune when appraising Antony; but the knottier problem remains that Plutarch can contradict himself by telling the same story in different *Lives* in quite different ways or with different details. Apparently, as his work developed, Plutarch used various sources based on Cicero, Caesar, Livy, Pollio, Augustus, Varro, and perhaps twenty-five other authors. Where he failed was in harmonizing them. Plutarch, unlike modern historians, viewed the problem as minor—providing that the moral lesson was clear in each *Life*.[39]

The biographies of Caesar and Augustus by Suetonius (c. A.D. 69-140) included Antony only incidentally; and at best Suetonius was superficial in his treatment of character motivation and in his political analysis. Nevertheless, the chance references to Antony are interesting because Suetonius, as secretary to the emperor Hadrian, had access to state documents, letters, private imperial files, and even gossipy reports. Some of the documents, including a pamphlet written by Antony, were uncomplimentary to Octavian, whom Suetonius—probably following sources like Pollio and Valerius—viewed critically before, although not after, Actium. Suetonius identifies his sources more generously than most ancient writers do.[40] Regrettably, few works from his long list of names are now extant, and it is hard to reconcile the many discrepancies he leaves in his account. His writings, like Plutarch's, were used by many later writers, such as Aurelius Victor and Eutropius.

Biographies are inevitably *disiecta membra* in a full account of any age. Connected narrative about Antony's era must depend on the complete histories written about the late republican period. The histories of Appian (c. A.D. 90–165) and Cassius Dio (c. A.D. 160–230), though late and derivative, are the fullest and most informative. Appian covers the civil wars from 44 to 35 B.C. in considerable detail. Unfortunately, his long section on his native Egypt from 35 to 30 B.C. is lost. He must have used a number of sources (Caesar, Varro, Cicero, Asinius Pollio, Livy, Messalla Corvinus, P. Volumnius, Munatius Plancus, Augustus, Nicolaus of Damascus) and could be critical enough to say of the reliability of the official annalists: "Lying, especially in a patriotic cause, was permitted even more than to the rhetorician." Nevertheless, Appian was sometimes not equal to the task of reconciling discrepancies in the sources and even contradicts himself. Moreover, he judged that details were not as important as a good moral tale, though he is less given to flamboyant moralizing than Plutarch. In general, Appian was a competent craftsman providing a good narrative of wars and, to a lesser extent, of changing political institutions. His special value for Antony's portrayal is that he used Asinius Pollio as a source down to Philippi. When Appian writes critically of Cicero and of the early years of Octavian and his overthrowing of liberty, while showing sympathy to Antony, one assumes the influence of Pollio. Some of Appian's best writing is in his speeches. Literary speeches can be manipulated for propaganda: in the debate between Cicero and Piso over branding Antony a public enemy, Piso's speech favoring Antony is much longer and more effective; Lucius Antonius's speeches at Perusia are carefully designed to present him in a favorable light. Appian was a lawyer and probably composed most of the orations himself. Yet he had memoranda about the originals. Certainly it is tempting to hope that Antony's funeral oration for Caesar almost repeats Antony's own words.[41]

Even more remote from Antony was our other main source, Cassius Dio, who in his eighty-book, thousand-year survey of Ro-

man history included the republic's fall. Dependent on his varied
and sometimes contradictory sources (such as Livy, Cicero, and
Augustus), he introduced no new facts or even acute analyses; but
he did combine the ages and the areas in a straightforward, fairly
reliable account. Despite some rhetorical speeches and flourishes,
he did not intentionally withhold or misrepresent facts. His sympathy lay with political order, and he saw benevolent monarchy as
tidier than the chaotic late republic. Yet his varied sources (including Asinius Pollio and perhaps some of Antony's propaganda like
the work of Timagenes) led him sometimes to praise, sometimes to
blame both Antony and Octavian. His most substantial criticism of
Antony appears in his presentation of Cicero's *Philippics*. Dio con-
centrates them all into one supposititious speech, including, in the
standard rhetorical tradition, many unproved charges against Antony. But even here, the hostility is attributed to Cicero, for whom
Dio has faint praise; and in the text proper a moderate if not highly
original picture of Antony is presented.[42]

"Last scene of all, That ends this strange eventful history, Is second childishness and mere oblivion."[43] After the third century,
only late, rhetorical, inaccurate epitimators of earlier historians repeated earlier tales, like Eutropius who epitomized Livy and like
Orosius who stressed Christian history. Yet they too warrant review; for occasional details, perhaps drawn from books of Livy
lost to us, can still add a small brush stroke to Antony's portrait.

The sources, then, are indispensable yet treacherous. The historian must study them closely yet in Antony's case attempt to discard the hostile propaganda and appreciate his achievements. Two
further examples of variant accounts in the sources recapitulate
these source problems:

The brutal proscriptions by the triumvirs in 43–42 B.C. took
the lives of many leading Romans. According to Livy (*Ep*. 120):
"Gaius Caesar made terms with Antony and Lepidus providing
that . . . each should proscribe his personal enemies . . . among
them Lucius Paulus, the brother of Lepidus, Lucius Caesar, the uncle of Antony, and Marcus Cicero."[44] Appian (*BCiv*. 4.5) reports:
"The triumvirs . . . put on the list those whom they suspected because of their power, and also their personal enemies, and they exchanged their own relatives and friends with each other for death,

both then and later."[45] Plutarch (*Ant*. 19.2-20.2) has it that "each demanded the privilege of slaying his enemies and saving his kinsmen. But at last their wrath against those whom they hated led them to abandon both the honour due to their kinsmen and the goodwill due to their friends, and Caesar gave up Cicero to Antony, while Antony gave up to him Lucius Caesar, who was Antony's uncle on the mother's side. Lepidus also was permitted to put to death Paulus his brother; although some say that Lepidus gave up Paulus to Antony and Caesar, who demanded his death . . . three hundred men were proscribed and put to death by them; moreover, after Cicero had been butchered, Antony ordered his head to be cut off, and that right hand with which Cicero had written the speeches against him. When they were brought to him, he gazed upon them exultantly, laughing aloud for joy many times; then, when he was sated, he ordered them to be placed on the rostra in the forum."[46] Florus (2.16.6), however, defends Octavian: "Although Antony by himself was a sufficient menace to peace and to the state, Lepidus joined him. . . . What could be done against two consuls and two armies? Octavian was forced to become a party to a horrible compact. . . . These crimes were the result of the proscription lists of Antonius and Lepidus; Octavian contented himself with proscribing his father's murderers, for fear lest his death might be considered to have been deserved if it had remained unavenged."[47] So too Velleius (2.66.1-2): "Then the vengeful resentment of Antony and Lepidus . . . renewed the horror of the Sullan proscription. Caesar [Octavian] protested, but without avail being but one against two. The climax of the shame of this time was that Caesar should be forced to proscribe any one."[48] And Cassius Dio (47.7.1-8.5): "These acts were committed chiefly by Lepidus and Antony; for . . . as they had been holding offices and governorships for a long time they had many enemies. But Caesar [Octavian] seems to have taken part in the business merely because of his sharing the authority, since he himself had no need at all to kill a large number, for he was not naturally cruel. . . . Moreover, as he was still a young man and had just entered politics, he was under no necessity in any case of hating many persons violently, and besides, he wished to be loved. . . . So Caesar saved the lives of as many as he could; and Lepidus allowed his brother Paulus to escape to Miletus and was not inexorable toward the others. But

Antony killed savagely and mercilessly, not only those whose names had been posted, but likewise those who had attempted to assist any of them. He always viewed their heads, even if he happened to be eating, and sated himself to the fullest extent on this most unholy and pitiable sight. . . . When, however, the head of Cicero also was brought to them, . . . Antony uttered many bitter reproaches against it and then ordered it to be exposed on the rostra more prominently than the rest, in order that it might be seen in the very place where Cicero had so often been heard declaiming against him, together with his right hand, just as it had been cut off. And Fulvia took the head into her hands before it was removed, and after abusing it spitefully and spitting upon it, set it on her knees."[49] Suetonius (*Aug.* 27.1) gives a more balanced account, saying that though Octavian "opposed his colleagues for some time and tried to prevent a proscription, yet when it was begun, he carried it through with greater severity than either of them. For while they could oftentimes be moved by personal influence and entreaties, he alone was most insistent that no one should be spared."[50] Tacitus's venomous attacks on Augustus (*Ann.* 1.10) include an intimation that he was specially responsible for the murders.

In sum, the bloody business was an ugly episode in the scramble for power in which the triumvirs all participated and shared for self-justification. But only Octavian survived to "doctor" the record in his own favor; and in the writings of Dio, Velleius, and Florus, the historians most fully in the pro-Augustan tradition, Octavian appears the unwilling accomplice of the luridly vengeful Antony.

Similar distortions, probably following Augustus's *Memoirs*, were used in attempts to dethrone Antony from his position as victor at Philippi. Appian (*BCiv.* 4.14–17 *passim*), reflecting Pollio's account, makes it clear that Antony, who was "everything and attacked everywhere," had full responsibility for the strategy and the battle, whereas Octavian because of illness and inexperience saw very little action. Even the republican leaders and soldiers acknowledged Antony's gallantry and disdained Octavian. Suetonius (*Aug.* 13.1–2) is even more damning of Octavian: "he finished the war of Philippi also in two battles, although weakened by illness, being driven from his camp in the first battle and barely making his escape by fleeing to Antony's division. He did not use his victory with moderation, but after sending Brutus's head to Rome to be cast at the feet of Caesar's statue, he vented his spleen upon the most distinguished of his captives."[51] For the pro-Augustan historians, Antony's role is so depreciated that one marvels that the battle was won! Plutarch (*Ant.* 22), although giving an accurate account of the campaign, indicates the existence of a hostile press: "no great achievements were performed by Caesar [Octavian], but it was Antony who was everywhere victorious and successful. In the first battle, at least, Caesar was overwhelmingly defeated by Brutus, lost his camp, and narrowly escaped his pursuers by secret flight; although he himself says in his *Memoirs* that he withdrew before the battle in consequence of a friend's dream. But Antony conquered Cassius; although some write that Antony was not present in the battle but came up after the battle when his men were already in pursuit."[52] Florus (2.17.10) enlarges the criticism: "Though on one side both generals were present, on the other side one had been kept away by illness, the other by fear and cowardice."[53] Velleius (2.70.1) does not mention Antony during the battle although "Caesar [Octavian] was performing his duties as commander although he was in the poorest of health."[54] In Cassius Dio's full account (47.42-49 *passim*) an ill Octavian remained in camp, while Antony lost courage after an abortive ambush attempt. Receiving this news, Octavian hurried to the site, giving Antony's men courage by his own bravery. In the light of Antony's clear domination of the empire after Philippi, Octavian's greatest boldness in the campaign appears to have been in manipulating its history, to clear himself of blame and to attach the stigma of coward on the bold Antony.

The chief contemporary sources, then, were Cicero and Augustus himself—the other major sources were discredited or suppressed. For a true picture of Antony, one must weed out the multiple influences of Cicero and Octavian, and—so far as possible—carefully weigh the facts reported by Livy, Valerius, and Pollio. As followers of these sources, Suetonius, Appian, and Plutarch are the most useful historians. But all the lesser and later historians must also be screened for possible truths. In the end, despite historians' best critical judgments, Octavian won his propaganda battle, for uncertainties in the sources make the drawing of a complete or wholly legitimate portrayal of Antony still a challenge.

XV

Marcus Antonius, Vir Vitalissimus

The most hostile judgments have never drained the life and power from this vital man. His physical appearance, as seen in sculpture and on coins, reflected his life and his personality. He was handsome in a rough, hearty, heavy way. His expression, not at all subtle, was normally direct and friendly.[1] His powerful physique withstood a lifetime of strenuous use as well as casual abuse and neglect. In his late forties he led the killing retreat through Parthian mountain snows, and to his last days he was heading his legions in the battle line after nights of revelry. His exceptional strength in itself permitted his military campaigning and multiple duties of leadership, although the hard living tempted him to the excesses of carouse.[2]

He was a man fitted by and for his own age. In almost every way he was the quintessential Roman aristocrat of the first century B.C. Yet in areas in which he determined to excel, he had the special genius and fire of passion to carry him beyond his contemporaries. For the rest, he could be irresponsible, indolent, disorderly, brutal. His excellent intellectual abilities were carelessly cultivated. He appreciated the arts fully enough in his mature years that he attended the philosophic schools and served as gymnasiarch when in Athens, he transferred part of the Pergamene library to Alexandria, and he patronized art and the theater. His oratorical and writing skills were impressive. Though his enemies criticized his style as ornate and bombastic,[3] he could sway his audiences and win his causes at will.

But his real interests were not academic, though he could appreciate the performance of others. It was more fun to explode his gargantuan energies with less than respectable actresses and dancers, in high-stake games of chance or in lavish and riotous banquets.[4] As a bluff good fellow, he could immerse himself so totally in such entertainments as to seem "insolent in prosperity and abandoned . . . to luxury and enjoyment."[5] Especially in Egypt he seemed dazzled by the fascinating elegancies of the queen's court.

But, though given to boisterous excess, he could discipline himself and turn to duty at will. Even his frank sensual attraction to women was tempered by prudent judgment, especially in marriage contracts. The shadowy freedwoman Fadia may have been a wife of youthful love or of social rebellion. Antonia was taken in a typically Roman family alliance. Fulvia brought a dowry of valuable political allies as well as astute political judgment and unbridled ambition. Octavia provided a necessary political tie. Cleopatra matched Antony in playing for the highest stakes of control of Egypt, the eastern Mediterranean, and the Roman empire. Even paramours like Glaphyra brought the power as well as the flattery of eastern kingdoms. Calculation does not exclude attraction, or love, and Antony relished being in love. But even Cleopatra who fulfilled his passion with "infinite variety" rarely endangered his political judgment, except when she persuaded him to concentrate on the eastern Mediterranean instead of keeping a firm hold on Italy.[6]

A born leader, Antony long held the unswerving loyalty of his troops by able command, courage, daring, and a popular bonhomie in good times and in hard. He had an acute eye for rewarding talent at every rank and was liberally, even extravagantly, generous to his supporters. He enjoyed a laugh at himself and could tolerate honest disagreement. Certainly he could be brutally ruthless, and the proscriptions especially show hot wrath, stark revenge, and conscienceless greed. But in the late republic, Antony was the product of a century of civil wars, the heir of Sullan and Marian proscriptions; and Caesar's murder was a potent demonstration of the dangers of mercy. Despite the cold-blooded selfishness common in his day, Antony rarely showed malice and responded readily to appeals. In an amoral, irreligious age, his virtues were those of an honest soldier. Normally, he was chivalrous to his enemies and tenaciously faithful to his friends. If anything, he suffered from too much loyalty to and trust of unprincipled, calculating men like Octavian. It must have been Antony's cruelest failure when troops and officers defected to Octavian in the final campaigns.

As a Roman born to an ancient noble family, Antony was trained to be ambitious for powers and honors and to be conscious of the family and his own *dignitas* (eminence and esteem). Only driving ambition could have enabled him to ride roughshod over men and institutions to reach his peak of power in the empire. Yet he never rode ruthlessly enough or saw the all-consuming purpose or accepted the total obligations the times demanded. Indeed, he was willing to be second to a man like Caesar whom he respected. Octavian finally vaulted over the less power-hungry Antony, who lost because he could have been content with half the empire.

The role of general was the one Antony filled best and most happily. He was an expert strategist on land or sea—though his prize force was the cavalry. He could even effect skillful retreats, as he did from Parthia. His finest qualities of daring courage, speed, and decisiveness appeared in stress of danger. His men were loyal because he won their respect and trust.

It is by government service to Rome that Antony must finally be judged. Again he seems truly representative of his century in goals and means. He was not a powerful political analyst, nor a bold economic or social reformer. Yet he had independence of mind and was so realistic, sane, and willing to compromise that for some critical problems he led his contemporaries to fresh, pragmatic solutions. To Rome itself, Antony was patriotically loyal. But the republican form of government had been disintegrating for a century, and honest men differed over possible settlements of the crises. Though Antony (like Octavian) used the political slogan "restoring the republic,"[7] he realistically accepted the need for strong unified leadership. His own grandfather had received the first *maius imperium* (superior command) from the state; and Antony had supported Caesar's moves toward autocratic rule. Antony saw no alternative to dictatorship backed by military force, and he used his army even against the established government. But, when practical, he did try to work through established forms. Given a chance, most traditional republicans supported Antony over Octavian, indicating Antony's known preference for evolutionary over revolutionary change. The people also generally gave him their support as long as he was in the west—though often in response to donations which are hard to distinguish from bribes. Peace and prosperity mattered far more to them than a theoretical liberty. Antony's years in Italy were too troubled with military conflicts and grabs for political power to permit well formulated economic or social reform policies. Sextus Pompey's near blockade of Italy may have led Antony to realize the urgency of sea commerce. The need to settle veterans on land allotments brought forward issues of land assignments and uses. Perhaps, even given time, Antony might not have shown the insight and steadiness to solve the rampant problems of the west as well as Octavian did; but his successes in the east suggest that he would have striven for order, prosperity, and moderate rule, albeit under his authoritarian control.

For such were his policies during his ten-year rule in the east. Here Pompey was his model in organization and development. The east was exhausted by the republican government's exploitation and by the exactions of the civil wars. Antony made army and government demands too; but he was serious about resettling borders, rulers, taxes, and armies. After Actium, his able organization was accepted by Augustus with few modifications and prevailed for generations in the empire. Most significant, he seemed Caesar's heir in breadth of vision of the empire. Rome was to unify the Mediterranean lands, Hellenistic Greek with western Roman. Provincials were not mere subjects for exploitation. Antony recognized the equality of his peoples, indeed was sympathetic and tactful about their traditions and feelings. Octavian's propaganda persuaded the west that Antony would let Egypt dominate Rome. The deceit was possible only because Antony lived up to his agreement with Octavian to take responsibility for eastern settlements, and thus let slip his ties with Italy. Perhaps Antony would have developed two centers for the empire, as later emperors were to find necessary. In all probability, he would have established one-man rule, less discreetly monarchical than Augustus's principate; but the failure of the republic and the craving of the people for order dictated one-man rule. These were the major trends of Antony's time, and he had helped mold them. But in realizing the essential equality of the peoples of the empire, he was ahead of his time. He knew that class lines and old traditions were fading. Without denying Rome, he would have striven to harmonize and equalize the east and the west.

Antony failed. But it was a failure worth the struggle. He had seized the chances which Fortune had presented him for ruling the empire. He had relished every adventure possible in a man's lifetime. He had fallen, but only at the hands of an unprincipled man to whom he had too long attempted to be conciliatory and loyal. Throughout triumphs and failures, even in excesses, Antony remained sane and pragmatic, with the ironic perspective of a sense of humor. "He made himself so great that men thought him worthy of greater things than he desired" (Plut. *Dem. and Ant.* 1.3).[8] The final words that Plutarch (*Ant.* 77.4) gave him ring true; he bade Cleopatra "not to lament him for his last reverses, but to count him happy for the good things that had been his, since he had become the most illustrious of men, had won greatest power, and now had been not ignobly conquered, a Roman by a Roman."[9]

Chronology

Dates (B.C.)	Events in the West	Events in the East
83 or 82	Antony's birth	
71		Death of Antony's father
63	Catilinarian Conspiracy; death of Antony's step-father	
60	First Triumvirate	
59	Caesar consul	
58	Caesar begins Gallic Wars	Antony studies in Greece, takes command of cavalry under Aulus Gabinius
57	Pompey controls Rome; Cicero recalled to Rome	Antony fights in Palestine and Arabia
56	Triumvirs' conference at Luca	Antony fights in Egypt
55	Pompey and Crassus consuls	Antony fights in Syria
54	Antony joins Caesar in Gaul; Clodius-Milo riots in Rome	

Dates (B.C.)	Events in the West	Events in the East
53	Antony campaigns for quaestorship in Rome	Death of Crassus in Parthia
52	Antony quaestor; Clodius murdered; Pompey sole consul; Revolt of Vercingetorix	
51	Gallic Revolts quieted	
50	Antony elected augur and tribune	
49	Caesar crosses the Rubicon; civil war; Antony tribune and propraetor, Caesar's commander in Italy	Pompey gathers eastern army
48	Campaign at Brundisium	Caesar, then Antony cross to Dyrrhachium; battle of Pharsalus
47	Caesar dictator; Antony Master of the Horse in Italy	Caesar fights in Egypt and installs Cleopatra as queen of Egypt
46	Caesar fights in Africa and Spain; Antony in charge in Italy, loses Caesar's favor, marries Fulvia	
45	Caesar's reforms in Rome; Antony reconciled with Caesar, named flamen dialis	Caesar prepares Parthian campaign
44	Ides of March; Antony seizes control, holds consulship, named imperator and flamen divi Julii, besieges Decimus Brutus at Mutina; Octavian arrives in Rome as heir to Caesar; Cicero delivers four *Philippics*	Cassius and Brutus go east to build republican army

Dates (B.C.)	Events in the West	Events in the East
43	Antony defeated at Mutina by Octavian and the consuls, retreats to Gaul; Octavian seizes Rome; Second Triumvirate; proscriptions; death of Cicero	Republicans raise forces and money; Brutus takes Macedonia
42	Lepidus consul; Sextus Pompey increases power	Antony wins battle of Philippi; takes charge of settling the east
41	Octavian's power challenged by Antony's brother and wife; siege of Perusia	Antony settles affairs in Asia and Greece; joins Cleopatra in Egypt
40	Fall of Perusia; death of Fulvia; Octavian takes Gaul; Pact of Brundisium; Antony marries Octavia; makes last visit to Rome	Parthians overrun Syria
39	Treaty of Misenum: Antony, Octavian, Sextus Pompey	Ventidius defeats Parthians; Herod king of Palestine
38	Antony nominal consul; Pompey extends dominion against Octavian	Antony besieges Samosata; from Athens and Syria prepares for war against Parthia
37	Pact of Tarentum: renewal of triumvirate	Antony continues preparations against Parthia
36	Octavian defeats Pompey at Naulochus; Lepidus demoted	Antony invades Parthia, retreats; marries Cleopatra
35	Octavian restores order and prosperity in Rome	Sextus Pompey killed; Antony in Egypt
34	Antony nominal consul; Octavian subdues Dalmatia	Antony conquers Armenia; Donations of Alexandria

Dates (B.C.)	Events in the West	Events in the East
33	Octavian consul; readying for war	Peace with Media; Antony and Cleopatra prepare for war
32	Antony's will revealed; Octavian declares war on Cleopatra; Octavia divorced	Antony and Cleopatra move to Greece, assemble army and navy
31	Maecenas in charge in Italy; Antony consul for the third time	Battle of Actium
30		Last battles at Alexandria; Antony and Cleopatra commit suicide

Notes and
Selected Bibliography

Abbreviations
Used in Notes
and Selected Bibliography

Ancient Authors and Texts

Aelian.	Aelianus (*Varia Historia*)
Amm.	Ammianus Marcellinus (*Res Gestae*)
App.	Appian
BCiv.	*Bella Civilia*
Ill.	*Illyria*
Lib.	*Libya*
Sic.	*Sicilia*
Syr.	*Syria*
Ascon.	Asconius
Divin.	Commentary on Cicero's *De Divinatione*
Mil.	Commentary on Cicero's *Pro Milone*
Athen.	Athenaeus (*Deipnosophists*)
Aug.	Augustus
R.G.	*Res Gestae*
Aur. Vict.	Aurelius Victor (*Caesares*)
(Ps.-Vict.)	(Pseudo-Aurelius Victor)
De Orig.	*De Origine Gentis Romanae*
Vir. Ill.	*De Viris Illustribus*

Caes.	Caesar
Afr.	*Bellum Africum*
Alex.	*Bellum Alexandrinum*
Civ.	*Bellum Civile*
Gall.	*Bellum Gallicum*
Hisp.	*Bellum Hispaniense*
Cass. Dio	Cassius Dio Cocceianus (*Roman History*)
Cens.	Censorinus (*De Die Natali Volumen Illustre*)
Cic.	Cicero
Ad Brut.	*Epistulae ad Brutum*
Ad Q. Fr.	*Epistulae ad Quintum Fratrem*
Arch.	*Pro Archia*
Att.	*Epistulae ad Atticum*
Balb.	*Pro Balbo*
Catil.	*In Catilinam*
De Div.	*De Divinatione*
De Or.	*De Oratore*
Div. in Caec.	*Divinatio in Caecilium*
Dom.	*De Domo Sua*
Fam.	*Epistulae ad Familiares*
Fin.	*De Finibus*
Flacc.	*Pro Flacco*
Font.	*Pro Fonteio*
Manil.	*Pro Lege Manilia*
Marc.	*Pro Marcello*
Mil.	*Pro Milone*
Off.	*De Officiis*
Orat.	*Orator ad M. Brutum*
Phil.	*Orationes Philippicae*
Pis.	*In Pisonem*
Planc.	*Pro Plancio*
Pro Cael.	*Pro Caelio*
Rab. Post.	*Pro Rabirio Postumo*

Red. Sen.	*Post Reditum in Senatu*
Sest.	*Pro Sestio*
Sull.	*Pro Sulla*
Tusc.	*Tusculanae Disputationes*
Verr.	*In Verrem*
Clem. of Alex.	Clemens Alexandrinus
Strom.	*Stromateis*
Diod.	Diodorus Siculus (*World History*)
Euseb.	Eusebius
Chron.	*Chronica*
Ecc. Hist.	*Historia Ecclesiastica*
Eutr.	Eutropius (*Breviarium ab Urbe Condita*)
Flor.	Florus (*Epitomae Bellorum Omnium Annorum DCC*)
Frontin.	Frontinus
Strat.	*Strategemata*
Gell.	Aulus Gellius (*Noctes Atticae*)
Hor.	Horace
Car.	*Carmina* or *Odes*
Epist.	*Epistulae*
Epod.	*Epodi*
Sat.	*Satirae* or *Sermones*
Jos.	Josephus
Ant. Jud.	*Antiquitates Judaicae*
Bell. Jud.	*Bellum Judaicum*
C. Ap.	*Contra Apionem*
Just.	Justinus (*Trogi Pompei Historiarum Philippicarum Epitoma*)
Juv.	Juvenal (*Satires*)
Lact.	Lactantius
Div. Inst.	*Divinae Institutiones*
Liv.	Livy (*Ab Urbe Condita Libri*)
Ep.	*Epitomae*

Lucan.	Lucanus (*Bellum Civile* [*Pharsalia*])
Macr.	Macrobius
Sat.	*Saturnalia*
Martial.	Martialis
Ep.	*Epigrammaton Libri*
Nep.	Nepos
Att.	*Atticus*
Eum.	*Eumenes*
Nic. Dam.	Nicolaus of Damascus (*Life of Augustus*)
Obseq.	Julius Obsequens (*De Prodigiis*)
Oros.	Orosius (*Historiae contra Paganos*)
Ov.	Ovid
Fast.	*Fasti*
Met.	*Metamorphoses*
Pont.	*Epistulae ex Ponto*
Paus.	Pausanias (*Description of Greece* [*Periegesis*])
Pl.	Pliny (the Elder)
N.H.	*Naturalis Historia*
Plut.	Plutarch
Ant.	*Antonius*
Brut.	*Brutus*
Caes.	*Caesar*
Cat. Min.	*Cato Minor*
Cic.	*Cicero*
Crass.	*Crassus*
Dem.	*Demetrius*
Dem. and Ant.	*Demetrius and Antonius*
Mor.	*Moralia*
Pomp.	*Pompey*
Q.R.	*Quaestiones Romanae*
Symp.	*Symposium*
Prop.	Propertius (*Elegies*)
Ps.-Vict.	(See Aur. Vict.)

Quint.	Quintilian
Inst.	*Institutio Oratoria*
Ruf. Fest.	Rufius Festus (*Breviarium Rerum Gestarum Populi Romani*)
Sall.	Sallust
Ad Caes.	*Epistulae ad Caesarem* (disputed work)
B.J.	*Bellum Jugurthinum*
Cat.	*Bellum Catilinae*
Hist.	*Historiae*
Sen.	Seneca the Elder
Suas.	*Suasoriae*
Sen.	Seneca the Younger
Benef.	*De Beneficiis*
Clem.	*De Clementia*
De Brev. Vit.	*De Brevitate Vitae*
De Cons.	*De Constantia Sapientis*
De Ira	*De Ira*
Dial.	*Dialogi*
Epist. Mor.	*Epistulae Morales*
Stat.	Statius
Silv.	*Silvae*
Strab.	Strabo (*Geography*)
Suet.	Suetonius
Aug.	*Divus Augustus*
Calig.	*Gaius Caligula*
Claud.	*Divus Claudius*
De Gr. et Rhet.	*De Grammaticis et Rhetoribus*
Galba	*Galba*
Gramm.	*De Grammaticis*
Jul.	*Divus Julius*
Ner.	*Nero*
Tib.	*Tiberius*
Tac.	Tacitus
Ann.	*Annales*

Germ.	*Germania*
Hist.	*Historiae*
Theophr.	Theophrastus
C. Plant.	*De Causis Plantarum*
Trog.	Pompeius Trogus
Prolog.	*Prologi*
Val. Max.	Valerius Maximus (*Factorum ac Dictorum Memorabilium Libri IX*)
Vell.	Velleius Paterculus (*Historiae Romanae*)
Verg.	Vergil
Aen.	*Aeneid*
Ecl.	*Eclogues*
G.	*Georgics*
Zon.	Zonaras (*Epitome of the Histories*)

Journals and Books

AAnt Hung	*Acta Antiqua Academiae Scientiarum Hungaricae*
AHR	*American Historical Review*
AJA	*American Journal of Archaeology*
AJP	*American Journal of Philology*
ANS	*American Numismatic Society*
ANSMusN	*American Numismatic Society Museum Notes*
ASNP	*Annali della Scuola Normale Superiore di Pisa*
BMC Phoenicia	*British Museum Coins of Phoenicia*
BMC Ptolemies	*British Museum Coins of the Ptolemies*
BMC Rom Emp	*British Museum Coins of the Roman Empire*
BMC Rom Rep	*British Museum Coins of the Roman Republic*

ABBREVIATIONS

CAH	*Cambridge Ancient History*
Cal. St. in Cl. Ant.	*California Studies in Classical Antiquity*
Cal. U. Pub. in Cl. Phil.	*California University Publications in Classical Philology*
C&M	*Classica et Mediaevalia*
CB	*Classical Bulletin*
CIL	*Corpus Inscriptionum Latinarum*
CJ	*Classical Journal*
CP	*Classical Philology*
CQ	*Classical Quarterly*
CR	*Classical Review*
CW	*Classical World*
FGH	*F. Jacoby: Die Fragmente der griechischen Historiker*
G&R	*Greece and Rome*
GRBS	*Greek, Roman, and Byzantine Studies*
HSPh	*Harvard Studies in Classical Philology*
HZ	*Historische Zeitschrift*
ILS	*Inscriptiones Latinae Selectae*
Jahrb. für Cl. Phil.	*Jahrbuch für classische Philologia*
Jahreshefte	*Jahreshefte des österreichischen archäologischen Instituts*
JDAI	*Jahrbuch des deutschen archäologischen Instituts*
JEA	*Journal of Egyptian Archaeology*
JHS	*Journal of Hellenic Studies*
JRS	*Journal of Roman Studies*
LEC	*Les études classiques*
NZ	*Numismatische Zeitschrift*
OGIS	*Orientis Graeci Inscriptiones Selectae*
PACA	*Proceedings of the African Classical Association*
PAMAAR	*Papers and Monographs of the American Academy in Rome*

Pap. Oxy.	*Oxyrhynchus Papyri*
PCPhS	*Proceedings of the Cambridge Philological Society*
QJS	*Quarterly Journal of Speech*
RA	*Revue Archéologique*
RE	*Paulys Real-Encyclöpadie der classischen Altertumswissenschaft*
RecPhL	*Recherches de philologie et de linguistique*
RFIC	*Rivista di filologia e di istruzione classica*
RhM	*Rheinisches Museum*
RIL	*Rendiconti dell'Istituto Lombardo*
RSI	*Rivista storica italiana*
SDHI	*Studia et Documenta Historiae et Iuris*
Smith Coll. Cl. St.	*Smith College Classical Studies*
SPh	*Studies in Philology*
TAPA	*Transactions and Proceedings of the American Philological Association*
U. of Missouri Stud. Soc. Sc.	*University of Missouri Studies in Social Science*

Notes

After the introductory survey chapter, the notes stress chiefly the primary sources and, in general, give priority to the most influential sources. However, when a major secondary work dominates historical thinking or when a question is an issue of important dispute, secondary works are cited. For a fuller listing of secondary studies, see the Bibliography.

Chapter I.
The Setting

1. Sound general works on Rome's early history include: A. E. R. Boak and William Sinnigen, *A History of Rome to A.D. 565*, 5th ed. (New York, 1965); Max Cary, *A History of Rome*, 2nd ed. (London, 1954); Howard H. Scullard, *A History of the Roman World, 753-146 B.C.*, 2nd ed. (London, 1951); Jacques Heurgon, *The Rise of Rome to 264 B.C.*, trans. James Willis (London, 1973); W. Drumann and P. Groebe, *Geschichte Roms*, 2nd ed., 6 vols. (Leipzig, 1899-1929), 46-384; Gugielmo Ferrero, *The Greatness and Decline of Rome*, trans. Alfred Zimmern, vol. I (London, 1907).

2. Howard H. Scullard, *Scipio Africanus* (London, 1970); Gavin R. De Beer, *Hannibal* (New York, 1969); Gilbert Charles-Picard, *Hannibal* (Paris, 1967); Edward T. Salmon, *Roman Colonization under the Republic* (London, 1969); Tenney Frank, *Roman Imperialism* (New York, 1921); Frank B. Marsh, *The Roman World from 146-30 B.C.* (London, 1963), 1-11; Matthias Gelzer, *Caesar: Politician and Statesman*, trans. Peter Needham (Oxford, 1968), 1-12; E. Huzar, "Egyptian Influences on Roman Coinage in the Third Century B.C.," *CJ* 61 (April, 1966), 337-46.

3. T. R. E. Holmes, *Caesar's Conquest of Gaul* (London, 1931); Holmes, *The Roman Republic*, vol. I (Oxford, 1923), 121-32; Richard E. Smith, *The Failure of the Roman Republic* (Cambridge, 1955), 47-56; Robert K. Sherk, *Roman Documents from the Greek East* (Baltimore, 1969); Sherk, "The Text of the *Senatus Consultum de Agro Pergameno*," *GRBS* 7 (1966), 361-69; G. Colin, *Rome et la Grèce* (Paris, 1905); David Magie, *Roman Rule in Asia Minor* (Princeton, 1950); R. Stevenson, "The Provinces and Their Government," *CAH* 9, (Cambridge, 1932), 438-52.

NOTES

4. L. R. Taylor, *Party Politics in the Age of Caesar* (Berkeley, 1964), 7-10; Ronald Syme, *The Roman Revolution* (Oxford, 1939), *passim*; A. Afzelius, "Zur Definition der römischen Nobilität vor der Zeit Ciceros," *C&M* 7 (1945), 150-200; Matthias Gelzer, *Die Nobilität der römischen Republic* (Berlin, 1912), 18-135; Friedrich Münzer, *Römische Adelsparteien und Adelsfamilien* (Stuttgart, 1920), *passim*; Christian Meier, *Res Publica Amissa* (Wiesbaden, 1966), 166-200; P. A. Brunt, "*Amicitia* in the Late Roman Republic," *PCPhS* 191 (1965), 1-20; A. E. Astin, *The Politics and Policies in the Roman Republic*, *Lecture at Queens University, Belfast* 41 (1968).

5. E. Badian, *Foreign Clientelae* (Oxford, 1958), *passim*; Syme, *Roman Revolution*, *passim*; Taylor, *Party Politics*, *passim*.

6. Michael Grant, *The World of Rome* (London, 1960), 36-42; E. Badian, *Roman Imperialism in the Late Republic* (Ithaca, 1968), 16-28, 60-89; Zvi Yavetz, "Living Conditions of the Urban Plebs in Republican Rome," *Latomus* 17 (1958), 500-517; Paul-Louis, *Ancient Rome at Work* (London, 1927), 131-51; L. Hutchinson, *The Conspiracy of Catiline* (London, 1966), 7-28.

7. The earlier, wholly plebeian Concilium Plebis was essentially merged with the Comitia Tributa.

8. L. R. Taylor, *The Voting Districts of the Roman Republic*, *PAMAAR* 20 (1960); Taylor, *Roman Voting Assemblies from the Hannibalic War to the Dictatorship of Caesar* (Ann Arbor, 1966); Timothy P. Wiseman, *New Men in the Roman Senate, 139 B.C.-14 A.D.* (London, 1971); George W. Botsford, *The Roman Assemblies* (New York, 1909); Leon Homo, *Roman Political Institutions from City to State* (London, 1924).

9. P. A. Brunt, "The Equites in the Late Republic," in *The Crises of the Roman Republic*, ed. R. Seager (Cambridge, 1969), 117-37; Frank, *Roman Imperialism*, 279-93; Badian, *Roman Imperialism*, 76-92; Badian, *Publicans and Sinners* (Ithaca, 1972), *passim*; R. H. Barrow, *Slavery in the Roman Empire* (New York, 1928), 208-29; Adrian N. Sherwin-White, *Racial Prejudice in Imperial Rome* (Cambridge, 1967), 13-32; Susan Treggiari, *Roman Freedmen during the Late Republic* (Oxford, 1969), 12-20; W. W. Fowler, *Social Life at Rome in the Age of Cicero* (New York, 1933), 213-36; T. Frank, *Economic Survey of Ancient Rome*, vol. I (Baltimore, 1933), 162-93; 327-46; 376-87; 394-99; M. Rostovtzeff, *Social and Economic History of the Hellenistic World*, vol II (Oxford, 1953), 960-74; 1014-25; Frank Cowell, *Cicero and the Roman Republic* (London, 1948), 52-77; P. A. Brunt, "The Army and the Land in the Roman Revolution," *JRS* 52 (1962), 69-87; Theodor Mommsen, *History of Rome*, ed. E. A. Saunders and J. H. Collins (Cleveland, 1958), 537-552.

10. Fowler, *Social Life at Rome*, 144-58; 180-84; 353-55; John Dickinson, *Death of a Republic* (New York, 1963), 378-89; Smith, *Failure of the Roman Republic*, 123-131; Ferrero, *Greatness and Decline*, 48-58.

11. Henry Boren, "The Urban Side of the Gracchan Economic Crisis," *AHR* 63 (1958), 890-902; Boren, *The Gracchi* (New York, 1968), *passim*; F. Cowell, *The Revolutions of Ancient Rome* (New York, 1963), 98-108; T. Frank, *An Economic History of Rome* (Baltimore, 1927), 127-40; Salmon, *Roman Colonization*, 112-25; M. Rostovtzeff, *History of the Ancient World* (Oxford, 1926), 105-15; R. Rowland, "C. Gracchus and the Equites," *TAPA* 96 (1965), 361-73; H. Heuss, "Der Untergang des römischen Republic," *HZ* 182 (1956), 1-28; Solomon Katz, "The Gracchi, an Essay in Interpretation," *CJ* 38 (1942), 71-82; Andrew Lintott, *Violence in Republican Rome* (Oxford, 1968), *passim*; A. Sherwin-White, "Violence in Roman Politics," *JRS* 46 (1956), 1-9; John Heaton, *Mob Violence in the Late Roman Republic, 133-49 B.C.* (Urbana, 1939), 5-20; 67-91; P. A. Brunt, *Social Conflicts in the Roman Republic* (London, 1971), *passim*; Badian,

Foreign Clientelae, 169-91; Badian, "From the Gracchi to Sulla," *Historia* 11 (1962), 197-245 provides an excellent survey of the 1940-59 literature on the period.

12. Thomas Carney, *Biography of C. Marius* (Assen, Netherlands, 1961), *passim*; Phillip Kildahl, *Gaius Marius* (New York, 1968), *passim*; Badian, *Foreign Clientelae*, 194-210; Badian, "Waiting for Sulla," *JRS* 52 (1962), 47-61; A. Passerini, *Caio Mario come uomo politico* (Pavia, 1934), *passim*; Howard H. Scullard, *From the Gracchi to Nero* (New York, 1959), 79-89; R. Smith, *Service in Post-Marian Army* (Manchester, 1958), 28-43; Henry Parker, *Roman Legions* (London, 1928), 21-26; Frank B. Marsh, *Founding of the Roman Empire* (Oxford, 1927), 21-49; P. Brunt, *Italian Manpower, 225 B.C.-A.D. 14* (London, 1971), *passim*; Brunt, "Army and Land," 69-84; Mason Hammond, *The Augustan Principate* (New York, 1968), 8-18; Chaim Wirszubski, *Libertas as a Political Idea at Rome* (Cambridge, 1950), *passim*; F. Marsh, "The Gangster in Roman Politics," *CJ* 28 (1932), 168-78; R. Smith, *Cicero the Statesman* (London, 1966), 36-45; Smith, "Anatomy of Force in Late Republican Politics," in *Ancient Society and Institutions*, ed. V. Ehrenberg (London, 1966), 257-70; E. Staveley, "The Fasces and *Imperium Maius*," *Historia* 12 (1963), 458-84; A. E. R. Boak, "The Extraordinary Commands from 80-48 B.C.," *AHR* 24 (1918), 1-25.

13. C. Wirszubski, *Libertas, passim*; D. R. Shackleton-Bailey, "The Roman Nobility in the Second Civil War," *CQ* 10 (1960), 253-67; R. Smith, "Pompey's Conduct in 80 and 77 B.C.," *Phoenix* 13 (1960), 1-10; E. Badian, "Caepio and Norbanus," *Historia* 6 (1957), 318-46; L. R. Taylor, "Caesar and the Roman Nobility," *TAPA* 73 (1942), 1-24; Mason Hammond, *City State and World State* (Cambridge, 1951), 81-97; Syme, *Roman Revolution*, 7-27; 47-60; K. von Fritz, "Emergency Powers in the Last Centuries of the Roman Republic," *Annual Report of the AHA* 3 (1942), 221-37; von Fritz, *The Theory of the Mixed Constitution in Antiquity*, 255-305; Smith, *Failure of the Roman Republic*, 81-103; J. Collins, "Caesar and the Corruption of Power," *Historia* 4 (1955), 445-65.

14. Taylor, *Party Politics*, 7-15; E. Gruen, "Pompey, the Roman Aristocracy, and the Conference of Luca," *Historia* 18 (1969), 71-108; Gruen, *The Last Generation of the Roman Republic* (Berkeley, 1974), *passim*; Christian Meier, "Populares," *RE* supp. 10 (1965), 550-615; H. Strasburger, "Optimates," *RE* 18.1 (1939), 773-98.

15. Smith, *Failure of the Roman Republic*, 123-31; Dickinson, *Death of a Republic*, 378-89; Fowler, *Social Life at Rome*, 144-58; 180-84; Ferrero, *Greatness and Decline*, 48-58; 139-58; Tac. *Hist.* 2.38; Tac. *Ann.* 3.26-28; Sall. *B.J.* 31.

16. Erich Gruen, *Roman Politics and the Criminal Courts, 149-74 B.C.* (Cambridge, Mass., 1968), *passim*; Taylor, *Party Politics*, 62-97; Syme, *Roman Revolution*, 149-61; Frank Cowell, *Cicero and the Roman Republic* (London, 1948), 341-60.

Chapter II.
Heir

1. Plut. *Pomp.* 24.6; Obseq. 24; Cic. *Manil.* 33; Cic. *De Or. passim*; Liv. *Ep.* 68; Val. Max. 3.7.9; 6.8.1; Trog. *Prolog.* 39; E. Gruen, "M. Antonius and the Trial of the Vestal Virgins," *RhM* 3 (1968), 59-63; Gruen, *Roman Politics and the Criminal Courts, 149-74 B.C.* (Cambridge, Mass., 1968), 129-31 and 188-95; P. Groebe, "Antonii," *RE* 1, 2591.

2. Plut. *Pomp.* 24.6; Plut. *Ant.* 1; Cic. *Verr.* 2.3.8; 3.91.213; Cic. *Orat.* 1.82; App. *Sic.* 6; Liv. *Ep.* 68; 97; Vell. 2.31.3-4; Tac. *Ann.* 12.62; Flor. 1.42.2-3; Sall. *Hist.* 3.2-3. The exact legal meaning of *imperium maius* and *imperium infinitum* are disputed. Most persuasive are those who argue that *imperium maius* in the first century B.C. meant a

command that exceeded the authority of other officials in a certain area, whereas *imperium infinitum* had no geographic limitations. See Theodor Mommsen, *Römisches Staatsrecht* 2[3], 3rd ed. (Graz, 1887-88), 233; Michael Grant, *From Imperium to Auctoritas* (Cambridge, 1946), 412-23; Hugh Last, *"Imperium Maius," JRS* 37 (1947), 157-64; Victor Ehrenberg, *Polis und Imperium* (Zurich, 1965), 587-606; E. S. Staveley, "The *Fasces* and *Imperium Maius," Historia* 12 (1963), 458-84; A. E. R. Boak, "Extraordinary Commands from 80-48 B.C.," *AHR* 24 (1918), 1-25; E. Badian, *Roman Imperialism in the Late Republic* (Ithaca, 1968), 52-53; W. M. Jashemski, *The Origins and History of the Proconsular and Propraetorian Imperium to 27 B.C.* (Rome, 1966), *passim*. E. Badian, *Foreign Clientelae* (Oxford, 1958), Chapter IX argues that as censor Antonius opened citizen lists to allies who had no right to the rank. P. A. Brunt, "Italian Aims at the Time of the Social War," *JRS* 55 (1965), 90-109 denies that the censors of 97/6 enrolled the Italians.

3. Cic. *Phil.* 3.6; Cic. *Div. in Caec.* 17; Lact. *Div. Inst.* 1.11; Cass. Dio 45.47.

4. Plut. *Ant.* 1 calls him not very distinguished but "a worthy, good man." An explanation for Antonius's appointment may be that the Senate tended to send commanders to areas where they had family connections—here secured by his father. See Vell. 2.31.2; Cic. *Verr.* 2.8; 2.206; 3.213; Sall. *Hist.* 3.2.

5. Pl. *N.H.* 8.53; Plut. *Cic.* 11-12; 16; Cass. Dio 38.10; Cic. *Phil.* 2.38; Cic. *Att.* 1.12.1; 1.14.7; Sall. *Cat. passim.*

6. Strab. 10.2.13.

7. The participation of Caesar and Crassus is disputed. See especially the arguments of A. Kaplan, *Catiline* (New York, 1968).

8. Perhaps the stipulation was included that Antonius share the booty. Or perhaps Cicero loaned him money directly. Whichever was the case, Antonius failed to pay debts owed Cicero. Cic. *Att.* 1.12.1; 1.14.7.

9. Antony later accused Cicero of not returning his body for burial, but apparently the charge was baseless. Plut. *Cic.* 17; Plut. *Ant.* 2; Cic. *Att.* 1.16.9; E. G. Hardy, "The Catilinarian Conspiracy in its Context," *JRS* 7 (1917), 153-228; Kaplan, *Catiline*, 51-77; Lester Hutchison, *The Conspiracy of Catiline* (London, 1966), 49-60; Charles Odahl, *The Catilinarian Conspiracy* (New Haven, 1971), 44-55.

10. Cic. *Catil. passim*; Ascon. *Divin.* 7.21; Plut. *Cic.* 17; Cass. Dio 37.30-36; 38.10.3; Gell. 5.6; Sall. *Cat. passim*; Cic. *Verr.* 1.14; Cic. *Flacc.* 5; 40; 95; Cic. *Pro Cael.* 15; 74; 78; Cic. *Phil.* 2.7; 2.56; 2.98-99; Cic. *Sull.* 25; Plut. *Ant.* 2; *ILS* 6204; Val. Max. 4.2.6; Erich Gruen, *The Last Generation of the Roman Republic* (Berkeley, 1974), 288-89.

11. Val. Max. 9.2.2; App. *BCiv.* 1.40-42; 1.45; 1.48-49; 1.72; Flor. 2.18; 2.21.14; Cic. *De Or.* 3.3; Cic. *Tusc.* 5.19; Cic. *Arch.* 5; Cic. *Balb.* 8; Cic. *Planc.* 21; Cic. *Font.* 15; Cic. *De Div.* 1.2; Vell. 2.15-16; Liv. *Ep.* 73; Pl. *N.H.* 2.29; 13.3; 14.14; Gell. 4.4; Obseq. 115; Oros. 5.18.

12. Sall. *Cat.* 17; App. *BCiv.* 4.37; 5.52; 5.63; Cass. Dio 48.15-16; 48.27; Cic. *Catil.* 4.13; Cic. *Phil.* 2.14; 2.58; Plut. *Ant.* 1.20-21.

13. App. *BCiv.* 3.32; 3.51; 5.52; 5.63; Plut. *Ant.* 19; Cass. Dio 47.8; 48.16; Cic. *Phil.* 2.14.

14. In *Ant.* 86.5 Plutarch gives a variant birth date of 86 B.C.; see also App. *BCiv.* 5.8.

15. Plut. *Ant.* 2.3; Pl. *N.H.* 14.148.

16. Plut. *Ant.* 2; Cic. *Phil.* 2.63; Cass. Dio 45.30. For coin portraits of Antony, see E. A. Sydenham, *Coinage of the Roman Republic* (London, 1952); H. A. Grueber, *Coins of the Roman Republic in the British Museum*, vol. II (London, 1970); M. Bieber, "The Development of Portraiture on Roman Republican Coins," *Aufstieg und Niedergang der Römischen Welt*, part I, vol. 4 (Berlin, 1973), 882-85.

17. Plut. *Ant.* 9.10; 10; 24.2; App. *BCiv.* 2.33; Cic. *Fam.* 9.26; Cic. *Pis.* 89; Cic. *Att.* 10.10.5; 10.16.5; Cic. *Phil.* 2.20; 2.24; 2.28; 2.31; 2.41; 2.58; 2.63; 2.69; 2.77; 2.105; 5.11; 6.4.

18. Cic. *Att.* 1.14; Cic. *Phil.* 2.3; 2.48; 3.11; Plut. *Ant.* 2.4.

19. Pl. *N.H.* 12.56; Cic. *Fin.* 2.8.23; Cic. *Phil.* 2.45; Diod. 37.3.4; Plut. *Ant.* 2; Cass. Dio 45.26.1-3. Cicero's bitter personal invective in *Phil.* 2.45 is evidently the source of these tales of a profligate youth, so that their accuracy must be held suspect.

20. Cic. *Att.* 16.11.1; Cic. *Phil.* 2.3; 3.17; 13.23.

21. Cic. *Phil.* 2.44-46.

22. Vell. 2.45.1-2; Cass. Dio 38.17.1-4; Cic. *Att.* 1.14.45; 2.48.3-5; App. *BCiv.* 2.15; Plut. *Cic.* 30-33.

23. Cic. *Phil.* 2.48-50.

24. Plut. *Ant.* 2.4-5; Suet. *Aug.* 86.3; Suet. *De Gr. et Rhet.* 25(4); 25(1).

Chapter III.
Lieutenant

1. App. *Syr.* 50-51; Jos. *Bell. Jud.* 1.8.1-2; Jos. *Ant. Jud.* 14.4.5-5.2; Michael Grant, *Jews in the Roman World* (New York, 1973), 57.

2. Jos. *Bell. Jud.* 1.8.2-5; Jos. *Ant. Jud.* 14.5.3-6.1; Plut. *Ant.* 3.1. Variant readings for Servilius are Servidius and Servianus.

3. Jos. *Bell. Jud.* 1.8.5-6; Jos. *Ant. Jud.* 14.5.4; 14.6.2-4.

4. Cass. Dio. 39.55.3-56.5; App. *Syr.* 51; Jos. *Ant. Jud.* 14.6.2.

5. Strab. 17.1.11; Cass. Dio 39.56.4-57.3; Plut. *Cat. Min.* 35.2-36.3.

6. Cass. Dio 39.56.3-5; Plut. *Ant.* 3.2; Cic. *Phil.* 2.48; Cic. *Att.* 4.10.1; Cic. *Pis.* 21.49; Strab. 17.1.11; App. *Syr.* 51.

7. Plut. *Ant.* 3.4; Jos. *Bell. Jud.* 1.8.7; Jos. *Ant. Jud.* 14.6.2; Cass. Dio. 39.58.1.

8. Cic. *Phil.* 2.48; App. *BCiv.* 5.8; Plut. *Ant.* 3.5-6; Strab. 12.3.34; 17.1.11; Cass. Dio 39.58.

9. Jos. *Ant. Jud.* 14.6; Jos. *Bell. Jud.* 1.8.7; Caes. *Civ.* 3.4.4; Cic. *Rab. Post.* 10.28; Oros. 6.15.33.

10. Cass. Dio 39.59-62.1; Cic. *Pis.* 22.

11. Cass. Dio 39.62.2-3; Cic. *Att.* 4.18; Cic. *Ad Q. Fr.* 3.1.15; 3.4.1-4; 3.6.5; 3.9.1-4.

12. Cass. Dio 39.59.2; 39.63.

13. Caes. *Gall.* 5.1-23; Cass. Dio 40.1-4.

14. Caes. *Gall.* 5.24-58; Cass. Dio 40.5-11.

15. Cic. *Phil.* 2.49.

16. Cass. Dio 39.64; 40.16-30; Plut. *Crass.* 17-32.

17. Charles Babcock, "The Early Career of Fulvia," *AJP* vol. 86, no. 341 (1965), 17; Cic. *Phil.* 2.21; 2.49; Cass. Dio 45.40.2; Cic. *Mil.* 15.

18. Cic. *Mil. passim*; Ascon. *Mil.* 11; Plut. *Cic.* 35.

19. Cic. *Att.* 6.6.4.

20. Cass. Dio 40.33-39; Caes. *Gall.* 7.1-68; Plut. *Caes.* 25-26.

21. Caes. *Gall.* 7.76; Plut. *Caes.* 27 says 300,000 Gauls.

22. Caes. *Gall.* 7.77; Plut. *Caes.* 27 says the population was 170,000.

23. Caes. *Gall.* 7.68-88; Vell. 2.47; Diod. 4.19; Strab. 4.2.3; Cass Dio 40.39-40; Tac. *Ann.* 11.23; Flor. 3.10; Plut. *Caes.* 27.

24. Cass. Dio 40.40.5; Caes. *Gall.* 7.81-82.

25. Caes. *Gall.* 7.83-89; Cass. Dio 40.41-43; Plut. *Caes.* 27.5-10.

26. Caes. *Gall.* 7.90; 8.2-5.

27. Caes. *Gall.* 8.24; 8.38-46.

28. Caes. *Gall.* 8.23; 8.46-48; Cass. Dio 40.42-43.

29. Cic. *Phil.* 2.50; Cic. *Fam.* 16.27; Caes. *Gall.* 8.50.

Chapter IV.
Across the Rubicon

1. Plut. *Ant.* 5.1 says that the office of tribune was won first. Cf. Cic. *Phil.* 2.4; Cic. *Fam.* 8.14.1; Caes. *Gall.* 8.50.1.

2. For the date see Jerzy Linderski, "The Aedileship of Favonius Curio and Cicero's Election to the Augurate," *HSPh* 76 (1972), 190-200.

3. Cic. *Phil.* 2.4.

4. Cic. *Fam.* 8.14.1; Cic. *Phil.* 2.4; Plut. *Ant.* 5.1-2; Caes. *Gall.* 8.50.1; App. *BCiv.* 3.7.

5. Cass. Dio 40.60-62; Plut. *Ant.* 5.1; Plut. *Caes.* 29.2; Caes. *Gall.* 8.52; Cic. *Phil.* 2.4; 5.9; Cic. *Dom.* 110; Cic. *Red. Sen.* 18; Cic. *Sest.* 53; Cic. *Fam.* 2.18.

6. App. *BCiv.* 2.62; Suet. *Jul.* 24.1; 29.2; Caes. *Civ.* 1.9.2; 1.32; Cic. *Fam.* 1.9.9; Cic. *Att.* 7.3.4; Plut. *Crass.* 14.6; Plut. *Caes.* 21.5; Plut. *Pomp.* 51.4; Sall. *Ad Caes.* 2.2.3.

7. Cass. Dio 40.44; 40.50; Suet. *Jul.* 26; Liv. *Ep.* 107.

8. The date for the legal end of Caesar's command in Gaul has been much disputed. Those arguing that the command was due to end in 49 B.C.: Theodor Mommsen, *Die Rechtsfrage zwischen Caesar und dem Senate* (Breslau, 1857), 1-58; T. R. Holmes, *The Roman Republic*, vol. II (London, 1923), 229-310; E. G. Hardy, *Some Problems in Roman History* (Oxford, 1924), 150-206; G. R. Elton, "The Terminal Date of Caesar's Proconsulate," *JRS* 36 (1946), 18-42; R. Sealey, "*Habe Meam Rationem*," *C&M* 18 (1957), 75-101; S. Jameson, "The Intended Date of Caesar's Return from Gaul," *Latomus* 29 (1970), 638-660. Those arguing for 50 B.C.: C. E. Stevens, "The Terminal Date of Caesar's Command," *AJP* 59 (1938), 169-208; C. G. Stone, "March 1, 50 B.C.," *CQ* 22 (1928), 193-201; F. B. Marsh, *The Founding of the Roman Empire* (Oxford, 1927), 265-89; O. Hirschfeld, "Der Endtermin der gallischen Statthalterschaft Caesars," *Klio* 4 (1904), 77-88.

9. Liv. *Ep.* 107-8; Suet. *Jul.* 26.1; 28.3; Cass. Dio 40.51.2; 40.56; 40.59.1; App. *BCiv.* 2.20; 2.25-26; Caes. *Civ.* 1.9; Caes. *Gall.* 8.53; Cic. *Att.* 7.3.4; 7.7.6; 7.33-34; 8.3.3; Cic. *Fam.* 6.6.5; 8.5.2-3; 8.8.9; 8.9.2; Plut. *Pomp.* 56.

10. Cic. *Fam.* 8.11.3; 8.14.2; App. *BCiv.* 2.28; Caes. *Gall.* 8.52.4; Caes. *Civ.* 1.9.5.

11. This and the following dates accept the contemporary chronology. But until the Julian calendar correction, the calendar ran about seven weeks ahead. December 1, in the Roman calendar, was our mid-October, and Caesar crossed the Rubicon on January 11 in the Roman calendar, November 23 in our calendar. The November date permitted a campaigning season before the army set up winter camp, although the fact that Italy normally has a rainy November may have persuaded Pompey that Caesar would not attempt to move.

12. App. *BCiv.* 2.4.30-31; Plut. *Pomp.* 58.4; 59.1; Plut. *Ant.* 5.4; Plut. *Caes.* 30.3; 31.1; Cass. Dio 40.64.4; 41.1.4; Cic. *Att.* 7.9; Cic. *Fam.* 2.18.2-3; 8.14; Oros. 6.15.1.

13. Plut. *Ant.* 5.2; Cic. *Att.* 7.8.5; Cic. *Fam.* 8.4.4.

14. Cass. Dio 40.66.5. The exact sequence of proposals cannot be determined from the disparate sources: Cass. Dio 41.1-4; App. *BCiv.* 2.30-32; 2.127; Cic. *Fam.* 16.11.2; Cic. *Att.* 7.8.4; Caes. *Civ.* 1.1-2; 1.9; Flor. 2.13-17; Plut. *Ant.* 5.3; Plut. *Caes.* 30.1-2; 30.4; 31.1; Plut. *Pomp.* 59.3-4; Vell. 2.49.3-4; Suet. *Jul.* 29.2.

15. App. *BCiv.* 2.34; Cic. *Att.* 7.8.5; 7.9; 10.8.8; Caes. *Civ.* 1.5; 1.7.2-5; Plut. *Ant.*

5.4; 5.8-9; Plut. *Caes.* 31.2; 33; Plut. *Pomp.* 61; Liv. *Ep.* 109; Lucan, 1.303-25; 2.16-44; Oros. 6.15.2.

16. Caes. *Civ.* 1.6; Cic. *Fam.* 16.11.2.

17. Suet. *Jul.* 31; 33; Plut. *Caes.* 31.1-33.4; Plut. *Ant.* 5.3-4; Flor. 2.13.19; App. *BCiv.* 2.33; 2.35; Vell. 2.49.4; Caes. *Civ.* 1.8.1; 1.9; Cic. *Fam.* 8.17.1; Cic. *Phil.* 2.22; 2.53; 2.55; Cic. *Att.* 11.7.1; Cass. Dio 41.4.1; Lucan. 1.231-395; Oros. 6.15.3.

18. Caes. *Civ.* 1.11.4; 1.16-29; Cic. *Att.* 7.12.2; 8.4.3; 9.19.1; Cass. Dio 41.10-12; 41.26; Plut. *Caes.* 34.3-35.1; Sen. *Benef.* 3.24; Suet. *Jul.* 34; Suet. *Ner.* 2; Oros. 6.15.3-4.

19. Plut. *Caes.* 34.2; Caes. *Gall.* 8.52; Cic. *Att.* 7.12.5; 8.13; 8.16; 9.7; Oros. 6.15.4.

20. Vell. 2.49.4; Caes. *Civ.* 1.8-11; Plut. *Caes.* 33.5-34.1; Plut. *Pomp.* 60; Cic. *Att.* 7.12.2; 7.14; Cic. *Fam.* 16.2; Cass. Dio 41.5.2-10.2; App. *BCiv.* 2.36.

21. Plut. *Caes.* 35.2.

22. The *pomerium* was the line marked out by the augurs as the boundary of the city. Religious prohibition forbade a promagistrate with *imperium* to cross the *pomerium*.

23. Cic. *Att.* 9.11.2; 9.18; 10.4.9; 10.8.8; Cic. *Fam.* 8.16; Sall. *Ad Caes.* 2.5; 4.2; Caes. *Civ.* 1.32-33.

24. Cic. *Att.* 9.19.1; Cass. Dio 41.18.2; 41.36.3; 43.47.3; 43.49.1; 44.47.4; Plut. *Caes.* 37.1; Suet. *Jul.* 41; Sall. *Ad Caes.* 6.1.

25. Pompey's property was auctioned at 50 million denarii although it was worth 70 million denarii. After Caesar's death, when Antony hoped to win the support of Sextus Pompey, he had the Senate vote to return to Sextus the 50 million Attic drachmae that the state treasury had received from the sale of his father's estate. Later Antony offered Sextus even the estate itself. After the battle of Actium, at least the villa at Misenum fell to Octavian.

26. Cass. Dio. 41.16.1; 43.50; 45.9.4; 45.10.6; 48.36.4; Cic. *Att.* 9.8; Cic. *Phil.* 2.48; 2.103-4; 13.10-11; Cic. *Fam.* 12.2.1; Vell. 2.77.1; App. *BCiv.* 3.4; 3.20-21; 5.79; Plut. *Caes.* 51.

27. Plut. *Pomp.* 62.2; Plut. *Caes.* 35.2-4; Flor. 2.13.21; Oros. 6.15.5; Pl. *N.H.* 33.56; App. *BCiv.* 2.41; Cic. *Att.* 10.4.8; Cass. Dio 41.17.1-2.

28. Cic. *Att.* 9.9.3; 9.15.2; 10.8a; 10.10.5; 10.11.4; 10.12a.1; 10.15.3; 10.16.5; Plut. *Ant.* 6.2; App. *BCiv.* 2.41; Caes. *Civ.* 3.1; *CIL* 1².2.787.

29. Cic. *Att.* 9.9; 10.8.4; Plut. *Ant.* 6.5; Plut. *Pomp.* 62; Caes. *Civ.* 1.25; 3.10.5; 3.67.5; Liv. *Ep.* 110; Flor. 2.13.31-33; Cic. *Fam.* 12.14; 12.15; Oros. 6.15.7-9; Lucan. 4.406-824; App. *BCiv.* 2.49; 2.191; Cass. Dio 41.40.

30. Plut. *Ant.* 6.6.

31. Cic. *Att.* 9.11.2; 9.18.2; 9.19; 10.8.8; 10.8.10; 10.8a; 10.9; 10.10.1; 10.18.

32. Gossip swelled even to claim that Antony's carriage was drawn by lions and that laurel-crowned lictors preceded him. The lions, at least, must have been a contemporary jest or an extravagant association of Antony with Hercules or with Dionysus whose chariot was drawn by leopards. Cicero's criticism of Antony's lictors appears based on his refusal to accept Antony's irregular propraetor status, since a praetor normally was entitled to lictors.

33. Plut. *Ant.* 9; Plut. *Q.R.* 81; Cic. *Att.* 10.10; 10.11; 10.12; 10.13; 10.15.3; Cic. *Phil.* 2.58; Sall. *Ad Caes.* 2.5; 4.2; 6.1 indicates that Cicero was not alone in his hostility to Antony's conduct.

34. Cic. *Att.* 10.12a; 10.16; 10.17; 10.18.

35. Caes. *Civ.* 1.34; 2.22; 2.32; Oros. 6.15.6-7; Flor. 2.13.26-30; App. *BCiv.* 2.42-43; Plut. *Caes.* 36; Suet. *Jul.* 34; Vell. 2.50.3.

36. App. *BCiv.* 2.44-48; Oros. 6.15.9-10; Caes. *Civ.* 2.23-44; 3.1-2; Plut. *Ant.* 7.1.

37. Cass. Dio 41.44; Caes. *Civ.* 3.6; Vell. 2.51.1-2; App. *BCiv.* 2.53. No record exists that Antony had an official title during this period, but probably he was a legate.

38. Caes. *Civ.* 3.18; 3.24; Cass. Dio. 41.48.3; Plut. *Caes.* 37; Oros. 6.15.10.

39. App. *BCiv.* 2.56-58; Plut. *Caes.* 38; Lucan. 5.476-702; Val. Max. 9.8.2; Flor. 2.13.37; Suet. *Jul.* 58; Cass. Dio 41.46.4; Zon. 10.8; Caes. *Civ.* 3; 25.

40. App. *BCiv.* 2.59; Cass. Dio 41.48; Plut. *Ant.* 7.2-4; Caes. *Civ.* 3.26; 3.29-30; 3.40.

41. Caes. *Civ.* 3.26; 3.30.

42. Caes. *Civ.* 3.34; 3.41; 3.43-46; 3.48-49; Oros. 6.15.18; App. *BCiv.* 2.60.

43. Caes. *Civ.* 3.46; 3.59-60; 3.63-71; Plut. *Ant.* 8.1; Plut. *Pomp.* 65.5; Plut. *Caes.* 39.3-5; App. *BCiv.* 2.61-62.

44. App. *BCiv.* 2.63; 2.65-69; Cass. Dio 41.51; Plut. *Caes.* 39.6-42.1; Plut. *Pomp.* 56; 67; Suet. *Ner.* 2; Lucan. 7.45-123; Caes. *Civ.* 3.82-83; Cic. *Fam.* 7.3.2; Cic. *Att.* 11.6.6; Vell. 2.52.1-2, in his pro-Caesar tradition, says that Pompey insisted on fighting despite the advice of the senators to the contrary.

45. Plut. *Caes.* 44.2 and *Pomp.* 69.1 says that Pompey opposed Antony, but Caes. *Civ.* 3.88 is the more reliable source. See Eutr. 6.20.4; Oros. 6.15.23-27; Plut. *Caes.* 42-46; Plut. *Pomp.* 56.3-57.4; 69.1-72.4; Plut. *Ant.* 8.2; Caes. *Civ.* 3.86-99; App. *BCiv.* 2.70-82; Suet. *Jul.* 35; Flor. 2.13.47-52; Cic. *Phil.* 2.59; 2.71; Cass Dio 41.53-61; App. *Ill.* 12.

46. App. *BCiv.* 2.82 says that 25,000 of Pompey's men were casualties, but Caesar *Civ.* 3.99 is more trustworthy. See Cic. *Phil.* 2.71; Oros. 6.15.27; Plut. *Pomp.* 72.3; Plut. *Caes.* 46.3; Vell. 2.52.3-5.

Chapter V.
Henchman to the Dictator

1. Plut. *Ant.* 8.3; Cic. *Phil.* 2.25.

2. Both the Nile cruise and Caesarion's paternity are disputed in ancient and modern sources, cf. App. *BCiv.* 2.90; Suet. *Jul.* 52; Nic. Dam. 20. Octavian judged him enough of a challenge as Caesar's heir to have him killed in 30 B.C.

3. Cass. Dio 42.7-9; 42.34-48; Lucan. 8-10; Vell. 2.53-54.1; Oros. 6.15.28-16.3; Caes. *Alex. passim*; Jos. *Bell. Jud.* 1.9.3-4; App. *BCiv.* 2.71; 2.83-88; 2.91; Suet. *Jul.* 35; Plut. *Caes.* 48-49; Liv. *Ep.* 112; Flor. 2.13.55-63; Caes. *Civ.* 3.106-7; 3.111.

4. A dictator was nominated by a consul on the senate's proposal. The nomination was confirmed by the Lex Curiata. The dictator appointed a magister equitum as his subordinate.

5. Cic. *Phil.* 2.59; 2.62-63; 2.71; Plut. *Ant.* 8.3; Cass. Dio 42.21; 45.27.5; 46.13.1; *CIL* IV, 191, no. 2894.

6. Cass. Dio 41.62; Cic. *Phil.* 2.38; Cic. *Att.* 11.7.3; Plut. *Cic.* 37-39.

7. Plut. *Ant.* 9.3-6; Plut. *Caes.* 51; Pl. *N.H.* 8.55; Cic. *Att.* 10.10.5; 13.19.4; Cic. *Phil.* 2.42; 2.61-63; 2.67-69; Cass. Dio 42.27-28; 45.28.

8. Cic. *Phil.* 2.62; Cass. Dio 41.38.

9. Cic. *Att.* 7.11.1; Cic. *Fam.* 8.17.2; 9.16.7; Cic. *Phil.* 6.11; 11.14; 13.26; Caes. *Civ.* 3.1; 3.20-22; Vell. 2.68.2-3; Cass. Dio 42.29-31; Plut. *Ant.* 9.1; Liv. *Ep.* 113.

10. Cic. *Att.* 11.12.4; 12.28; 14.21.3; Cic. *Phil.* 2.99; Plut. *Ant.* 9.1-2.

11. Cic. *Phil.* 6.11; 10.22; 11.15-16; Cass. Dio 42.29.3-4; 42.31.3-32.1; 46.16; Plut. *Ant.* 9.2; App. *BCiv.* 2.92.

12. Cass. Dio 42.30-31.1.

13. Cass. Dio 42.30-32.1.

14. Cass. Dio 42.32.2-3; Liv. *Ep.* 113.

15. Cass. Dio 42.33; 42.50-51; App. *BCiv.* 2.92; Cic. *Off.* 2.23.83; Cic. *Fam.* 8.17.2; 13.7.2; Plut. *Ant.* 10.

16. Cic. *Att.* 12.18a.1; Cic. *Phil.* 2.64-69; 2.71-74; 13.10-11; Plut. *Ant.* 10; Cass. Dio 42.50.5.

17. Cic. *Att.* 11.21.2; 11.22.2; App. *BCiv.* 2.92-94; Cass. Dio 42.52-55; Plut. *Caes.* 51; Suet. *Jul.* 70.

18. There remains some question whether Caesar himself ordered the execution, cf. Suet. *Jul.* 75.3; Caes. *Afr.* 89.

19. Caes. *Afr. passim*; Vell. 2.54.2-55.2; App. *BCiv.* 2.14.95-100; Liv. *Ep.* 113-14; Oros. 6.16.3-6; Suet. *Jul.* 59; 75.3; Plut. *Caes.* 52-54; Plut. *Cat. Min.* 56-72; Flor. 2.13.64-72; Cass. Dio 42.56-43.13; Cic. *Phil.* 2.48.

20. Plut. *Caes.* 55; 59.5-6; App. *BCiv.* 2.101-2; 2.154; Cic. *Phil.* 1.19; 8.28; 14.23; Macr. *Sat.* 1.14.1-3; Cens. 20.4.7; Pl. *N.H.* 7.92; 18.211; Cass. Dio 43.19-26; Suet. *Jul.* 37-38; 40-42; Oros. 6.16.6; Flor. 2.13.88-89 and Vell. 2.56.1-2 place the triumphs after the Spanish War.

21. Plut. *Ant.* 10.1-2; Plut. *Caes.* 56; Cass. Dio 43.1.1; 43.28-45; 43.51.8; App. *BCiv.* 2.103-7; Cic. *Phil.* 2.74; Vell. 2.55.2-4; Oros. 6.16.5-9; Caes. *Hisp. passim*.

22. The younger Curio was killed at Actium as a follower of Antony. Cass. Dio 51.2.5.

23. For an estimate of Fulvia, see Charles Babcock, "The Early Career of Fulvia," *AJP* 86 (1965), 1-32. See Vell. 2.74; 2.100.4; Plut. *Ant.* 9-10; 57.3; 81; 87.1; Cass. Dio 51.2-5; 51.15; 54.26; Cic. *Phil.* 3.16; Sen. *De Brev. Vit.* 5.4.

24. Plut. *Ant.* 10.3-4; App. *BCiv.* 4.29; Cic. *Phil.* 2.11; 2.113; 5.11; 6.4; 13.18. About this time Marcus Brutus was taking a new, strong-minded wife, Porcia, the daughter of the anti-Caesarian Cato the Younger. She would similarly influence his career.

25. Cic. *Phil.* 2.34; 2.78; Plut. *Ant.* 10.4; 11.1-2; 13.1.

26. Plut. *Ant.* 11.1-2; Plut. *Brut.* 18; Plut. *Caes.* 61; Cass. Dio 43.49.1; 45.9.2; 45.11.2; 45.40.3; Cic. *Fam.* 11.2.1; Cic. *Phil.* 2.70; 2.79; 2.85; 2.106; Liv. *Ep.* 116-17; App. *BCiv.* 2.107; 2.109; 2.114; 2.118; 3.28; Vell. 2.56; 2.58; 2.60.

27. Suet. *Jul.* 83; Liv. *Ep.* 116 says that Octavian received only half of Caesar's estate. Plut. *Caes.* 64.1; Plut. *Ant.* 2.1; Plut. *Brut.* 22.1; Pl. *N.H.* 35.21; Cass. Dio 44.35.2; Oros. 6.18.1; Flor. 2.15.1; App. *BCiv.* 2.143; 3.11; 3.13; 3.22-23; 3.94; Vell. 2.59.1; Nic. Dam. 8; 13.

28. Cic. *Phil.* 2.98 later blamed Antony for not using his influence with Caesar to recall his uncle in 49 B.C.

29. App. *BCiv.* 2.94; *Lib.* 136; Nic. Dam. 17; Suet. *Jul.* 42; 81.1; Cic. *Off.* 1.43; 2.27; Cic. *Att.* 14.6.1; 14.12.1; 16.16a.4-5; Cic. *Fam.* 9.17.2; 13.4-5; 13.7.2; 13.8; Plut. *Caes.* 57.5; Cass. Dio 43.50.3-4; Liv. 34.9.3; Strab. 17.3.15. Caesar initiated the large overseas colonies which became common in the empire. See E. T. Salmon, *Roman Colonization under the Republic* (London, 1969), 113.

30. Suet. *Jul.* 41; 44; Suet. *Claud.* 20.1; Pl. *N.H.* 4.10; Cic. *Phil.* 5.7; Cic. *Att.* 13.33a.1; Plut. *Caes.* 58; Cass. Dio 43.49.2-50.1; 44.5.

31. Cass. Dio 41.24.1; 47.15; 47.31.5; Liv. *Ep.* 110; Suet. *Jul.* 52; 76; 79; Suet. *Aug.* 17.5; *CIL* I2.1, no. 206; Cic. *Fam.* 6.18.1; Cic. *Att.* 4.4; 14.7.1-8; 14.8; 14.18.1; 14.20.2; 15.4.4; 15.15; 17.2; 20.2; App. *BCiv.* 2.102; Nic. Dam. 20 calls Caesarion Cyrus; Plut. *Ant.* 54.4; Plut. *Caes.* 49.

32. Cass. Dio 43.27.1; Cic. *Fam.* 4.6.3; 6.16; 7.30.1; 9.15.3-4; 13.77.1; 15.19.4.

33. App. *BCiv.* 2.112; Cic. *Phil.* 7.16; Suet. *Jul.* 41.2; 76; Cass. Dio 43.51.3.

34. Caesar, to check the building up of military and political power in a province

such as he had achieved in Gaul, had limited proconsular governorships to two years, propraetorian governorships to one year. Cass. Dio 43.25.3; Cic. *Phil.* 1.19; 5.7; 8.28.

35. Plut. *Ant.* 11.3; App. *BCiv.* 2.122; 2.128-29; 2.138; Vell. 2.58.2; Cass. Dio 43.51.8; Cic. *Phil.* 2.79-84; 2.88; 3.37-39; Nic. Dam. 22; Suet. *Jul.* 76.3.

36. Cass. Dio 44.6.4 calls it Julian Jupiter.

37. Plut. *Caes.* 57.1; App. *BCiv.* 2.102; 2.106; 2.124; 2.134; 2.137; 2.139; 2.144; Suet. *Jul.* 76; 84.2-5; Cass. Dio 42.20.3; 43.14; 43.22.2; 43.44-45; 44.4.4; Cic. *Phil.* 2.110; Cic. *Att.* 13.44.1. For a full account of Caesar's role as divinity, see S. Weinstock, *Divus Julius* (London, 1971), *passim*.

38. See pp. 25, 77.

39. The Lex Cassia of 45 B.C. gave Caesar the right to create patrician families (*gentes*). Besides Antony's, a number of other patrician *gentes* were created at this time to refill the shattered patrician ranks: Tac. *Ann.* 11.25.3; Suet. *Jul.* 41.1.

40. Cic. *Phil.* 285; 2.110; 13.41; 13.47; Cass. Dio 44.6.4; 45.30.2; Liv. 1.20.2; 27.8.2-12.

41. Or consul, if the date were more accurately January 44 B.C. App. *BCiv.* 2.107; Plut. *Caes.* 60 refer to "consuls" plural.

42. Cic. *Fam.* 3.4; 4.3; 4.4; 4.5.2-6; 5.15.4; 6.1.1; 6.7.4; 6.9; 9.16.3; 9.26.1-3; 11.27.8; 12.18; 13.68; 13.77.1; 21.3; Cic. *Att.* 12.21.4; 12.23.1; 13.50.1; 13.51.1; 28.2-3; 37.2; Cass. Dio 44.8.1-4; Plut. *Caes.* 60; Eutr. 6.25; Nic. Dam. 20-22; Liv. *Ep.* 116; Suet. *Jul.* 78; App. *BCiv.* 2.107.

43. Here, among the slightly divergent accounts, Appian seems most reliable. Nic. Dam. 20 compresses the two incidents into one. Plut. *Ant.* 12; *Caes.* 61 place the incident of the diadems after the Lupercalia and state that the tribunes were taken to prison. Cass. Dio 44.9-10 states that the deposition of the tribunes came only after further provocation. App. *BCiv.* 2.108 says that the diadems were placed on the statues to discredit Caesar and that Caesar was well pleased with their removal. Suet. *Jul.* 79 states that the criticism of the tribunes followed the removal of the diadems. Cf. Cic. *Att.* 13.37.2; 13.44.1; Cic. *Fam.* 6.19.2; Cic. *Phil.* 13.31; Strab. 2.68.4-5; Liv. *Ep.* 116; Vell. 2.68.3-4.

44. A. K. Michels, "Topography and Interpretation of the Lupercalia," *TAPA* 84 (1953), 35. For the alternative interpretation of a fertility rite, cf. H. J. Rose, "Two Notes on Roman Religion," *Latomus* 8 (1949), 9-17. See Cic. *Att.* 12.5.1; *Phil.* 13.31; Suet. *Aug.* 31.4; *CIL* 1².310.

45. Cass. Dio 43.49.2; 44.11.1-3; 45.30.2; 46.5.2; 47.19.4-7 (distorted in the speech of Calenus); Plut. *Caes.* 60-61; Plut. *Ant.* 12; Liv. *Ep.* 116; Suet. *Jul.* 79.2; App. *BCiv.* 2.109; Cic. *De Div.* 1.52.119; 2.16.37; Cic. *Phil.* 2.84-87; 3.5; 3.12; 5.38; 13.15; 13.17; Val. Max. 1.6.13; Quint. *Inst.* 9.3.61; Flor. 2.13.91; Ps.-Vict. *De Orig.* 22.1; Vell. 2.56.4; Nic. Dam. 21 adds a number of details which, without further corroboration, appear a late Augustan addition; Antony was director of the festival; Licinius, then Cassius and Casca offered the diadem to Caesar; next Antony twice offered the crown; when it was rejected, Antony embraced Caesar and had the diadem placed on one of Caesar's statues. A. Alföldi, "The Portrait of Caesar on the Denarii of 44 B.C.," *Centennial Volume of the American Numismatic Society* (1958), 27-42 argues that coins show the diadem hung on a peg in the temple.

46. Cic. *Phil.* 13.41; Cic. *Fam.* 10.28.1; Cass. Dio 46.17.5-7; 46.19.4-7; Plut. *Ant.* 12; Nic. Dam. 19-20.

47. Cic. *Phil.* 2.26; 2.34; 2.74; Cic. *Marc.* 21-23; App. *BCiv.* 2.107; 2.109; 2.146; Suet. *Jul.* 75.5; 80; 86; Plut. *Ant.* 11.3; 13.2; Plut. *Caes.* 57; 62.5; Plut. *Brut.* 8.1; 10; Eutr. 6.25; Sen. *De Ira* 3.30.4-5; Nic. Dam. 19 says that over eighty men were in the

conspiracy; 22-23; Cass. Dio 44.7.4. One loyal follower of Caesar was Matius: Cic. *Fam.* 11.28.

48. Plut. *Brut.* 18.2-5; Plut. *Ant.* 13; Cic. *Phil.* 2.34; Cic. *Fam.* 10.28.1; 12.4.1; Cic. *Ad Brut.* 1.4.2; 2.5.1; 25.1; Cic. *Att.* 9.2; 11.1; 14.21.3; 15.4.2; 15.11.2; 15.12.2; 20.2 App. *BCiv.* 2.114; Cass. Dio 44.19.

49. Plut. *Ant.* 11.2; 13.2; 14.1; Plut. *Caes.* 62-66; Plut. *Brut.* 17.1; 18; Cass. Dio 43.51.8; 44.15-19; 44.22.2; Suet. *Jul.* 80.4-82.3; Cic. *Phil.* 2.32-33; 2.79-88; 13.22; 14.14.2; 14.21.3; 14.34; Cic. *Ad Brut.* 2.5.1; Cic. *Att.* 14.4.4; 15.4.2; Cic. *Fam.* 10.28.1; Cic. *De Div.* 2.23; App. *BCiv.* 2.111-18; Nic. Dam. 23-24; 26; Liv. *Ep.* 116; Flor. 2.13.93-95; Vell. 2.56-58; Oros. 6.17.1-3; Zon. 10.11D; Eutr. 6.25; Val. Max. 4.5.6.

50. Cic. *Att.* 9.18.1; Suet. *Jul.* 77-78.

Chapter VI.
Caesar's Successor

1. Plut. *Brut.* 18; Plut. *Ant.* 14.1; Cic. *Phil.* 2.89; Cass. Dio 44.22.2; App. *BCiv.* 2.118; Nic. Dam. 26.

2. Cic. *Att.* 6.1; 9.2; 11.1; 14.4.2; 14.9; 14.10.1; 14.12.1; 14.13.2; 14.14.2-3; 14.17a; 14.21; 14.22; 15.3.2; Cic. *Fam.* 6.15; 10.28.1; 12.1.1; 12.3.1; Cic. *Phil.* 2.28; 2.34; 2.89; Plut. *Cic.* 42.1; Plut. *Brut.* 12; 18; Plut. *Caes.* 67; Cass. Dio 44.20-22; Flor. 2.17.1-3; Oros. 6.17.9; Liv. *Ep.* 116; Nic. Dam. 17; 25-27; App. *BCiv.* 2.118-23.

3. Liv. *Ep.* 117; App. *BCiv.* 2.118; 2.131-32 (Appian inaccurately states that the republicans offered the office of pontifex maximus to Lepidus); Cass. Dio 43.49.1; 44.16.2; 44.22; 44.34; 44.53.6-7; Nic. Dam. 17; 26b-27; Suet. *Jul.* 82.4; Pl. *N.H.* 7.147; *CIL* 1.440; 466; Plut. *Brut.* 12.

4. App. *BCiv.* 2.125; 3.5; Cic. *Phil.* 1.17; 2.35; 2.93; 4.14; 5.11; 5.15; 8.26; 12.12; Cic. *Att.* 14.10.1; 14.13a & b; 14.14; 16.14.3; Nic. Dam. 28; Plut. *Ant.* 15.1; Vell. 2.60.4.

5. App. *BCiv.* 1.123-25; Nic. Dam. 17; 27; Cic. *Fam.* 11.1.

6. App. *BCiv.* 2.126-29; Jos. *Ant. Jud.* 14.10.9-10; Plut. *Cic.* 42.3; Plut. *Caes.* 67.9; Plut. *Brut.* 19.1; Plut. *Ant.* 14.2; Cass. Dio 44.22-34; Vell. 2.58.2-4; Cic. *Att.* 14.6.2; 14.9.2; 15.4.3; 16.14.1; Cic. *Phil.* 1.1; 1.31; 2.89; Cic. *Fam.* 12.1.2.

7. App. *BCiv.* 2.129-35; Plut. *Ant.* 14.2; Cic. *Phil.* 2.100; Cic. *Fam.* 12.1; Cic. *Att.* 14.10; 14.14.2; Flor. 2.17.4.

8. Cass. Dio 44.34-35.1; App. *BCiv.* 2.134; 2.136; 2.142; 3.15; Suet. *Jul.* 82.4; Plut. *Brut.* 19.2; 20.1; Plut. *Ant.* 14.1; Vell. 2.58.3; Liv. *Ep.* 116; Cic. *Phil.* 1.31; 2.90.

9. Liv. *Ep.* 116 reports that Octavian received only half the estate. Cf. Pl. *N.H.* 35.21; Cic. *Phil.* 2.71; 2.109; Vell. 2.59; Flor. 2.15.1; Suet. *Jul.* 83; App. *BCiv.* 2.143; 3.11; 3.17; 3.22-23; 3.94; Cass. Dio 44.35 gives an alternative sum of 120 sesterces; 44.53.5; Aug. *R.G.* 15; Tac. *Ann.* 2.41; Nic. Dam. 8 says that Octavian knew of his adoption, but in 13 he contradicts this by saying that Caesar hid his decision; see 17; 29.

10. Suet. *Jul.* 84; Plut. *Brut.* 20.1-4; Plut. *Caes.* 68.1; Plut. *Cic.* 42.4; Plut. *Ant.* 14.3-4; Oros. 6.17.3; Nic. Dam. 13; 16-7; Cic. *Att.* 14.10.1; 14.14.3; Cic. *Phil.* 2.90-91; 3.30; Cass. Dio 44.35.4-49.4; Val. Max. 9.9.1; App. *BCiv.* 2.143-47; 3.15; 3.35; see M. Deutsch, "Antony's Funeral Speech," *Cal. U. Pub. in Cl. Phil.* vol. 9, no. 6 (1926-29), 127-58; G. Kennedy, "Antony's Speech at Caesar's Funeral," *The Quarterly Journal of Speech* 54.2 (April 1968), 99-108.

11. Suet. *Jul.* 85; Tac. *Ann.* 1.8; Plut. *Brut.* 20.5-21.1; Plut. *Caes.* 68; Plut. *Cic.* 42.4-5; Plut. *Ant.* 14.4-15.1; Cic. *Att.* 14.7.1; 14.10.1; Cic. *Phil.* 2.91; 10.7; Liv. *Ep.* 116; Cass. Dio 44.50-52; App. *BCiv.* 2.147-48; 3.2; 3.15; 3.35.

NOTES

12. Suet. *Jul.* 85; App. *BCiv.* 2.148; 3.2-3; 3.16; Cass. Dio 44.51; Cic. *Att.* 12.49.1; 14.6.1; 14.8.1; Cic. *Phil.* 1.5; Liv. *Ep.* 116.

13. App. *BCiv.* 3.3-4; Cic. *Att.* 14.15.1; Cic. *Phil.* 1.5; Val. Max. 9.15.1; Nic. Dam. 14.

14. Cic. *Fam.* 10.30.1; Cic. *Att.* 16.8.2; Cic. *Phil.* 1.27; 2.100; 2.108; App. *BCiv.* 3.4-5 says that the guard was composed wholly of centurions, but such a number of officers is unrealistic; see 3.46; 3.57.

15. Cic. *Att.* 14.15.1; 14.16.2; 14.17a; 14.18.1; 14.19.2; 14.20; 14.21; 14.22; 15.1; 15.5.1; 15.6; 15.22; 16.1; 16.15.1; 16.27; Cic. *Fam.* 9.14; 11.2.2; 12.1.1; 12.2.2; Cic. *Phil.* 1.5; 1.29; 2.107; 11.10; 13.2-3; 13.5; 13.26-28; 13.47; Cass. Dio 44.53.7; 45.9.2; Liv. *Ep.* 117; Vell. 2.63.1; Nic. Dam. 14.

16. Cic. *Att.* 14.3.2; 14.6.2; 14.10.1; 14.13.4; 14.17.3; 14.18.4; 14.19.1; 15.20.2-3; 15.22; 16.4; 16.7; Cic. *Fam.* 11.1.2-4; 11.3; 11.14.

17. App. *BCiv.* 3.4; 3.36; 4.83-84; Cic. *Att.* 14.13.2-6; 15.29.1; 16.4; 16.7; 16.11; Cic. *Phil.* 1.8; 5.39-41; Cass. Dio 45.9-10.

18. Cass. Dio 44.51; Liv. *Ep.* 116; Cic. *Phil.* 1.3-4; 1.32; 2.91; 5.10; App. *BCiv.* 3.25.

19. App. *BCiv.* 3.5; Cass. Dio 44.53; 45.23; 46.23; Plut. *Ant.* 15; Vell. 2.60.4; Cic. *Att.* 14.6.1-2; 14.10; 14.12.1-2; 14.14.2-4; 14.22; 15.4.4; 16.16c; Cic. *Fam.* 12.1-2; Cic. *Phil.* 1.3; 1.24; 2.93-100; 3.30; 5.10-12; 7.15; 12.12.

20. Cic. *Att.* 14.21.2-3; 15.5; Cic. *Phil.* 2.100; 2.108; 5.18; App. *BCiv.* 2.94; 2.125; 2.135; 3.87.

21. Cic. *Att.* 15.17.1; 15.19.2; Cic. *Fam.* 11.2.3; Cic. *Phil.* 1.6; 2.43; 2.100-4; 5.3; 5.7; 5.10; 5.20-21; 5.33; 6.12-14; 7.17; 8.25-26; 10.22; 11.13; 13.5; 13.31; 13.37.

22. Cic. *Att.* 14.17.2; 14.19.4; 14.20.2-3; 15.1.2; 15.2.1-3; 15.3.1; 15.4; 15.12.1; 15.14.2-3; 15.15.1; 15.18.2; 15.19.1; 15.29.3; 16.1.2; 16.2.1; 16.4.3; 16.16a-f; Cic. *Phil.* 2.101-4; 5.7; 13.37; 14.10; Cass. Dio 45.9.1; *CIL* II Supp. 5439; 1^2.594.

23. App. *BCiv.* 2.125; Plut. *Ant.* 15; Vell. 2.60.4; Suet. *Aug.* 35.1; Cass. Dio 44.53.3; Cic. *Phil.* 2.92-4; 5.11; 12.12.

24. Cic. *Phil.* 2.97 states that the freedom of Crete depended on the departure of Marcus Brutus, who was supposed to get Macedonia. Cass. Dio 45.32.4, in what appears to be his version of the *Second Philippic*, says the same. In Cass. Dio 46.23.3, Calenus, in a defense of Antony, seems to cast doubt on the freeing. K. W. Drumann and P. Groebe, *Geschichte Roms in seinem Übergang* (Berlin-Leipzig, 1899-1929), 81 accept the freedom of Crete. Drumann-Groebe, 101 give Brutus Crete and Cassius Cyrene, without mentioning the earlier freeing of Crete, which they suggest did not go through. Drumann-Groebe seem to cast doubt on the genuineness of the commission for Brutus and Cassius. Possibly all that was done for Crete was temporary relief from direct taxes, not self-government—i.e., like a "free and immune" city, which the governor could not interfere with but which remained part of the empire.

25. App. *BCiv.* 3.5; 3.12; Jos. *Ant. Jud.* 14.10.9-10; Cass. Dio 44.53.5-7; Cic. *Att.* 14.12.1; 14.13.6; 14.13a; 14.14; 14.14a; 14.19.2; Cic. *Phil.* 1.24; 2.94-98; 3.10; 5.11-12. Cleopatra did not appear in Antony's foreign policies at this time. She had been in Rome as Caesar's guest when he was killed. Antony must have known her there, or, perhaps, even earlier in Egypt (App. *BCiv.* 5.8), but there is no evidence of close ties. She had hoped that her son Caesarion would be acknowledged in Caesar's will. Disappointed, she fled Rome in April (Cic. *Att.* 14.8.1).

26. Cic. *Phil.* 1.19-23; 5.12-16; 8.27; 12.12; 13.3; 13.5; 13.37.

27. App. *BCiv.* 2.124; 3.2; 3.8; 3.12; 3.16; 3.24-25; 3.35-38; 3.66; and Flor. 2.17.4 state that Macedonia and Syria had been assigned to Brutus and Cassius. The chief argument against this is Cicero's silence about seizure of the provinces. Cic. *Phil.* 11.27-28; Cass. Dio 45.9.3; 45.20.3; 47.21.1; Nic. Dam. 16.

28. Lex de permutatione provinciarum (Liv. *Ep.* 117) is the same law as Lex tribunicia de provinciis (Cic. *Phil.* 5.7).

29. Cass. Dio 47.21.1 says Crete and Bithynia; App. *BCiv.* 3.8 says Cyrenaica and Crete to Cassius, Bithynia to Brutus.

30. Plut. *Ant.* 14; Plut. *Cic.* 42; Plut. *Brut.* 19-21 makes the distribution of provinces fall on March 17. Nic. Dam. 28; 30.4; Liv. *Ep.* 117; Nep. *Att.* 8; App. *BCiv.* 3.6-8; 3.12 indicates the action fell in May; 3.16; 3.24; 3.27-31; 3.37-38; 3.52; 3.55; Cass. Dio 44.51.2; 45.9.3; 45.20.1; 45.20.3; 46.23.4; 46.24.3; 47.20.3-21.1; Cic. *Att.* 11.3; 14.14; 14.22.2; 15.4-6; 15.9-12; 15.17; 16.4; Cic. *Ad Brut.* 1.15.4-6; Cic. *Phil.* 1.6; 1.19; 1.25; 2.31; 2.97; 2.108; 5.7-10; 7.3; 8.27-28; 11.27-30; Cic. *Fam.* 11.2; 11.10.5.

31. Cic. *Phil.* 1.6; 1.11; Cic. *Fam.* 11.3; 16.23.2; Cic. *Att.* 10.10; 12.2; 14.3.2; 14.6.2; 14.7; 14.11.1; 14.13a-b; 14.20-21; 15.5; 15.8; 15.11.3; 15.20; 15.29.1; 16.7.

Chapter VII.
Challenged by Octavian

1. Vell. 2.59.1-3; Suet. *Aug.* 1-2; 4; 8.1; Plut. *Ant.* 11.1; Nic. Dam. 13; 15-18; 30; Nic. Dam. 15 says that Octavian was made patrician by the Senate, but see Suet. *Jul.* 41.1; Cass. Dio 43.47.3; 45.1.5; 45.2.7.

2. App. *BCiv.* 3.11; Cic. *Phil.* 5.46; Liv. *Ep.* 117.

3. Cic. *Att.* 14.12.1; 15.12.2; Cic. *Fam.* 16.24.2.

4. Vell. 2.59.4-60.2; Liv. *Ep.* 117; Suet. *Aug.* 8.2-3; Plut. *Ant.* 16.1; Plut. *Cic.* 43.8; Plut. *Brut.* 22.1-3; Cass. Dio 43.41.3; 45.3; Oros. 6.18.1; App. *BCiv.* 3.9-14; Cic. *Att.* 14.5.3; 14.6.1; 15.12.2.

5. Plut. *Ant.* 16.1-2; Plut. *Mor.* 206F-207; Vell. 2.60.3-4; Suet. *Aug.* 10.1-2; Cic. *Att.* 14.10.3; 14.11.2; 14.12.2; 15.3.2; 15.12.2; Cic. *Phil.* 13.24; App. *BCiv.* 3.12-20; 3.31; Cass. Dio 45.5-9; Hugh Last, "On the *Tribunicia Potestas* of Augustus," *RIL* 84 (1951), 93-110 maintains that the people elected Octavian tribune against his wishes.

6. Plut. *Ant.* 16.3-4; Suet. *Aug.* 10.3; Flor. 2.15.1-4; App. *BCiv.* 3.21; 3.29-30; Nic. Dam. 18; 29.

7. Cic. *Att.* 14.20.5; 14.21.4; 15.2.3; Cass. Dio 45.5.3-6.2; 45.24; App. *BCiv.* 3.14; 3.17; 3.20-23; 3.94; Nic. Dam. 18; 28; Vell. 2.60.4; Plut. *Mor.* 207A; Plut. *Brut.* 22.3; Plut. *Cic.* 43.8.

8. Cic. *Phil.* 3.15; 13.24; Cic. *Att.* 14.10.3; 14.12.2; 15.12.2; App. *BCiv.* 3.61-62; Liv. *Ep.* 117; Plut. *Brut.* 22.3-4; Plut. *Cic.* 43.4; 45.1-2; Tac. *Ann.* 1.10.

9. Plut. *Ant.* 16.2; Nic. Dam. 28; Cic. *Phil.* 1.8; 1.13; Cic. *Att.* 15.2.3; 15.3.2; 15.11.2; 16.1.1; 16.4.1; 16.5.3; 16.7.1; App. *BCiv.* 3.28; Cass. Dio 44.5.2; 45.6.4; 45.7.2; Suet. *Jul.* 76.1; *BMC Rom Rep* III, p. 486, nos. 87-88.

10. Cic. *Phil.* 1.36; 2.31; Cic. *Att.* 15.12.1; 15.18.2; 15.26.1; 16.2.3; App. *BCiv.* 3.23-24; Cass. Dio 47.20.2 incorrectly says that Cassius was praetor; Plut. *Brut.* 21.3-6.

11. Cic. *Phil.* 2.110; Cic. *Fam.* 12.3.1; Cass. Dio 45.7.1-2; Suet. *Jul.* 88; Ov. *Met.* 15.847-50; Val. Max. 3.2.19; Pl. *N.H.* 2.23; 2.94.

12. Cic. *Ad Brut.* 1.17.5-6; Cic. *Fam.* 10.28.1; 12.1; 12.25a.3-4; Cic. *Att.* 14.13.4; 14.13a; 14.13b; 15.12.2; 15.20; 16.2.4; 16.5.3; 16.6.1-2; 16.11.6; 16.13b; 16.14.1-2; 16.15.3; Cass. Dio 45.15; 46.22; 46.28.

13. Cic. *Phil.* 1.11; 8.22; 8.31-32; Cic. *Ad Brut.* 1.16; Cic. *Fam.* 10.1.1; 11.5; 12.2-5; Cic. *Att.* 14.4; 14.9.2; 14.13.1-3; 14.13.6; 14.14.2-7; 15.4; 15.11; 15.12.1; 15.20.2; 15.29.1; 16.2.3.

14. Plut. *Cic.* 43; Cic. *Phil.* 1.8; 1.11-13; 5.18-19; Cic. *Fam.* 9.24.4; 10.1; 12.24-25; Cic. *Att.* 15.12; 16.7.

15. Cic. *Phil.* 1 *passim*; 5.19; Cic. *Att.* 15.1A.2.

16. Cic. *Fam.* 12.1–3.1; 12.25A.4; Cic. *Phil.* 2.7; 2.25; 2.112; 5.19–20.

17. Cic. *Phil.* 2 *passim*; other examples of Philippic invective are in 3.28–29; 3.34–35; 5.10; 6.3; 7.15; 13.5; 13.17; Cic. *Fam.* 12.25.4; Cic. *Att.* 15.13.1; 16.11. Regrettably, in November Cicero's correspondence with Atticus ended, and for events after that date, we miss this excellent source. Cass. Dio. 46.1–29.1.

18. Nic. Dam. 29–31; App. *BCiv.* 3.29–30; 3.39–40; Plut. *Brut.* 23; Plut. *Ant.* 16; and Cass. Dio 45.7.3–8.3; 45.11 doubt that Octavian made the attempt; rather, Antony was spreading a malicious rumor. Suet. *Aug.* 10; Sen. *Clem.* 1.9.1; Vell. 2.60–63; Cic. *Fam.* 12.23.2; 12.28.2; Cic. *Phil.* 11.11–16; 13.26–28 accept the story.

19. Liv. *Ep.* 117; Tac. *Ann.* 1.10: Cic. *Phil.* 3.3–8; 3.27; 4.3; 5.21; 5.43–44; 14.27; 14.31; Cic. *Att.* 15.13.2; 16.8; 16.11.6; 16.14.1–2; Suet. *Aug.* 10.3; Flor. 2.15.4; Cass. Dio 45.12–13; Vell. 2.61.2; Nic. Dam. 30–31; App. *BCiv.* 3.31; 3.40–42; Aug. *R.G.* 1.1–3.

20. Liv. *Ep.* 117; Cic. *Phil.* 3.4–8; 3.10–11; 3.31; 4.4–6; 5.22–23; 12.12; 13.18; Cic. *Att.* 16.8; 16.10; Cic. *Fam.* 12.23.2; Cass. Dio 45.13; 55.38.3–5; Plut. *Ant.* 10.3; 16.3–4; Vell. 2.61.2–3; App. *BCiv.* 3.43–48.

21. Cic. *Att.* 16.8–9; 16.11; 16.15; Cic. *Phil.* 13.19; App. *BCiv.* 3.41–42; Cass. Dio 45.12; Nic. Dam. 31; Vell. 2.64.3.

22. Cic. *Phil.* 3.19; 13.19.

23. App. *BCiv.* 3.45–46; 3.58; Suet. *Aug.* 68; Cic. *Phil.* 3.1; 3.6; 3.9; 3.15–17; 3.19–21; 3.23–26; 4.6; 5.23–24; 5.46; 5.52–53; 13.19; Cic. *Fam.* 10.28.3; 11.7; Cass. Dio 45.13; 45.42; 46.37; Liv. *Ep.* 117; Vell. 2.61.2.

24. Personal alliances shifted rapidly at this time. Besides his cousins, Lucius Pinarius Scarpus and Quintus Pedius, Octavian's leading henchmen were able nonnobles: Publius Servilius Rufus, Quintus Salvidienus Rufus, Marcus Vipsanius Agrippa, and Gaius Maecenas. Nic. Dam. 16; Vell. 2.59.5; Suet. *Aug.* 94.12.

25. Antony's noble supporters included Lucius Cassius Longinus, who owed Antony for the favor of recalling his son from exile; Lucius Sempronius Atratinus, consul suffectus in 34 B.C.; Lucius Julius Caesar, consul in 64 B.C., Antony's uncle whom Antony had made praefectus urbi in 47 B.C.; Gaius Sempronius Rufus, recalled from exile by Antony in 44 B.C.; Gaius Antonius, consul in 63 B.C.; Quintus Fufius Calenus, Caesar's general, orator, and politician; Aulus Hirtius, consul in 43 B.C., the soldier and historian of Caesar's campaigns; Lucius Calpurnius Piso, consul in 58 B.C., censor, the father-in-law of Caesar and the executor of his will; Lucius Decidius Saxa, tribune in 44 B.C.; and Gaius Sallustius Crispus, governor of Africa and historian. See Nic. Dam. 28; Cass. Dio 45.11; 46.34; Cic. *Fam.* 10.28.3; 11.7–8; 11.20.1; 11.22.1; Cic. *Ad Brut.* 1.3.1; 1.15.7; 1.16–17; Cic. *Phil.* 3.15–21; Cic. *Att.* 15.12; 15.20; 16.8–9; 16.11.6; 16.14–15; Plut. *Cic.* 45; Plut. *Brut.* 22.

26. Cic. *Fam.* 12.7; 12.23.

27. App. *BCiv.* 2.48; 3.27; 3.46; Cic. *Fam.* 11.9; 11.10.3; Cic. *Phil.* 3.31; Suet. *Aug.* 10.2; Nic. Dam. 22–23; 28; Cass. Dio 45.13.5.

28. App. *BCiv.* 2.48; 2.115; 2.124; 2.143; 2.146; 3.2; 3.27; Suet. *Jul.* 81; Cic. *Att.* 14.13.2; Cic. *Fam.* 11.1.1; 11.9; 11.10.5; Cic. *Phil.* 3.37–38; 10.15; Vell. 2.58.1–2; 2.60.5; Cass. Dio 44.14.4; Plut. *Caes.* 64.1; Plut. *Ant.* 11.1; Plut. *Brut.* 19.5.

29. App. *BCiv.* 4.84; Cic. *Fam.* 10.1–10; 10.32; 11.9; 11.10.4; Cic. *Phil.* 3.38; 5.5; Cass. Dio 43.51.8; 45.10.3.

30. Cic. *Att.* 15.4; Cic. *Fam.* 12.5; Cic. *Phil.* 3.8; 7.23; 11.37; 12.9–10; 12.24; 12.36; App. *BCiv.* 3.49; Cass. Dio 46.35; Oros. 6.18.3; Macr. *Sat.* 1.11.22; Nic. Dam. 28.

31. Cic. *Att.* 15.5; 15.6; 15.22; Cic. *Fam.* 11.1; 12.22.2.

NOTES

32. Cic. *Att.* 15.4.1; Cic. *Fam.* 10.28; 11.5; 11.6; 12.22.3; 12.25a.2-4; Cic. *Phil.* 3 and 4 *passim*; 5.3; 5.28; 5.30; 10.23; Cass. Dio 45.14-15; 46.47.1-4.

33. Cass. Dio 45.18-46.29 and App. *BCiv.* 3.52-59 quote Cicero's speeches and the rebuttals of Calenus and Calpurnius Piso at length; but the speeches are created by the historians, although drawn in part from the *Philippics*, Cicero's letters, Antony and Pollio's invectives against Cicero, and other contemporary and later writers. See Fergus Millar, *A Study of Cassius Dio* (London, 1964). 52-55.

34. Cic. *Phil.* 3.37; 5 *passim*; 10.21; Cic. *Fam.* 12.24.2; App. *BCiv.* 3.47; 3.50; Cass. Dio 45.17-47; 46.1-29; 46.35.

35. Cic. *Fam.* 11.20.3; Cic. *Phil.* 5 *passim*; 11.37; 14.8; Aug. *R.G.* 1; Vell. 2.61.3-4; Tac. *Ann.* 1.10.1-2; Suet. *Aug.* 10.2-3; Plut. *Cic.* 45.4; Plut. *Ant.* 17.1; Liv. *Ep.* 118; Cass. Dio 46.29.2-3; App. *BCiv.* 3.48; 3.51-61; 64.

36. Cic. *Ad Brut.* 1.18.5; 2.4.4; Cic. *Phil.* 6 and 7 *passim*; Liv. *Ep.* 118; Cass. Dio 46.29.4; 46.31.3-4.

37. Cic. *Phil.* 8.22-28; 9 *passim*; Cic. *Fam.* 12.4.1; 12.5.3; 12.24.1; App. *BCiv.* 3.62-63; Cass. Dio 46.30; 46.35.5-6.

38. Cic. *Phil.* 8.24; 8.28-29; Cic. *Fam.* 12.4.1; App. *BCiv.* 3.63; Cass. Dio 46.30-31; Oros. 6.18.3.

39. Cic. *Phil.* 3.3-8; 3.19; 4.2-6; 5.6; 5.23; 5.42-51; 7.22-24; 8.6; 8.11-19; 10.2-6; 11.15; 12.18; 14.25; Cic. *Fam.* 10.28.3; 11.8.2; 12.4.1; 12.25.4; Plut. *Cic.* 45.3.

40. Cic. *Phil.* 5.38-41; 8 *passim*; Cic. *Fam.* 12.4.1; Cass. Dio 46.32.3-4; App. *BCiv.* 3.63.

41. Cic. *Phil.* 3.31; 10 and 11 *passim*; App. *BCiv.* 3.63-64; 3.77-79; Oros. 6.18.6.

42. Cic. *Phil.* 1.25-26; 3.31; 5.7-16; 13.5; 13.31.

43. App. *BCiv.* 3.63-64.

44. Cic. *Phil.* 12 and 13 *passim*; Cic. *Fam.* 10.7-10.

45. Cic. *Fam.* 12.5.2; Cic. *Phil.* 14.4-7; App. *BCiv.* 3.65; Cass. Dio 46.36; Plut. *Cic.* 45.4; Plut. *Ant.* 17.1; Suet. *Aug.* 10.3-4; Oros. 6.18.4-5.

46. Cic. *Fam.* 10.30; 10.33.3-4; 12.6.2; Cic. *Ad Brut.* 1.3.1-3; Cic. *Phil.* 14.26-27; 14.36-38; App. *BCiv.* 3.66-70; Cass. Dio 46.37.

47. Cic. *Phil.* 14 *passim*; App. *BCiv.* 3.74; Cass. Dio 46.38-39.

48. Eutr. 7.1; Oros. 6.18.4-5; App. *BCiv.* 3.71.

49. App. *BCiv.* 3.71-72; 3.80; Cic. *Fam.* 10.33; 11.9-10; 11.13-14.1; 11.18; Cic. *Phil.* 3.31; 13.48; Cic. *Ad Brut.* 1.5.1; 3 and 4; Ov. *Fast.* 4.625-28; Cass. Dio 46.38-39; Plut. *Ant.* 17; Tac. *Ann.* 1.10; Oros. 6.18.5; Vell. 2.61; Flor. 2.15.4-5.

50. Cass. Dio 46.39; 46.50; Suet. *Aug.* 11; Tac. *Ann.* 1.10.1-2; the deaths may well have been natural: Vell. 2.61.4; App. *BCiv.* 3.71; 3.74-76; Cic. *Phil.* 14.26; 14.36; Cic. *Fam.* 10.23.4-24; 11.13a.1-2; 12.25; others were also accused of the unnatural deaths of the consuls; Suet. *Aug.* 11; Cic. *Ad Brut.* 1.6.2; 1.16.

51. Cic. *Fam.* 11.9-13; 11.19-20; Cic. *Ad Brut.* 1.10; App. *BCiv.* 3.73; Oros. 6.18.5.

52. Cass. Dio 46.29; 46.40; App. *BCiv.* 3.51; 3.58; 3.63; Cic. *Ad Brut.* 1.3.2; 1.3a.4; 1.5.1; 2.5; Cic. *Fam.* 12.10.1; Liv. *Ep.* 119; Vell. 2.64.4; Nep. *Att.* 9.2.

Chapter VIII
Avenger of Caesar

1. Cic. *Fam.* 10.33.4; 11.10.3-4; 11.13.3; Cic. *Phil.* 12.23; App. *BCiv.* 3.66; 3.80; 3.84.

2. Cic. *Fam.* 10.1; 10.7-9; 10.11-24; 10.27; 10.31-34; 11.10.4-5; 11.11.1; 11.13.4-5;

11.18; 11.24; Cic. *Phil.* 13.14-17; Plut. *Ant.* 18; Cass. Dio 44.53; 46.50-51; Vell. 2.63; Ascon. *Mil.* 43c.

3. Ps.-Vict. *Vir. Ill.* 85.2; Liv. *Ep.* 119; Cic. *Fam.* 10.17.1; 10.21; 10.23.2; 10.34-35; 12.8-10; 12.30.2; Cic. *Phil.* 16 fragments; Cic. *Ad Brut.* 1.15.4; 1.15.9; Eutr. 7.2; App. *BCiv.* 3.83-84; Cass. Dio 46.51; 46.53; Plut. *Ant.* 18; Vell. 2.63.1-2; 2.64.4.

4. Plut. *Ant.* 18; Plut. *Brut.* 27-28; Cic. *Fam.* 10.23-24; App. *BCiv.* 3.81; 3.96-98; Vell. 2.63-64; Cass. Dio 46.53-54; Oros. 6.18.7; Val. Max. 9.13.3; Liv. *Ep.* 120-21; Sen. *De Cons.* 16.1-2.

5. App. *BCiv.* 3.80; 3.82; Cic. *Fam.* 11.14.1.

6. Cass. Dio 46.40-42; 46.50; Suet. *Aug.* 12; 26.1; Cic. *Fam.* 11.14.2; 11.19-20; 12.15.1; 12.30.4; Cic. *Ad Brut.* 1.3.2; 1.5.3-4; 1.10.3; 1.15-18; Liv. *Ep.* 119-20; App. *BCiv.* 3.74; 3.76; 3.80; 3.82-89; Plut. *Cic.* 45.4-5; Vell. 2.62.4-5.

7. Plut. *Cic.* 46.1-2; Cass. Dio 46.41-43; Cic. *Fam.* 10.23-24; Cic. *Ad Brut.* 1.17; App. *BCiv.* 3.80-82.

8. Suet. *Aug.* 12; App. *BCiv.* 3.80; Cass. Dio 46.39-41.

9. App. *BCiv.* 3.88-93; 3.97; Cic. *Ad Brut.* 1.9.3; 1.10; 1.12.2; 1.14.2; Suet. *Aug.* 26.1; 31.2; 95; Cass. Dio 46.43-45; Liv. *Ep.* 119.

10. App. *BCiv.* 3.94-95; Vell. 2.65.2; 2.69.5; Plut. *Brut.* 27; Suet. *Ner.* 3.1; Suet. *Galba* 3.2; Liv. *Ep.* 119-20; Aug. *R.G.* 1-2; Cass. Dio 46.45-49; 46.51; 47.22; Tac. *Ann.* 1.9.1; 1.10.2; *CIL* I 2.1, 466. See Chapter XII, "Breaking with Octavian," pp. 200-1, and 207.

11. Iullus was a cognomen among the Julii in the fifth century B.C. Antony's claim to the name could also come through his mother Julia.

12. Flor. 2.16.6; Suet. *Aug.* 12; 27; 96.1; App. *BCiv.* 3.96; 4.2; Liv. *Ep.* 120; Plut. *Brut.* 27.5; Plut. *Cic.* 46.2-3; Plut. *Ant.* 19.1; Oros. 6.18.6; Eutr. 7.2; Cass. Dio 46.42; 46.52; 46.54-55; Vell. 2.65.

13. Cicero criticized Antony for not seeing to his recall earlier: *Phil.* 2.56; 2.98-99.

14. Fergus Millar, "Triumvirate and Principate," *JRS* 63 (1973), 50-65; Vell. 2.65.3; App. *BCiv.* 4.2; 4.7; Cass. Dio 43.47.3; 46.55; Eutr. 7.2; *CIL* I, 440, 446; Aug. *R.G.* 1. The First Triumvirate was totally informal; the Second Triumvirate was set up by law and can be called a committee dictatorship. The results may have been similar but the legal practices were very different. The First Triumvirate had to act within the legal framework of magistrates and assemblies. The Second Triumvirate had the power to act directly.

15. Aug. *R.G.* 1; Cass. Dio 46.55-56; 47.13.3-4; 47.15.4.

16. Zon. 10.21; App. *BCiv.* 4.2.

17. App. *BCiv.* 4.3.

18. Vell. 2.65.2; Cass. Dio 46.55-56; 47.1-2; 47.14-15; 47.18-20; 48.21; Oros. 6.18.8-9; Plut. *Ant.* 20.1; 21.4; Suet. *Aug.* 62.1; App. *BCiv.* 4.3; 4.7.

19. Cass. Dio 46.40; Cic. *Fam.* 10.32.4; 12.30.4; Cic. *Phil.* 5.53; App. *BCiv.* 3.45; 4.5; 4.35; 4.99.

20. Val. Max. 8.3.3; Plut. *Ant.* 21; App. *BCiv.* 4.5; 4.31-34; 4.96; Cass. Dio 47.14-17.

21. Cass. Dio 46.56.1; 47.3-5; Pl. *N.H.* 34.2.6; App. *BCiv.* 4.3; 4.8-11; Sen. *Clem.* 1.9.2-3; Eutr. 7.2; Val. Max. 9.5.4.

22. Plut. *Ant.* 19; 21 identifies Antony as the most guilty for the proscriptions; Cass. Dio 46.56.1; 47.3-7 says that Antony was the most responsible, Octavian the least. Suet. *Aug.* 27.1-2; 72.2 describes Octavian as the most bloodthirsty and greedy. Sen. *Clem.* 1.11.1 notes Octavian's hot, youthful passions. Flor. 2.16 makes Octavian the least violent. Cf. Vell. 2.66; 2.86.2; App. *BCiv.* 4.3; 4.5-7; 4.11; Eutr. 7.2; Pl. *N.H.* 7.147 Ps.-Vict. *Vir. Ill.* 85.3.

NOTES

23. The numbers of the proscribed vary in the sources: App. *BCiv.* 3.94-95; 4.5-7; 4.12-18; 4.21-51; 4.95-96; Val. Max. 5.7.3; Oros. 6.18.9-12; Vell. 2.67; Liv. *Ep.* 120; Flor. 2.16.4; Sen. *Clem.* 1.9.1; Plut. *Ant.* 19-20; Plut. *Cic.* 46; Plut. *Brut.* 27; Caes. *Gall.* 7.65; Caes. *Civ.* 1.8; Cass. Dio 37.10; 42.30; 46.49; 47.5-13; Macr. *Sat.* 2.4.21.

24. Cic. *Att.* 11.7.2; 14.19; Val. Max. 5.3.4; Eutr. 7.2; Juv. 10.118-26; Oros. 6.18.11; Liv. *Ep.* 120; Vell. 2.64.4; 2.66.4-5; Flor. 2.16.5; App. *BCiv.* 4.19-20; Plut. *Cic.* 46-49; Plut. *Brut.* 27-28; Plut. *Ant.* 19-20; Cass. Dio 47.8; 47.11.

25. App. *BCiv.* 4.19-20; 4.51; Plut. *Brut.* 24; Plut. *Cic.* 47; Cass. Dio 47.10; Cic. *Ad Brut.* 1.5.3; 2.3.6; 12.3; 14.2; Cic. *Phil.* 3.17; Cic. *Att.* 11.8; 14.14.1; 14.17.3; 14.19-20; 15.19.2; 15.21; 15.29.2; 16.1.6; 16.5.2; 16.14.4.

26. Nep. *Att.* 8-11.

27. Cass. Dio 47.11-13; Cic. *Phil.* 2.40-41.

28. Cass. Dio 47.15-20; App. *BCiv.* 4.7.

29. Cic. *Att.* 15.11; 15.26; 15.28-29; 16.1-5; 16.7; Cic. *Fam.* 11.3; 11.7; Cic. *Phil.* 1.9; 2.97; 10.8; Vell. 2.62.2-3; Plut. *Brut.* 21; 23; App. *BCiv.* 3.1; 3.5-6; 3.8; 3.24; Cass. Dio 47.20; Ps.-Vict. *Vir. Ill.* 82.

30. Plut. *Brut.* 24-26; 28; Plut. *Ant.* 22.4; Cass. Dio 47.20-25; App. *BCiv.* 3.26; 3.63; 3.79; 4.75; Cic. *Ad Brut.* 1.2.3; 1.4; 2.3-5; Cic. *Fam.* 12.5.1; 12.15.1; Cic. *Phil.* 10 *passim*; 11.26-27; 13.32; Liv. *Ep.* 118; 121; Vell. 2.69.3; Hor. *Epist.* 2.2.43-49; Hor. *Sat.* 1.6.48-50; *BMC Rom Rep* II, p. 470, nos. 37-40, 46.

31. Plut. *Brut.* 22; 28.2; Cic. *Ad Brut.* 1.2; 1.4.3-6; 1.11.1; 1.16-17; Liv. *Ep.* 122; Cass. Dio 46.51.5; 47.25; App. *BCiv.* 4.75. For coins of the liberators, see H. Grueber, *Coins of the Roman Republic in the British Museum*, vol. II (London, 1970). For Cassius, nos. 71, 72, 82, 83, 84. For Brutus, nos. 57, 58, 62, 68, 69, 70, 79, 80, 81.

32. Oros. 6.18.13; Liv. *Ep.* 120; App. *BCiv.* 3.26; Cass. Dio 40.28.1; 45.15.2; 47.21.2; 47.26.1-2; 47.28.1-30.7.

33. Cic. *Fam.* 12.5.1; 12.7.1; 12.11-15; Cic. *Att.* 15.13.4; 15.15; Cic. *Ad Brut.* 1.2.1; 1.5.2; 1.6.3; 2.4.2; Cic. *Phil.* 11 *passim*; Liv. *Ep.* 119; 121; App. *BCiv.* 3.77-78; 4.57-64; 5.8; Vell. 2.69.1-2; Cass. Dio 47.26-31 says that Cleopatra did send ships and money; Plut. *Brut.* 28.3; Strab. 16.2.9; Jos. *Ant. Jud.* 14.10.11-12; 14.11.2; 14.11.6-7; 14.12.1.

34. Cass. Dio 47.32.1-33.2.

35. Cic. *Fam.* 12.14.2-3; 12.15.2-5; Cic. *Phil.* 2.94-96; 10.13; 11.27; Cic. *Att.* 14.12.1; 14.19.2; Oros. 6.18.13; Plut. *Brut.* 28.3-5; 29.1-33.1; Cass. Dio 46.40.3; 47.32-34; App. *BCiv.* 3.63; 4.65-82; 4.94; 4.100; 5.17; Vell. 2.65.1; 2.69.6; 2.73.2.

36. Liv. *Ep.* 122; Plut. *Brut.* 28.6-7; 34-37; Cass. Dio 47.35.1; 48.24.4-5; App. *BCiv.* 4.86; 4.88-89; 4.108; Val. Max. 1.5.8; *BMC Rom Rep* II, pp. 480-85, nos. 71-86.

37. Liv. *Ep.* 123; Cass. Dio 47.36.2-37.1; 48.17-18; Flor. 2.18.1; App. *BCiv.* 4.74; 4.82; 4.85-86; 4.99-100; Vell. 2.72.4-5.

38. The numbers must be approximate. The sources vary widely. App. *BCiv.* 4.88 essentially doubles the numbers. Cf. App. *BCiv.* 4.108; Vell. 2.65; Cic. *Fam.* 11.13.2; P.A. Brunt, *Italian Manpower, 225 B.C.-A.D. 14* (London, 1971), 486-88.

39. Cass. Dio 47.35-38; Flor. 2.17.5-6; App. *BCiv.* 4.87-88; 4.102-9; Plut. *Brut.* 38; Jos. *Ant. Jud.* 14.12.3.

40. Plut. *Brut.* 39-44 describes the battle as planned by the republicans, urged on especially by Brutus; cf. Plut. *Caes.* 69; Plut. *Ant.* 22; Liv. *Ep.* 124; Cass. Dio 47.41-46; Flor. 2.17.9-13; App. *BCiv.* 4.109-13; Suet. *Aug.* 13; Val. Max. 6.8.4; 9.9.2; Vell. 2.70.1-3; Ps.-Vict. *Vir. Ill.* 83.6-7.

41. Plut. *Caes.* 69.2-3; Plut. *Brut.* 44-48; Cass. Dio 47.47-48.2; App. *BCiv.* 4.114-24.

42. Plut. *Cat. Min.* 73.3-4; Plut. *Caes.* 69.6-14; Plut. *Brut.* 28.2; 29.7-11; 49-53; Vell. 2.70.4-5; Oros. 6.18.14-17; Liv. *Ep.* 124; Cass. Dio 47.48.3-49.4; Val. Max. 1.4.7;

NOTES

4.6.5; 5.1.11; Eutr. 7.3; Flor. 2.17.14; App. *BCiv.* 4.125-136; 5.14; 5.53; 5.58; Suet. *Aug.* 13.1-2; Suet. *Tib.* 5; Ps.-Vict. *Vir. Ill.* 82.6; Jos. *Ant. Jud.* 14.12.3. Antony later taunted Octavian about his absence from the fighting (Cass. Dio 50.18.3; Pl. *N.H.* 7.148), an accusation so painful that Octavian charged that Antony too avoided the battle and took part only in the pursuit. Plut. *Ant.* 22; Aug. *R.G.* 2.

43. Liv. *Ep.* 124; Cass. Dio 47.48-49; 48.1; 48.19-20; Suet. *Aug.* 13; Eutr. 7.3; App. *BCiv.* 4.135-36; 5.3; 5.58-59; Vell. 2.71; 2.86.2; Aug. *R.G.* 3.1.

44. The revolt against Nero in A.D. 68 started as a "restoration of the republic," but Galba soon assumed imperial powers.

45. Cass. Dio 47.42; 48.1; App. *BCiv.* 4.137-38; *BMC Rom Rep* II, pp. 474-84, nos. 48-85.

Chapter IX.
Relinquishing the West

1. Cass. Dio 48.1-3; 48.12; 48.24; 48.27-28; App. *BCiv.* 5.1; 5.3; 5.7; 5.12; 5.22; Jos. *Ant. Jud.* 14.12.2; Eutr. 7.4; Zon. 10.21; Plut. *Dem. and Ant.* 1.2.

2. App. *BCiv.* 5.3; Cass. Dio 48.2.3.

3. Plut. *Ant.* 23.1; Cass. Dio 48.7; Liv. *Ep.* 125; App. *BCiv.* 5.4; Nep. *Eum.* 8.2.

4. Cass. Dio 47.19.4; 48.3; 48.7-9; App. *BCiv.* 5.18; 5.67; 5.74; Strab. 7, frag. 41; Pl. *N.H.* 4.42.

5. Verg. *Ecl.* 1.6-10; 9.1-29; Cass. Dio 47.14; 48.6-9; 48.15; 51.4; Hor. *Car.* 2.7.9-10; Hor. *Epist.* 2.2.46-54; App. *BCiv.* 4.3; 5.5; 5.12-15; 5.19; 5.22; 5.27; 5.43.

6. Cass. Dio 48.3; App. *BCiv.* 5.5-6; 5.12-14; 5.22;

7. See p. 153 of this volume. App. *BCiv.* 5.66; Martial. *Ep.* 11.20.3-8 adds that Fulvia was angry with Octavian for having rejected her advances when Antony had turned to Glaphyra.

8. *BMC Rom Rep* II, p. 394, no. 40; pp. 400-401, nos. 65-68; pp. 491-92, nos. 106-8; Michael Grant, *From Imperium to Auctoritas,* 2nd ed. (London, 1971), pl. XI, coin 52; p. 350; p. 368; *BMC Phoenicia* CXVIII.

9. Perhaps Lucius did see long-term prudence in a return to republican forms: so claims Emelio Gabba, "The Perusine War and Triumviral Italy," *HSPh* 75 (1971), 139-60.

10. Vell. 2.74-75; Cic. *Phil.* 2.113; 5.11; 5.22; 5.64; 13.18; Liv. *Ep.* 125; App. *BCiv.* 5.14; 5.19; 5.27-31; 5.39; 5.43; 5.54; 5.66; Cass. Dio 48.4-12; Flor. 2.16; Suet. *Aug.* 13-14; 62.1; 68; Plut. *Ant.* 28; 30; Zon. 10.21.

11. Vell. 2.74.2; Macr. *Sat.* 1.11.22; App. *BCiv.* 5.14; 5.17; 5.19-23; Liv. *Ep.* 125; Cass. Dio 48.11-12.

12. Vell. 2.74.3; App. *BCiv.* 5.21; 5.24; 5.29; Cass. Dio 48.10.

13. App. *BCiv.* 5.24; 5.26-27; 5.30-31; Liv. *Ep.* 125; Cass. Dio 48.13; 48.22.

14. Vell. 2.74; Lucan, 1.41; Liv. *Ep.* 126; Flor. 2.16; App. *BCiv.* 5.31-46; Suet. *Aug.* 14; Suet. *Tib.* 4.2; Cass. Dio 48.13-14; 48.16; Eutr. 7.4.

15. Plut. *Ant.* 28; 30; Cass. Dio 48.27; Zon. 10.22.

16. Cass. Dio 48.14; 48.20-23 and Suet. *Aug.* 15 unreliably state that 300 equestrians and many senators were sacrificed on the altar of Caesar on the anniversary of the Ides. The tale shows how harsh Octavian appeared in the general view. Vell. 2.74 and App. *BCiv.* 5.48-49 say that the soldiers, not Octavian, were responsible for the slaughter. See App. *BCiv.* 5.40-54; 5.60; Cass. Dio 48.15; Liv. *Ep.* 126; Plut. *Ant.* 30.1; Suet. *Tib.* 4.2; Vell. 2.74.4; 2.76.2; Sen. *Clem.* 1.11.1.

17. App. *BCiv.* 5.50-51; 5.53; 5.75; Plut. *Ant.* 30.4; Eutr. 7.3; Zon. 10.21.

18. Plut. *Ant.* 30.3 says that Fulvia died en route, at Sicyon, without seeing Antony. Zon. 10.21-22.

19. Cass. Dio 48.27-28; Oros. 6.18.17-18; App. *BCiv.* 5.50; 5.52; 5.55; 5.59; 5.62; Vell. 2.74.2; 2.76.2; Plut. *Ant.* 30; Zon. 10.22.

20. App. *BCiv.* 5.51 states that this news reached Antony at Alexandria.

21. Cass. Dio 48.15.2; 48.27; App. *BCiv.* 5.51-54; 5.59-62; Plut. *Ant.* 32.1; Zon. 10.22.

22. Cass. Dio 45.10.1-5; 47.12; 48.7.4; 48.15.1-2; 48.17-20.1; 48.31; Aug. *R.G.* 25.1; Hor. *Epod.* 4.19; Ps.-Vict. *Vir. Ill.* 84; Vell. 2.73.3-74.3; Caes. *Hisp.* 3; 34; Flor. 2.13.2; 2.18.1-4; Liv. *Ep.* 127; Plut. *Ant.* 32.1; Lucan. 8.87-97; 9.117; App. *BCiv.* 4.36; 4.39; 4.83-86; 5.25; 5.139; 5.143; Cic. *Att.* 14.1.2; 14.4.1; 14.8.2; 14.13.2; 15.20.3; 16.4.2; Oros. 6.18.19-20; Zon. 10.21.

23. Cass. Dio 45.10.6; 46.40.3; 47.12.2; 48.17.3; 48.31.4-5; 48.48.5-6; Hor. *Epod.* 9.7-10; Vell. 2.74.2; Suet. *Aug.* 16.2; Flor. 2.18.3; App. *BCiv.* 4.70; 4.84; 4.94; 4.96; 5.26; 5.100; 5.143; Cic. *Phil.* 5.38-39; 5.41; 13.10; 13.13; 13.50.

24. Cass. Dio 48.30.4 claims that Antony and Sextus agreed to wage war against Octavian. See Cass. Dio 48.15.2; 48.16.3; 48.20.1-3; 48.27; Plut. *Ant.* 32.1; Suet. *Aug.* 62.2; App. *BCiv.* 5.51-54; 5.59-62; Zon. 10.21.

25. Cass. Dio 48.7.4; 48.16.2-4; 48.29; Cic. *Phil.* 2.11.27; 2.12.30; Suet. *Ner.* 3.1; App. *BCiv.* 5.26; 5.50; 5.52; 5.55; 5.59; 5.62; Vell. 2.72.3; 2.76.2; *BMC Rom Rep* II, pp. 487-88, nos. 93-97; pp. 494-95, nos. 111-13; Zon. 10.21; E. A. Sydenham, *Coinage of the Roman Republic* (London, 1952), p. 191, nos. 1176-79.

26. Cass. Dio 48.27.5-28 says that Octavian's adherents did hold Brundisium on his orders, and that war between Antony and Octavian was being mobilized. Cf. Vell. 2.76.3; App. *BCiv.* 5.26; 5.56-58; 5.60-61.

27. Vell. 2.76.3; Aug. *R.G.* 5.29; Plut. *Ant.* 30.3-4; App. *BCiv.* 5.59-64; Cass. Dio 48.25-28; Zon. 10.22. Hor. *Sat.* 1.5 reflects the popular joy in the peaceful meeting of Antony and Octavian at Brundisium.

28. Cass. Dio 48.28-29; 50.6.2; App. *BCiv.* 5.65; 5.93; Plut. *Ant.* 30.4; Liv. *Ep.* 96; Cic. *Phil.* 2.102; Suet. *Gramm.* 7; Suet. *Aug.* 17.2.

29. Plut. *Ant.* 30.4; Cass. Dio 48.28.4-29.1; 48.32-35 adds that several officials were named in each year to increase the number of friends honored.

30. Liv. *Ep.* 127; App. *BCiv.* 5.65-66; Vell. 2.76.4; Suet. *Aug.* 66.2; Sen. *Clem.* 1.9.5.

31. Liv. *Ep.* 127; Plut. *Ant.* 31; Cass. Dio 48.31.3; App. *BCiv.* 5.64; 5.93; Vell. 2.78.1; Tac. *Ann.* 1.10; *BMC Rom Rep* II, p. 499; Zon. 10.24.

32. Plut. *Ant.* 31.3; 33.1 also calls Antony pontifex maximus; Cass. Dio 48.30-33; App. *BCiv.* 5.66; Aug. *R.G.* 4; Suet. *Aug.* 22; *CIL* I 1.180; *BMC Rom Rep* II, pp. 497-99, nos. 114-30; Sydenham, *Coinage*, pp. 192-93, nos. 1189, 1192-98; Sen. *Suas.* 1.6.

33. Cass. Dio 48.30.2-4; 48.31; 48.34 describes the attack as directed against Antony, who was saved by Octavian. Cf. App. *BCiv.* 5.18; 5.67-68; 5.77; Liv. *Ep.* 127; Vell. 2.73.2-3; 2.77.1; Plut. *Ant.* 32; Oros. 6.18.19-20; Suet. *Aug.* 70.2; Zon. 10.22.

34. Cic. *Att.* 16.4.1; App. *BCiv.* 5.69-73; Cass. Dio 48.31.6; 48.36; 48.38.3; 48.46.1; 50.10.1; Plut. *Ant.* 21.2; 32.2-3; Vell. 2.77; Liv. *Ep.* 127; Oros. 6.18.20; Zon. 10.21-22.

35. App. *BCiv.* 5.71-72; Cass. Dio 48.36.3-37.1; Vell. 2.77.2-3.

36. Appian calls him Menodorus; Plutarch and Dio use the name Menas.

37. Plut. *Ant.* 32.4-5; 33.3; 87.3; Vell. 2.77.2; Cass. Dio 48.37-39.1; 48.46.1; Ps.-Vict. *Vir. Ill.* 84.3; App. *BCiv.* 5.73-76; Flor. 18.8.4; Zon. 10.22; Sydenham, *Coinage*, p. 193, nos. 1196-1200; *BMC Rom Rep* II, p. 499; pp. 502-3, nos. 133-37; pp. 507-8, nos. 144-45.

38. App. *BCiv.* 5.77; Cass. Dio 48.44–46.1; Suet. *Aug.* 62.2; 69.1; Suet. *Claud.* 1.1; Vell. 2.79.2; Zon. 10.23.

39. App. *BCiv.* 5.76–94; Cass. Dio 48.46–48; Zon. 10.23; Pl. *N.H.* 33.132; *BMC Rom Rep* pp. XLVI–XLVII.

40. App. *BCiv.* 5.80; Liv. *Ep.* 128 calls Octavian's defeats "drawn battles"; Plut. *Ant.* 35.1; Suet. *Aug.* 16.1; Hor. *Epod.* 1; Oros. 6.18.21–22; Zon. 10.23–24.

41. Zon. 10.24; App. *BCiv.* 5.93–94; Plut. *Ant.* 35; Cass. Dio 48.54.3; *BMC Rom Rep* II, pp. 509–19, nos. 147–71.

42. App. *Ill.* 28; App. *BCiv.* 5.95.

43. Plut. *Ant.* 35.4–5; App. *BCiv.* 5.55; 5.95; Suet. *Aug.* 63.2.

44. App. *BCiv.* 5.95; 5.98; 5.134–35. Cass. Dio 48.54 says that Octavian did give Antony the legions; *BMC Rom Rep* II, pp. 511–15; Zon. 10.24; Sydenham, *Coinage*, pp. 197–99, nos. 1255–70.

45. Cass. Dio 48.54.5; App. *BCiv.* 5.95; Plut. *Ant.* 35.5.

46. Flor. 2.18.5–6; Vell. 2.79.1–2; Suet. *Aug.* 16.1; Cass. Dio 48.49–51; Oros. 6.18.21.

47. App. *BCiv.* 5.98 says that the number of ships was 130.

48. Flor. 2.18.7; Liv. *Ep.* 129; App. *BCiv.* 5.96–122; Vell. 2.79.2–5; 2.80.1; Aug. *R.G.* 5.25; Suet. *Aug.* 16.1–3; 70.2; Cass. Dio 49.1–10; Oros. 6.18.25–29; *CIL* I 1.180; Hor. *Epod.* 9.7–10; Eutr. 7.4–5; Zon. 10.21; 10.23–25.

49. Oros. 6.18.29; 6.19.2; App. *BCiv.* 5.133–39; Zon. 10.25.

50. Dio says Titius and Furnius, App. says the Pisidians.

51. Strab. 3.2.2–141; Oros. 6.19.2; Flor. 2.18.8–9; Liv. *Ep.* 131; App. *BCiv.* 5.122; 5.127–29; 5.133–44; Cass. Dio 48.30.5–6; 49.11.1; 49.14.6; 49.17–18; 50.1.3; Vell. 2.79.5–6; Eutr. 7.6; Zon. 10.25.

52. App. *BCiv.* 5.91; 5.100; 5.134–35; 5.143.

53. Cass. Dio 49.8.3–4; 49.11.2–12.4; 49.15.3; 50.1.3; App. *BCiv.* 5.75; 5.122–26; 5.131; Suet. *Aug.* 16.4; Vell. 2.80; Oros. 6.18.30–32; Plut. *Ant.* 55; Zon. 10.25.

54. Liv. *Ep.* 129; Oros. 6.18.32–34; 6.20.6; Aug. *R.G.* 25.1; 27.3; Cass. Dio 49.12.4–15.6; 50.1.3; App. *BCiv.* 5.127–29; 5.132; Vell. 2.81.1–2; Plut. *Ant.* 55.

Chapter X.
Reorganizing Eastern Provinces and Allies

1. Plut. *Ant.* 23.1.

2. Suet. *Aug.* 13.3; App. *BCiv.* 5.3; Liv. *Ep.* 125; Vell. 2.74.1; Cass. Dio 48.2; 48.24; Plut. *Ant.* 23.1; *BMC Rom Rep* II, pp. 486–531, nos. 87–229 *passim*.

3. Cass. Dio 48.24; App. *BCiv.* 4.74; Plut. *Ant.* 23.

4. Plut. *Ant.* 24.3–4; 60.2–3.

5. App. *BCiv.* 4.74; 5.4–5.

6. Plut. *Ant.* 24; App. *BCiv.* 4.74; 5.5–6 exaggerates the amounts claimed by the Romans.

7. *BMC Rom Rep* II, pp. 502–31, nos. 133–229.

8. App. *BCiv.* 4.75; 5.5; Plut. *Ant.* 24; Cass. Dio 48.24.1; Antony's coinage in these years showed the globe for breadth of conquest, cornucopiae and caduceus for plenty and commerce: *BMC Rom Rep* II, p. 495, nos. 114–15.

9. Plut. *Ant.* 24; App. *BCiv.* 4.74; 5.5–6; Strab. 14.1.23; 14.1.41; Jos. *Ant. Jud.* 14.12.3–4.

10. App. *BCiv.* 5.4; 5.7; 5.9; 5.10 notes that Antony awarded Cappadocia to Sisira because his mother, Glaphyra, was beautiful. Cass. Dio 49.32.3 calls him Archelaus. For-

tunately, he proved an able ruler. See Cass. Dio 47.31; 47.36.4; 48.24.1; Strab. 14.1.41; 14.5.14; Martial. *Ep.* 11.20; Zon. 10.22.

11. App. *BCiv.* 4.74; 4.82; 5.8; Plut. *Ant.* 25; Cass. Dio 47.13; Suet. *Jul.* 52.1-2; Suet. *Aug.* 17.5; Cic. *Att.* 14.20.2; Strab. 17.1.11; Zon. 10.22.

12. Jos. *Ant. Jud.* 14.13.1; Socrates of Rhodes in Athen. 4.147f-148b; Plut. *Ant.* 26-28.1; App. *BCiv.* 5.8; Cass. Dio 48.24.

13. Cass. Dio 48.24.2-3 identifies the relatives killed as Cleopatra's brothers. Jos. *C. Ap.* 2.57; Jos. *Ant. Jud.* 15.4.1; App. *BCiv.* 5.9-10; Plut. *Ant.* 28.1; Zon. 10.22; *CIL* 6.1316; 10.6087.

14. Plut. *Ant.* 28-29; Zon. 10.22; Cass. Dio 48.24.3.

15. App. *BCiv.* 5.10-11; 5.26; Cass. Dio 48.45.1-3.

16. Cass. Dio 48.22-27; Plut. *Ant.* 28.1; 30.1-2; 33.2-3; Vell. 2.78.1; Liv. *Ep.* 127; Strab. 12.8.9; 14.2.24; Zon. 10.22-23.

17. See Chapter IX, "Relinquishing the West."

18. Cass. Dio 48.39.2 says that the dowry was four million sesterces; Sen. *Suas.* 1.6 gives six times that amount (1,000 talents). Zon. 10.23; Socrates of Rhodes in Athen. 148b-c; App. *BCiv.* 5.76; Vell. 2.82.4; *BMC Rom Rep.* II, pp. 502-3, nos. 133-37; Plut. *Ant.* 60.2-3; E. A. Sydenham, *Coinage of the Roman Republic* (London, 1952), p. 193, nos. 1196-1200.

19. Cic. *Phil.* 5.4.11; Cass. Dio 48.39.2.

20. Antony's distribution of the legions is discussed in W. W. Tarn: "Antony's Legions," *CQ* 26 (1932), 75-81. Cf. Plut. *Ant.* 61; Cass. Dio 48.41.7; App. *BCiv.* 5.75.

21. Antony's friends could also be generous; the number of families carrying his name indicates that when Gnaeus Domitius Ahenobarbus was Antony's legate in Bithynia he granted citizenship liberally. App. *BCiv.* 5.7; *OGIS* 377.

22. *OGIS* 448; 453-55; Victor Ehrenberg and A. H. M. Jones: *Documents Illustrating the Reigns of Augustus and Tiberius,* (Oxford, 1949), pp. 122-23, nos. 299-300; App. *BCiv.* 5.75; Plut. *Ant.* 24.1-4; 37.3; 67.7; Cass. Dio 48.40.6; Strab. 14.1.41.

23. App. *BCiv.* 5.7; Cass. Dio 49.21.3; 49.22.1-3; Strab. 12.3.35; 14.2.19; 14.2.24; 14.5.10; 14.5.14; 14.8.8-9; Plut. *Ant.* 34. Octavian also tried to maintain prominence in the east by sending letters and decrees on behalf of temples and for other popular measures: R. K. Sherk, *Roman Documents from the Greek East* (Baltimore, 1969), pp. 294-307, no. 58.

24. App. *BCiv.* 5.75; Plut. *Ant.* 61.1; Cass. Dio 49.25.4; 49.33.2; 49.44.2-3; Strab. 11.2.18; 12.3.29; 12.8.16; 13.4.3; 14.2.24.

25. Plut. *Ant.* 37.3; 61.2; 63.3; Cic. *Att.* 14.12.1; 14.19.2; 16.3.6; Cic. *Phil.* 2.94; Cass. Dio 47.48.2; 48.33.5; 49.32.3; 53.26.3; Vell. 2.84.2; Strab. 12.3.6; 12.3.41; 12.5.1; 12.5.4; 12.6.1; 12.6.3; 12.7.3; 14.5.6.

26. App. *BCiv.* 5.7; Plut. *Ant.* 61.1; Martial. *Ep.* 11.20; Cass. Dio 49.32.3; 54.9.2; Strab. 12.2.11.

27. J. Rufus Fears, "Princeps a Diis Electus," *PAMAAR* 26 (1977), 62-83.

28. Plut. *Ant.* 36.1-2; Jos. *Ant. Jud.* 14.13.1.

29. Cass. Dio 48.45.1-3; 49.32.5; Plut. *Ant.* 61.

30. Jos. *Ant. Jud.* 10.10; 14.7.3-8.5; 14.9.3-10; 14.11.2-6; Jos. *Bell. Jud.* 1.7.6; 1.8.3-4; 1.8.9-10.4; 1.11.4-8; Euseb. *Ecc. Hist.* 1.6-7.

31. Jos. *Ant. Jud.* 14.9.2-5; 14.11.2; 14.12.1-13.1; Jos. *Bell. Jud.* 1.10.4-9; 1.12.4-6; Cass. Dio 49.22.6.

32. Jos. *Ant. Jud.* 14.13.2; Jos. *Bell. Jud.* 1.12.6-7; Liv. *Ep.* 128.

33. Zon. 10.22; Tac. *Hist.* 5.9; Oros. 6.18.23; Flor. 2.19.5-7.

34. Jos. *Ant. Jud.* 14.13.3-14.3; 15.2.1-4; Jos. *Bell. Jud.* 1.13.1-14.

35. Jos. *Bell. Jud.* 1.14.3-4; Jos. *Ant. Jud.* 14.14.3-4.

36. Euseb. *Ecc. Hist.* 6-7; Tac. *Hist.* 5.9; Oros. 6.18.24; App. *BCiv.* 5.75; Jos. *Bell. Jud.* 1.14.4; 1.15.3; Jos. *Ant. Jud.* 14.14.4-15.1.

37. Jos. *Ant. Jud.* 14.12.1; 14.14.6-16.4; 15.1.1; Jos. *Bell. Jud.* 1.15.1-18.3; Cass. Dio 49.22; Plut. *Ant.* 34.2-4; Tac. *Hist.* 5.9: Oros. 6.18.23-24; *BMC Rom Rep* II, p. 504, nos. 138-40; p. 508, no. 146; Sydenham, *Coinage*, p. 199, no. 1272.

38. Jos. *Ant. Jud.* 14.12.1; 14.15.14-16.4; 15.1.1-2.4; Jos. *Bell. Jud.* 1.17.8-9; 1.18.3-4; Cass. Dio 49.22.6; Plut. *Ant.* 36.2.

39. Jos. *Ant. Jud.* 15.2.4.

40. Jos. *Ant. Jud.* 15.2.5-3.3.

41. Jos. *Ant. Jud.* 15.3.2-5; Euseb. *Ecc. Hist.* 1.8.

42. Jos. *Ant. Jud.* 15.3.5-9.

43. Nic. Dam. 90, fragments 68, 130.

44. Jos. *Bell. Jud.* 1.18.4; Strab. 14.5.3; 14.5.6; 14.6.6; Plut. *Ant.* 36.2; Cass. Dio 49.32.4-5; Diod. 19.98.

45. Jos. *Bell. Jud.* 1.18.4; 7.8.4; Jos. *Ant. Jud.* 15.4; Strab. 17.1.15; Plut. *Ant.* 36.2; Cass. Dio 49.32.4-5; Theophr. *C. Plant.* 9.6; Just. 36.3.1; Euseb. *Chron.* 1.70; Zon. 10.26; Michael Grant, *From Imperium to Auctoritas*, 2nd ed. (London, 1971), 371.

46. Later anti-Cleopatra gossip (Jos. *Ant. Jud.* 15.3.8; 15.4.2) reported that Cleopatra had tried unsuccessfully to seduce Herod, but the stakes were too high for either party to risk Antony's jealousy.

47. Plut. *Ant.* 35.5-36.1; Plut. *Dem. and Ant.* 4.1; Josephus uses the less probable date 35-34 B.C.; Euseb. *Chron.* I 170 = *FGH* III 724.

48. Plut. *Ant.* 36.3; Liv. *Ep.* 132; Cass. Dio 49.32.4-5. Linda Ricketts, in a personal note, agrees that the new system of dating could have been meant to mark the new era which Antony's territorial gifts was to have initiated. She quotes her thesis: "The chronologist Porphyry attributed the double numeration to Cleopatra's acquisition of the territories which she gained in 37 B.C., and this view is generally accepted." The double numeration appears also in papyri and inscriptions. However, it has been demonstrated that the second date has nothing to do with Caesarion in the documents. See T. C. Skeat, *The Reigns of the Ptolemies* (Munich, 1954), 42; H. Heinen, "Cäsar und Kaisarion," *Historia* 18 (1969), 188-89.

Chapter XI.
Parthia Invicta

1. Just. 41. Two recent surveys of Parthian history are: Malcolm Colledge, *The Parthians* (New York, 1967) and Neilson Debevoise, *A Political History of Parthia* (New York, 1968).

2. Liv. *Ep.* 106; Just. 42.4; Plut. *Crass.* 16.2-33.4 *passim*; App. *BCiv.* 5.10; 5.65; Flor. 2.19.3; Jos. *Ant. Jud.* 14.7.3; Strab. 16.1.28.

3. Suet. *Jul.* 44.3; 79.3; Nic. Dam. 18; Flor. 2.19.4; Plut. *Brut.* 25; Plut. *Caes.* 58.5-6; 60; App. *Syr.* 51; App. *BCiv.* 2.110; 4.58; 4.63; 4.88; 4.99; Cass. Dio 44.15.3-4; 48.24.3-6; Cic. *De Div.* 2.110; Just. 42.4.

4. App. *BCiv.* 5.9-10.

5. Flor. 2.19.4-5; Vell. 2.78.1; Cass. Dio 48.24.4-26.5; Liv. *Ep.* 127; Plut. *Ant.* 28.1; 30.1; Just. 42.4; Ruf. Fest. 18; Jos. *Ant. Jud.* 14.13.3-14.3; 15.2.1-4; Jos. *Bell. Jud.* 1.13-14; Strab. 12.9.9; 14.2.24; Frontin. *Strat.* 2.5.36; Tac. *Ann.* 3.62; App. *BCiv.* 5.65;

5.133; App. *Syr.* 51; *BMC Rom Rep* II, p. 500, nos. 131-32; Zon. 10.22; R. K. Sherk, *Roman Documents from the Greek East* (Baltimore, 1969), pp. 310-12, no. 60.

6. Ruf. Fest. 18; Eutr. 7.3-4; Plut. *Ant.* 30.3; Vell. 2.74-78.1; Cass. Dio 48.27-39; App. *BCiv.* 5.55-76.

7. Cass. Dio 48.24.3; 48.24.8; 48.39.2-41.7; 49.19.1-20.5; App. *BCiv.* 5.75; Gell. 15.4.4; Eutr. 7.5; Flor. 2.19.5-7; Frontin. *Strat.* 1.1.6; 2.5.36-37; Tac. *Germ.* 37; Tac. *Hist.* 5.9; Jos. *Ant. Jud.* 14.15.1-5; 14.15.7; Jos. *Bell. Jud.* 1.15.2; 1.16.4; Just. 42.4; Juv. 7.199; Liv. *Ep.* 127-28; Oros. 6.18.23; Pl. *N.H.* 7.44; Plut. *Ant.* 33.1; 33.4-34.2; Ruf. Fest. 18; Strab. 11.13.3; 16.1.28; 16.2.8; Val. Max. 6.9.9; Vell. 2.78.1; Hor. *Car.* 3.6.9-12; Zon. 10.18; 10.22-23; 26; *BMC Rom Rep* II, p. 505.

8. Plut. *Ant.* 34.2-3; Cass. Dio 48.41.5; 49.20.3-5.

9. Val. Max. 6.9.9; Juv. 7.199-201; Jos. *Ant. Jud.* 14.15.8-9; Jos. *Bell. Jud.* 1.16.7; Oros. 6.18.23; Plut. *Ant.* 34.3-4; Cass. Dio 49.21.1; 49.22.1-2; Zon. 10.26.

10. Plut. *Ant.* 34.4-5; Cass. Dio 49.21.2-3; Gell. *Noc. Att.* 15.4.4; Vell. 2.65.3; Ruf. Fest. 18; *CIL* I.180. See p. 207 of this volume.

11. Plut. *Ant.* 35; Cass. Dio 48.54.1-6; 49.23.1; App. *BCiv.* 5.95.

12. Jos. *Ant. Jud.* 14.16; 15.1; Jos. *Bell. Jud.* 1.17.2; 1.18.2-3; Plut. *Ant.* 34.6; 37.1-2; Plut. *Dem. and Ant.* 1.2; Cass. Dio 49.23.2-24.5; Just. 42.5.1; *BMC Rom Rep* II, p. 508, no. 146; Zon. 10.26; E. A. Sydenham, *Coinage of the Roman Republic* (London, 1952), p. 194, no. 1202.

13. There is a substantial variation in the number of legions the ancient authorities list: Flor. 16; Aur. Vict. 15; Liv. 18; Vell. 13. T. R. Holmes, *The Architect of the Roman Empire* (London, 1928), I, 223 argues the accuracy of 16. Plut. *Ant.* 35.4; 40.5; 42.3; Cass. Dio 49.24.5; 50.1.3; Liv. *Ep.* 130; Vell. 2.82.1; Flor. 2.20.10; Strab. 11.13.4; 11.14.9; 16.1.28.

14. There is a debate over the date of the marriage of Cleopatra. The year 36 B.C. seems most probable; other authors suggest as late as 32 B.C. when Antony divorced Octavia. Cf. Plut. *Ant.* 37.3; Jos. *Bell. Jud.* 1.18.5; Aur. Vict. 85; Just. 42.5; Eutr. 7.6.

15. Strab. 11.13.3-4; 16.1.28; Jos. *Ant. Jud.* 15.4.2; Pl. *N.H.* 5.21; Plut. *Ant.* 37.3-38.1; Cass. Dio 49.25.1-2; Suet. *Jul.* 44.3; Aur. Vict. 85.4.

16. Plut. *Ant.* 38.2; Cass. Dio 49.25.2; Zon. 10.26.

17. Ruf. Fest. 18; Plut. *Ant.* 38.2-39.1; 50.2-3; Cass. Dio 49.25.3-26.2; Zon. 10.26; Vell. 2.82.2.

18. Plut. *Ant.* 39.1-7; Cass. Dio 49.26.3-27.2; Liv. *Ep.* 130; Frontin. *Strat.* 4.1.37.

19. Cass. Dio 49.27.3; Plut. *Ant.* 40.

20. Liv. *Ep.* 130; Vell. 2.82.2-3; Ruf. Fest. 18; Flor. 2.20.4-10; Plut. *Ant.* 17.2; 41-49; Frontin. *Strat.* 2.13.7; Tac. *Hist.* 3.24; Cass. Dio 49.28.1-31.2; 50.27.5; Zon. 10.26; Eutr. 7.6.

21. Flor. 2.20.9-10; Plut. *Ant.* 50.2-51.2; Cass. Dio 49.31.2-32.1; Strab. 11.13.4; Zon. 10.26; Liv. *Ep.* 130.

22. Plut. *Ant.* 50.1; Vell. 2.82.3; Flor. 2.20.10; Liv. *Ep.* 130; Frontin. *Strat.* 2.3.15; Eutr. 7.6; Oros. 6.19.1; Strab. 11.13.3-4; Suet. *Aug.* 21.3; *BMC Rom Rep* II, pp. 506-8, nos. 141-45; Cass. Dio 49.32.1-2.

23. Vell. 2.79.5; 2.87.2; App. *BCiv.* 5.1; 5.133-45; Plut. *Ant.* 52; Eutr. 7.6; Oros. 6.19.2; Flor. 2.18.8; Cass. Dio 49.17-18; 49.33.1-2; Liv. *Ep.* 131; *BMC Rom Rep* II, p. 520, no. 172.

24. App. *BCiv.* 5.133-44; Cass. Dio 49.18.4-6; Vell. 2.79.

25. App. *BCiv.* 5.95; 5.134-35; 5.138; 5.145; Plut. *Ant.* 53.1-54.2; Zon. 10.26; Cass. Dio 49.33.3-4. See p. 157 of this volume.

26. Plut. *Ant.* 50.2-4; Plut. *Dem. and Ant.* 5.2; Cass. Dio 49.33.2; 49.39.1-40.4; 50.1.4; 50.27.7; 51.5.5; Liv. *Ep.* 131; Tac. *Ann.* 2.3; Zon. 10.27; Vell. 2.82.3; Jos. *Ant. Jud.* 15.4.2-3; Jos. *Bell. Jud.* 1.18.5; Oros. 6.19.3; App. *BCiv.* 5.145; Strab. 11.13.4; 11.14.15; Sydenham, *Coinage*, p. 194, nos. 1205-07; *BMC Rom Rep* II, pp. 520-21, nos. 172-74.

27. Plut. *Ant.* 55.2; Cass. Dio 49.39.6-40.2; Tac. *Ann.* 2.3; Zon. 10.27; Jos. *Ant. Jud.* 15.4.3.

28. Cass. Dio 49.40.2-41.3; 50.1.5; Plut. *Ant.* 50.4; 54.3-6; 55.2; Pl. *N.H.* 33.24; Liv. *Ep.* 131; Strab. 11.14.15; Vell. 2.82.4; Zon. 10.27.

29. Cass. Dio 49.33.2; 49.40.2; 49.44; Plut. *Ant.* 53.6; Zon. 10.27.

30. Cass. Dio 51.16.2; Plut. *Ant.* 55.2; 56.1; Just. 42.5; Hor. *Car.* 3.8.19.

Chapter XII.
Breaking with Octavian

1. Shakespeare, *Antony and Cleopatra*, Act II, Scene 2.

2. E.g., Nicolaus of Damascus, friend of Herod. Also Josephus, who drew heavily from Nicolaus of Damascus. Horace, Vergil, Propertius were poets under the patronage of Augustus and were themselves recoiling from the recent dangers of war. Velleius, Florus, and Cassius Dio were all influenced by hostile propaganda. Plutarch used her as a lesson against immorality, although in the account of her last days, he seems to have accepted the more sympathetic account of her physician, Olympus. Only Suetonius and Appian are reasonably fair.

3. Hor. *Car.* 1.37.21.

4. E. Badian, *Roman Imperialism in the Late Republic* (London, 1968), *passim* argues that the senate avoided adding new provinces as long as possible.

5. Plut. *Ant.* 27.3-4; App. *BCiv.* 5.9; Ps.-Vict. *Vir. Ill.* 86; Cass. Dio 48.24.2; Jos. *Ant. Jud.* 15.4.1.

6. App. *BCiv.* 5.7; Cass. Dio 48.24.1; 49.32.3-5.

7. App. *BCiv.* 5.7-8; Flor. 2.13.56; Cass. Dio 42.34-45; 49.32.3-5; Ps.-Vict. *Vir. Ill.* 86; Eutr. 6.22.

8. Plut. *Ant.* 25-29; 58.5-6; Oros. 6.15.28-16.2; App. *BCiv.* 5.8; 5.11; Cass. Dio 42.38.2; 48.24.1-2; 48.24.8; Amm. 22.16.13; Sen. *Dial.* 9.9.5; Jos. *Bell. Jud.* 1.18.4-5 Jos. *Ant. Jud.* 15.4.1; Gell. 7.17.3.

9. An excellent recent account of the city of Alexandria during this period is P. M. Fraser, *Ptolemaic Alexandria*, 3 vols. (London, 1972). Cleopatra's divine titles included *nea Isis, thea neotera*, and *thea philopator*; Cass. Dio 50.5.3. She also wore the apparel of Isis at state celebrations; Plut. *Ant.* 54.6.

10. Pl. *N.H.* 33.14; Macr. *Sat.* 3.17.14-18.

11. Eutr. 7.6-7; Cass. Dio 50.5.4; Hor. *Car.* 1.37.6.

12. Liv. *Ep.* 132; Jos. *Bell. Jud.* 1.18.4; Flor. 2.21.11; Hor. *Car.* 1.37.21; Plut. *Ant.* 58.5-6.

13. Juv. 15; Hor. *Car.* 1.37. See pp. 242-52 of this volume.

14. Strab. 17.1.11; Juv. 15.44-50; Cass. Dio 50.5; 50.27.2-7; 51.15.4; Vell. 2.83.2; Hor. *Car.* 1.37.14; Plut. *Ant.* 4; 27-29; Plut. *Dem. and Ant.* 3; Sen. *Epist. Mor.* 83.25; 91.13; Prop. 3.11.29-33; Lucan. 10.109-72; Pl. *N.H.* 9.58; 33.50; 36.32. Experimenters more casual about their pearls than I report that Antony and Cleopatra could not have wasted wealth by dissolving pearls in wine as reported since their experiments indicate that wine will not act on pearls.

NOTES

15. Plut. *Ant.* 4; App. *BCiv.* 5.11; *OGIS* 195.

16. *OGIS* 195; Lily Ross Taylor, *The Divinity of the Roman Emperor* (Middletown, Connecticut, 1931), 1–77 *passim*; Stephan Weinstock, *Divus Julius* (London, 1971).

17. Verg. *Ecl.* 1.7; 1.41–43; App. *BCiv.* 5.100; Cass. Dio 48.31.5; 48.48.5; 49.15.5; Suet. *Aug.* 70; Taylor, *Divinity*, 78–141 *passim*.

18. Verg. *G.* 2.385; Plut. *Ant.* 4.1–2; G. Wissowa, *Religion und Cultus d. Römer*, 2 (Munich, 1912), 138, 299; F. Altheim, *History of Roman Religion* (London, 1938), 125, 149; Vell. 2.82.4; *BMC Rom Rep* I, p. 578, no. 4255; II, p. 394, no. 40; p. 396, no. 48; p. 505; Liv. 39.8.1–19.4; 39.41.6; 40.19.9–11; E. A. Sydenham, *Coinage of the Roman Republic* (London, 1952), p. 189, nos. 1160, 1163; *Pap. Oxy.* 1629.

19. Val. Max. 3.4; Juv. 15; Prop. 3.11.39–44.

20. Plut. *Ant.* 24.3; 26.1–3; 60.2–3; Cass. Dio 48.39.2; 50.5.3; Sen. *Suas.* 1.6; *BMC Rom Emp* pp. 14, 52, 355; *BMC Rom Rep* II, pp. 502–3, nos. 133–37; pp. 505–7, nos. 141–43; Sydenham, *Coinage*, p. 193, nos. 1199–1201.

21. Cass. Dio 50.5.3; 50.25; 51.15.5; Zon. 10.28; Plut. *Ant.* 54.6.

22. Cass. Dio 49.27.4; 49.40.3; 50.5.2–3; 50.25.4; Flor. 2.21.3; Vell. 2.82.4; Plut. *Mor.* 56 E-F; Strab. 17.1.11; Athen. 5.200C; Macr. *Sat.* 2.17.14–18; Pl. *N.H.* 14.148.

23. Plut. *Ant.* 54.3; Cass. Dio 49.41; Aug. *R.G.* 27; Taylor, *Divinity*, 127.

24. *BMC Rom Rep* II, p. 509, no. 147; p. 521, nos. 173–74; *BMC Rom Emp* pp. 60, 92; Sydenham, *Coinage*, p. 194, nos. 1206–7; Plut. *Ant.* 28.4–7.

25. Strab. 14.5.3–6; 14.6.6; Plut. *Ant.* 54.4; Cass. Dio 49.41.1–2; *BMC Rom Rep* II, p. 394, no. 40; pp. 502–3, nos. 133–37; pp. 507–8, nos. 144–45; pp. 510–19, nos. 150–71; *BMC Rom Emp* p. 15; *BMC Phoenicia* p. CXVIII; *BMC Ptolemies* p. LXXXIV; Michael Grant, *From Imperium to Auctoritas*, 2nd ed. (London, 1971), pl. IX, no. 29.

26. Plut. *Ant.* 54.4; Suet. *Jul.* 49.5; 52.1–2; Suet. *Aug.* 17.5; Cic. *Att.* 14.20.2; Cass. Dio 47.31.5; 49.41.1–2; 50.1.5. I am grateful to Linda Ricketts for her personal notes arguing against following Cass. Dio 49.41.1, who calls Caesarion King of Kings, matching his co-ruler Cleopatra, Queen of Kings. Ricketts accepts Plut. *Ant.* 54, who says that Antony conferred the title upon his own sons, because the title, originally held by the ancient Persian dynasts, and more recently by Tigranes I of Armenia, would more appropriately fit Antony's sons, who now received these territories. For other positions cf. Michael Grant, *Cleopatra* (London, 1972), 161–72; M. A. Levi, *Ottaviano Capoparte* (Florence, 1933), 146; John Carter, *The Battle of Actium* (New York, 1970), 175–77; O. von Wertheimer, *Cleopatra: A Royal Voluptuary* (London, 1931), 259; Ernle Bradford, *Cleopatra* (London, 1971), 198–201; Marie-Thérèse Lenger, *Corpus des ordonnances des Ptolémées* (Brussels, 1964), pp. 210–15, nos. 75–76: Letter of Cleopatra VII and Ptolemy Caesarion, April 12, 41 B.C.

27. Plut. *Ant.* 54; Cass. Dio 49.32.4–5; 49.41.3; 50.25.3–4; 50.26.2; *BMC Rom Rep* II, p. 525, nos. 179–82; Strab. 17.1.11; Sydenham, *Coinage*, pp. 194–95; nos. 1210–11. The title King of Kings was not unprecedented, e.g., Pompey had granted it to Tigranes in 65 B.C.; Cass. Dio 37.6.2.

28. Hor. *Epod.* 9.11–16.

29. Cass. Dio 49.41.4–6; Plut. *Ant.* 55.1.

30. Plut. *Ant.* 55; Cass. Dio 49.41.1; 49.43.6; 50.1.3–2.2; Oros. 6.18.19–32; Suet. *Aug.* 69.

31. Plut. *Ant.* 58.2–6; Plut. *Dem. and Ant.* 3.3; Cass. Dio 49.41.5; 50.24.5–25.4; Zon. 10.27; Pl. *N.H.* 9.15; Macr. *Sat.* 3.17.14--18; Suet. *Aug.* 70.

32. Plut. *Ant.* 25.2–3; Cass. Dio 49.17.5; 49.39.2; App. *BCiv.* 4.42; 4.38; 4.104; 4.136; 5.132; 5.137; 5.139; 5.144; Suet. *Ner.* 3.2; Macr. *Sat.* 2.4.29; *BMC Rom Rep* II, p. 514.

33. Nep. *Att.* 12; 20.

34. Cass. Dio 48.3.3–5; 49.13.1–14.3; 49.34.3; Liv. *Ep.* 131; Vell. 2.81.1; Aug. *R.G.* 1.3.

35. App. *BCiv.* 5.145; App. *Ill.* 16–28; Flor. 23.6–25.12; Cass. Dio 49.35–38; 50.24.4; 50.28.4; 51.21.6; Zon. 10.27; Strab. 4.6.10; Liv. *Ep.* 131–33; Oros. 6.18–19; Vell. 2.78.2; Suet. *Aug.* 20; 22; Aug. *R.G.* 5.29–30.

36. Cass. Dio 47.7–8; 49.15.3; 49.43.6; App. *BCiv.* 5.132.

37. Cass. Dio 43.44.2–6; 44.4.2–7.3; 48.42.3–5; 49.15.6; 49.43.6–8; Liv. *Ep.* 116; Suet. *Jul.* 76.1; Suet. *Aug.* 29.1–3; App. *BCiv.* 2.106; 5.132; Aug. *R.G.* 1.4; 1.7; 2.10; 3.19; Verg. *Ecl.* 1.6.

38. Cass. Dio 49.14.4–5; 49.42.1–43.5; 50.24.5–25.4; Vell. 2.81.3; Suet. *Aug.* 29.5; Pl. *N.H.* 7.45; 36.24.

39. Suet. *Aug.* 28.1; Liv. *Ep.* 132; Cass. Dio 49.41.6; 50.1; Aug. *R.G.* 7; *BMC Rom Rep* II, pp. 526–31, nos. 183–229; Carter, *Battle of Actium*, 143.

40. Suet. *Aug.* 17.2; Cass. Dio 49.41.4; 50.2.2–4; Plut. *Ant.* 59.1.

41. Aug. *R.G.* 25; Suet. *Aug.* 17.2; Cass. Dio 50.2.5–7; 50.3.2; 50.20.6; Zon. 10.28.

42. Plut. *Dem. and Ant.* 4.1; Plut. *Ant.* 57; Cass. Dio 49.38.1; 50.3.2.

43. Eutr. 7.6; Oros. 6.19.4; Plut. *Ant.* 53.4–54.2; 57.3; 59.3; Liv. *Ep.* 131–32; Cass. Dio 50.3.2; Strab. 17.1.11; Suet. *Aug.* 69.2.

44. Plut. *Ant.* 58.2–4; Vell. 2.83; Cass. Dio 50.3; 50.20.7; Zon. 10.28; Suet. *Aug.* 17.1; 17.4; Grant, *Cleopatra*, 192–93.

45. Prop. 3.11.29–49; Cass. Dio 50.3.5–4.1.

46. Plut. *Ant.* 60.1; Cass. Dio 50.4.2–5; 50.6.1; 50.10.1; 50.21; 50.24.3–27.7; 51.19.5; *BMC Rom Rep* II, p. 531.

Chapter XIII.
The Lion at Bay

1. Aug. *R.G.* 25; Cass. Dio 50.4.5; 57.3.2; *CIL* I, 160.

2. Plut. *Mor.* 56E; Plut. *Ant.* 58.1–2; Suet. *Aug.* 17.2; Cass. Dio 50.7.2–3; 50.9.1; 50.10.4–6; 51.3.5; 51.4.6.

3. Cass. Dio 50.6.2–4; 50.11.1; 50.11.4–6; 51.3.5; Flor. 2.21.4; Oros. 6.19.6; Plut. *Ant.* 61.2; App. *BCiv.* 5.127; *CIL* I, 160; Zon. 10.28–29.

4. Plut. *Ant.* 56.1; Val. Max. 1.1.19; Cass. Dio 51.8.3; Lact. *Div. Inst.* 2.7.17; Oros. 6.19.5; E. A. Sydenham, *Coinage of the Roman Republic* (London, 1952), p. 195, nos. 1212–19.

5. Plut. *Ant.* 56.1.; Cass. Dio 49.44.

6. Even within one ancient author the numbers may vary: e.g., Plut. *Ant.* 56 = 100,000; 61.1 = 80,000; 68 = 19 legions. P. Brunt, *Italian Manpower, 225 B.C.–A.D. 14* (London, 1971), 505 reasonably calculates 23 legions for the total force in the east.

7. Jos. *C. Ap.* 2.61; Jos. *Bell. Jud.* 1.19–20; Jos. *Ant. Jud.* 15.5–7; Plut. *Ant.* 61.1–2; 71.1; 72.2–3; Strab. 12.8.9; 16.2.46; *BMC Rom Rep* II, pp. 526–27.

8. Plut. *Ant.* 56.2–3.

9. Plut. *Ant.* 56.4–57.1; Strab. 14.14; *BMC Rom Rep* II, pp. 526–33, nos. 183–233.

10. Plut. *Ant.* 54.1–3; 57; 60; Suet. *Aug.* 2.3; 4.2; 7.1; 16.2; 63.2; 68–70; Cass. Dio 50.6.6–7.1; 50.8.6; Martial. *Ep.* 11.20; 22.1–2; Pl. *N.H.* 14.148; Aug. *R.G.* 25; Vell. 2.83.

11. Cass. Dio 50.7.3; 50.9.1; 50.10.3–6 states that Antony intended to invade Italy but was discouraged by finding Octavian's fleet ready to oppose him.

12. Plut. *Ant.* 58.2; 59; 62.1; Strab. 12.8.9; Sen. *Clem.* 1.10.1; *BMC Rom Rep* II, p. 531.

13. Flor. 2.215-17; Cass. Dio 50.9.2-3; 50.29; Hor. *Epod.* 1.1; Zon. 10.28. *BMC Rom Rep* II, p. 531, nos. 227-29.

14. *ILS* 2672. The primary, and therefore the secondary, sources differ widely in giving the sizes of the armies and the numbers of ships. I have closely followed the calculations of John Carter, *The Battle of Actium*, (New York, 1970), 202.

15. Plut. *Ant.* 62.3; Liv. *Ep.* 132; Cass. Dio 50.11.3-12.7; Flor. 2.21.4; Oros. 6.19.6.

16. Plut. *Ant.* 62.1; 62.3-63.2; 68.4-5; Vell. 2.84.2; Cass. Dio 50.12.8-13.5; 50.30.1; Flor. 2.21.4; Zon. 10.29; Oros. 6.19.7; Strab. 8.4.3.

17. Plut. *Ant.* 59.4; 63.3; Vell. 2.84; Cass. Dio 50.11.2; 50.13.8-14.2; 50.23.1; 50.23.3; 50.30.2-3; Oros. 6.19.7; Hor. *Epod.* 9.17-20; Sen. *Suas.* 1.7; *BMC Rom Rep* II, p. 527.

18. Suet. *Ner.* 3; Cass. Dio 50.12.8; 50.13.5-7; Vell. 2.84.2; Plut. *Ant.* 63.2-3; App. *BCiv.* 4.38; Strab. 12.8.9; Pl. *N.H.* 33.132.

19. Cass. Dio 50.14.4-15.4; 50.23.2-3; 50.30.3-4; 50.32.2; Vell. 2.84.1; 2.85.2. Flor. 2.21.5-7 says that Antony had fewer than 200 ships; Oros. 6.19.8 says 170 ships; Plut. *Ant.* 61.1; 63.3-5; 64 says 500 ships.

20. Plut. *Ant.* 65; Vell. 2.85.1-2; Cass. Dio 50.31; 51.1.1.

21. Cass. Dio 50.18.5-6; 50.19.5; 50.29; 50.32-33. Dio gives a set battle piece and describes Cleopatra's breakthrough as due to unplanned panic which broke Antony's will. Plut. *Ant.* 65.5-66.5; Flor. 2.21.5-7; Zon. 10.29.

22. Hor. *Epod.* 1.1; Hor. *Car.* 1.37; although expressing grudging admiration of Cleopatra's courage, Horace erroneously reports that scarcely one of Cleopatra's ships escaped. Prop. 3.11; 4.6.15-68; Plut. *Ant.* 68.1; Plut. *Dem. and Ant.* 3.4; 6.1; Zon. 10-29; Liv. *Ep.* 133; Vell. 2.85.3; Cass. Dio 50.31.1--33.3; 51.3.1; Pl. *N.H.* 19.22; 32.3; Eutr. 7.7; Verg. *Aen.* 8.671-713; Flor. 2.21.8; Oros. 6.19.9-12. Numbers of casualties and modern interpretations of these varying accounts differ widely. My description is based largely on the analysis presented in Carter, *Battle of Actium*, 200-27, and followed also in Michael Grant, *Cleopatra* (London, 1972), 203-12. Carter persuades me that the purpose of the action was to escape with a minimum of loss and that Cleopatra and Antony were leading rather than deserting their troops. For other interpretations, see especially: W. W. Tarn, "The Battle of Actium," *JRS* 21 (1931), 174-96; and in *CAH* X, 100-6; J. Kromeyer, "Kleine Forschungen zur Geschichte des zweiten Triumvirats," *Hermes* 34 (1899), 1-54; Kromeyer, "Actium, ein Epilog," *Hermes* 68 (1933), 361-83; A. Ferrabino, "La battaglia d'Azio," *RFIC* 52 (1924), 433-72; and 53 (1925), 131-35; G. W. Richardson, "Actium," *JRS* 27 (1937), 153-64; T. R. Holmes, *The Architect of the Roman Empire* (Oxford, 1928-31), 255-58.

23. Hor. *Epod.* 9.17-20; Plut. *Ant.* 68.1-2; Vell. 2.85.4-6; Cass. Dio 50.33.4-35.6; Suet. *Aug.* 17.2.

24. Strab. 17.1.11; Verg. *Aen.* 8.675-713; Jos. *C. Ap.* 2.59; Cass. Dio 50.33.1-4; Plut. *Ant.* 66.3-5; Prop. 2.16.38-40; Gell. 2.22.23; Vell. 2.84.1.

25. Plut. *Ant.* 67.1-5; Cass. Dio 51.1.4; Zon. 10.29.

26. Aug. *R.G.* 1.3; Vell. 2.85.6-86.2; App. *BCiv.* 4.42; 4.49; Plut. *Ant.* 67.5; 68.2-3; 71.1.

27. Val. Max. 1.1.19; Aug. *R.G.* 1.3; 3.15; App. *BCiv.* 4.51; Cass. Dio 51.1.1-5; 51.3.1; 51.5.3; Zon. 10.30.

28. Verg. *Aen.* 8.695-706; Plut. *Ant.* 68.4; Paus. 5.23.3; 7.18.8; Cass. Dio 51.1.2-3; Strab. 7.7.6; 10.2.2; Aug. *R.G.* 13; 24; Pl. *N.H.* 4.1.5; Suet. *Aug.* 18.2; Zon. 10.30; Tac. *Ann.* 2.53; 5.10; Jos. *Bell. Jud.* 1.398; Victor Ehrenberg and A. H. M. Jones, *Documents Illustrating the Reigns of Augustus and Tiberius* (Oxford, 1949), p. 56, no.12.

29. App. *BCiv.* 4.42; Cass. Dio 51.4.1–3; 51.7.2–7; 51.9.1; Zon. 10.30; Jos. *Bell. Jud.* 1.20.2; Jos. *Ant. Jud.* 15.6.7; Suet. *Aug.* 17.3; R. K. Sherk, *Roman Documents from the Greek East* (Baltimore, 1969), pp. 297–307, no. 58, sections 3–4.

30. App. *BCiv.* 4.51; Suet. *Aug.* 17.3; 26.3; Oros. 6.19; 14; Vell. 2.88; Liv. *Ep.* 133; Plut. *Ant.* 73.3; Cass. Dio 51.3.2–5.1.

31. Plut. *Ant.* 69.1–4; 72.1; 73.1–2; Cass. Dio 51.5.3–5; 51.6.3–7.1; 51.8; 51.10.4; Zon. 10.30; Verg. *Aen.* 8.709–13; Flor. 2.21.9; Strab. 2.5.12; 15.1.4; 17.1.13.

32. Plut. *Ant.* 69.1–2; 71.1; Cass. Dio 51.5.6; 51.9.1; Zon. 10.30; Hor. *Epod.* 9.17–20; Oros. 6.19.15; App. *BCiv.* 4.107; *BMC Rom Emp* I, p. 111, nos. 686–89.

33. Cass. Dio 51.6.1; 51.8.2–4 gives an account, that Antony sent Antyllus to Octavian with gold offering to retire from active life in return for safety, which is probably spurious. So too his other petitions to Octavian and his betrayal of his friend Publius Turullius. Hostile propaganda strove to make Antony appear craven and treacherous. Cf. Plut. *Ant.* 69.4–71.3; 72.1; 73.3; Strab. 17.1.9.

34. Oros. 6.19.15; Flor. 2.21.9; Cass. Dio 51.9.1–4; Suet. *Aug.* 17.3.

35. Flor. 2.21.9; Plut. *Ant.* 74; Cass. Dio 51.9.5–10.4; Jos. *Bell. Jud.* 1.20.3; Jos. *Ant. Jud.* 15.6.7; Suet. *Aug.* 17.3.

36. Antony was now 52 or 53 years old, Octavian 33, and Cleopatra 37.

37. Strab. 17.1.10; Suet. *Aug.* 17.4; Jos. *C. Ap.* 2.60; Vell. 2.87.1; Oros. 6.19.16; Plut. *Ant.* 75.1–76.2; Zon. 10.30.

38. Plut. *Ant.* 81.2; Oros. 6.19.13 says that she and Antony sent all their children away from Alexandria.

39. Cass. Dio 51.8; 51.10.5; Zon. 10.30; Plut. *Ant.* 74.1–2.

40. Vell. 2.87.1; Plut. *Ant.* 76.2–4; Plut. *Dem. and Ant.* 6.2; Liv. *Ep.* 133; Suet. *Aug.* 17.4; Oros. 6.19.17. Flor. 2.21.9.

41. Cass. Dio 51.10.6–11.1; Zon. 10.30; Aur. Vict. 85–86; Plut. *Ant.* 76.5–77.4; Eutr. 7.7; Oros. 6.19.17; Clem. of Alex. *Strom.* 1.21.145.

42. Plut. *Ant.* 78–79; 82; Cass. Dio 51.11.1–5; Zon. 10.31.

43. Flor. 2.21.9; Plut. *Ant.* 83; Cass. Dio 51.11.6–13.2; Strab. 17.1.10; Zon. 10.31.

44. Plut. *Ant.* 84.1; Cass. Dio 51.13.1–4. For the opposite arguments, that Octavian wanted Cleopatra alive, cf. especially W. R. Johnson, "Cleopatra," *Arion* 6 (1967), 387–400. Three centuries later the emperor Aurelian dared to march Queen Zenobia in triumph.

45. Perhaps, as the sources tell, she died by the bite of poisonous snakes. The evidence was never found. The ancient symbol of royal rule in Egypt was the cobra-headed crown; and the snake was associated with Isis. The asp is sometimes identified as a small African cobra—which could have been smuggled into the chamber easily. In all probability, the snake symbols were associated with Cleopatra and transferred into the cause of her death. Those who mention snakes: Vell. 2.87.1; Suet. *Aug.* 17.4; Oros. 6.19.18; Strab. 17.1.10; Verg. *Aen.* 8.697; Eutr. 7.7; Aur. Vict. 86; Hor. *Car.* 1.37.21–32; Flor. 2.21.11; Aelian. 9.11; Prop. 3.11.53; Stat. *Silv.* 3.2.119–20; Cass. Dio 51.11.2; 51.13–15.1; 51.15.4; Zon. 10.31; Plut. *Ant.* 71.4–5; 84.2–86.4; Pl. *N.H.* 7.2.14; Lucan. 9.891–937; cf. Liv. *Ep.* 133; Liv. *Frag.* 54; Martial. *Ep.* 4.59.5–6; Jos. *C. Ap.* 2.60.

46. Sen. *Suas.* 7.13; Sen. *Benef.* 4.30.2; Cass. Dio 51.19.3–6; Zon. 10.31; App. *BCiv.* 4.51; Plut. *Ant.* 86.5; Plut. *Cic.* 49; Clem. of Alex. *Strom.* 1.121.143; *Pap. Oxy.* 1635; *CIL* I, 160; Suet. *Claud.* 11.3; Ehrenberg and Jones, *Documents*, p. 56, nos. 14–15; for dating, see T. Skeat, "The Last Days of Cleopatra," *JRS* 43 (1953), 98–100. Tac. *Ann.* 3.18 gives evidence that Antony's name remained in public records during the reign of Tiberius; and Caligula ostentatiously honored Antony over Augustus; Cass. Dio 59.20.1–2;

Suet. *Calig.* 23. Michael Grant, *From Imperium to Auctoritas*, 2nd ed. (London, 1971), 268. For the chronology see Charles Babcock, "Dio and Plutarch on the *Damnatio* of Antony," *CP* 57 (1962), 30-31.

47. Cass. Dio 51.15.6 says that Caesarion was killed in Ethiopia. Cf. 48.54.4; 51.2.2-6; 51.6.2; 51.8.2-3; 51.15.5; Zon. 10.31; Aug. *R.G.* 3-4; Suet. *Aug.* 17.5; Plut. *Ant.* 72.2-3; 81-82.1; 87.1; Oros. 6.19.20; Vell. 2.87.2-3 says that Octavian killed no one.

48. Pl. *N.H.* 3.4.35-37; 5.1.20; Aug. *R.G.* 3.15-16; Plut. *Mor.* 207.2-3; Cass. Dio 51.16; 53.1.1; Macr. *Sat.* 2.4.29; Sen. *Benef.* 2.25.1; Sen. *Clem.* 1.10;*ILS* 8780; Strab. 14.6.6.

49. Pl. *N.H.* 34.8.14; Strab. 13.1.30; 14.1.14; 17.1.10; Cass. Dio 51.17.1-3; 51.17.6-18.1; Zon. 10.31; Suet. *Aug.* 18.2; Jos. *Bell. Jud.* 1.20.3; Aug. *R.G.* 24; 27; Eutr. 7.7; Tac. *Hist.* 5.9.

50. Vell. 2.89.1-4; Liv. *Ep.* 133; Prop. 3.11.25-55; Oros. 6.19.21-20.1; Aug. *R.G.* 4; 15; Suet. *Aug.* 22; Cass. Dio 51.19.1-20.4; 51.21.5-22.9; Zon. 10.31; *ILS* 91; *BMC Rom Rep* II, pp. 535-37, nos. 236-55; *CIL* I, 76, 180, 248.

51. Pl. *N.H.* 5.1.2; 5.1.11; 5.1.16; 5.1.20; Strab. 17.3.7; Cass. Dio 51.15.6; 59.25.1; Plut. *Ant.* 87.1; Tac. *Ann.* 4.23; 4.26.

52. Tac. *Ann.* 2.56; 2.67; 3.38; Strab. 12.3.29; 12.3.31; 12.3.37; 14.1.42; Cass. Dio 59.12.2; 60.8.2. For a full study of Antony's descendents, see Ernestine Leon, "One Roman's Family," *CB* 6 (April 1959), 61-64. Cf. p. 157 of this volume.

53. Cass. Dio 51.15.7; 54.26.2; 55.10.18; Tac. *Ann.* 4.44; Vell. 2.100.4; Plut. *Ant.* 57.3; 87.1-3; Strab. 12.3.37; Sen. *De Brev. Vit.* 4.5.

54. Shakespeare, *Macbeth* 1.3.69; see Tac. *Hist.* 5.9; Tac. *Ann.* 4.44; 11.37; 12.65.2; Plut. *Ant.* 87.3-4; Cass. Dio 51.15.7; Suet. *Ner.* 4-7; Suet. *Calig.* 1.1.7; Suet. *Claud.* 11.3.

Chapter XIV.
"My Fame is Shrewdly Gored"

1. Shakespeare, *Troilus and Cressida* 3.3.228.

2. *Nicolaus of Damascus' "Life of Augustus,"* trans. Clayton Morris Hall, *Smith Coll. Cl. St.* 4 (Northampton, 1923), 65-69.

3. *Appian's "Roman History,"* trans. Horace White (London, 1913), IV, 27-29.

4. *Cicero: "The Letters to his Friends,"* trans. W. Glynn Williams (London, 1928), II, 595-97.

5. *Velleius Paterculus; "Compendium of Roman History,"* trans. Frederick W. Shipley (London, 1967), 181.

6. *Suetonius: "The Lives of the Caesars,"* trans. J. C. Rolfe (London, 1914), I, 135.

7. *Plutarch's "Lives,"* trans. Bernadotte Perrin (London, 1968), IX, 173.

8. The standard collection and commentary on literature of this age is Martin von Schanz and Carl Hosius, *Geschichte der römischen Literatur bis zum Gesetzgebungswerk der Kaisers Justinian* (Munich, 1914-35). For the Augustan writers see especially Vol. II, 8-30, 397-400.

9. Good studies of invective and its effects are found in Kenneth Scott, "The Political Propaganda of 44-30 B.C.," *Memoirs of the American Academy in Rome* 11 (1933), 7-50; Lily Ross Taylor, *Party Politics in the Age of Caesar* (Berkeley, 1964); Ronald Syme, *The Roman Revolution* (London, 1956).

10. *Cicero: "Philippics,"* trans. Walter C. A. Ker (London, 1963), 205.

11. *Suetonius*, trans. Rolfe, I, 127.

12. Sen. *Clem.* 1.9-11; Tac. *Ann.* 1.10; Plut. *Ant.* 55; Plut. *Mor.* 1.56E; Cass. Dio 48.44.3; 50.1.2-3; Suet. *Aug.* 16.2; 27.3-4; 28.1; 63.2; 69.1-2; 71.1.

13. Plut. *Ant.* 33.2.

14. *Horace; The "Odes" and "Epodes,"* trans. C. E. Bennett (London, 1968), 99.

15. Cass. Dio 51.19.3.

16. Cic. *Phil.* 2.74-77.

17. *Cicero*, trans. Ker, 593.

18. Plut. *Brut.* 40-45; App. *BCiv.* 4.38; 4.136; 5.112-13; Cass. Dio 49.16.1; 49.38.3; 50.10.1.

19. Martial. *Ep.* 11.20.

20. Aug. *R.G.* 1.1.

21. *Augustus: "Res Gestae,"* trans. Frederick W. Shipley (London, 1967), 385; see Schanz-Hosius, *Geschichte der römischen Literatur*, II, 14-18.

22. E.g., App. *BCiv.* 4.110; Schanz-Hosius, *Geschichte der römischen Literatur*, II, 8-14.

23. E.g., Cass. Dio 48.34; 48.44; 51.22.8; Suet. *Aug.* 70; see Philip Harsh, "The Role of the Ghost of Cicero in the Damnation of Antony," *CW* 47 (1954), 99-101; M. P. Charlesworth, "Some Fragments of Propaganda of Mark Antony," *CQ* 27 (1933), 175-76.

24. Plut. *Ant.* 55.1; 58.2; Ov. *Pont.* 1.1.23; Tac. *Ann.* 4.34; Suet. *Aug.* 2.3; 4.2; 7.1-2; 10.4; 15; 16.2; 28.1; 69.1-2.

25. Pl. *N.H.* 14.147-48; Schanz-Hosius, *Geschichte der römischen Literatur*, II, 398; Kenneth Scott, "Octavian's Propaganda and Antony's *De sua ebrietate*," *C.P.* 24 (1929), 133-41.

26. R. Syme, *Roman Revolution*, 320.

27. E.g., App. *BCiv.* 2.119. Other writers mentioned as moderates or favorable to Antony were Julius Saturninus, Aquilius Niger, Timagenes of Alexandria, and Cassius Parmensis; but little is known of their works. See E. Kornemann, "Die historische Schriftstellerei des G. Asinius Pollio," *Jahrb. für Cl. Phil.* Supp. 22 (1896), 557-691; G. Thouret, *De Cicerone, Asinio Pollione, C. Appio rerum Caesarianarum scriptoribus* (Leipzig, 1878); E. Gabba, "Note sulla polemica anticiceroniana di Asinio Pollione," *RSI* 69 (1957), 317.

28. Plut. *Ant.* 58-59; Plut. *Mor.* 1.50E; Sen. *Suas.* 1.7; Strab. 11.523.

29. E. Fraenkel, *Horace* (London, 1957); B. Snell, "Die 16 *Epode* von Horaz und Vergils 4 *Eclogue*," *Hermes* 73 (1938), 237-40.

30. Jos. *Ant. Jud.* 16.7.1; Plut. *Symp.* 8.4; Athen. 14.652a; *Nicolaus of Damascus' "Life of Augustus,"* trans. Clayton Norris Hall, *Smith Coll. Cl. St.* 4 (Northampton, 1923).

31. E.g., Vell. 2.56.4; 2.60-61; 2.66-67; A. Dihle, "C. Velleius Paterculus," *RE* 2nd ser., 8 (1955), part 1, sect. 1, pp. 637-59; A. J. Woodman, "Velleius Paterculus," *Empire and Aftermath: Silver Latin*, vol. II, ed. T. A. Dorey (London, 1975), 1-25.

32. Patrick Walsh, *Livy: His Historical Aims and Methods* (Cambridge, 1961); Walsh, "Livy and Augustus," *PACA* 4 (1961), 26-37; M. L. W. Laistner, *The Greater Roman Historians* (Berkeley, 1947), 83-88; Ronald Syme. "Livy and Augustus," *HSPh* 64 (1959), 27.

33. Tac. *Ann.* 4.34-35; Suet. *Calig.* 16.1; Suet. *Claud.* 41.1-2.

34. *Seneca: "Epistulae Morales,"* trans. Richard M. Gummere (London, 1962), II, 273.

35. Plut. *Ant.* 23-33 *passim*; 68.6-8.

36. Plut. *Cic.* 46.1-6; Plut. *Brut.* 27.1-5; 39.8; 46.2-3; Plut. *Ant.* 19.1-4; 22.1-2; 53.1; 89.2.

37. Plut. *Dem.* 1.7.

38. *Plutarch's "Lives,"* trans. Perrin, IX, 135.

39. Plut. *Dem. and Ant.* 1.8; Plut. *Ant.* 25.1; Walsh, *Livy*, 110-72; R. H. Barrow, *Plutarch and His Times* (London, 1967), 61-63, 150-62; C. P. Jones, *Plutarch and Rome* (London, 1971), *passim*; A. J. Gossage, *Latin Biography*, ed. T. A. Dorey (London, 1967), 45-78; Alan Wardman, *Plutarch's Lives* (Berkeley, 1974), 34-36, 154-68.

40. E.g., Cremutius Cordus, Aquilius Niger, Junius Saturninus, Junius Novatus, Cassius of Parma. See Suet. *Aug.* 2.3; 4.2; 7.1; 13.1-2; 14; 15; 16.2; 27.1-2; 35.2; 63.2; 68-71. The degree to which Suetonius consulted the imperial archives is unknown. He may have found his material, except for the autograph documents he cites, in public libraries. See G. B. Townend, "Suetonius and His Influence," *Latin Biography*, ed. T. A. Dorey (London, 1967), 79-112; W. Steidle, *Sueton und die antike Biographie* (Munich, 1951), *passim*.

41. App. *BCiv.* 3.15-20; 3.94-95; 4.51; 5.53; Nicolae Barbu, *Les sources et l'originalité d'Appién* (Paris, 1934), *passim*; E. Hannak, *Appianus und seine Quellen* (Vienna, 1869), *passim*.

42. Fergus Millar, *A Study of Cassius Dio* (London, 1964), 32-38; E. Schwartz, *Griechische Geschichtsschreiber* (Leipzig, 1957), 394-450; H. A. Andersen, *Cassius Dio und die Begründung des Principates* (Berlin, 1938), 1-66 *passim*.

43. Shakespeare, *As You Like It* 2.7.163-65.

44. *Livy*, trans. Alfred C. Schlesinger (London, 1959), XIV, 153.

45. *Appian's "Roman History,"* trans. White, IV, 147.

46. *Plutarch's "Lives,"* trans. Perrin, IX, 179-81.

47. *Lucius Annaeus Florus: "Epitome of Roman History,"* trans. Edward Seymour Forster (London, 1966), 305.

48. *Velleius Paterculus*, trans. Shipley. 191.

49. *Dio's "Roman History,"* trans. Earnest Cary (London, 1917), V, 129-133.

50. *Suetonius*, trans. Rolfe, I, 161.

51. *Suetonius*, trans. Rolfe, I, 139.

52. *Plutarch's "Lives,"* trans. Perrin, IX, 183-85.

53. *Lucius Annaeus Florus*, trans. Forster, 309.

54. *Velleius Paterculus*, trans. Shipley, 201.

Chapter XV.
Marcus Antonius, Vir Vitalissimus

1. Plut. *Ant.* 2.4; 4.

2. Cass. Dio 45.30; Cic. *Phil.* 2.63.

3. Suet. *Aug.* 86.

4. Plut. *Ant.* 29.1; 33.3; Plut. *Mor.* 319 F.

5. Plut. *Dem. and Ant.* 2.1.

6. Prop. 3.11.27-56; Liv. *Ep.* 130; Plut. *Dem. and Ant.* 2; Sen. *Epist. Mor.* 25; 83.

7. Suet. *Aug.* 28; App. *BCiv.* 5.132; Cass. Dio 49.41.6; 50.7.1.

8. *Plutarch's "Lives,"* trans. Perrin, IX, 335.

9. *Plutarch's "Lives,"* trans. Perrin, IX, 315.

Selected Bibliography
of Secondary Works

Abbott, Frank Frost. *Roman Political Institutions*. Boston: 1911.
———. *Roman Politics*. New York: 1932.
———. *Society and Politics in Ancient Rome*. New York: 1909.
Accame, S. "Decimo Bruto dopo i funerali di Cesare." *RFIC* 62 (1934), 201–8.
Adcock, Frank Ezra. *Marcus Crassus, Millionaire*. Cambridge: 1966.
———. *The Roman Art of War*. New York: 1960.
———. *Roman Political Ideas and Practice*. Ann Arbor: 1959.
Afzelius, A. "Zur Definition der römischen Nobilität vor der Zeit Ciceros." *C&M* 7 (1945), 150–200.
Alföldi, A. "Der neue Weltherrscher der vierten Ekloge Vergils." *Hermes* 65 (1930), 369–84.
———. "The Portrait of Caesar on the Denarii of 44 B.C." *Centennial Volume of the ANS* (1958), 27–42.
Allen, W., Jr. "Sallust's Political Career." *SPh* 51 (1954), 7–21.
Altheim, Franz. *A History of Roman Religion*. London: 1938.
Andersen, H. A. *Cassius Dio und die Begründung des Principates*. Berlin: 1938.
Anderson, A. "Heracles and His Successors." *HSPh* 39 (1928), 7–58.
Anderson, William S. *Pompey, His Friends, and the Literature of the First Century B.C.* Cal. U. Pub. in Cl. Phil. vol. 19, no. 1 (1963).
Arnold, William Thomas. *Studies of Roman Imperialism*. Manchester: 1906.
Astin, A. E. *The Politics and Policies in the Roman Republic. Lecture at Queens University, Belfast* 41 (1968).
Babcock, Charles. "Dio and Plutarch on the *Damnatio* of Antony." *CP* 57 (1962), 30–32.
———. "The Early Career of Fulvia." *AJP* 86 (1965), 1–32.
Badian, Ernst. "Caepio and Norbanus." *Historia* 6 (1957), 318–46.
———. "The Early Career of A. Gabinius (cos. 58 B.C.)." *Philologus* 103 (1959), 87–99.
———. *Foreign Clientelae*. London: 1958.
———. "From the Gracchi to Sulla." *Historia* 11 (1962), 197–245.
———. *Publicans and Sinners*. Ithaca: 1972.

SELECTED BIBLIOGRAPHY

————. *Roman Imperialism in the Late Republic*. London, 1968.

————. "Waiting for Sulla." *JRS* 52 (1962), 47-61.

Bahrfeldt, M. von. "Die Münzen der Flottenpräfekten des Marcus Antonius." *NZ* 37 (1905), 9-53.

Balsdon, John P. V. D. "Consular Provinces of the Late Republic." *JRS* 29 (1939), 57-73.

————. "The Ides of March." *Historia* 7 (1958), 80-94.

————. *Julius Caesar*. New York: 1967.

————. *Life and Leisure in Ancient Rome*. New York: 1969.

————. "Roman History, 58-56 B.C. Three Ciceronian Problems." *JRS* 47 (1957), 15-20.

————. *Roman Women*. London: 1974.

Barbu, Nicolae I. *Les sources et l'originalité d'Appien*. Paris: 1934.

Barrow, R. H. *Plutarch and His Times*. London: 1967.

————. *Slavery in the Roman Empire*. New York: 1928.

Becher, I. *Das Bild der Kleopatra in der griechischen und lateinischen Literatur*. Berlin: 1966.

————. "Octavians Kampf gegen Antonius und seine Stellung zu den Ägyptischen Göttern." *Altertum* 11 (1965), 40-47.

Bengtson, H. "Die letzten Monate der römischen Senatsherrschaft." In *Aufstieg und Niedergang der römischen Welt*, edited by Hildegard Temporini, part I, vol. 1, pp. 967-81. Berlin: 1972.

Berchem, D. Van. "La fuite de Decimus Brutus," In *Mélanges Carcopino*, edited by J. Heurgon, G. Picard, and W. Seston, pp. 941-53. Paris: 1966.

Bevan, Edwyn. *A History of Egypt under the Ptolemaic Dynasty*. London: 1927.

Bieber, Margaret. "The Development of Portraiture on Roman Republican Coins." In *Aufstieg und Niedergang der römischen Welt*, edited by Hildegard Temporini, part I, vol. 4, pp. 882-85. Berlin: 1973.

Boak, Arthur E. R. "Extraordinary Commands from 80 to 48 B.C." *AHR* 24 (1918), 1-25.

Boak, Arthur E. R., and Sinnigen, William. *A History of Rome to A.D. 565*. 5th ed., revised. New York: 1965.

Boissier, Gaston. *Cicero and His Friends*. London: 1897.

Boren, Henry Charles. *The Gracchi*. New York: 1968.

————. "The Urban Side of the Gracchan Economic Crisis." *AHR* 63 (1958), 890-902.

Botermann, Helga. *Die Soldaten und die römische Politik in der Zeit von Caesars Tod bis zur Begründung des zweiten Triumvirats*. Munich: 1968.

Botsford, George Willis. *The Roman Assemblies from Their Origin to the End of the Republic*. New York: 1909.

Bouché-Leclercq, A. *L'histoire des Lagides*.Vol. II. Paris: 1904.

Bowersock, Glen Warren. *Augustus and the Greek World*. London: 1965.

————. "Eurycles of Sparta." *JRS* 51 (1961), 112-18.

Božić, I. M. Garrido. "Quintus Filius." *G&R* 20 (1951), 11-25.

Bradford, Ernle D. S. *Cleopatra*. London: 1971.

Brandis, Carl Georg. "Ein Schreiben des Triumvirn Marcus Antonius an den Landtag Asiens." *Hermes* 32 (1897), 509-22.

British Museum. *Catalogue of Coins of the Roman Republic*. London: 1910.

Broughton, Thomas Robert S. "Cleopatra and 'The Treasure of the Ptolemies'." *AJP* 63 (1942), 328-32.

————. "The *Elogia* of Julius Caesar's Father." *AJA* 52 (1948), 323-30

SELECTED BIBLIOGRAPHY

————. *The Magistrates of the Roman Republic*. 2 vols. New York: 1951-52.

————. "Notes on Roman Magistrates." *TAPA* 77 (1946), 35-43.

————. "Notes on Roman Magistrates. The Augurates of Two Marci Antonii." *Historia* 2 (1953-54), 209-13.

Brunt, Peter Astbury. "*Amicitia* in the Late Roman Republic." *PCPhS* 191 (1965), 1-20.

————. "The Army and Land in the Roman Revolution." *JRS* 52 (1962), 69-84.

————. "The Equites in the Late Republic." In *The Crises of the Roman Republic*, edited by R. Seager, pp. 117-37. Cambridge: 1969.

————. "Italian Aims at the Time of the Social War." *JRS* 55 (1965), 90-109.

————. *Italian Manpower (225 B.C.-A.D. 14)*. London: 1971.

————. *Social Conflicts in the Roman Republic*. New York: 1971.

————. "Sulla and the Asian Publicans." *Latomus* 15 (1956), 17-25.

Buchan, John. *Augustus*. London: 1947.

————. *Julius Caesar*. London: n.d.

Buchheim, H. *Die Orientpolitik des Triumvirn M. Antonius*. Heidelberg: 1960.

Burns, Alfred. "Pompey's Strategy and Domitius' Stand at Corfinium." *Historia* 15 (1966), 74-95.

Busch, Fritz Otto. *The Five Herods*. Translated by E. W. Dickes. London: 1958.

Buttrey, Theodore V., Jr. "*Thea Neotera* on Coins of Antony and Cleopatra." *ANSMusN* 6 (1954), 95-109.

Cameron, A. "Caelius on C. Antonius." *CR* n.s. 16 (1966), 17.

Carcopino, Jérome. "César et Cléopâtre." *Annales de l'École des Hautes-Études de Gand* 1 (1937), 37-77.

Carney, Thomas. *Biography of C. Marius*. Assen, Netherlands: 1961.

Carson, R. A. G. "Caesar and the Monarchy." *G&R* series 2, vol. 4 (1957), 46-53.

Carson, R. A. G., and Sutherland, C. H. V., eds. *Essays in Roman Coinage*. London: 1956.

Carter, John M. *The Battle of Actium*. New York: 1970.

Cary, Max. *A History of Rome*. 2nd ed. London: 1954.

————. "The Municipal Legislation of Julius Caesar." *JRS* 27 (1937), 48-53.

Casson, Lionel. *The Ancient Mariners*. London: 1959.

————. *Ships and Seamanship in the Ancient World*. Princeton: 1971.

Charles-Picard, Gilbert. *Augustus and Nero*. Translated by Len Ortzen. London: 1962.

Charlesworth, Martin Percival. *The Roman Empire*. London: 1951.

————. "Some Fragments of the Propaganda of Mark Antony." *CQ* 27 (1933), 172-77.

————. *Trade Routes and Commerce of the Roman Empire*. Cambridge: 1924.

Chilver, G. E. F. "Augustus and the Roman Constitution." *Historia* 1 (1950), 408-35.

Ciaceri, E. *Cicerone e i suoi tempi*. 2 vols. Milan: 1939.

Cobban, J. M. *Senate and Provinces, 78-49 B.C.* Cambridge: 1935.

Colin, G. *Rome et la Grèce*. Paris: 1905.

Colledge, Malcolm A. R. *The Parthians*. New York: 1967.

Collins, John H. "Caesar and the Corruption of Power." *Historia* 4 (1955), 445-65.

————. "Caesar as Political Propagandist." In *Aufstieg und Niedergang der römischen Welt*, edited by Hildegard Temporini, part I, vol. 1, pp. 922-66. Berlin: 1972.

————. "On the Date and Interpretation of *Bellum Civile*." *AJP* 80 (1959), 113-32.

Cook, S. A.; Adcock, F. E.; and Charlesworth, M. P., eds. *The Cambridge Ancient History*. Vols. 9 and 10. Cambridge, 1932.

Corpus Inscriptionum Latinarum. Berlin: 1863-

Cowell, Frank Richard. *Cicero and the Roman Republic*. London: 1948.

————. *The Revolutions of Ancient Rome*. New York: 1963.

Craven, L. *Antony's Oriental Policy until the Defeat of the Parthian Expedition. U. of Missouri Stud. Soc. Sc.* series 3, no. 2 (1920).

Crook, John. *Consilium Principis.* Cambridge, 1955.

———. "A Legal Point about Mark Antony's Will." *JRS* 47 (1957), 36-38.

Cuntz, O. "Legionäre des Antonius und Augustus aus dem Orient." *Jahreshefte* 25 (1929), 70-81.

Davis, A. T. "Cleopatra Rediviva." *G&R* series 2, vol. 16, no. 1 (1969), 91-93.

Davis, H. H. "Cicero's Burial." *Phoenix* 12 (1958), 174-77.

De Beer, Gavin R. *Hannibal.* Paris: 1967.

Debevoise, Neilson Carel. *A Political History of Parthia.* New York: 1968. (First published, Chicago: 1938.)

Dessau, Hermann, ed. *Inscriptiones Latinae Selectae.* 3 vols. Berlin: 1954. (First published, Berlin: 1892-1916.)

Deutsch, Monroe E. "Antony's Funeral Speech." *Cal. U. Pub. in Cl. Phil.* vol. 9, no. 5 (1926-29), 127-58.

———. "Caesar's Son and Heir." *Cal. U. Pub. in Cl. Phil.* vol. 9, no. 6 (1926-29), 149-200.

Devijver, H. "De Aegypto et Exercitu Romano." In *Studia Hellenistica.* Louvain: 1975.

Dickinson, John. *Death of a Republic.* New York: 1963.

Dihle, A. "C. Velleius Paterculus." *RE* second series, vol. 8, part 1, section 1, pp. 637-59.

Dobias, J. "La Donation d'Antoine à Cléopâtre en l' an 34 av. J.-C." In *Mélanges Bidez,* pp. 287-314. Brussels: 1934.

Dorey, Thomas Alan. "Cicero *Philippic* 14.18." *CP* 65 (1970), 98-99.

———. "A Note on Cicero *Philippic* 8.16." *CP* 63 (1968), 214.

———, ed. *Cicero.* London: 1965.

———, ed. *Latin Biography.* London: 1967.

Drumann, K. W., and Groebe, P. *Geschichte Roms in seinem Übergangs von der republikanischen zur monarchischen Verfassung,* vol. 1, part 2 to vol. 6, part 2. Berlin-Leipzig: 1899-1929.

Dubnov, Simon. *History of the Jews.* Vol. I. Translated by Moshe Spiegel. South Brunswick, N.J.: 1967.

Dunkle, J. Roger. "The Greek Tyrant and Roman Political Invective of the Late Republic." *TAPA* 98 (1967), 151-71.

Dyson, Stephen L. "Caesar and the Natives." *CJ* 63 (May 1968), 341-46.

Echols, Edward. "The Roman City Police." *CJ* 53 (1958), 377-84.

Ehrenberg, Victor. "*Imperium Maius* in the Roman Republic." *AJP* 74 (1953), 113-36.

———. *Polis und Imperium.* Zurich: 1965.

Ehrenberg, Victor, and Jones, Arnold H. M. *Documents Illustrating the Reigns of Augustus and Tiberius.* London: 1949.

Elton, G. R. "The Terminal Date of Caesar's Proconsulate." *JRS* 36 (1946), 18-42.

Fears, J. Rufus. "*Princeps a Diis Electus,*" *PAMAAR* 26 (1977), 62-83.

Ferguson, John. *Moral Values in the Ancient World.* New York: 1959.

Ferrabino, A. "La battaglia d'Azio." *RFIC* 52 (1924), 433-72.

Ferrero, Guglielmo. *Characters and Events of Roman History from Caesar to Nero.* New York: 1909.

———. *Greatness and Decline of Rome.* Translated by Alfred Zimmern. New York: 1907-9. (First published as *Grandezza e decadenza di Roma.* 1901-7.)

———. *The Life of Caesar.* London: 1933.

Finlay, George. *Greece under the Romans.* Edinburgh: 1857.

SELECTED BIBLIOGRAPHY

Fontaneau, R. "César et Cléopâtre." *Bulletin de l'Association G. Budé* (1954), 341–59.

Fowler, William Warde. *Social Life at Rome in the Age of Cicero*. 2nd ed. New York: 1933.

Fraenkel, E. *Horace*. London: 1957.

Frank, Tenney. *Aspects of Social Behavior in Ancient Rome*. Cambridge, Mass.: 1932.

————. *An Economic History of Rome*. Baltimore: 1927.

————. *Roman Imperialism*. New York: 1921.

————, ed. *An Economic Survey of Ancient Rome*. 5 vols. Baltimore: 1933–40.

Fraser, P. M. "Mark Antony in Alexandria—a Note." *JRS* 47 (1957), 71–73.

————. *Ptolemaic Alexandria*. 3 vols. London: 1972.

Frederiksen, M. W. "Caesar, Cicero, and the Problem of Debt." *JRS* 56 (1966), 128–41.

Friedlander, Ludwig. *Roman Life and Manners under the Early Empire*. Vol. 2. Translated by J. H. Freese and L. A. Magnus. London: 1908.

Frisch, Hartvig. *Cicero's Fight for the Republic*. Translated by Niels Halslund. Copenhagen: 1946.

Gabba, Emilio. "The Perusine War and Triumviral Italy." *HSPh* 75 (1971), 139–60.

————. "Note sulla polemica anticiceroniana di Asinio Pollione." *RSI* 69 (1957), 317.

————. "Ricerche sull' esercito professionale romano da Mario a Augusto." *Athenaeum* 29 (1951), 171–272.

Ganter, L. "Die Provinzialverwaltung der Triumvirn." Dissertation, Universität Strassburg. Strassburg: 1892.

Gelzer, Matthias. *Caesar: Politician and Statesman*. Translated by Peter Needham. Oxford: 1968. (First published, Wiesbaden: 1960.)

————. *The Roman Nobility*. Translated by Robin Seager. Oxford: 1969. (First published as *Die Nobilität der römischen Republik*. Stuttgart: 1912.)

Glauning, A. E. "Die Anhängerschaft des Antonius und des Octavian." Dissertation, Universität Leipzig. Leipzig: 1936.

Goodfellow, Charlotte Elizabeth. *Roman Citizenship*. Lancaster: 1935.

Graindor, Paul Simon. "La date de la bataille du Nile." *In Mélanges Paul Thomas*, pp. 364–68. Bruges: 1930.

————. *La guerre d'Alexandrie*. Cairo: 1931.

Grant, Michael. *Cleopatra*. London: 1972.

————. *Herod the Great*. New York: 1971.

————. *From Imperium to Auctoritas*. Cambridge, 1946.

————. *The Jews in the Roman World*. New York: 1973.

————. *The World of Rome*. London, 1960.

Grimal, Pierre. *The Civilization of Rome*. Translated by W. S. Maguinness. New York: 1963. (First published, Paris: 1960.)

Groag, E. "Beiträge zur Geschichte des zweiten Triumvirats." *Klio* 14 (1914), 43–68.

Grueber, Herbert Appold. *Coins of the Roman Republic in the British Museum*. Vol. II. London: 1970.

Gruen, Erich S. "Clodius: Instrument or Independent Agent?" *Phoenix* 20 (1966), 120–30.

————. *The Last Generation of the Roman Republic*. Berkeley: 1974.

————. "The *Lex Varia*." *JRS* 55 (1965), 59–73.

————. "M. Antonius and the Trial of the Vestal Virgins." *RhM* 111 (1968), 59–63.

————. "Pompey and the Pisones." *Cal. St. in Cl. Ant.* 1 (1968), 155–70.

————. "Pompey, the Roman Aristocracy, and the Conference of Luca." *Historia* 18 (1969), 71–108.

————. "The Quaestorship of Norbanus." *CP* 61 (1966), 105–6.

————. *Roman Politics and the Criminal Courts, 149-78 B.C.* Cambridge: 1968.

————. "The Trial of C. Antonius." *Latomus* 32 (1973), 301–10.

Gyles, Mary Francis. *Laudatores temporis acti: Honoring Wallace Caldwell.* Chapel Hill: 1964.

Hadas, Moses. *Hellenistic Culture: Fusion and Diffusion.* New York: 1959.

————. *Sextus Pompey.* New York: 1930.

Hahn, I. "Das Legionsorganisation des zweiten Triumvirats." *AAntHung* 17 (1969), 199–222.

Hall, Clayton Morris. *Nicolaus of Damascus' "Life of Augustus."* Smith Coll. Cl. St., no. 4. Northampton: 1923.

Hammond, Mason. *The Augustan Principate.* Enl. ed. New York: 1968.

————. *City State and World State.* Cambridge, Mass.: 1951.

Hannak, E. *Appianus und seine Quellen.* Vienna: 1869.

Hardy, E. G. "The Catilinarian Conspiracy in Its Context: a Restudy of the Evidence." *JRS* 7 (1917), 153–228.

————. *Some Problems in Roman History.* London: 1924.

Harmand, Jacques. *L'armée et la soldat à Rome de 107 à 50 avant notre ère.* Paris: 1967.

————. *Une campagne Césarienne, Alesia.* Paris: 1967.

Harsh, Philip. "The Role of the Ghost of Cicero in the Damnation of Antony." *CW* 47 (1954), 97–103.

Haywood, Richard M. "Some Traces of Serfdom in Cicero's Day." *AJP* 54 (1933), 145–53.

Heaton, John. *Mob Violence in the Late Roman Republic, 133–49 B.C.* Urbana: 1939.

Heichelheim, Fritz Moritz. *An Ancient Economic History.* Vol. 3. Leiden: 1958–70.

Heinen, Heinz. "Cäsar und Kaisarion." *Historia* 18 (1969), 181–203.

————. "Rom und Ägypten von 51 bis 47 v. Chr." Dissertation, Eberhard-Karls-Universität. Tübingen: 1966.

Heurgon, Jacques. *The Rise of Rome to 264 B.C.* Translated by James Willis. London: 1973.

Heuss, H. "Der Untergang des römischen Republic." *HZ* 182 (1956), 1–28.

Hill, Herbert. *The Roman Middle Class in the Republican Period.* London: 1952.

Hirschfeld, O. "Der Endtermin der gallischen Statthalterschaft Caesars." *Klio* 4 (1904), 77–88.

Hoehner, Harold W. *Herod Antipas.* Cambridge, 1972.

Holmes, Thomas Rice Edward. *The Architect of the Roman Empire.* 2 vols. London: 1928–31.

————. *Caesar's Conquest of Gaul.* London: 1931.

————. *The Roman Republic.* 3 vols. London: 1923.

Homo, Léon. *Roman Political Institutions from City to State.* London: 1929.

Hutchison, Lester. *The Conspiracy of Catiline.* London: 1966.

Huzar, E. G. "Egyptian Influences on Roman Coinage in the Third Century B.C." *CJ* 61 (April 1966), 337–46.

Instinsky, Hans Ulrich. "Bemerkungen über die ersten Schenküngen des Antonius an Kleopatra." In *Robinson Studies,* edited by G. E. Mylonas and D. Raymond, vol. 2, pp. 975–79. St. Louis: 1953.

Jacoby, Felix, ed. *Die Fragmente der griechischen Historiker.* Leiden: 1923–

Jameson, Shelagh. "The Intended Date of Caesar's Return from Gaul." *Latomus* 29 (1970), 638–60.

SELECTED BIBLIOGRAPHY

Jashemski, Wilhelmina Mary. *The Origins and History of the Proconsular and Propraetorian Imperium to 27 B.C.* Rome: 1966.

Jeanmaire, Henri. *Dionysos: Histoire du culte de Bacchus.* Paris: 1951.

————. "La politique religieuse d'Antoine et de Cléopâtre." *RA* 19 (1924), 241-61.

Jerome, Thomas Spencer. *Aspects of the Study of Roman History.* New York: 1962. (First published, New York: 1923.)

Johnson, W. R. "A Quean, a Great Queen? Cleopatra and the Politics of Misrepresentation." *Arion* vol. 6, no. 3 (1967), 387-402.

Jones, Arnold Hugh Martin. *Augustus.* New York: 1970.

————. *The Cities of the Eastern Roman Provinces.* London: 1937.

————. *The Herods of Judaea.* London: 1938.

————. "The *Imperium* of Augustus." *JRS* 41 (1951), 112-19.

Jones, Christopher Prestige. *Plutarch and Rome.* London: 1971.

Jones, H. Stuart. "A Roman Law Concerning Piracy." *JRS* 16 (1926), 155-73.

Jouguet, Pierre. *L'Égypte ptolémaique.* Histoire de la nation Égyptienne, vol. 3. Paris: 1933.

Kaplan, Arthur. *Catiline.* New York: 1968.

Katz, Solomon. "The Gracchi, an Essay in Interpretation." *CJ* 38 (November 1942), 71-82.

Kennedy, George. "Antony's Speech at Caesar's Funeral." *QJS* vol. 54, no. 2 (April 1958), 99-108.

Kenyon, F. G. "A Rescript of Marcus Antonius." *CR* 8 (1893), 476-78.

Kildahl, Phillip. *Gaius Marius.* New York: 1968.

Kloevekorn, H. "De proscriptionibus a.a. Chr. 43 a M. Antonio, M. Aemilio Lepido, C. Iulio Octaviano triumviris factis." Dissertation, Albertus-Universität Königsberg. Königsberg: 1891.

Knight, Donald W. "The Political Acumen of Cicero after the Death of Caesar." *Latomus* 27 (1968), 157-64.

————. "Pompey's Concern with Preeminence after 60 B.C." *Latomus* 27 (1968), 878-83.

Kornemann, E. "Die historische Schriftsstellerei des C. Asinius Pollio." *Jahrb. für Cl. Phil.* supp. 22 (1896), 557-691.

Kraft, Konrad. "Zu Sueton, *Divus Augustus* 69.2: M. Anton und Kleopatra." *Hermes* 95 (1967), 496-99.

Kromayer, J. "Actium: ein Epilog." *Hermes* 68 (1933), 361-83.

————. "Die Entwicklung der römischen Flotte vom Seeräuberkriege des Pompeius bis zur Schlacht von Actium." *Philologus* 56 (1897), 426-91.

————. "Kleine Forschungen zur Geschichte des zweiten Triumvirats." *Hermes* 29 (1894), 556-85; 31 (1896), 70-104; 33 (1898), 1-70; 34 (1899), 1-54.

Lacey, W. K. "The Tribunate of Curio." *Historia* 10 (1961), 318-29.

Laistner, M. L. W. *The Greater Roman Historians.* Berkeley: 1947.

Last, Hugh. "*Imperium Maius.*" *JRS* 37 (1947), 160-62.

————. "On the *Tribunicia Potestas* of Augustus." *RIL* 84 (1951), 93-110.

Laughton, Eric. "Cicero and the Greek Orators." *AJP* 82 (1961), 27-49.

Lenger, Marie-Thérèse. *Corpus des ordonnances des Ptolémées.* Brussels: 1964.

Leon, Ernestine F. "One Roman's Family." *CB* 35 (1959), 61-65.

————. "Scribonia and Her Daughters." *TAPA* 82 (1951), 168-75.

Leroux, Jacqueline. "Les problèmes stratègiques de la bataille d'Actium." *RecPhL* 2 (1968), 29-61.

Levi, Mario Attilio. "La battaglia d'Azio." *Athenaeum* 10 (1932), 3-21.

———. *Ottaviano Capoparte.* 2 vols. Florence: 1933.

Liegle, J. "Die Münzprägung Octavians nach dem Siege von Aktium und die augusteische Kunst." *JDAI* 56 (1941), 91-119.

Linderski, Jerzy. "The Aedileship of Favonius, Curio the Younger, and Cicero's Election to the Augurate." *HSPh* 76 (1972), 181-200.

Lintott, Andrew William. *Violence in Republican Rome.* London, 1968.

Löfstedt, Einar. *Roman Literary Portraits.* London: 1958.

Lord, E. "The Date of Julius Caesar's Departure from Alexandria." *JRS* 28 (1938), 19-40.

Lozinski, Bohdan Philip. *The Original Homeland of the Parthians.* Gravenshage: 1959.

Luce, T. James. "Appian's *Egyptian History.*" *CP* 59 (1964), 259-62.

MacKay, L. A. "Horace, Augustus, and *Ode* I 2." *AJP* 83 (1962), 168-77.

MacMullen, Ramsay. *Enemies of the Roman Order.* Cambridge: 1966.

Maffii, Maffio. *Cleopatra contro Roma.* Florence: 1939.

Magie, David. *Roman Rule in Asia Minor to the End of the Third Century after Christ.* Princeton: 1950.

Mahaffy, J. P. "Cleopatra." *JEA* 2 (1915), 1-4.

Malcovati, E. *Clodia, Fulvia, Marzia, Terenzia.* Rome: 1945.

Marsh, Frank Burr. *The Founding of the Roman Empire.* London: 1927.

———. "The Gangster in Roman Politics." *CJ* 28 (December 1932), 168-78.

———. *A History of the Roman World from 146-30 B.C.* 3rd ed. London: 1963.

Mattingly, Harold. *Coins of the Roman Empire in the British Museum.* Vol. 1. London: 1962.

Mattingly, Harold, and Sydenham, E. A. *The Roman Imperial Coinage.* Vol. 1. London: 1923.

Meier, Christian. *Res Publica Amissa.* Wiesbaden: 1966.

Meiklejohn, K. W. "Alexander Helios and Caesarion." *JRS* 24 (1934), 191-95.

Meyer, Eduard. *Caesars Monarchie und das Principat des Pompejus.* Stuttgart: 1922. (Reprinted, 1963.)

Meyer, Paul Martin. *Das Heerwesen der Ptolemäer und Römer in Ägypten.* Stuttgart: 1966.

Michel, D. *Alexander als Vorbild für Pompeius, Caesar, und Marcus Antonius, archäologische Untersuchungen.* Brussels: 1967.

Michels, Agnes Kirsopp. "The Topography and Interpretation of the Lupercalia." *TAPA* 84 (1953), 35-59.

Millar, Fergus. *A Study of Cassius Dio.* London: 1964.

———. "Triumvirate and Principate." *JRS* 63 (1973), 50-67.

———, ed. *The Roman Empire and Its Neighbors.* New York: 1967.

Momigliano, Arnaldo. *Ricerche sull'organizzazione della Giudea sotto il dominio romano.* *ASNP* series 2, vol. 3 (1934).

Mommsen, Theodor. *The History of Rome.* Edited by E. A. Saunders and J. H. Collins. Cleveland: 1958. (Exerpted from *Römische Geschichte.* 3 vols. Berlin: 1854-56. Translated by William P. Dickson, 1887.)

———. *The Provinces of the Roman Empire.* Edited by T. R. S. Broughton. Chicago: 1968. (Selections from *Römische Geschichte.* Vol. V, book 8. Berlin: 1885. Translated by William P. Dickson, 1887.)

———. *Die Rechtsfrage zwischen Caesar und dem Senat.* Breslau: 1857.

———. *Römisches Staatsrecht.* 3rd ed. Graz: 1887-88.

311

SELECTED BIBLIOGRAPHY

Münzer, Friedrich. *Römische Adelsparteien und Adelsfamilien.* Stuttgart: 1920.
Nilsson, Martin Persson. *The Dionysiac Mysteries of the Hellenistic and Roman Age.* Lund: 1957.
————. *Imperial Rome.* Translated by G. C. Richards. London: 1926.
Nock, Arthur Darby. "Notes on Ruler Cult." *JHS* 48 (1928), 21–43.
Odahl, Charles. *The Catilinarian Conspiracy.* New Haven: 1971.
Oliver, James H. "Attic Text Reflecting the Influence of Cleopatra." *GRBS* vol. 6, no. 4 (1965), 291–94.
————. "Octavian's Inscription at Nicopolis." *AJP* 90 (1969), 178–82.
Oman, Charles William Chadwick. *Seven Roman Statesmen.* New York: 1927.
Orientis Graeci Inscriptiones Selectae. Edited by Wilhelm Dittenberger. Hildesheim: 1960.
The Oxyrhynchus Papyri. Edited by B. P. Grenfell and A. S. Hunt. London: 1899–1976.
Packer, Mary N. "The Question of Cicero's Sincerity in His Addresses to Caesar." *TAPA* 77 (1946), 321.
Paget, R. F. "The Naval Battle of Cumae in B.C. 38." *Latomus* 29 (1970), 363–69.
Paoli, Ugo Enrico. *Rome: Its People, Life, and Custo⁊ns.* Translated by R. D. Macnaghten. New York: 1963. (First published as *Vita Romana.* Florence: 1940.)
Parker, Henry Michael Denne. *The Roman Legions.* New York: 1958. (First published, London: 1928.)
Passerini, A. *Caio Mario come uomo politico.* Pavia: 1934.
Paul-Louis. *Ancient Rome at Work.* London: 1927.
Pauly, A.; Wissowa, F.; and Kroll, W. *Real-Encyclopädie der classischen Altertumswissenschaft.* Stuttgart: 1894– .
Payne, Pierre Stephen Robert. *The Roman Triumph.* London: 1962.
Petersson, Torsten. *Cicero, a Biography.* New York: 1963. (First published, Berkeley: 1919.)
Radin, Max. *Marcus Brutus.* London: 1939.
Radista, Leo. "Julius Caesar and His Writings." In *Aufstieg und Niedergang der römischen Welt,* edited by Hildegard Temporini, part I, vol. 3, pp. 417–56. Berlin: 1972.
Rand, Edward Kennard. *Building of Eternal Rome.* Cambridge: 1943.
Raubitschek, Anthony E. "Brutus in Athens." *Phoenix* 11 (1957), 1–11.
————. "Octavia's Deification at Athens." *TAPA* 77 (1946), 146–50.
Rawlinson, George. *The Story of Parthia.* New York: 1893.
Rawson, Elizabeth. *Cicero, a Portrait.* London: 1975.
Reid, J. S. "Roman Ideas of Deity." *JRS* 6 (1916), 170–84.
Reinhold, M. *Marcus Agrippa, a Biography.* Geneva, N.Y.: 1933.
————. "The Perusine War." *CW* 26 (1933), 180–82.
Richards, George Chatterton. *Cicero: a Study.* Boston: 1935.
Richardson, G. W. "Actium." *JRS* 27 (1937); 153–64.
Richmond, I. A. "Palmyra under the Aegis of Rome." *JRS* 53 (1963), 43–54.
Robert, L. *Hellenica.* Vol. 7. Paris: 1949.
Rose, H. J. "Two Notes on Roman Religion." *Latomus* 8 (1949), 9–17.
Rossi, F. R. *Marco Antonio nella lotta politica della tarda republica romana.* Trieste: 1959.
Rostovtzeff, Michail Ivanovich. *History of the Ancient World.* London: 1926.
————. *The Social and Economic History of the Hellenistic World.* 3 vols. London: 1941.
————. *The Social and Economic History of the Roman Empire.* 2 vols. 2nd ed. London: 1957. (First published, London: 1926.)
Rowell, Henry Thompson. *Rome in the Augustan Age.* Norman, Okla.: 1962.

SELECTED BIBLIOGRAPHY

Rowland, R. J. "C. Gracchus and the Equites." *TAPA* 96 (1965), 361-73.

———. "Crassus, Clodius, and Curio in the Year 59 B.C." *Historia* 15 (1966), 217-23.

Sachs, E. "Some Notes on the Lupercalia." *AJP* 84 (1963), 266-79.

Salmon, Edward Togo. *Roman Colonization under the Republic.* London: 1969.

Samuel, Alan Edouard. *Ptolemaic Chronology.* Munich, 1962.

Sanders, Henry A. "The Origins of the Third Cyrenaic Legion." *AJP* 62 (1941), 84-87.

———. "The So-called First Triumvirate," *PAMAAR* 10 (1932), 55-68.

Sanford, Eva M. "The Career of Aulus Gabinius." *TAPA* 70 (1939), 64-92.

———. "Political Campaigns in the Roman Municipalities." *CJ* 25 (1930), 453-63.

Schanz, Martin von, and Hosius, Carl. *Geschichte der römischen Literatur bis zum Gesetzgebungswerk des Kaisers Justinian.* Munich: 1914-35.

Schmidt. Otto Eduard. *Der Briefwechsel des M. Tullius Cicero.* Leipzig: 1893.

———. "Die letzten Kämpfe der römischen Republik," *Jahrb. für Cl. Phil.* supp. 13 (1884), 665-722.

———. "P. Ventidius Bassus," *Philologus* 51 (1892), 198-211.

Schmitthenner, Walter. "The Armies of the Triumviral Period." Dissertation, Oxford University. Oxford: 1958.

———. *Oktavian und das Testament Cäsars.* Munich: 1952.

———. "Oktavians militärische Unternehmungen in den Jahren 35-33 v. Chr." *Historia* 7 (1958), 189-236.

———, ed. *Augustus.* Darmstadt: 1969.

Schulz, O. Th. "Das dritte Triumvirat Oktavians." *Zeitschr. für Num.* vol. 7, no. 4 (1932), 101-27.

Schwartz, E. *Griechische Geschichtsschreiber* pp. 394-450. Leipzig: 1957.

———. "Die Vertheilung der römischen Provinzen nach Caesars Tod." *Hermes* 33 (1898), 185-244.

Scott, Kenneth. "The Deification of Demetrius Poliorcetes." *AJP* 49 (1928), 137-66, 217-39.

———. "Octavian's Propaganda and Antony's *De sua ebrietate.*" *CP* 24 (1929), 133-41.

———. "Plutarch and the Ruler Cult." *TAPA* 60 (1929), 117-35.

———. "The Political Propaganda of 44-30 B.C.." *PAMAAR* 11 (1933), 7-50.

———. "*Sidus Iulium* and the Apotheosis of Caesar." *CP* 36 (1941), 257-72.

Scullard, Howard Hayes. *From the Gracchi to Nero.* 4th ed. London: 1976. (1st ed., New York: 1959.)

———. *A History of the Roman World, 753-146 B.C.* 2nd ed. London: 1951. (1st ed., New York: 1935.)

———. *Scipio Africanus in the Second Punic War.* 2nd ed. London: 1970. (1st ed., London: 1930.)

Seager, Robin. "Lex Varia de Maiestate." *Historia* 16 (1967), 37-43.

———, ed, *The Crisis of the Roman Republic.* Cambridge: 1969.

Sealey, R. "Habe Meam Rationem." *C&M* 18 (1957), 75-101.

Shackleton-Bailey, David Roy. *Cicero.* New York: 1971.

———. "The Roman Nobility in the Second Civil War." *CQ* n.s. 10 (1960), 253-67.

Shatzman, Israel. "The Egyptian Question in Roman Politics, 59-54 B.C." *Latomus* 30 (1971), 363-69.

Shepard, Arthur MacCartney. *Sea Power in Ancient History.* Boston: 1924.

Sherk, Robert K. "Der Brief des Antonius an Plarasa-Aphrodisias." *Historia* 15 (1966), 123-24.

———. *Roman Documents from the Greek East.* Baltimore: 1969.

———. "The Text of the *Senatus Consultum de Agro Pergameno.*" *GRBS* vol. 7, no. 4 (1966), 361–69.

Sherwin-White, Adrian. *Racial Prejudice in Imperial Rome.* Cambridge: 1967.

———. "Violence in Roman Politics." *JRS* 46 (1956), 1–9.

Showerman, Grant. *Rome and the Romans.* New York: 1931.

Singer, Mary White. "Octavia's Mediation at Tarentum." *CJ* 43 (December 1947), 173–77.

———. "The Problem of Octavia Minor and Octavia Maior." *TAPA* 79 (1948), 268–74.

Skeat, Theodore Cressy. "The Last Days of Cleopatra." *JRS* 43 (1953), 98–100.

———. "Notes on Ptolemaic Chronology." *JEA* 46 (1960), 91–94.

———. *The Reigns of the Ptolemies.* Munich: 1954.

Smethurst, S. E. "Cicero and the Senate." *CJ* 54 (1958), 73–78.

———. "Mark Antony, Reluctant Politician." *Thought from the Learned Societies of Canada* (1960), 155–70.

Smith, Richard Edwin. "Anatomy of Force in Late Republican Politics." In *Ancient Society and Institutions*, presented to V. Ehrenberg on his 75th birthday, pp. 257–73. London: 1966.

———. *Cicero the Statesman.* Cambridge: 1966.

———. *The Failure of the Roman Republic.* Cambridge: 1955.

———. "The Greek Letters of M. Junius Brutus." *CQ* 30 (1936), 194–203.

———. "Pompey's Conduct in 80 and 77 B.C." *Phoenix* 14 (1960), 1–10.

———. *Service in the Post-Marian Army.* Manchester: 1958.

Snell, B. "Die 16 *Epode* von Horaz und Vergils 4 *Eclogue.*" *Hermes* 73 (1938), 237–42.

Stadter, P. *Plutarch's Historical Methods.* Cambridge: 1965.

Starr, Chester G. *Civilization and the Caesars.* New York: 1965.

———. *The Roman Imperial Navy.* 2nd ed. Cambridge: 1960.

———. "Virgil's Acceptance of Octavian." *AJP* 76 (1955), 34–46.

Stauffer, Ethelbert. "Augustus und Kleopatra," In *Christus und die Cäsaren,* pp. 43–76. Hamburg: 1948.

Staveley, E. S. "The *Fasces* and *Imperium Maius.*" *Historia* 12 (1963), 458–84.

Steidle, W. *Sueton und die antike Biographie.* Munich: 1951.

Stevens, C. E. "The Terminal Date of Caesar's Command." *AJP* 59 (1938), 169–208.

Stevenson, George Hope. *Roman Provincial Administration.* London: 1939.

Stockton, David. *Cicero: a Political Biography.* London: 1971.

Stone. C. G. "March 1, 50 B.C." *CQ* 22 (1928), 193–201.

Sumner, G. V. "*Lex Aelia, Lex Fufia.*" *AJP* 84 (1963), 337–58.

Sydenham, Edward A. *Coinage of the Roman Republic.* London: 1952.

Syme, Ronald. "Imperator Caesar: a Study in Nomenclature." *Historia* 7 (1958), 172–88.

———. "Livy and Augustus." *HSPh* 64 (1959), 27.

———. "Pollio Salonius and Salonae," *CQ* 31 (1937), 39–48.

———. *The Roman Revolution.* London: 1952. (First published, London: 1939.)

———. "Sabienus the Muleteer." *Latomus* 17 (1958), 73–80.

———. *Sallust.* Berkeley: 1964.

———. "Who Was Decidius Saxa?" *JRS* 27 (1937), 127–37.

———. "Who Was Vedius Pollio?" *JRS* 51 (1961), 23–30.

Tarn, William Woodthorpe. "Actium: a Note." *JRS* 28 (1938), 165–68.

———. "Alexander Helios and the Golden Age." *JRS* 22 (1932), 135–60.

———. "Antony's Legions." *CQ* 26 (1932), 75–81.

———. "The Battle of Actium." *JRS* 21 (1931), 173–99.

———. *Hellenistic Civilization.* 3rd ed. Revised by W. W. Tarn and G. T. Griffith. London: 1952. (First published, London: 1927.)

SELECTED BIBLIOGRAPHY

Taylor, Lily Ross. "Caesar and the Roman Nobility." *TAPA* 73 (1942), 1-24.

———. "Caesar's Colleagues in the Pontifical College." *AJP* 63 (1942), 385-412.

———. "Caesar's Early Career." *CP* 36 (1941), 113-32.

———. *The Divinity of the Roman Emperor.* Middletown, Conn.: 1931.

———. *Party Politics in the Age of Caesar.* Berkeley: 1949.

———. "The Rise of Julius Caesar." *G&R* series 2, vol. 4, no. 1 (1957), 10-17.

———. *Roman Voting Assemblies.* Ann Arbor: 1966.

———. *The Voting Districts of the Roman Republic. PAMAAR* 20 (1960).

Thompson, L. A. "Cicero's Succession Problem in Cilicia." *AJP* 86 (1965), 375-86.

Thouret, G. *De Cicerone, Asinio Pollione, C. Appio rerum Caesarianorum scriptoribus.* Leipzig: 1878.

Tibiletti, G. "The Comitia during the Decline of the Roman Republic." *SDHI* 25 (1959), 94-127.

Tidman, Brenda M. "On the Foundation of the Actian Games." *CQ* 44 (1950), 123-25.

Townend, G. B. "Suetonius and His Influence." In *Latin Biography,* edited by T. A. Dorey, pp. 79-111. London: 1967.

Toynbee, Jocelyn Mary Catherine. *Death and Burial in the Roman World.* Ithaca: 1971.

Treggiari, Susan. *Roman Freedmen during the Late Republic.* London: 1969.

Volkmann, Hans. *Cleopatra, a Study in Politics and Propaganda.* Translated by T. J. Cadoux. New York: 1958. (First published as *Kleopatra: Politik und Propaganda.* Munich: 1953.)

Von Fritz, Kurt. "Emergency Powers in the Last Century of the Roman Republic." *Annual Report of the AHA* 3 (1942), 221-37.

———. "The Mission of L. Caesar and L. Roscius in January, 49 B.C." *TAPA* 72 (1941), 125-56.

———. *The Theory of the Mixed Constitution in Antiquity.* New York: 1954.

Vulic, N. "La guerre d'Octave en Illyrie, 35-33 av. J.C." *Acropole* (1932), 115-22.

Waddy, Lawrence. *"Pax Romana" and World Peace.* London: 1950.

Walbank, F. W. "Nationality as a Factor in Roman History." *HSPh* 76 (1972), 145-68.

Walsh, Patrick. "Livy and Augustus." *PACA* 4 (1961), 26-37.

———. *Livy: His Historical Aims and Methods.* Cambridge: 1961.

Walter, Gérard. *Brutus et la fin de la Republique.* Paris: 1938.

———. *Caesar, a Biography.* Translated by Emma Craufurd. New York: 1952.

Wardman, Alan. *Plutarch's Lives.* Berkeley: 1974.

Watson, George Ronald. *The Roman Soldier.* London: 1969.

Webster, Graham. *The Roman Imperial Army.* London: 1969.

Weigall, Arthur. *The Life and Times of Cleopatra, Queen of Egypt.* New York: 1924.

———. *The Life and Times of Marc Antony.* New York: 1931.

Weinrib, E. J. "The Prosecution of Roman Magistrates." *Phoenix* 22 (1968), 32-56.

Weinstock, Stephan. "Clodius and the *Lex Aelia Fufia.*" *JRS* 27 (1937), 215-22.

———. *Divus Julius.* London: 1971.

———. "The Image and Chair of Germanicus." *JRS* 47 (1957), 144-54.

———. "*Pax* and the *Ara Pacis.*" *JRS* 50 (1960), 44-58.

Wertheimer, Oscar von. *Cleopatra, a Royal Voluptuary.* Translated by Huntley Patterson. London: 1931.

Welwei, Karl-Wilhelm. "Das Angebot des Diadems an Caesar und das Luperkalienproblem." *Historia* 16 (1967), 44-69.

Wheeler, Marcus. "Cicero's Political Ideal." *G&R* 21 (1952), 49-56.

Wiehn, E. "Die illegalen Heereskommanden in Rom bis auf Caesar." Dissertation, Universität Leipzig. Leipzig: 1926.

315

SELECTED BIBLIOGRAPHY

Wilcken, Ulrich. "Octavian after the Fall of Alexandria." *JRS* 27 (1937), 138–44.

Williams, Richard Stanley. "Aulus Gabinius: a Political Biography." Dissertation, Michigan State University. East Lansing, Michigan: 1973.

Winkler, Iudita. "A propos de la penetration en Dacia des derniers romains èmis par Marc Antoine." *Istorie Veche* 22 (1971), 97–107.

Wirszubski, Chaim. *Libertas as a Political Idea at Rome during the Late Republic and Early Principate*. Cambridge: 1950.

Wiseman, Timothy Peter. "The Ambitions of Quintus Cicero." *JRS* 56 (1966), 108–115.

———. "The Last of the Metelli." *Latomus* 24 (1965), 52–61.

———. *New Men in the Roman Senate, 139 B.C.–14 A.D.* London: 1971.

———. "Pulcher Claudius." *HSPh* 74 (1970), 207–21.

Wissowa, G. *Religion und Cultus d. Römer*. Vol. 2. Munich: 1912.

Wistrand, E. *Horace's Ninth Epode and Its Historical Background*. Göteborg: 1958.

Witherstine, Ruth. "Where the Romans Lived in the First Century B.C." *CJ* 21 (1926), 566–79.

Woodman, A. J. "Velleius Paterculus." In *Empire and Aftermath: Silver Latin*, vol. II., edited by T. A. Dorey, 1–25. London: 1975.

Wright, Frederick Adam. *Marcus Agrippa*. London: 1937.

Wurzel, F. "Der Krieg gegen Antonius und Kleopatra in der Darstellung der augusteischen Dichtung." Dissertation, Universität Heidelberg. Heidelberg: 1941.

Yavetz, Zvi. "Living Conditions of the Urban Plebs in Republican Rome." *Latomus* 17 (1958), 500–17.

———. *Plebs and Princeps*. London: 1969.

Zwaenepoel, A. "La politique orientale d'Antoine." *LEC* 18 (1950), 3–15.

316

Glossary

Glossary

Aediles: Four public officials elected annually by the Comitia Tributa. They served as commissioners of public works: roads, sewers, markets, festivals.

Amicitia: Friendship. In Roman politics *amicitia* meant a responsible association which provided support at the polls and in public office.

Augur: A priest, member of the college of augurs. Romulus created the first augurs to interpret omens and auspices. They were consulted for all important state matters, so they could aid or block any official action by their interpretations.

Auxilia: Military forces recruited from the provincials to supplement the Roman legions.

Campus Martius: A large plain outside the walls of Rome dedicated to Mars and frequently used for military exercises. The Comitia Centuriata met there.

Censors: The two highest Roman officials who were elected every five years from among former consuls. During their eighteen months of service they took a census of citizens and property and assigned each citizen to his proper tribe, class, and century. They also supervised public morals and could remove a senator or equestrian from his rank for misconduct.

Client: A free man in an ancient hereditary relationship with his patron. The patron granted land to his client, as well as economic, military, and legal protection. In return, the client loyally supported his patron, especially in political life.

Comitia: Assemblies of adult, male Roman citizens which met to elect officials or to vote on legislative matters.

GLOSSARY

Comitia Centuriata: An assembly of Roman citizens meeting in "centuries," the ancient military units which weighted power and the vote toward the wealthy. This Comitia met in the Campus Martius under a magistrate with *imperium*. It voted on legislation, elected consuls and praetors annually, and declared war or peace.

Comitia Curiata: The most ancient assembly of Roman citizens meeting according to family groupings of curiae. Later, its functions were diminished as the state absorbed family duties but still included priestly installations, family wills and adoptions, and the conferring of the *imperium* on magistrates.

Comitia Tributa: An assembly of Roman citizens voting in thirty-five tribes. The Comitia Tributa met in the Forum under a tribune, consul, or praetor. It elected tribunes, aediles, and quaestors and could initiate and pass legislation independent of the Senate. Populares political leaders usually worked their measures through this more democratic Comitia.

Concilium Plebis: An assembly of Roman plebeians meeting as tribes under plebeian magistrates. After 287 B.C. measures passed by the Concilium Plebis had the right of law without approval of the Senate. The Concilium Plebis elected plebeian magistrates.

Consul: One of two chief executive magistrates elected annually by the Comitia Centuriata. The consuls presided over the Senate and commanded the army. Election to the consulship gave a plebeian hereditary rank as a noble.

Consul suffectus: A consul appointed to complete the year of a consul who resigned, died, or was incapacitated.

Consular: A man who had previously held the consulship. He served in the Senate and had great prestige.

Curia: A building intended for holding public meetings. Caesar was slain in one such building, the Curia Pompeii.

Cursus honorum: Regular succession of major public offices held in a public career, from quaestorship through censorship.

Curule magistrate: A senior official at Rome (aediles and above) or a triumphant general, who had the right to sit in a ceremonial chair inlaid with ivory during public assemblies.

Denarius: A Roman silver coin, about four grams in weight during Antony's period. It equaled four sesterces, was close to the Greek drachma in value, and, very roughly, can be valued at about 40 cents.

Dictator: A magistrate with supreme military and judicial authority, elected for six months, on the nomination of the consuls, to meet a special emergency. After Sulla, the tenure of office could be extended. Antony abolished the office after Caesar's murder.

GLOSSARY

Equestrians: Citizens of nonsenatorial rank whose property amounted to at least 400,000 sesterces. Not politicians but businessmen and capitalists, they were the wealthy middle class.

Ethnarch: The governor of a province or a people. In Judaea, the ethnarch may have represented all Jews to the Romans politically and to the Sanhedrin spiritually.

Factio: A political clique whose members had shared objectives. The word often carries an opprobrious sense of self-interest.

Fasces: An ax and bundle of rods, carried by an official's lictors, which provided an emblem of magisterial authority.

Imperium: The magisterial power of command over the army and execution of the law. It was held by consuls, proconsuls, praetors, propraetors, dictators, Masters of the Horse, and military tribunes. The power could be enforced by capital punishment. *Imperium maius*: a command superior to that of other holders of *imperium*. *Imperium infinitum*: an extraordinary command superior to that of other holders of *imperium* and not confined to one province or even one theater of war. *Maius imperium infinitum*: a supreme command over other holders of the *imperium* and without temporal or geographic restrictions. These exceptional extensions of the traditional powers of the *imperium* were granted only during the emergencies of the late republic and prepared citizens for the autocracy of the Roman Empire.

Interrex: A temporary ruling magistrate appointed by the Senate if both consuls were ill or dead. He performed all the duties of the consulship until new consuls were elected.

Julian calendar: Caesar as pontifex maximus revised the civic calendar which, because of the inexact ancient calculations, had become about three months out of conformity with the solar calendar. The year 46 B.C. was lengthened to 445 days. Thereafter the civic and solar calendars coincided.

Laticlavia: The wide purple stripe on a senator's clothing marking his rank.

Legion: A levy of citizen soldiers, in full complement 6,000 men, uniformly equipped, armed, and trained. In each legion there were ten cohorts, in each cohort three maniples. An eagle was the standard of each legion.

Lictors: A bodyguard for Roman magistrates who held the *imperium*. They carried the fasces and represented the authority of the officials.

Magister equitum: Master of the Horse. A dictator's appointed assistant, bound absolutely to obey his commands.

Optimates: "The Best People," men of noble families who allied politically and led their followers to vote for policies maintaining senatorial dominance.

GLOSSARY

Patres conscripti: Official list of senators, often used to designate senators whose families had risen from the plebeians and who were therefore plebeian nobles.

Patricians: Aristocratic members of a hereditary privileged class composed of the members of a few ancient families.

Patron: The protector of clients, supplying them with land and military, economic, and legal protections in return for personal and political loyalty.

Pontifex: A priest, a member of a board (*collegium*) advising the magistrates on religious responsibilities.

Pontifex maximus: Head of the state religion by virture of being head of the college of pontiffs. He performed both a civic and a religious role, choosing some of the priests and presiding over the Comitia Curiata. The office was held for life.

Populares: Political leaders who sought the support and the votes of the people with popular measures. They usually worked through the Comitia Tributa and the Concilium Plebis with the aid of the tribunes.

Praetor: An annually elected magistrate, one of eight who presided over the courts and had the *imperium* to lead an army.

Praetor peregrinus: An annually elected magistrate responsible for the administration of legal justice between citizens and noncitizens.

Praetorians: The crack bodyguard assigned to protect a general (later an emperor) and his headquarters.

Proconsul: An ex-consul who continued to hold the official powers and privileges of a consul, normally during a tour of duty as a provincial governor.

Propraetor: An ex-praetor retaining the official powers and privileges of a praetor, who served as a governor of a minor province.

Quaestor: A lower official elected by the Comitia Tributa as the first step in the *cursus honorum*. Quaestors served as state treasurers and assistants to higher magistrates.

Quaestor pro praetore: Treasury official serving in the judicial role of the praetor or acting as governor of a praetorian province.

Senate: A senior council of nobles, drawn from ex-magistrates, who served for life. It had informal but very great powers in foreign relations, legislation, judicial cases, finances, and religion.

Senatus Consultum Ultimum: "The last decree of the Senate." Declared that the state was in danger and that the magistrates should "see to it that the republic takes no harm." Essentially, it imposed martial law.

GLOSSARY

Sesterce: A small silver coin, worth six asses, or ¼ denarius, in the first century B.C. Its value, by very rough approximation, was about 10 cents.

Talent: A Greek unit of weight and value also used by the Romans. The weight in silver ranged from 57 to 83 pounds. Very roughly, its value was approximately $5,000.

Tarpeian Rock: A rock high on the Capitoline Hill from which condemned criminals for certain crimes were hurled to their death.

Tetrarch: A ruler over a limited territory, like a small principality.

Toga praetexta: A toga bordered with a purple stripe distinguishing curule magistrates and priests.

Tribunes: Ten officials elected annually by the Comitia Tributa to act as protectors of the people. They had the power of veto over the acts of other magistrates and presided over the Concilium Plebis. Their persons were sacrosanct. They became important supporters of late republican leaders.

Triumph: The festive celebration of a general's victories over foreign foes. It included a procession of the victor in a four-horse chariot, his soldiers, booty, and captives, traveling from the Campus Martius to the Temple of Jupiter on the Capitoline Hill to present the victory to the God.

Dramatis Personae

Dramatis Personae

The list is alphabetized according to the familiar usage of the names in the text; e.g., Caesar rather than Julius.

Agrippa, Marcus Vipsanius: Consul 37 B.C. Octavian's strong supporter, general, and admiral. Victor over Antony at Actium.

Ahenobarbus, Gnaeus Domitius: Consul 32 B.C. Republican who became a close counselor of Antony until the Actium campaign.

Ahenobarbus, Lucius Domitius: Consul 54 B.C. Brother-in-law of Cato. Optimate leader, defeated by Caesar at Corfinium. Killed at Pharsalus.

Alexander Helios: Elder son of Antony and Cleopatra.

Alexandra: Mother of Mariamne and Aristobulus III. Hated her son-in-law, Herod the Great.

Ambiorix: Chief of the Eburones tribe in Gaul during Antony's campaigns.

Amyntas: King of Galatia, ally of Antony. Deserted to Octavian at Actium.

Antigonus: Pro-Parthian king of Judaea, of the Hasmonean dynasty hostile to Herod the Great.

Antiochus: Pro-Parthian king of Commagene whom Antony besieged at Samosata.

Antipater: Father of Herod the Great. Collaborated with the Romans.

Antonia: Antony's first cousin and second wife.

Antonia: Antony and Antonia's daughter who married Pythodorus of Tralles.

Antonia Major: Antony and Octavia's elder daughter.

Antonia Minor: Antony and Octavia's younger daughter.

Antonius, Gaius: Praetor 44 B.C. Brother of Mark Antony. Commanded forces against the republicans in Illyricum where he was defeated and killed.

Antonius, Iullus: Antony and Fulvia's younger son. Reared by Octavia.

Antonius, Lucius: Tribune 44 B.C., consul 41 B.C. Brother of Mark Antony. Led the war against the republicans at Perusia.

Antonius, Marcus: Consul 99 B.C., censor 97 B.C. Fought pirates in Cilicia. Leading orator. Grandfather of Mark Antony.

Antonius "Antyllus," Marcus: Antony and Fulvia's elder son. Killed in Egypt.

Antonius Creticus, Marcus: Praetor 74 B.C. Father of Mark Antony. Held command in Crete against the pirates.

Antonius "Hybrida," Gaius: Consul 63 B.C. Uncle of Mark Antony. Favored Catiline.

Arsinoë: Sister of Cleopatra. Opposed Cleopatra and was killed by Antony.

Artavasdes: King of Armenia. Betrayed Antony in campaign against Parthia, 36 B.C. Antony invaded Armenia and took him captive to Egypt in 34 B.C.

Artavasdes: King of Media Atropatene, hostile to Artavasdes of Armenia.

Artaxes: King of Armenia, son of Artavasdes.

Atticus, Titus Pomponius: Financier and man of learning who was the diplomatic friend of all important men, especially of Cicero.

Balbus, Lucius Cornelius: Quaestor 44 B.C., consul 40 B.C. Ally of Caesar.

Bibulus, Lucius Calpurnius: Grandson of Cato. Served Antony as governor of Syria, 32 B.C.

Bocchus: King of Mauretania who supported current winners in the civil war.

Brutus, Marcus Junius: Praetor 44 B.C. A Pompeian, he was pardoned by Caesar after Pharsalus and made governor of Cisalpine Gaul. Assassinated Caesar and became the moral leader of the republicans and a general in the east. Died at Philippi.

Brutus Albinus, Decimus Junius: Praetor 45 B.C. Caesar's aide who was one of his assassins. Besieged by Antony at Mutina and executed by Antony's order.

Caesar, Gaius Julius: Consul 59 B.C., proconsul in Gaul and Illyricum 58–49 B.C., dictator 49–48 and 47–44 B.C. Antony's commander in Gaul and in the civil war. Murdered in 44 B.C.

Caesarion: Son of Cleopatra and supposed son of Caesar. Killed by Octavian in 30 B.C.

Calenus, Quintus Fufius: Consul 47 B.C., Antony's governor of Gaul 43–40 B.C.

Calpurnia: Wife of Caesar, daughter of Lucius Calpurnius Piso. Collaborated with Antony after Caesar's death.

Calpurnius Bibulus, Marcus: Consul 59 B.C. with Caesar. Supported Pompey against Caesar in the civil war. Died patrolling the Adriatic Sea.

Calpurnius Piso, Lucius: Consul 58 B.C., censor 50 B.C. Father-in-law of Caesar. Political moderator between Pompey and Caesar.

Canidius Crassus, Publius: Consul 40 B.C. Antony's loyal commander in the east and at Actium.

Capito, Gaius Fonteius: Consul 33 B.C. Antony's ambassador to Rome.

Cassius Longinus, Gaius: Praetor 44 B.C. Opposed Caesar and was pardoned by him. Assassin of Caesar. General in the east for the republicans. Died at Philippi.

Cassius Longinus, Quintus: With Antony, tribune for Caesar in 49 B.C. Legate in Spain for Caesar during the civil war.

Catiline, Lucius Sergius: Led a revolution against the state (in 63 B.C.) which was crushed by Cicero.

Cato, Marcus Porcius: Praetor 54 B.C. Conservative leader of the republicans. Fought the Second Triumvirate. Died a republican martyr at Utica.

Cicero, Marcus Tullius: Consul 63 B.C. Rome's greatest orator. Republican supporter of Pompey. Later favored Octavian and denounced Antony in the *Philippic Orations*.

Cicero, Quintus Tullius: Nephew of Cicero the orator. Fought with Caesar, then Antony, then the republicans. Executed by the Second Triumvirate.

Claudia: Daughter of Fulvia, stepdaughter of Antony.

Cleopatra VII: Queen of Egypt, fifth wife of Antony.

Cleopatra Selene: Daughter of Antony and Cleopatra.

Clodius Pulcher, Publius: Tribune 58 B.C., consul 54 B.C. Married to Fulvia. Popular leader who was bitter toward Cicero, sometimes friendly to Antony, sometimes hostile. Leader of street gangs. Killed by Milo in a brawl.

Commius: Gallic chieftain of the Atrebates. Defeated by Antony.

Cotiso: King of the Getae. Supporter of Antony.

Crassus, Marcus Licinius: Consul 70 and 55 B.C., censor 65 B.C. Member of the First Triumvirate. Died fighting the Parthians at Carrhae in 53 B.C.

Curio, Gaius Scribonius: Tribune 50 B.C. Boyhood friend of Antony. Agent for Caesar. Died fighting for Caesar in Africa.

Cytheris: Roman actress, mistress of Antony.

Decidius Saxa, Lucius: Tribune 44 B.C. Antony's governor of Syria, killed fighting the Parthians.

Deiotarus: King of Galatia. Supported Pompey, then Antony.

Dellius, Quintus: Historian friend and diplomatic agent of Antony in the east. Deserted at Actium.

Dolabella, Publius Cornelius: Consul with Antony in 44 B.C. Cicero's son-in-law. Supporter of Caesar and leader of the Caesarians in the east, where he was killed.

Eurycles, Gaius Julius: Ruler of Sparta who attacked Antony after Actium.

Fadia: Antony's first wife.

Fulvia: Third wife of Antony.

Furnius, Gaius: Praetor 42 B.C., Antony's governor of Asia 36 B.C.

Gabinius, Aulus: Consul 58 B.C., proconsul in Syria 57–54 B.C. Antony served under him in Syria and in illegally restoring Ptolemy XII to the throne of Egypt. Gabinius died fighting for Caesar in the civil war.

Glaphyra: Antony's mistress, to whose son he gave the throne of Cappadocia.

Herod the Great: King of Judaea who received his throne from Antony and fought for him.

Hirtius, Aulus: Consul 43 B.C. Close supporter of Caesar; he completed Caesar's *Commentaries*. Died fighting the Antonians at Mutina.

Horatius Flaccus, Quintus (Horace): Republican soldier who fought under Brutus. Became Augustan poet.

Hortensius Hortalus, Quintus: Praetor 45 B.C., governor of Macedonia 44 B.C. Republican executed by Antony after Philippi.

Hyrcanus II: High priest of the Jews under Pompey and Gabinius, ethnarch under Caesar.

Iotape: Daughter of Artavasdes of Media, betrothed to Alexander Helios.

Juba II: King of Numidia and Mauretania, married to Antony and Cleopatra's daughter.

Julia: Mother of Antony.

Labienus, Quintus: Republican son of the Pompeian Titus Labienus. Fled to Parthia for sanctuary and led a Parthian army against Syria in 40 B.C.

Lentulus Sura, Publius Cornelius: Consul 71 B.C. Antony's stepfather. Leader in Catilinarian conspiracy of 63 B.C. Executed by Cicero.

Lepidus, Marcus Aemilius: Patrician magister equitum under Caesar 46–44 B.C., consul 46 B.C., pontifex maximus for life. Member of the Second Triumvirate. Defeated in Sicily by Octavian and deposed from the triumvirate.

Livia Drusilla: Third wife of Octavian.

Lucullus, Lucius Licinius: Consul 74 B.C. Commander against Mithridates. Arranged the affairs of many states of Asia Minor while proconsul in Bithynia and Pontus, 73–67 B.C.

Maecenas, Gaius: Close friend and diplomatic agent for Octavian.

Malchus: King of the Nabataeans. Hostile to Herod the Great and Cleopatra, although he sent troops to Antony.

Marcellus, Gaius Claudius: Octavia's first husband, supporter of Pompey.

Mariamne: Wife of Herod the Great.

Menodorus: Admiral of Sextus Pompey.

Messalla Corvinus, Marcus Valerius: Consul 31 B.C. A republican who became loyal to Octavian.

Metellus, Quintus Caecilius: Consul 52 B.C. Pompeian supporter who died fighting the Caesarians in Africa.

Milo, Titus Annius: Tribune 57 B.C., praetor 55 B.C. A street brawler whom Pompey used to oppose Clodius's gangs. Convicted for Clodius's murder despite Cicero's attempts to defend him.

Mithridates VI: King of Pontus who waged repeated wars against Rome, 88–68 B.C.

Monaeses: Parthian noble who defected for a time to Antony and encouraged his Parthian campaign.

Nicolaus of Damascus: Tutor for Antony's children in Alexandria. Court historian for Herod the Great. Biographer of Augustus.

Octavia: Grandniece of Caesar, sister of Octavian, fourth wife of Antony.

Octavianus, Gaius Julius Caesar (Octavian): Grandnephew and heir of Caesar. Member of the Second Triumvirate. Victor over Antony at Actium and Alexandria. Emperor Augustus.

Orodes II: King of Parthia whose troops defeated Crassus and took many of Rome's eastern lands.

Pacorus: Prince of Parthia. Invaded Roman-held Syria.

Pansa, Gaius Vibius: Consul 43 B.C. Supporter of Caesar. Died fighting the Antonians at Mutina.

Pedius, Quintus: Consul 43 B.C. Caesar's grandnephew and minor heir.

Phasael: Tetrarch of Judaea and brother of Herod the Great.

Phraates IV: King of Parthia. Murdered his father, Orodes II, for the throne. His troops defeated Antony in Media Atropatene.

Pinarius, Lucius: Grandnephew of Caesar and his minor heir.

Plancus, Lucius Munatius: Consul 42 B.C. Military leader, shifting sides to his own advantage during the civil war, but generally aiding Antony.

Polemo: King of Pontus. Supported Antony. Married Antony's granddaughter.

Pollio, Gaius Asinius: Consul 40 B.C. Supported Caesar, then Antony. In 38 B.C. he left political-military life to become a historian, poet, and patron of Vergil and Horace.

Pompeius, Gnaeus: Elder son of Pompey the Great. Led the Pompeians fighting in Spain.

Pompeius, Sextus: Younger son of Pompey the Great. Seized Sicily and other lands of the western Mediterranean after Pharsalus, and his camp became a center for anti-Caesarians. Defeated by Octavian and died by order of Antony.

Pompeius Magnus, Gnaeus: Consul 70, 55, 52 B.C. Member of the First Triumvirate. Broke with Caesar in 49 B.C. and was vanquished at Pharsalus in 48 B.C. Died in Egypt.

Porcia: Daughter of Cato, wife of Marcus Brutus.

Ptolemy XI Auletes: King of Egypt restored to his throne by Gabinius and Antony, Father of Cleopatra.

Ptolemy XII: Joint ruler of Egypt with his sister Cleopatra. Died fighting Caesar in 47 B.C.

Ptolemy XIII: Joint ruler of Egypt with his sister Cleopatra. Murdered by Cleopatra in 44 B.C.

Ptolemy Philadelphus: Younger son of Antony and Cleopatra.

Pythodorus: Rich Greek of Tralles. Married Antony's eldest daughter, Antonia.

Rabirius Postumus, Gaius: Extortionate financial agent for Ptolemy XII in Egypt.

Sallustius Crispus, Gaius (Sallust): Tribune 52 B.C. Lieutenant of Caesar. Governor of Numidia 46–45 B.C. Retired from political life to write history.

Salvidienus Rufus, Quintus: Consul designate 39 B.C. Octavian's longtime friend and military officer. Defected to Antony in 40 B.C. Executed by Octavian.

Scribonia: Second wife of Octavian, Sextus Pompey's aunt.

Scribonius Libo, Lucius: Consul 34 B.C. Father-in-law of Sextus Pompey. Hostile to Caesar. Agent between Sextus and Antony.

Servilia: Mother of Marcus Brutus. Strong political influence in republican councils.

Servilius Isauricus, Publius: Consul 48 and 41 B.C. Supporter of Caesar, then of Octavian and Antony. A trimmer.

Sosius, Gaius: Consul 32 B.C. Antony's agent in Greece, Syria, and Palestine.

Titius, Marcus: Consul 31 B.C. Antony's lieutenant against the Parthians and Sextus Pompey. Defected to Octavian in 32 B.C.

Titius, Publius: Tribune 43 B.C. Proposed the *Lex Titia* which established the Second Triumvirate.

Trebellius, Lucius: Tribune 47 B.C. Lieutenant for Antony at Mutina.

Trebonius, Gaius: Consul 45 B.C. Officer under Caesar in Gaul. Then republican supporter who spoke of Caesar's murder to Antony and detained Antony outside the Curia Pompeii on the Ides of March.

Varro, Marcus Terentius: Praetor before 67 B.C. Librarian and historian. A Pompeian, forgiven by Caesar, proscribed but not killed by the Second Triumvirate.

Vatinius, Publius: Consul 47 B.C. Useful agent for Caesar and the Second Triumvirate.

Ventidius Bassus, Publius: Consul 43 B.C. Antony's general who fought in Perusia and against the Parthians.

Vercingetorix: Chief of the Arverni tribe. Led a revolt of the Gauls against Rome. Besieged and defeated by Caesar and Antony at Alesia.

Index

Index

Roman men are listed by their clan names (*nomina gentiles*). Since normally a woman's only name was her father's name in the feminine form, identifying phrases have been added for the women. Similarly, non-Romans with single names have been further identified. Julio-Claudian emperors are listed by their standard imperial titles.

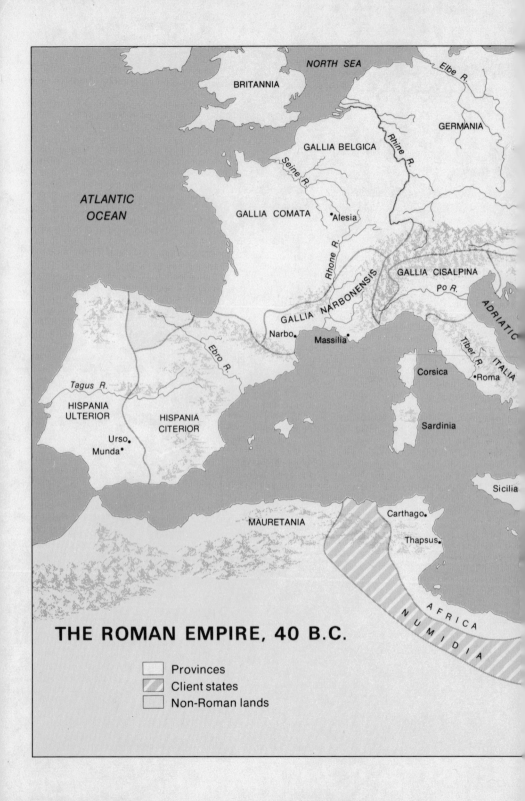

THE ROMAN EMPIRE, 40 B.C.

Provinces
Client states
Non-Roman lands

Map labels:

NORTH SEA
BRITANNIA
GERMANIA
Elbe R.
GALLIA BELGICA
Rhine R.
Seine R.
ATLANTIC OCEAN
GALLIA COMATA
•Alesia
Rhone R.
GALLIA CISALPINA
Po R.
ADRIATIC
GALLIA NARBONENSIS
Narbo.
Massilia•
Tiber R.
ITALIA
•Roma
Corsica
Ebro R.
Tagus R.
HISPANIA ULTERIOR
HISPANIA CITERIOR
Urso•
Munda•
Sardinia
Sicilia
MAURETANIA
Carthago•
Thapsus•
AFRICA
NUMIDIA